FOOTBALL FOR FUN

DIAG. 3

IN MOTION

ABOUT
3½ YDS.

3 TO 4
YARDS

DIAG. 3

IN MOTION

DIAG. 5

THE STORY OF COACH STEWART "FERGIE" FERGUSON

FOOTBALL FOR FUN

BILL BELL & PETER OLTCHICK

SOUTH DAKOTA HISTORICAL SOCIETY PRESS

PIERRE

Library of Congress Control Number: 2023937120

ISBN 9781941813478

Printed in the United States of America

The paper in this book meets the guidelines for permanence and durability of the Committee on Production Guidelines for Book Longevity of the Council on Library Resources.

Please visit our website at sdhspress.com

27 26 25 24 23   1 2 3 4 5

Cover and book design by Mike Corrao, Mayfly Design

"Those are my principles, and if you don't like them . . . well I have others."

—Groucho Marx

For Diana, Amanda, and Sarah

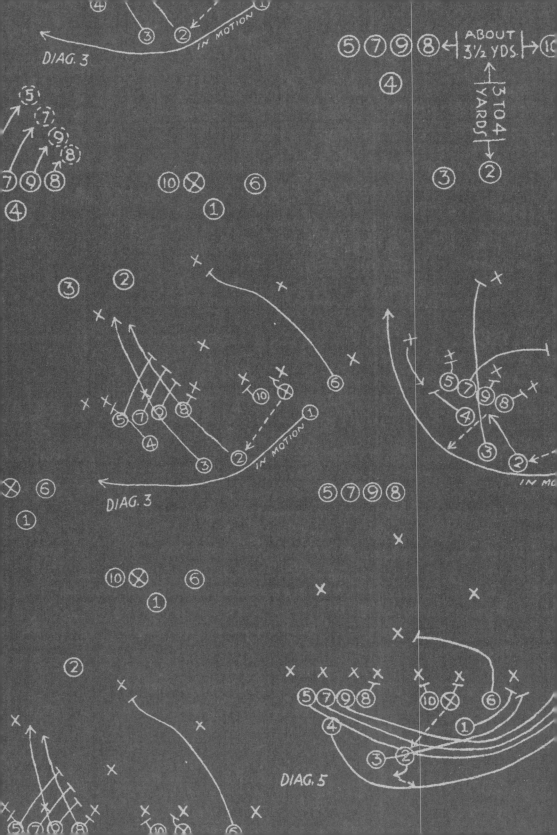

DIAG. 3

ABOUT 3½ YDS.

3 TO 4 YARDS

IN MOTION

DIAG. 3

IN MOTION

DIAG. 5

CONTENTS

Preface xi

PART 1: PUGNACIOUS PK

Chapter 1. Conversion 3
Chapter 2. The End of Boyhood 9
Chapter 3. Football Takes a Back Seat 19
Chapter 4. "Teaching or Preaching" 24
Chapter 5. The Prodigal Son 33
Chapter 6. Stuck 39
Chapter 7. Methodist Meat 50

PART 2: FINDING FUN—AND FAME

Chapter 8. Damn Yankee 59
Chapter 9. Southern Showdown 67
Chapter 10. A Hero's Welcome—For Bo 75
Chapter 11. Rough Boys 82
Chapter 12. Strangest. Contract. Ever. 88
Chapter 13. "Going Crazy" 94
Chapter 14. "A Dizzy Liar" 103
Chapter 15. Epiphany 110
Chapter 16. Marx Brothers of Football 121
Chapter 17. Busology 101: The Wandering Weevils 133
Chapter 18. Hershey Kisses 140
Chapter 19. California Dreamin' 146

Chapter 20. "Paid in Full" 153

Chapter 21. Handsprings, Backflips—and a "W" 158

Chapter 22. Detour 165

Chapter 23. Ditching the Green Dawg 170

Chapter 24. *Collier's* 176

Chapter 25. Fork in the Road 183

Chapter 26. Hamburger & Bananas 188

Chapter 27. Drunken Rainbows 200

Chapter 28. (Almost) Calling it Quits 205

Chapter 29. Fireside Fool 214

PART 3: HOME

Chapter 30. Back to (Flight) School 221

Chapter 31. Welcome Mat 225

Chapter 32. Lovefeasts 234

Chapter 33. New Additions 240

Chapter 34. Papa Bear 248

Chapter 35. Winning, Actually 256

Chapter 36. Cue the Corn Palace 265

Chapter 37. Transition 272

Chapter 38. A Special Season 280

Chapter 39. Sidelined 289

Chapter 40. Back in Action 299

Chapter 41. Celebrating Fergie 307

Author's Note 311

Acknowledgements 313

Notes 317

PREFACE

It all started in 2000, in Arkansas, at the annual Bell family reunion. The conversation turned to sports, and an uncle of Bill's mentioned that when he was a young man, a nutty nearby football team—with a strange sort of coach—was one of the most famous college outfits in the United States. Neither his uncle nor any other family members seemed sure of the names, dates, or anything else for that matter, but Bill was intrigued. Back home, he dug further and confirmed his uncle had it right: Starting in 1939, a tiny cow college from Monticello, Arkansas, and its coach, Stewart Ferguson, were somehow becoming a big deal in college football. Yet, surprisingly, over the years—beyond the occasional newspaper and magazine feature—there wasn't a single complete recounting of the bananas, barnstorming team commonly known as the Wandering Weevils. Bill was hooked and decided this was a story he needed to tell.

After forty years in the newspaper business and over twenty-five at the New York *Daily News*, Bill partially retired (continuing to write a weekly column, review books, and do other assorted chores) and got to work. Over the next few years, he traveled to Arkansas and South Dakota (where Coach Stewart Ferguson grew up and eventually resurfaced); found Ferguson's unpublished memoirs; tracked down some surviving former players and family members of former players; and amassed all the accounts he could find about Ferguson and his squad, the Arkansas A & M Boll Weevils, that from 1939 to 1941 had indeed become famous, and in certain circles infamous, for playing and losing—from coast to coast—for fun.

Bill did the heavy lifting in crafting a complete telling of the story of ringmaster Ferguson and his travelling band of Boll Weevils; however, he and his literary agent increasingly pictured a bigger book, one centered on a slight, mild-mannered but fiery ex-college coach turned full-time history teacher. The hard-to-fathom story of Coach Stewart Ferguson—later known as Fergie—was in motion. Battling failing health, Bill would make a strong push to capture Coach Ferguson's turbulent and defining earlier years.

As touched upon in the book, "Every now and then, even a blind hog finds an acorn." This bit of Arkansas backwoods wisdom very much captures how I felt staring some years later at a big, dusty box in my mother-in-law's Connecticut basement. Having recently finished some school visits for a children's picture book, I decided it was finally time to take a peek inside. The contents contained a perfect mess of chicken scratch scribbles across mounds of cocktail napkins, backs of envelopes, bits of small sheets—including Bill's amorously-graphic *A faire aujourd'hui* (to do today) papers, scattered index cards, sectioned thick spirals (via fraying Post-it notes), and of course, his trusty eight-by-four-inch *Daily News* notebooks.

I can recall only one casual chat with Bill, years earlier, about the book. But soon enough, I, too, was hooked by the fascinating Fergie and felt a strong pull to dive in. I reset to full-research mode, channeled my days as sports editor of a college newspaper, and went about trying to walk in Bill's—and Fergie's—footsteps, which led me to Arkansas, Louisiana, and across South Dakota. During two trips to the breathtaking Black Hills, highlighted by critical interviews made possible by two passionate Deadwood High School alumni (and discussed further in this book's acknowledgments), I drank in Fergie's lasting impact on the community of Deadwood. And his full tale fell into focus.

Shaping the book into a biography has been a true labor of love, and I'm thrilled to share and celebrate Fergie's wild ride. In Bill's words, it's a helluva story.

—*Peter Oltchick*

PART 1

PUGNACIOUS PK

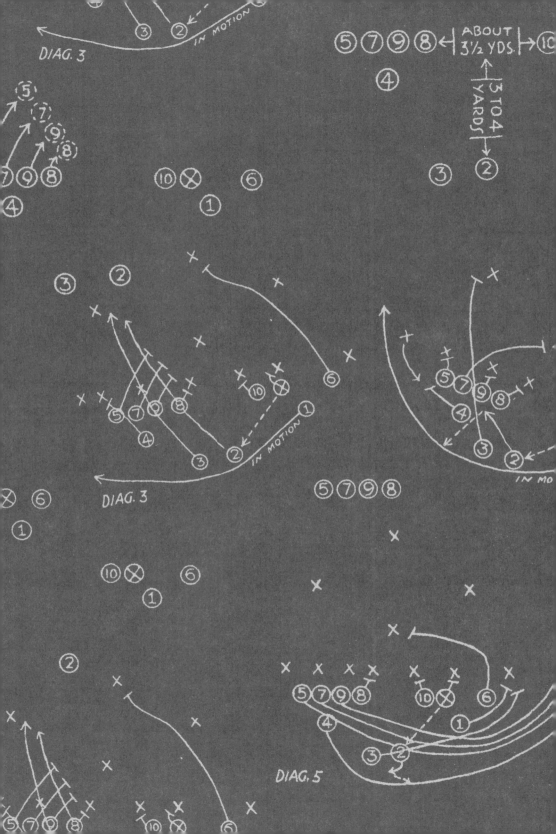

DIAG. 3

ABOUT 3½ YDS.

3 TO 4 YARDS

IN MOTION

DIAG. 3

IN MOTION

IN MO

DIAG. 5

CHAPTER 1

CONVERSION

One afternoon in the troubled, anxious fall of 1916, Stewart Ferguson borrowed his mother's bicycle and pedaled over ten miles of dusty, rutted roads from his home in Mount Vernon, South Dakota, to the county seat of Mitchell to watch a football game between Dakota Wesleyan College and Madison State Teachers College. He had never seen a game nor expressed any interest in the sport. For one thing, there weren't enough boys at Mount Vernon's high school to field a team, nor was there any support for one from parents. For another, his father, the Reverend William T. Ferguson—like many other clergymen of the day—considered football morally damaging, socially frivolous, and physically dangerous.

His father's opinions carried weight with the townspeople, and not just with the 114 members of his own Methodist flock. Reverend Ferguson was the most prominent and popular citizen of Mount Vernon, a farm town with a two-block-long main street and a water tower built to supply the Chicago & North Western Railroad, which ran along one side of town. He was deemed so trustworthy by the community at large that when the editor of the local weekly newspaper went on vacation or was sick, Reverend Ferguson was left in charge.

Although sixteen-year-old Stewart was the oldest of the four Ferguson boys, he rarely went anywhere by himself and his father, a strict and pious patriarch, was reluctant to allow him to do so this Saturday afternoon. But circumstances at the family's modest home, one door away from the Mount Vernon Methodist Church, made it difficult for the Reverend to refuse Stewart's plea to go into Mitchell.

Hanging over every moment of life in the Ferguson home was a terrible crisis shared not only by the members of the Reverend Ferguson's flock but by everyone else in town. Citizens learned of it on August 18 in a brief, chilling item in that week's issue of the *Mount Vernon News*: "Paul, the little son of Mr. and Mrs. W. T. Ferguson, is sick with infantile paralysis, but is reported some better at this writing," it read. "The house is quarantined and every precaution will be used to prevent the spread of the disease."

The youngest of the boys, Paul had celebrated his eighth birthday less than three weeks earlier and his affliction struck Mount Vernon with cyclonic force. The muscle-crippling disease poliomyelitis, polio for short, or infantile paralysis because so many of its victims were children, had afflicted humans since ancient times. Before the twentieth century, it was fairly rare. But now polio was sweeping America, and the overwhelming percentage of its victims were, like little Paul, less than ten years old.

Doctors were not sure what caused the disease, which some called the summer plague because it struck hardest during the warmest months. One prominent expert blamed it on horse flies; more credible researchers asserted the polio virus traveled in water, leading parents to forbid their children from swimming in public ponds and pools. No one knew how Paul contracted the disease, and there was shock and sadness that such an ordeal should befall a man of God and his family.

The Ferguson family was far from alone in its sorrow. The 1916 polio epidemic, the first in the United States in six years, claimed about six thousand lives and left thousands more paralyzed. At the time, treatment consisted mainly of immobilizing the affected limbs in splints and plaster and preventing any contact between victims and outsiders. Health officials imposed quarantines, usually lasting one month, and ordered the burning of any items that they thought might spread the disease. Paul sobbed at the window as strangers burned his toys and clothing in the backyard. His brothers and parents wept, too, feeling a sense of unshakable melancholy, and neighbors left flowers and prepared meals on the porch as signs of their solidarity.

For Reverend Ferguson and especially for his wife Edith, it was the second terrible blow in their life together. In 1900, the year that Stewart was born, their first child, Mary, died mysteriously in her crib.

One week after its initial report, the *Mount Vernon News* published a follow-up item: "Reverend Ferguson reports that his little son, who has been sick with infantile paralysis, is getting along pretty well. They expect to be out of quarantine by next Tuesday."

The quarantine, in fact, was lifted just in time for the start of the new school year. Stewart, a sophomore, had enrolled as one of forty-eight high school students. Some of them did not start classes immediately because of a lingering fear of polio in the community, and soon, Stewart would suffer the consequences in another way.

Robert Wilson, a fellow sophomore and the son of L. A. Wilson, the principal, taunted Stewart about his "crippled" brother. Hurt and enraged, Stewart beat up Robert in the schoolyard. As punishment, the principal told Stewart to go the library during the lunch hour. A few minutes later, when entering the room, he found Stewart sleeping and woke him up by throwing a piece of chalk at him. Stewart retaliated by hurling an inkpot that struck Principal Wilson, who immediately expelled the preacher's son.

Whatever his feelings, the Reverend Ferguson kept them to himself. A few days after Stewart's expulsion, he went to the school to speak to the fifth and sixth grades, coincidentally on the same day that another of his sons, Marion, who had been held out of class until the polio scare abated, enrolled in the seventh grade. Ministers often accepted invitations to address students on various moral and practical virtues, and relations were especially close between the school and the Methodist church. When the school burned the following year, the result of an accidental late night fire in the basement, classes for grades one through six were held temporarily in Reverend Ferguson's sanctuary.

The expulsion led to intense arguments at home and sullen bouts of rebellion by Stewart, whose standing as a preacher's son subjected him to bullying and unrealistic expectations. He had plenty of company. All preachers' kids—PKs, in the slang of the day—were held to impossibly high standards by members of their fathers' flocks and were expected to be models of filial obedience and respect. Many sons reacted, as Stewart did, by ignoring or defying the images, values, and rules exemplified by their fathers. To the disappointment and dismay of the Fergusons, Stewart's defiance included smoking hand-rolled cigarettes, profanity, fooling around with the family's Bohemian maid, and brawling with other town toughs.

Out of school and out of favor at home, Stewart campaigned to work his way back into the good graces of his parents by washing dishes and performing other chores around the house. At every meal, after he said grace, Reverend Ferguson lectured his son about the error of his ways, and carefully, very carefully, encouraged Stewart to consider the ministry. Just as carefully, Stewart implied that he would not rule it out.

Now, like an omen, came an unexpected invitation. The son of a Methodist minister in Mitchell asked Stewart if he would like to see Dakota Wesleyan play football. To the Reverend Ferguson, the invitation was a mixed blessing. On the one hand, exposure to Dakota Wesleyan, a Methodist school with a sizable enrollment of young men preparing for the ministry, might inspire Stewart to think more seriously about his future. On the other hand, it was, after all, a football game.

Stewart did not know it but affiliated with the college was a newly established high school, the Dakota Wesleyan Academy, and the Fergusons—who did know—thought maybe their son would find himself there. Money was a problem; Reverend Ferguson was paid only $1,114 a year, but he and Edith thought the sacrifice was worth it. The big question was whether a visit to the college campus might lead Stewart to enroll in the academy, which would remove him from the bad influences in Mount Vernon and at the same time put him in the company of wholesome young Christian men who might inspire him to follow their path to the pulpit.

At dinner on September 28, his parents informed him he could go to the game. They did not know that Stewart had accepted the invitation partly because it came with the promise that at halftime, he and the other minister's son could prowl under the bleachers, looking up girls' skirts.

Just after noon the next day, Stewart set off, pumping furiously on the pedals of his mother's open-framed bicycle down Main Street, past the stores where his parents shopped, to the railroad tracks, and then along a bumpy two-lane road past familiar farms and woods. He felt free for the first time in weeks and a bit curious, because although he had never seen a game, he had read about the sport and knew it was becoming a dominant feature of South Dakota's collegiate life. Nationally, the sport claimed the enthusiastic loyalties of hundreds of thousands of collegians and, increasingly, ordinary Americans who enjoyed its spectacle, noise, and color.

Stewart was not overly impressed by his first views of the university. In an unpublished memoir he wrote many years later, he remembered his arrival, weary and sweating, on Dakota Wesleyan's campus. "I passed between two buildings resembling the aroused tits of a middle-aged virgin, springing brownish-red from the drab prairie," Stewart wrote, adding that as far as he was concerned, the whole place seemed to exist in a "theological stupor."

The game was already underway when he arrived. Drawn by the cheering, he steered his bicycle to the stadium, with its wooden bleacher seats. After a shout of welcome from his host, Stewart took a seat.

What followed, in a simile that his preacher father might well appreciate, was a conversion as instant and lasting as the one Paul the Apostle experienced along the road to Damascus. Almost as soon as he sat down, Stewart was entranced with everything: the cheers, the pageantry, and above all, the ritualized violence. He was so taken that he passed on the chance to peek at coeds' panties and remained in the stands at halftime to watch the players exercise or relax. "The chance to sock with reward rather than penalty," he wrote later, "seemed like a Jack Dempsey dream."

Dakota Wesleyan won the game, 14–6. The Methodists lost their remaining seven games, but by then Stewart was obsessed with an ambition to play. "This," he said, "would be considerably more red blooded and a lot more fun than following the pattern my father quite eloquently and quite personally set for me each Sunday morning."

While talking with some other boys, Stewart learned that Wesleyan Academy was organizing its first football team. As he cycled home, he was seized with the exciting possibility that he might have found the solution to his—and his parents'—problems.

"I knew that my father's professional pride was being embarrassed by having his 16-year-old boy out of school," Stewart wrote later. "Too, my mother's beautiful face was becoming a bit more grim with the growing realization that her oldest son did not seem likely to carry on the religious passion of her life."

He had been smoking cigarettes furtively in an old, abandoned blacksmith shop and had engaged in a "rather frightening" amatory experience with the maid. He had found the road to hell, as described each Sunday from the pulpit by the Reverend Ferguson, more inviting than the stairway to heaven. But now, for the chance to play football, Stewart was ready to renounce all worldly pleasures and fleshy desires.

That night at supper, he excitedly reported on the football game and announced he wanted to enroll in Wesleyan Academy as the first necessary step to becoming a Methodist minister. His mother's eyes lit up with delight. His father hesitated, then after a few agonizing moments of reflection, nodded his head.

"If football is the way to the Lord's work," he said, "your mother and I will help."

Stewart Ferguson's first prayer had been answered.

CHAPTER 2

THE END OF BOYHOOD

It had been some time since Stewart Ferguson felt anything like the spark from watching his first game of football. In October 1913, the Reverend William Ferguson left the frontier ways of Gregory, South Dakota, called to the windswept prairie town of Mount Vernon, moving his wife and four sons into a setting so unfamiliar that he might as well have migrated to the moon. It was particularly hard for his oldest boy, Stewart.

A parody version of the hymn "Beulah Land" summed up the feeling of many of the town's 541 citizens:

> We've reached the land of drought and heat,
> Where nothing grows for man to eat,
> The wind, it blows with fervent heat,
> Across the plains that are hard to beat.

In truth, by the time the Fergusons arrived, Mount Vernon was a fairly prosperous town largely populated by the sons and daughters of Norwegian, German, and other hardworking, reliably solid immigrants. The Chicago, Milwaukee & St. Paul Railroad made several stops a day to load grain and take on water, and the two-block-long Main Street was lined with shops selling everything from hand-rolled cigars and buggies to Model Ts.

The most famous citizen the year the Fergusons arrived was James E. Fraser, an increasingly renowned sculptor and artist raised on the frontier who designed the buffalo nickel to commemorate the bison and the American Indians.

Mount Vernon was a quarter the size of Gregory, but far more important to a restless teenager, the new town lacked all the excitement and adventure that Stewart Ferguson had known in Gregory. There, the cowboys and Indians he saw every day on the streets seized his imagination, as did—in defiance of his Methodist minister father—the saloon floozies, card sharks, and other unsavory characters that received the Reverend Ferguson's stern wrath every Sunday from his pulpit. Contrasted with all those forbidden delights, Stewart found Mount Vernon suffocating and dull. The only escape was Mitchell—incorporated in 1881 and named for Milwaukee railroad president Alexander Mitchell—about a dozen miles away, with its famous Corn Palace, Dakota Wesleyan College, and a lively commercial and social life. The Ferguson family, like most families in surrounding towns, traveled to Mitchell on Saturdays to shop and catch up on the latest gossip. For Stewart, whose favorite Mitchell activity was walking its vibrant streets, Saturday window shopping was the reward for surviving another week in Mount Vernon.

He hated school, partly because then, as now, most teenaged newcomers to a small town find it hard to win quick acceptance. Making it worse for Stewart, he did not play sports and was not particularly interested in any extracurricular activities. Above all, he was a preacher's kid, a PK, and thus fair game for bullies. Despite his father's advice, he was not inclined to turn the other cheek—he frequently came home covered in dust, in torn clothing, and sometimes with a bloody nose from playground scraps.

He also fought back by embracing some of the antisocial behavior that Reverend Ferguson condemned so publicly. He smoked, cussed, mocked religious convictions, sassed his teachers, and engaged in mischievous pranks—all symbolic acts of rebellion intended to distance himself from his father and establish his independence. The more prominence Reverend Ferguson achieved, the more obstreperous his oldest son became. But Stewart's conduct was more or less harmless. He learned to skirt the thin line between the unorthodox and the unacceptable, neither disgracing the family nor attracting the attention of the police.

Just as he had in Gregory, Reverend Ferguson quickly became a prominent figure in Mount Vernon, and not just because his church, with nearly one in four of the town's citizens, was the town's largest institution. He was a founder of the town library in 1915 and donated one of its first six volumes. He was also a popular speaker at school events and civic holidays; at one farmers' picnic, Reverend Ferguson chose hog cholera as his topic. More often, though, he spoke of farmers' difficult relations with everyday life in a fast-changing world. He was so admired that he delivered the eulogy for a Lutheran farmer who said on his deathbed that he wished the Reverend Ferguson would speak at his funeral.

During his five years in Gregory, Reverend Ferguson preached every Sunday at a small Methodist church attended mostly by the Sicangu Lakota residents of the Rosebud Indian Reservation and formed warm relations with many Indians. Before his transfer to Mount Vernon, a delegation from his Rosebud congregation asked Reverend Ferguson to undertake a pastoral visit to Canton, near the border with Nebraska, the site of the Hiawatha Asylum for Insane Indians. Many of its forgotten and neglected inhabitants were Lakotas.

Shortly after he settled into Mount Vernon, the reverend drove to Canton to minister, as best he could, to the patients there. The asylum, which opened in 1903 and was the country's only such institution for Native Americans, was one of South Dakota's most unusual institutions, and virtually unknown outside the state. (Its true horrors—a facility run through rampant abuse and neglect in which many inhabitants "were locked up because they had clashed with white men, a school or an agency, not because they were mentally ill"—were not revealed until 1929 after a thorough inspection and subsequent report. Somehow, the asylum remained open until 1935, and today, at least 121 bodies lie in unmarked graves in the middle of a golf course.)

Since he was on a winter break from school, Stewart accompanied his father. It was a trip that, despite his conventional attitudes toward Indians— generally considered savages—left Stewart troubled by the way they were treated by supposedly superior white men.

The years in Mount Vernon coincided with Stewart's coming of age, at least by most definitions of maturity at the time. It also coincided with a remarkable social, industrial, communal, political, and technical revolution that seemed to bring something new every day.

The two daily newspapers in Mitchell brought the outside world to Mount Vernon, and with it, the looming shadow of World War I, overseas in lands many citizens had long left behind. Within a year of the arrival of the Ferguson family, the bewildering, bloody conflict was engulfing not only Europe but parts of Africa, Asia, and elsewhere, and threatening to suck in the United States as well. In Mount Vernon, as in many other towns, the war seemed senseless.

For Stewart, though, the fall of 1916 centered squarely on a reboot of his high school education. Early on the morning of October 2, the Reverend Ferguson drove Stewart to the campus of Dakota Wesleyan College and enrolled him in the school's affiliated high school. Stewart was bursting with enthusiasm, which his father interpreted hopefully as a sign that his unhappy, lonely son might fall under the sway of the young men there who might convince Stewart to join them in studying for the Methodist ministry.

Falling under the spell of the Methodists, however, was not at the front of Stewart's mind. His parents might not understand his new obsession with football, but thousands of other young men around the country did and were, like Stewart, determined to become gridiron heroes. The sport was spreading fast—a few weeks earlier, the Pacific Coast Conference was formally established, giving the West Coast a league of its own for the first time. Small colleges were embracing the game, with the wholehearted support of local businessmen who recognized its commercial possibilities. The big schools in the East built large new stadiums, concrete bowls that could hold many thousands of howling fans. Newspapers were adding special reports to their sports pages and sending reporters to distant cities to cover the most successful and famous squads.

But not everybody was smitten. The ritualized violence of the game that seduced the tempestuous teenage Ferguson had a decade earlier driven calls for serious reforms to football. As a 1993 *Journal of Sports History* article detailed, the sport's brutality dated to 1892. On the Saturday before Thanksgiving, a packed crowd of over twenty thousand spectators at Hampden Park in Springfield, Massachusetts, watched Harvard and annual archrival Yale, both defensive-minded teams, struggle to a scoreless first half.

To open the second half, with rugby-like football rules then governing the college game, a Harvard player could either "kick the ball deep to the opposition, or to lightly touch the ball with his foot, then pick it up and pass it to a teammate." Harvard captain Benny Trafford chose the latter, tossing the football to a speedy halfback lurking just behind, as two groups of teammates on opposite sides of the ball ran "full tilt in a 'V' formation from a position some yards behind the ball . . . and directed their three-quarter ton of mass momentum toward one man on the opposing line (ten yards away) who would catch the brunt of their attack." The Harvard ball carrier followed fast and found a hole created by the flying bodies, making it all the way to Yale's twenty-five-yard line.

Designed by a Boston engineer, Lorin Deland—who was enthralled by the sport, though he had never played it, and spent hours revisiting Napoleon's military tactics and devising plays—the play came to be known as the 'flying wedge,' and "an already violent game brought forth the most revolutionary football play ever developed."

While the flying wedge (and its adaptations beyond kickoffs) was officially banned in 1894, coaches creatively skirted the legal rules, and the play melded into an increasingly violent kind of football characterized as "mass play" with endless rugby-like scrums and pile-ups. According to an October 15, 1905, article in the *Washington Post*, at least forty-five football players had died in the previous five years, many from internal injuries, broken necks, concussions, or broken backs. Additional reports cited as many as twenty-one deaths caused by football in 1905, though due to the extreme lack of medical knowledge at the time, it is impossible to pinpoint an exact number with any accuracy. But the November death of Union College halfback Harold Moore—who reportedly died of a cerebral hemorrhage after being kicked in the head while trying to tackle a

New York University player—was likely the final catalyst to demands for reform. By some accounts, Moore had recently recovered from a separate head injury sustained in a game a month earlier.

New rules intended to de-brutalize football, with an eye on creating more open play and eliminating mass formations like the flying wedge, were enacted for the following season. By early 1907, a football rules committee was in place, represented by a couple of the leading coaches in the game and Walter Camp, the "father of American football."

Though efforts to improve the sport continued, there was a separate, rising concern about the quickly escalating school funds considered necessary to compete at the highest level.

By the fall of 1916, top coaches commanded inflated salaries. A highly critical report from a special Yale committee on the school's excessive, overemphasized football and rowing budgets made national headlines. As the report argued, "The continually increasing competition for supremacy among rival universities, as exemplified in the employment of expensive staffs of coaching . . . if unchecked, may so increase as to make intercollegiate athletics an unprofitable scramble for the raising of large sums of money for the payment of the disproportionate salaries demanded by expert coaches."

If Stewart Ferguson was aware of the sport's critics, which included his father, he disregarded them. He was going to play football. But to do this, he had to stay in school, and to do that, he had to earn enough money to pay for room, board, and books. His father had paid the costs for the first month. Given his family's straitened financial circumstances, this constituted sacrificial giving, as Stewart well knew, and so he had promised he would pay all other costs of his education.

"I beat rugs, raked lawns, fired furnaces, delivered newspapers, shoveled snow and was a will-o'-the-wisp for a middle-aged, somewhat nymphomaniac widow," he wrote later. Stewart fit all this into a schedule built around football and, less importantly, his sophomore class studies.

Within minutes after completing registration, he rushed to the school gymnasium to sign up for the Dakota Wesleyan Academy's first-ever football team. It was four days before the opening game. A cluster of boys were waiting for someone to show up and tell them what to do.

"At last, the Academy coach, a Professor Wilds of the speech department, arrived," Stewart recalled later with undisguised admiration. "Wilds was a tall, nice-featured fellow with an inherent compulsion to be tragically dramatic, even when buttoning the fly of his pants." The sixteen-year-old Stewart had found his first role model.

Stewart suspected Elmer Wilds was not especially interested in coaching but very much enjoyed the opportunity to address audiences of any size. As a result, there was little practice that day or the days that followed. Most days, Wilds assembled his squad and delivered orations. "He would pose at the slightest opportunity, clasp hands together, and appeal to the gods for recognition in a truly beautiful voice," the deeply impressionable Stewart later remarked. "His tones were so delightful that generally, I was mesmerized into forgetting about football after the first sentence."

Wilds's love of flowery discourse was no accident. He not only chaired the department of public speaking and coached the college debate team, but he was also a onetime Pennsylvania oratory champion and a Harvard man. Fancy talk was as natural as breathing.

Asked how he felt about athletics in general and football in particular, Wilds told the weekly campus newspaper, the oddly named *Phreno Cosmian* (interpreted by the school as "the mind of the world" or "well ordered mind," and named after its first literary society) that "athletics has its place in every college and is a potent factor in shaping the reputation and standard of that school. There is another field of activity, which does, or at least should, reflect the strength of a college, even to a greater extent than does athletics. Connected most intimately with the primary purpose for which every school is founded are forensic contests."

In other words, give Wilds a good lively debate every time. Plenty of people agreed with him, too. At many colleges, literary and forensic skills were at least as important as the organized melees that passed for football contests. When Dakota Wesleyan won its second straight South Dakota collegiate debating competition the following spring, the news was proclaimed in large black type on page one of the *Phreno Cosmian*, followed by seven pages of biographies and details. In a way, this was payback for a decision made a week earlier by the college committee that awarded "W" letters to qualifying competitors on various sports teams; the committee had voted to end the traditional presentation of letters to students who excelled in debate and literary and other non-athletic competitions. The result of the vote roiled the campus—and downtown Mitchell—for months.

Dakota Wesleyan started playing football in 1897, twelve years after the college's founding by a committee of Methodist church leaders. (The school was initially named Dakota University before changing in 1904 to distinguish it from the state university in Vermillion and to assert its Methodist affiliation.) Students organized a team that year and played one game, which it lost. The next fall, the college assigned an instructor to coach part-time. The team was known simply as the Methodists.

Until 1915, when the college changed its eligibility rules, boys who were enrolled in the academy could play for the college. It was this change that prompted the academy to organize its own team in 1916 and to appoint Elmer Wilds as coach.

When Stewart turned up, seeking a place on the squad, he learned that the academy had scheduled a half dozen games with other teams around eastern South Dakota. To his surprise, he also learned that Wilds was so indifferent about the team that he had not even scheduled a practice. Like everyone else who wanted to play, Stewart made the team and was told that he would play end. He had worried that his small stature, light weight, slow speed, and lack of athletic ability would disqualify him. The only thing that saved him, as he later put it, was the cowardly nature of some of his teammates.

The Academy season opened October 5 with a 28–0 win over Alexandria High School. Stewart played right end. Two weeks later, the Academy won again, 6–0, over Columbus College, a prep school in Chamberlain, and for the first time, Stewart's play was noted in the school paper: "Ferguson, the diminutive right end, played a fast defensive game, tackling hard and low and several times bringing his man down for a loss."

But it was the third game, a 31–0 loss to Augustana College, a Lutheran prep school, that gave Stewart a certain notoriety on campus. At a postgame meeting with the team, Coach Wilds spoke with characteristic flamboyance of Stewart's performance. Asking Stewart to stand, Wilds pointed to him and proclaimed: "This young boy, with courage and determination shining from his face, looked at the enemy hosts and tackled, tackled, tackled as the rest of you so-called men did what? The answer is a black mark on your hearts and brains, which has been recorded forever in the great book of history. It is so." The academy ended the season with a record of three wins, two losses, and one tie. Shortly thereafter, the *Phreno Cosmian* commended Ferguson's overall play: "In spite of his small stature and lack of experience, Ferguson, by his consistent hard work and sure tackling, proved to be an essential feature of [the] team's success." Stewart was also rewarded a football letter before going home for the Christmas holidays.

What his parents, his three brothers, or anyone else in Mount Vernon thought about Stewart's football feats were not mentioned in his memoir. The *Mount Vernon News* did not mention them, either.

In any case, there were other, more important things distracting his family. In early March, during a snowstorm, Stewart's father was asked to call on a sick parishioner who lived in the country. Reverend Ferguson—who had spent his childhood working in a Pennsylvania coal mine, where, he suspected, he had contracted some kind of lung disease—went without hesitation but came home complaining he felt weak.

Over the following days, his condition grew more serious. Within a week, his doctor diagnosed the reverend with pneumonia. For a month, ignoring a suggestion that he stay in bed and rest, Reverend Ferguson struggled to fulfill his pastoral duties. A steady stream of neighbors and members of his church came to the door of the Ferguson home with flowers and food, the traditional gifts to homemakers who were beset by domestic crises that distracted them from cooking meals.

Then, at 7:45 p.m. on Sunday, April 22, with his family at his bedside and his Bible pressed into his right hand, Reverend Ferguson passed wordlessly away. He was only fifty-one years old.

The news of his death reached the offices of the *Mount Vernon News* too late for a full report in the issue dated April 27, but following the funeral, the *News* published in its May 11 issue an extensive and flowery account of Reverend Ferguson's life under a page one headline that read, "Last Sad Rites." His funeral was the largest in the town's history. All amusements, including the high school senior class play, a Civil War melodrama titled *Down in Dixie*, and all social engagements were cancelled during the week Reverend Ferguson's embalmed body lay in repose for visitors to the Ferguson home. An honor guard of his fellow Masons and Odd Fellows—organizations that, respectively, emphasized self-improvement and service in the community—stood at the coffin, a representative of the Sioux Nation came from the Rosebud reservation with a floral tribute, and the school and all businesses closed on the day of the funeral itself. The *News* devoted almost two thousand words to its story, extolling Reverend Ferguson as a role model.

"He has passed," editor Roy Herrick wrote, "but he left the world better for having lived in it. Through others he touched by his devotion, his life shall continue to bless men through the ages. He has not died. He cannot so long as men live and honor manhood, unselfishness and service for one's fellow man. May we so live that we leave behind us such a benediction."

For his eldest son, boyhood had ended.

CHAPTER 3

FOOTBALL TAKES A BACK SEAT

Stewart stayed away from classes until the end of the school year. Despite missing final examinations, he advanced from tenth to eleventh grade at Dakota Wesleyan Academy. During the summer, he worked odd jobs around Mitchell, worried that this uncertain income might not cover his tuition and other costs in the fall.

Edith Ferguson and her four sons had left the parsonage in Mount Vernon, though they were told they could stay until a successor to the late Reverend Ferguson arrived. They moved into a rented house on Wisconsin Street in Mitchell, not far from the Dakota Wesleyan campus. The family found itself surviving on the charity of friends and a thirty-three-dollar-per-month pension paid by the Methodist church to ministers' widows.

Whatever happened, Stewart was determined to return to the academy. Above all, he wanted to play football. It was his chief interest and afforded him welcome respite from the stress and sadness at home. But a few weeks prior to his father's passing, Congress had voted overwhelmingly to declare war on Germany, and suddenly football did not seem so important. At seventeen, Stewart was safe from induction into the armed services—all boys under the age of twenty-one were exempt—but that did not free him from doubts about his future. If the war dragged on, as some observers thought it would, he might find himself in uniform far from home, even in combat.

Even before the fall semester began, the academy announced it was suspending the football program for the duration of the war. The news crushed Stewart. When he arrived on campus a few days later, however, he learned that a loophole might make it possible for him to play. The Dakota Wesleyan board of trustees had voted to make all boys seventeen and older eligible for the college team.

Stewart went out for the team and made it, despite his limited experience and small size—at 135 pounds, he was lighter than some of the cheerleaders. His prospects had been greatly improved by the absence of competition; the war left the college with fewer than 130 male students, and almost anybody who could wear a uniform without provoking laughter stood a good chance of making the squad. Also working in Stewart's favor was his reputation for rough play, which he attributed to a "preacher-son complex" that made him want to "kick hell" out of opposing players. Still, Ray McLean, the college's new coach, was not overly impressed. He thought Ferguson was too green.

In any case, it was a so-so season for Ferguson, McLean, and Wesleyan, which won three games, including a 91–0 rout of long-time rival Augustana College, and lost three games, including one to Yankton College, the most hated of all rivals. There also were two ties. Ferguson spent most of the season on the bench, as the second-string left end.

The war overshadowed everything. Mitchell newspapers did not even report some of the football games, and like many small-town papers of the day, sports were not given special treatment. There were no sports pages and except for the World Series, which was important enough to publish on the front page, results and details of most sporting events were usually scattered throughout the paper—in Mitchell, sports stories often shared a page with late-breaking financial news about the grain and livestock markets.

By the end of the 1918 spring semester, Stewart had earned enough credits to graduate and made plans to enroll for college in the fall. He lived at home, where the financial situation had become even more precarious. His mother's pension had been reduced to $25 a month, and he gave her most of what he earned every week at his various odd jobs to help cover household expenses. This would end when he started classes, because he would need every cent he earned to pay tuition and other expenses.

A week before registration for classes at Dakota Wesleyan College, Stewart was notified that he and every other male student age eighteen to twenty-one would undergo military training in the Student Army Training Corps (SATC). There were eighty-four members, virtually every boy who was not studying for the ministry. The Department of War would issue them rifles, uniforms, and other equipment, conduct regular drills, and each SATC candidate would take four mandatory "military" courses per semester. To Stewart's relief, physical education courses were classified as "military." He was even more relieved when he learned the government would pay his tuition and other expenses. Stewart and his new comrades were not officially soldiers, but they were told if the war lasted much longer, they faced a call-up to active duty. Stewart's reaction was to say he was more interested in knocking out opposing football players than German soldiers.

He did not look beyond the war. Nobody did. Huge daily headlines made it difficult to think of the future. Stewart, like everyone else, found himself studying the war maps in Mitchell's *Evening Republican*, puzzling over the names of obscure villages in countries that until the war were as alien as distant stars. By the summer of 1918, front pages blossomed with promises of an impending Allied victory and a steady drumbeat of propaganda depicting German troops—invariably "Vile Huns" or "Treacherous Boche" in the headlines—as beasts who bayoneted the wounded, bombed hospitals, and even tortured cats on the battlefield to spread confusion among Allied forces.

It was a stressful time for the state's German residents, who formed the second largest ethnic bloc in South Dakota after people who identified themselves as "American." A law forbade the speaking of German on the telephone or in public, a particular hardship for the many immigrants who could not speak English. Eight communities appealed unsuccessfully for an exemption on grounds that not a single resident spoke English. Another controversial law banned worship services in German. Dachshunds became "liberty pups" and sauerkraut "liberty cabbage."

Along with the anti-German propaganda and laws, action was taken against able-bodied men—so-called "slackers"—who refused to register for the draft, as well as merchants engaged in non-essential businesses. All pool halls were closed. Production of brass beds, deemed non-essential, was halted. Beef was rationed, and all businesses closed on Sundays. The state Council of Defense asked churches to close their doors from November 1 to March 1, 1919, in order to save coal. Some churches objected and the Metropolitan Theater offered not to show movies on Sundays to let churches use its facilities.

As more South Dakota boys went overseas, news of their exploits filtered home. "Mitchell Boys Cover Selves with Glory, Says Col. Shade," the *Evening Republican* reported, quoting from a letter written to the Elks Club by Lieutenant Colonel Myron Lewis ("M. L.") Shade, the commander of an Allied supply train in France. A July headline brought grimmer news: "Mitchell Soldier Gassed in Battle." A month later, Harvey Coacher, who had played football with Stewart at the academy and attended the same Methodist church, was killed in action at the Second Battle of the Marne. Then the Reverend C. E. O'Flaherty, pastor of Mitchell's only Roman Catholic church and chaplain of a South Dakota unit, died in France. To bolster home front morale, there were feature stories about newsworthy military units or activities—one, about African American troops in France, appeared under the racist headline, "Yaw'sa, Dem Dere Darkey Boys Sure Can Battle Some."

On September 19, the newspapers bannered a story that pushed aside even all the war news. It was the first mention of the "Spanish plague," or 1918–1919 influenza pandemic. Shortly, it would bring panic and death to South Dakota, as it did everywhere; at least 50 million people died in the pandemic, with an estimated 650,000 deaths in the United States. One week after the first reports, South Dakota recorded its first flu death; a week after that, Mitchell recorded its first fatality. Schools and movie houses were closed. Church services were cancelled, including one for the funeral of a soldier slain in France. The mayor ordered the city's streets watered to keep down the dust, which many suspected spread flu germs. From the western half of the state came the news that Deadwood had declared itself quarantined, off-limits to outsiders, and had posted warning signs at all roads into town. Officials banned all public meetings, except livestock auctions, which were too economically important to scrub.

Before the end of October, one of Stewart's SATC classmates died and Dakota Wesleyan, reporting twenty cases of influenza in the women's dormitories alone, closed its doors. The Department of War, which had taken control of the college's athletic activities as part of its military training routine, called off a football game scheduled against the University of South Dakota.

On November 11, the announcement that the war had ended was bannered in a special edition of the *Evening Republican* under a headline six inches high—"Fighting Ends at 11 a.m." Despite the ban on public gatherings, Mitchell exploded in celebration. People formed a mile-long conga line to dance while an effigy of Kaiser Wilhelm burned on Main Street.

Five days later, the Mitchell Board of Health lifted its influenza bans, schools reopened, churches held special prayer services, and Dakota Wesleyan welcomed students back on campus after thirty-three days. Thirty-one people had died in the outbreak in Mitchell alone, and over 1,800 South Dakotans died—accounting for 28 percent of the entire year's deaths in the state—by the end of 1918.

Mitchell High School decided to cancel its entire football schedule for the year, and Dakota Wesleyan cut its season to one game. As originally scheduled, it would play the University of South Dakota, at Vermillion. The two teams played on November 23, and Dakota Wesleyan lost 33–0. Stewart started at left end, but was knocked down on one play, carried to the dressing room, and discovered to have suffered a broken ankle. Football at Dakota Wesleyan would return to normal the next season, and Stewart, undaunted by his injury, promised himself he would become a star.

CHAPTER 4

"TEACHING OR PREACHING"

Stewart Ferguson had every reason to look forward to the autumn of 1919 and the start of his college life at Dakota Wesleyan College. The war was over, the influenza pandemic abated, and despite his freshman status, his prospects for making the football team were good. Adding to his high spirits and hopes was the arrival of a new head football coach, which to Stewart signaled a fresh start. From now on, he resolved to play hard but fair—no more of the unnecessary rough stuff. When he arrived on campus, Stewart was determined to try out for quarterback, a position he believed would bring him the attention and acclaim that he felt he so richly deserved.

The new coach was Richard ("Bud") Dougherty, a recently discharged U.S. Army lieutenant who had played freshman football at Notre Dame. If the stories about him were true, he was a strict but fair disciplinarian with a keen dedication to traditional formations and strategies. He also hated to lose, as he made clear when he was hired to fill the coaching position that stood empty since Ray McLean's departure overseas the prior spring. (Sadly, McLean had recently died from pneumonia while part of the U.S. Army occupation in Germany.) McLean had sized Stewart up as too small, raw, and undisciplined for the college game, but used him as a substitute left end. Stewart thought Dougherty was more likely to appreciate his talents.

Stewart was also cheered by the flattering assessment published in the 1919 edition of *The Tumbleweed*, the college yearbook. At the time, *The Tumbleweed* was published every other spring, and its summaries of the football team covered the past two seasons—in this case, 1917 and 1918. In this edition, an unsmiling Stewart stands rigidly at attention in his uniform. He is mistakenly identified as a guard, while his weight is listed correctly as 135 pounds, making him the lightest player on the team. "Although small and light in weight," the caption reads, "'Fergie' never shows himself to be handicapped by either feature. There is no doubt that he would have earned his 'W' had he not sustained a broken ankle during the early part of the season. From a 'natural born football player' such as he, we certainly have a right to look for great things in the future."

The note about the broken ankle mistakenly referred to the 1917 season, but Stewart was flattered. Not bad, he thought, for a high school kid who had played as a substitute in only a handful of games, and then only because a wartime exemption made him eligible to play for the college. Football practice started early in September, and on October 9, four days before the opening game of the 1919 season, the college newspaper reported on the team's prospects for the season. Among the players it mentioned was Stewart. "Ferguson of Mount Vernon," it said, "is showing up well." Though the newspaper, and his coach, did not know it, "Ferguson of Mount Vernon" was already scheming something big: Stewart had developed an obsession to set a national record for scoring with a drop kick and was convinced that this would bring him national attention. If, in fact, he succeeded, it certainly would result in great publicity.

The idea did not come out of the blue. Four years earlier, on October 9, 1915, in a game with the Northern Normal & Industrial School in Aberdeen (now known as Northern State University), a Dakota Wesleyan player named Mark Payne had scored on a drop kick of sixty-three yards. It was the longest formally listed drop kick and was recognized as a national record. (Today, it is still listed as the record by the National Collegiate Athletic Association, and is likely to remain so, since drop kicks long ago went the way of the outlawed flying wedge.) Payne, a three-sport star, had broken the previous record of sixty-two yards, set in 1898 by Pat O'Dea of Wisconsin. One of the first things Stewart Ferguson heard about when he enrolled at the Dakota Wesleyan Academy was Payne's marvelous feat. Gradually, the idea of bettering the record took hold and Stewart began planning to do so at an appropriate time and place.

At the time, the drop kick was a popular offensive weapon, but because of the unpredictable bounces footballs take when dropped, it was a devilishly tricky feat to do effectively. Anyone who could drop kick with any degree of success was valuable. It looked deceptively simple: a player dropped the ball and as it bounced up from the ground, kicked it. Usually, it was used as a scoring play after a touchdown, or to score a field goal. Sometimes, it was used as a surprise punt to catch defenders off guard and leave them at a territorial disadvantage. In college play, drop kicks were common until the 1950s, but in the National Football League they fell out of favor much earlier. Before New England Patriots backup quarterback Doug Flutie converted an extra point drop kick in the 2006 New Year's Day game, the last points scored on a drop kick in the NFL were in 1941, by a Chicago Bears player coincidentally named Ray McLean (no relation to the late Dakota Wesleyan coach).

"One of my worst personality defects," Stewart recalled years later, "has been the nursing of preposterous dreams. None except myself could possibly suspect that I had determined to break the world record. Even though I felt lucky when able to clear the [goal post] bar from 20 yards, I knew from reading the classics and listening to my father's sermons that a faint heart seldom did anything but faint, but that with a will and God's help most anything can be accomplished."

Despite his high hopes, Stewart was not the starting quarterback in 1919, but he did start at left end, his old position, and doubled as a substitute defensive back. It was a highly successful season for Dougherty and the Methodists. Winning six of eight games, they were South Dakota Association of Colleges conference champions. One game, in Rapid City against the South Dakota School of Mines, took place in weather so cold the two coaches agreed to reduce the four quarters to five minutes apiece and not to call any timeouts; Dakota Wesleyan won 7–0. In the conference championship game, against archrival Yankton College, the stadium lights failed and the field was illuminated, after a fashion, by the headlights of cars parked in a circle around the field.

Stewart's chance for the immortality that he plotted came on November 23. The fates had decided this was the time, he reckoned. The opponent was Northern Normal, and the site was Aberdeen—the very team and the very town where Mark Payne had booted his way into the record books. Stewart pleaded with Dougherty to let him play quarterback, and the coach, who could never have suspected the reason for Stewart's dogged insistence, acquiesced. Years later, Ferguson ruefully recalled what happened:

> As we trotted on the field at Aberdeen before the game, I noticed with thrilling anticipation that a stiff gale was blowing down the length of the gridiron and knew that any ball kicked high in the air would travel far, provided it was kicked with the wind.
>
> We won the toss and chose the goal with the wind at our backs. It seemed to me that some sort of providence was unlocking the doors to glory in giving me the most perfect of conditions for the greatest drop kick in history.
>
> We kicked off to Northern, and they kicked back to me in the safety position after a couple of plays. I let the ball roll nearly to the goal line before picking it up and then carefully and deliberately starting back up the field. I cautioned myself as I ran not to carry it beyond the 30-yard line, for I wanted the drop kick that would make me famous to travel 70 yards in distance. People better remember even numbers. I dropped exactly on the 30-yard line after a weak tackle. I didn't worry whether or not it appeared that I went down intentionally—I sort of wanted people to remember that I coolly and calculatingly set up the kick. I wanted them to compliment me afterward on not being fool enough to try and gain an extra 10 or 12 yards and so spoil a new world's record.
>
> The teams lined up. I barked the signals for the play: 22, 46,

94, 35. The linemen turned their heads around and looked back at me in astonishment. I repeated the signals a little slower and considerably louder. After all, I reasoned, one must really be a quarterback or else play some other position.

I stretched out my arms and snapped my fingers for the [backward] pass [from center]. It was beautiful. Quickly, I dropped the ball and kicked. The ball sliced away, barely to the line of scrimmage.

Like a knife through my mind, fuddled with disappointment, [came] the scorching words of Bud Dougherty, the fiery Irishman who coached us, "You, you, you dumb son of a bitch. Come off that field."

Jesus wept, and so did I.

There was one game left, the championship game with Yankton, and despite his fears that Dougherty would bench him, Stewart again started at left end and played with enough fierce intensity to earn favorable mention in the college newspaper.

Back at home, the situation was not good. Money was extremely tight and his mother, who had never worked, now supplemented her twenty-five-dollar monthly widow's pension by devoting a few hours each week to administrative chores at the First Methodist Church of Mitchell. The war was over, and with it, his service in the Student Army Training Corps, so Stewart had lost the federal stipend that covered the cost of his tuition and books. His brothers Marion and William, at fifteen and seventeen, were still in high school. Little Paul, eleven, was crippled by the polio that had stunted his growth. The situation left Stewart, technically the man of the house, struggling to pay not only his share of the family's living expenses but his own college costs.

He was still doing odd jobs around town, but now he came up with another idea that he was sure would solve the Fergusons' financial pinch. He would organize and manage a dance band. Since he knew the basic banjo chords, he would play in his band, too. He called it the Dakota Kings. The band, with upright bass, drums, clarinet, trombone, guitar, and Stewart on banjo, played mostly at weekend parties in Mitchell. In its handbills, distributed in Mitchell stores, the band claimed it could play every popular song of the day. Stewart wrote its flamboyant promotions, a talent that would bring him unexpected benefits years later under extraordinarily different circumstances. The Dakota Kings did not earn much money, but it did give Stewart more visibility and made him more than just another guy on the football team. He began dating the daughter of a widowed Mitchell seamstress, and also joined the theatre program and debate team.

Among all his other interests, football still ruled. In a review of the 1919 season, published on January 15, 1920, the campus newspaper praised his play. "Though small," it declared, "he has all the requirements of a good end. He showed this in the Yankton game, when his tackling was almost spectacular." In March, Stewart was among nineteen players awarded their "W" letters in an elaborate chapel ceremony.

All the more surprising, then, that Stewart did not show up for football practice when classes began in September. He had, in fact, dropped out of school. The straitened financial situation finally forced him to seek full-time employment. He soon landed a job washing boilers for the Chicago, Milwaukee & St. Paul Railroad. It was hard, dirty work—when engines pulled into the roundhouse in Mitchell, Stewart would clean them of soot and grime, a chore that sometimes required him to dismantle and reassemble the parts. His brother William, now graduated from high school, went to work running errands and doing other menial tasks for the Federal System of Bakeries.

Stewart continued his college studies, however, taking classes when his job permitted. Still dreaming of becoming a football star, he told Coach Dougherty that he would return to school full-time for the 1921 season. But at the first practice in late August, Stewart failed to report. Once again, he would skip football. This time, though, there was a reason beyond his job: he wasn't eligible to play because he was not enrolled in enough classes.

By the following fall, however, Stewart—after a full summer school course load—was back. Dougherty installed him as starting right end, and in the first game of the 1922 season, his defensive play was a highlight as Wesleyan fell to Creighton College, 7–0, in Omaha, Nebraska. Things were looking up at long last, he believed. But once again, bad luck struck.

The campus newspaper reported on October 20: "Stewart Ferguson, right end, lost the little finger of his left hand while working at the roundhouse last week. In some manner, it became caught in a pump and was so badly cut that it was necessary to have it amputated. His hand is very sore and in all probability he will be kept out of the lineup for the rest of the season. His absence will be keenly felt." It was a devastating blow, and not only physically. For one thing, the injury ended his banjo playing—it was his left hand that formed the chords. For another, he was left with a lifetime of embarrassment about the injury. Whenever he could, he hid his left hand in a pocket or behind his back.

But the paper was wrong about one thing: Stewart did not miss the rest of the season. He returned to action in less than a month and was back starting at right end on November 30, in the vital annual match against Yankton College. In a game that Wesleyan won 12–0, Stewart was cited for his defensive play. The recap in the school paper said, "He had his man down on every play." Two weeks later, he sat in the front row in the team picture. Sporting a sly grin, he was one of six players wearing a helmet.

As his senior year in college approached, Stewart was determined to go out with a bang. The 1923 season began with Stewart as one of eighteen players on the traveling squad. He was not the starting right end, though, but was playing second string to Mark Payne's brother. Wesleyan lost its first game badly, however, and Payne was demoted in the second game. While Ferguson competed for playing time, there was some exciting news mounting around the overall athletic program—for the first time, Dakota Wesleyan would have a nickname. Spurred by action from the school's athletic board, a committee of five—comprising the football and basketball team captains,

the "yell leader," the *Phreno Cosmian* editor, and a faculty representative—brainstormed many ideas including the Weasels, Tumblers,
and Galloping Deacons. Although there were no announced criteria
or voting details, the group chose the name Tigers, saying it was the
"most descriptive of the spirit" displayed by Dakota Wesleyan teams.

For the rest of the Tigers' season, Payne and Stewart alternated
as starting and second-string right end. But it was once again the big
game against Yankton that gave Stewart a final chance to shine. With
the score tied 7–7 in the fourth quarter, he fell on a fumbled punt
on the Yankton five-yard line. Two plays later, Wesleyan scored the
winning touchdown.

Years later, Stewart looked back on his college playing days. "I
was generally a player with spirit and ambition but without the juice
that could spark me to glory," he wrote. However, he noted, he had
"strikingly" helped his team win his last college game and as a result had been named to "several" all-conference teams. That was an
exaggeration that would follow him the rest of his life, with his encouragement. All-conference teams were selected by South Dakota
sports writers with input from conference coaches, and one of them
did list Stewart on its first team, while another included him on its
honor roll of forty of the state's star players. Curiously, he never mentioned a more significant honor. He was nominated in November, a
week or so before the big Yankton game, for a Rhodes scholarship.
At the time, each of the eleven colleges in South Dakota forwarded
one name to the Rhodes selection committee. The news of Stewart's
nomination caused a stir on campus, but he was not chosen.

Like most small colleges, Dakota Wesleyan struggled to make its
athletic program, football above all, pay for itself. And like at most
small colleges, football rarely showed a profit. At the end of the 1923
season, the college reported that its football program for that season
lost $601.42. It was not enough to bring calls to balance the books
or abandon the sport—that was something that Stewart would hear
later, under more dire circumstances.

Because he had interrupted his studies over the past two years,
there was some uncertainty about Stewart's academic status. In fact,

he had accumulated enough credits to graduate in the summer of 1924, a belated surprise to the editor of *The Tumbleweed* yearbook. In its edition published in the spring of 1925, eight months after he had left college, the yearbook published a photograph of Stewart—leather helmet perched loosely on his head, hands coupled behind his back, face set in a mischievous grin—in the section devoted to the football team. His name was misspelled "Steward" Ferguson, and beneath it was a caption reading, "'Fergie' may seem shy in everyday life, but he is always where he should be and, according to Yanktonites, sometimes where he shouldn't be. Fergie also placed on the all-conference team. We are glad that Fergie will be with us next year."

The *Tumbleweed*'s mistakes were far from Stewart's thoughts in the spring of 1925. By then, he was thousands of miles away, employed in the profession that would eventually lead to a crazy kind of fame. "Preachers' sons, like myself, graduating from small denominational colleges in the 1920s, had but limited choices in vocations," he recalled later. "Those choices were most often either teaching or preaching, and few sons of ministers, except when in deliriums of self-denial, ever considered following their fathers' vocational sacrifice. So most of us became teachers or coaches. My only personal desire was to find a position with as little teaching as possible and with plenty of coaching. The glamour of directing the winning of games left me starry-eyed."

For months, Stewart had mailed applications to school superintendents all over the country, and just before graduation, he received an offer. It was from the superintendent of schools in someplace called De Ridder, in the "mysterious" state of Louisiana. It paid $150 a month but offered Stewart something he valued more—adventure. "I knew it was Frenchy, which harmonized perfectly with the then Gay Paree day dream epoch of my youth," he said later. "I accepted the position eagerly."

CHAPTER 5

THE PRODIGAL SON

Stewart Ferguson daydreamed as he traveled south in a railway coach towards De Ridder, Louisiana, and his first job. There were stops in Sioux City and Omaha, then a transfer to the Kansas City Southern line for the rest of the trip. As he rode, he fantasized about the great successes that lay ahead. Dripping perspiration in the muggy August weather, he walked from the rail station to the Beauregard Parish courthouse to meet the superintendent of schools. He screwed up his courage, pulling his fedora down over one ear and swaggered into the building. "I'm the new coach from South Dakota," he announced.

The superintendent, a man named Lunsford, genially greeted Ferguson and then with some puzzlement asked, "What made you think we'd put you in a Negro school?" Like the rest of the South, Louisiana practiced rigid segregation of the races and assigning a white teacher to a Black school was unthinkable. Ferguson, who grew up in a state with few Black residents, hadn't known that. But now, he remembered that on his application he had asked not to work in a Black school. He explained. "I just wanted to be sure that my first job would give me a chance to do some real coaching," Ferguson said, "and I would not know how to begin with Negroes."

"You have a white school in a good community," Lunsford said, "and I'm sure with your help, they'll have another good basketball team this year."

"I don't know much about basketball," Ferguson replied, "but I'm sure I'll give them a hustling football team."

"I'm sorry, but Dry Creek has never had a football team."

Dry Creek, Lunsford quickly explained, was a small, rural school about twenty-two miles from De Ridder, a fairly large town with several lumber mills, a cotton gin, and connections with four separate railways. Most importantly, it was where Ferguson had expected to coach.

Crestfallen, Ferguson protested that he was not a hick coach and impulsively said, "I quit." Lunsford sighed and asked him to stay on until he could find someone else, adding hopefully that Ferguson might be "surprised" when he saw Dry Creek.

The road from De Ridder was a rutted sandy track, and the fields were littered with stumps of trees cut for the timber companies. To his surprise, Ferguson did warm to Dry Creek, which he captured in a letter at the time to his "sincere friend" Professor Judson Owen, head of Dakota Wesleyan's English department:

> The scene here is very picturesque: quaint Louisianan cottages with the galleries running through the center, swamps strangled with Spanish moss, red hills, and deep green pine forests. I live less than two hundred yards from [a] swamp full of alligators, poisonous snakes, wild cats, and tarantulas. This is a dangerous country, but carries more than the usual thrill with it.

One of those thrills, he wrote years later, included boarding with a family in a ramshackle house with cracks in the walls big enough for Ferguson to watch the stars and moon. On his first Saturday night there, while taking a bath in a zinc tub in his room, he looked up to see the entire family staring back at him through the cracks. Another thrill? A certain blonde colleague. They soon struck up a romance, and Ferguson cherished their long walks around the countryside.

Ferguson taught Latin, a surprising subject in a town where, as he noted, few people seemed able to speak English properly. It turned out that Latin was introduced many years earlier, apparently by Catholic missionaries, to help Cajun speakers learn English grammar. Ferguson also was appointed to be the drama coach and assistant principal. Basketball was the only sport, as Lunsford said, and the season ran from September to the following June. It also was played on an outdoors dirt court, which, in Ferguson's acerbic words, was often used as a "boudoir for diabetic hogs." The Dry Creek five, he boasted later, never lost a game on its own court, even to larger schools with indoor courts. Maybe, he thought, that was Dry Creek's edge; its players could dribble on a bumpy, often muddy, surface.

In April, a month or so before the end of the school year, Ferguson (who by now owned a car) drove over to De Ridder for a track meet. By chance, he found himself sitting next to Ward Anderson, superintendent of schools in Lake Charles, a major business center. The two men talked about sports and a few days later, Ferguson was offered a job coaching there, starting in September 1925. "My promotion was like a jump from the Five & Ten to the First National Bank," Ferguson wrote later.

Over the years, he often rued leaving Dry Creek. While staying likely meant a life wearing boots but no necktie and bathing in a washtub every Saturday night, there was one significant benefit: fans left the coaching to the coaches. Some parents, he said, might even have named babies after him.

Contrast that, Ferguson went on, with what happened later. "Probably," he said, "I wouldn't have peeked out of doors before going downtown, to avoid the most obvious contempt of those buzzard fans whose meat is the coach after a lost game." But he went to Lake Charles to teach history and serve as an assistant coach, in charge of the running backs, where he stayed for three highly successful years. A paradise for coaches, he called the city, because of the outstanding athletes who passed through high school while he was there, such as Bill Banker, who played without a helmet (which was not required at the time) and was called the "Blond Blizzard" for his long light-colored hair that blew in the wind as he ran for touchdown after touchdown. He would go on to set records at Tulane University and become an all-American (and later, a bit player in Hollywood cowboy movies). There was also Don Zimmerman, another future all-American running back at Tulane, and Walter "Dobie" Reeves, a soon-to-be star back for Louisiana State University. The list went on and on.

"Lake Charles was acres of four-leaf clovers for me," Ferguson said. "The place changed me in a year from a hick country coach to a smooth dealer in touchdowns." It would also lead to bigger things, although Ferguson knew it was the natural talent of his athletes more than any "coaching brilliance" that made his progression possible.

He was still capable of wild whims, and on September 20, 1927, astounded everybody who knew him back in Mitchell, South Dakota, as well as colleagues at Lake Charles High. He eloped. The bride was Alice Ione Raben, a classmate he had dated at Dakota Wesleyan. "Ione," as she was called, was a member of Wesleyan's theatre and debate societies with Ferguson, a dark-eyed beauty who was considered an oddball. A caption under her photograph in *The Tumbleweed* yearbook, a direct, smoldering come-on pose, read: "Ione is an odd creature, but when you know her, she is fine." Neither she nor Ferguson told anybody they were a current item, or for how long, before they drove to Houston to tie the knot. Like so many other things in his life, marriage would prove a trial.

In the fall of 1928 came another move, to Bolton, Louisiana. Many educators considered the high school there a model for the South, with an excellent academic record and a wide variety of extra-curricular activities. Most important to the recently married Ferguson, its pay scales were among the highest in state schools. Another factor behind Ferguson's decision to leave Lake Charles was S. M. Brame, the Bolton principal and a fellow little fellow. Ferguson admired Brame greatly because, he later said, the principal didn't care if Bolton won or lost games as long as it played fair. He later wrote, "[Brame] was easily the greatest educator I ever met."

Bolton did not produce the kind of athletes Ferguson found in Lake Charles— "no school did," he said—but there were a few memorable standouts. One was a sprinter named Pete Spera, a squat bullet who ran the hundred-meter dash in 9.9 seconds despite tape wrapped around his thighs to protect him from rubbing them raw. Another was Percy Barber, a basketball star who became the object of a frantic recruiting battle that was won, to the surprise of Louisiana coaches, by Columbia University in New York.

Bolton was a revelation to Ferguson—hired there as a history teacher and track coach, with no ties to football—who for the first time began thinking about the relationship between athletics and education. He said he felt at the end of each day that he had accomplished something for both sports and scholastics. It was a "wonderful" year, in the classroom and on the field. Pivoting sharply from his combative teenage years, he sponsored the school's Hi-Y Club, which aimed "to create, maintain, and extend high standards of Christian character in the school and community." If not for a Western Union telegram that arrived in the late winter of 1929 with a job offer he could not refuse, he might well have stayed in Bolton.

The offer came from Dakota Wesleyan, where only five years earlier he graduated with a major in English and a determination, shared with everyone on campus, to coach football. The position was athletic director, a prize for any twenty-nine-year-old whose job experience was limited to Louisiana high schools, and was something of a surprise to Ferguson, considering the significant amount of time he missed from school before finally accumulating sufficient credits to graduate.

The news broke in the South Dakota papers at end of February. Yet, Alexandria's hometown paper, the *Town Talk*, did not run a story on Ferguson's new job until May 24. Maybe Ferguson wanted to eliminate any possibility of distraction from his joyous school year at Bolton, including the imminent start of track season. Whatever the reason, the local paper made it clear that Ferguson left a strong mark in a short period of time. "A likable, clean, and honest young man" the paper said, and "his many friends join in wishing him much success in his new position." Principal Brame added that if he ever needed a job down the road, to call him. It was an offer Ferguson would not forget.

Back in Mitchell, the *Evening Republican* reported that the college's trustees had voted unanimously to hire him. It also reported, almost entirely falsely, that Ferguson was a four-year letterman in football for Dakota Wesleyan, had been twice named to the state's all-college team, played football for an American Legion team in Louisiana (technically true: he played once, in 1924 on Armistice Day) and was elected in 1927 to the all-time Dakota Wesleyan team.

What inspired these grandly inflated feats is anyone's guess. Ferguson may have made the claims, which later were repeated in publicity handouts sent to other newspapers. But in his own sketchy memoirs, he never referred to any such honors.

In fact, he continued to express wonder at Dakota Wesleyan for taking a chance on him (seemingly dismissing that the university did nominate him for a Rhodes Scholarship), given his prior penchant for misbehavior. This included sneaking into the girls' dorm with a friend one night, dressed in women's clothing, and another time tricking a history professor into reading a saucy excerpt from the novel *Tom Jones*, a definite violation of decorum at the strictly orthodox Methodist school.

The trustees did not explain why they hired Ferguson, except to say that they turned to him to revive Dakota Wesleyan's athletic fortunes, which certainly could use some improvement. His predecessor, Elliott Hatfield, resigned after just two football seasons. After a 5–1 record in 1927, his team went winless in nine games, the first season in school history without at least one win. Another report said that Ferguson's selection was also partly based on his ability to "develop track as a major sport at the Methodist school."

On the way back from Louisiana, Ferguson remembered a Bible story that he had heard from his father's pulpit many times—the story of the Prodigal Son, who after years of dissolute living, returns home to find forgiveness and a feast with a fatted calf. It was, he thought, an appropriate parallel with his own situation. He even found an apt metaphor. His fatted calf, he said, was in the form of a contract. "Never have I been more thrilled over obtaining a job," said Ferguson.

Then another thought occurred to him, one more grounded in reality and, like the story of the Prodigal Son, based on a scriptural image. It was quite possible, he thought, that his head was swelling into a tight fit for a crown of thorns.

CHAPTER 6

STUCK

Despite his outward air of swaggering confidence, Stewart Ferguson felt decidedly apprehensive about returning to Dakota Wesleyan College, and not only because his record for mischief and misconduct as an undergraduate undoubtedly remained fresh among instructors who now were his colleagues. The other, more serious, reason was contained in the language of the announcement that he would become the director of men's athletics, "to regain the athletic prestige the school temporarily lost this year." That word "temporarily" struck him as a very short leash.

His predecessor, Elliot Hatfield, lasted only two seasons and was dismissed after Dakota Wesleyan lost all nine of its football games in 1928, finishing dead last in the ten-college South Dakota Intercollegiate Athletic Conference. The prior year, Dakota Wesleyan had gone 5–1. Ferguson figured if a single bad season could cost somebody as respected as Hatfield his job, the trustees were unlikely to exercise much patience with a rookie coach.

It was late in the summer of 1929 when Ferguson arrived by rail. As he stepped down from the Main Street station, his legs literally trembled with nervousness. "I was frigidly afraid I couldn't make good," he wrote later. He also remembered someone saying that it was always tougher to make good in one's hometown. Still, as he walked toward the campus, he willed himself to swagger as he imagined legendary Notre Dame coach Knute Rockne did. "I thought it might not hurt to pretend to be a coach."

A voice called out, "Hey, Fergie, glad to see you back. You must have been a plenty hot coach down south." Ferguson grinned weakly and kept moving. A couple of blocks later, he walked onto campus and into College Hall, the administrative center, where he found Dakota Wesleyan president Earl A. Roadman waiting for him.

An accomplished rural teacher, pastor, and in-demand public speaker, Roadman was entering his third year leading the university and quickly got to the point. He wasted no time putting Ferguson on guard, telling him that his new job was a challenge, "A favorite expression of Methodists," Ferguson noted, "meaning you either produce miracles or get the hell out." Roadman reinforced Ferguson's anxiety as they talked about the school's poor performance on the field, which the president blamed on Coach Hatfield. He added with a smirk, "But, we let him finish the season." Ferguson wondered if the trustees would do that again.

A formal welcome followed a couple weeks later, hosted by President Roadman. Ferguson was the honored guest at a lakeside feast while fellow faculty served steaks off the grill and assorted Mitchell businessmen swapped stories of past Wesleyan football glory and yearnings for future success.

His first meeting with the football squad, a few days later, dismayed Ferguson. The players were smaller than the boys he had coached in Louisiana. What he needed, he decided, was an ally. He telephoned Glenn ("Hub") Hubbard, who played football with Ferguson at Dakota Wesleyan and now sold used cars in Huron and convinced him to come to Mitchell as his assistant, focusing on the linemen. They agreed that some serious psychology was required—trumpeting up team spirit and "a fanatical desire to win," wrote Ferguson. "We would persuade, convince, deceive and exploit the boys for the glory of Ferguson and Hubbard and, incidentally, Dakota Wesleyan."

On September 18, Ferguson told reporters he felt confident and enthusiastic. Two weeks later in the season opener in Brookings, South Dakota State College thumped Dakota Wesleyan 49–0. The following week, Ferguson worked in all twenty players who made the second straight out-of-conference trip to Sioux City, Iowa, in an

18–0 loss to Trinity College. The rookie head coach was upbeat coming out of the game, feeling that he had uncovered some new lineup combinations and told the state's most widely circulated paper, the *Sioux Falls Argus-Leader*, that he "believes the team will show marked improvement with each game." His optimistic forecast proved prescient. Wesleyan strung together four straight conference wins, outscoring the opposition 89 to 18 and setting up for a leap from worst to first in South Dakota's intercollegiate conference.

Spearfish Normal, the defending conference champ, sat at 4–0 in the conference, like Wesleyan, but was done for the season. Ferguson's Tigers had one game left, versus archrival Yankton College. The Yankton game, traditionally the last of the season for both schools, was always hotly contested, and this year, Ferguson's Tigers needed a win to complete a perfect conference record and share of the title. There were ten colleges in the conference, but schools needed to play only four to qualify for conference honors.

One annual pregame ritual for the Yankton battle was a pep talk delivered by a committee of prominent Mitchell alumni. This year, it was a lawyer, a doctor, and a merchant, and their emotional calls to glory made Ferguson privately promise never to let outsiders into his dressing room again—a vow he would later break several times and under some bizarre circumstances.

Played on a snow-covered field, in freezing weather, the game was a scoreless tie, featuring plenty of fumbles and little sustained offense. Although the Tigers didn't win, they also didn't lose, and given the conference rules of the day, that was enough to share the conference championship. Ferguson found himself a hero; as part of Mitchell's full acceptance, he was invited to join the Kiwanis Club and strangers slapped him on the back.

Basketball was not as important as football—it wasn't on many college campuses and its growing popularity, sparked in part by double headers in New York's Madison Square Garden, was still five years away—but Dakota Wesleyan fans expected Ferguson to produce a winner in that sport, too. Hatfield's team only played eleven games in the 1928–1929 season and lost seven of them. Ferguson improved on that, winning ten games while losing five. More importantly, Wesleyan's 9–2 record in the conference was good enough to win the title.

What impressed school officials more was that several games at the World's Only Corn Palace (initially built in 1892 as a wooden structure, twelve years after the founding of Mitchell, and where Wesleyan played its home games) lured capacity crowds. The idea to cover a building with corn emanated from the desire of Mitchell's early leaders to put the city "on the map." William Clark, during his famous expedition with Meriwether Lewis and the Corps of Discovery in 1804–1806, reported that the upper Missouri region "may with propriety . . . be termed the Deserts of America, as I do not Conceive any part can ever be Settled, as it is deficient in water, Tim[b]er & too steep to be tilled." The Corn Belt Real Estate Association thought otherwise and wanted to attract settlers to the area; therefore, they "built the first Corn Palace to showcase all the crops that could be grown in the rich Dakota soil."

In 1921, the third and present-day palace was built, completely of steel and brick due to safety laws that prevented large groups from gathering in wooden structures. By 1929, the associated annual Corn Palace Festival was in its thirty-seventh year. Held in late September to celebrate the harvest, the festival booked assorted entertainment acts and invited representatives from neighboring counties to display their grown crops and manufactured goods.

The final, signature, undertaking was (and still is) a yearly panoramic design of the entire outside of the palace, with decorative materials made from local corn, grasses, and grain. When the corn matured in late summer, a local artist led the intense effort to replace the prior design and get to work on a new celebratory theme, selected in conjunction with the Corn Palace Committee. In the late twenties, the artist and director was W. A. Kearney, who did not use blueprints or scales; he sketched the designs on panels with chalk, indicating the color scheme and combination to be used, a truly giant "corn-by-number project."

The 1929 theme centered on Mitchell's early history and the development of the surrounding territory, and over one hundred men and women—using corn cutting machines to slice the ears in half the long way before nailing in the panel designs (seven varieties of corn totaling over two thousand bushels, along with twenty tons of grains and grasses)—painstakingly made Kearney's creation come to life. Upon completion in the fall, the detailed historical panels led up to the central picture, a view of a modern South Dakota farm home.

Inside the Corn Palace, basketball was a top attraction. In the spring of 1930, Wesleyan administrators were drawn not only by a team likely to win but by the playing style Ferguson brought from Louisiana, which emphasized speed and lots of passing, a necessity at Dry Creek, where dribbling had been out of the question on its outdoor, bumpy dirt court.

During basketball season, Ferguson sprang another surprise and basked in more admiring applause. The *Argus-Leader* headline read, "Wesleyan Grid Team Will Play At Baton Rouge." Dakota Wesleyan, it turned out, would open its 1930 football schedule in Baton Rouge against powerful Louisiana State University, a deal that Ferguson struck with Coach Russ Cohen, an old friend from his Louisiana days. In exchange for $1,500 in expenses, Wesleyan—in its first ever intersectional game, namely outside a school's usual competition or conference—would take the longest trip to date by any South Dakota college team in any sport. Both men stood to gain something. For Ferguson, it was adventure, publicity, and a pointed reminder to college officials that he was a coach of considerable intersectional standing. For Cohen, it was an easy workout, and a sure victory, for his team.

The Wesleyan team set off by train, with the marching band, cheerleaders, and pep squad leading a noisy sendoff at the station. Several hours later, in Chicago, the players transferred to an Illinois Central sleeper, and suddenly, to the surprise of Ferguson and his players, Earl A. Roadman appeared to deliver a personal, presidential pep talk. He slipped on board unnoticed, and after speaking to the team, he disembarked to return to Mitchell.

The only time Ferguson was at a loss for words on the trip was during a meal stop in Fulton, Missouri, where the train had stopped for an hour. On the ride south from Chicago, Ferguson had been thinking he was "becoming quite a coach" and though "homely enough," was wondering whether he had graduated to the coach-like appearance of the "master" Rockne. He didn't have to wait long to find out. Near the end of the meal, the proprietor of the station restaurant asked where the coach was sitting. One of his players pointed to Ferguson, and the proprietor slapped his leg, guffawed, and finally said, "You can't fool me, kid, I've seen coaches before."

Before leaving South Dakota, Ferguson told the papers his goal was to hold Louisiana State to fewer than fifty points and noted that halfback Walter ("Dobie") Reeves, the captain of the Louisiana team, was one of the Lake Charles boys he had coached a few years earlier. Louisiana State won 76–0, with Reeves chipping in for two touchdowns.

Dakota Wesleyan ended the season with six wins and three losses as Ferguson generally leaned on the strength of some talented running backs (enabling him to work in a sophisticated double-wing back formation, an offensive innovation attributed to the illustrious Coach Glenn ("Pop") Warner, then at Stanford, which emphasized deception and power) in a fluid week to week rotation to keep them fresh, while also going with the hot hand. Wesleyan missed its chance at another conference title with a Thanksgiving loss to Yankton. One of the wins, 33–6 over Augustana College, came in the first night game played in Sioux City, with two thousand spectators attracted more for the novelty than the action. The field was lighted by twenty 2,000-watt lamps and Ferguson and Augustana coach H. Paul Dee were so worried the lamps would fail that they agreed win or lose, the score would not count in conference standings.

After the Yankton loss, Ferguson proudly stated that the annual football banquet, open to the public for seventy-five cents, including dinner, would feature Bill Banker, the "Blond Blizzard" all-American star at Tulane University and another of the boys who had played at Lake Charles High School. As it turned out, Banker was a no-show, but nobody appeared to care. Wesleyan's players presented their slick-haired coach with a big bottle of hair tonic, and Ferguson announced two recently received intersectional contracts—Springfield College, in Springfield, Massachusetts, and Gonzaga, in Spokane, Washington—were under consideration for the following season.

The 1930–1931 basketball season immediately got under way and brought Wesleyan, and Ferguson, great acclaim. An undefeated conference season, sparked by freshman center sensation Jake Beier, led to an invitation to compete in the annual National Amateur Athletic Association (AAU) tournament, the only such competition at the time and a gathering for the top independent and college teams in the country. Dakota Wesleyan battled through a snowstorm in Iowa and barely reached Kansas City, Missouri, in time for the tip off in its opening AAU game. The tough trip didn't seem to affect them. They raced to a big lead and cruised to a victory over Louisville, Kentucky's Brown Hotel, who had qualified for the tournament by winning the combined independent basketball title of Indiana and Kentucky. Ferguson's crew lost a tight one in the next round to Oklahoma's East Central Teachers, who had placed third the prior year, but a new precedent had been set: Dakota Wesleyan had competed at the national level.

Three weeks later, Ferguson opened the track season by taking four students to the Minnesota Relays in Minneapolis, where the boys finished an incredible second in the mile, the first time a Dakota Wesleyan track team ever placed in a big meet. Heck, he had even scored some quality bonding time with President Roadman at an evening the president hosted to celebrate the school's newest organization and one at the core of Ferguson's soul—the PKs, forty-six strong at its inception with Ferguson one of the two faculty members.

In addition, Ferguson submitted a 309-page thesis to Louisiana State University, his final requirement for a master's degree in history. Ferguson had started his graduate work in the summer of 1927. His thesis, A History of the City of Lake Charles, now sits in the archives of McNeese State University and is often consulted by historians and others.

Stewart Ferguson was riding high, and when he asked for money to pay for the publication of an athletic guide, the first in school history, President Roadman quickly said yes. Roadman did know that Ferguson mainly wanted to promote himself. He wrote almost every word in the forty-eight-page guide, and, in his own memoirs later noted, "You may be sure that I hid no Ferguson fame." On the first page of the guide, Ferguson credited himself with turning out "the most brilliant backfield in conference history," "the best basketball team in Wesleyan history," and "some of the greatest track stars in state history."

The pumped-up coach also convinced himself that he was too good for Dakota Wesleyan and Mitchell. "I felt I was cheating the world and myself by remaining at such a small college," he wrote later. Ferguson mailed various applications to other universities—"all of them I considered big enough for my talents." His ruminations around an evolving big-time coach was not the only reason driving him to move on from Mitchell. His marriage to Ione Raben, a Mitchell native, was falling apart. They had married impulsively in Houston, Texas, while he was working in Louisiana, but now, only a few years later, it was clear to him that he and Ione were going their separate ways. In April 1931, she sued for a divorce. He filed a suit of his own a few weeks later.

On July 23, a Davison County, South Dakota circuit court judge, upon having reviewed all the submitted evidence and the arguments of both lawyers, dismissed all of Ione's claims—including that her husband had caused her a nervous breakdown on December 29, 1930—and awarded Stewart "an absolute divorce . . . on the ground of extreme cruelty." There were no children and Ione was working as a schoolteacher, but she said she needed financial help and asked for sixty dollars a month in alimony. Ferguson's salary was $2,600 a year and he listed his assets as $12.50 in a bank account and a DeSoto coupe worth one hundred dollars. The court awarded her the sixty dollars per month, and on August 3, Stewart Ferguson was once again a single man.

Though successful in court, Ferguson did not get any real bites from the coaching applications he had sent a few months earlier. He was, however, confident enough of his standing to take a bold step—especially amid soaring unemployment in the intensifying depression—at the start of the 1931 academic year. He asked Roadman for a raise.

"I'm sure [that] other colleges will pay me more than I'm receiving here," he said. Roadman smiled thinly. "You can?" he said. "I'm always glad when our faculty can better themselves financially." This was not what Ferguson counted on. "I guess you understand that I like Wesleyan and would never leave just for more money," he said.

"Do you mean you really love Wesleyan?" Roadman asked.

"I sure do," Ferguson said.

"Splendid. Splendid," Roadman replied. "I'm so glad because we are suggesting our most loyal faculty members contribute one hundred dollars each to our new financial campaign, and I know that those who love Wesleyan will not fail her."

Ferguson left the office, one hundred dollars poorer, determined never to ask for another raise. He ended his career at Dakota Wesleyan with the same salary that he received when he was hired (other than a 10 percent across faculty decrease for the 1932–1933 school year), but the $2,600 was only on paper. In fact, as the Great Depression deepened and money grew tighter, he was partially paid in goods and services, among them, potatoes, dental treatment, and cords of wood.

As the Tigers' 1931 football season approached, hurt by losses in the line and backfield, Ferguson delivered a downbeat prediction about Dakota Wesleyan's prospects. "No kidding," he said, "prospects are worse than they've been since I came here." Nevertheless, he had scheduled ten games, the first South Dakota conference team to do so, and proudly announced to reporters a new offensive style for the season. He said it was "based on the old Louisiana Line Divide," though there was no ink around that name to date and he didn't go into any details at the time. It may have had some roots in Alabama's John William Hobbs ("Doc") Pollard's secret 1906 "Military Shift," in which every player but the center lined up on the line of scrimmage and joined hands before turning right or left to form an unbalanced line. Further, it was a possible offshoot of the shift formations that had grown in popularity across college football, largely due to Minnesota's long-time head man, Dr. Henry Williams, and Notre Dame's Knute Rockne.

While he didn't discuss it back then, Ferguson, while coaching in Louisiana, had also been influenced and intrigued by the more open-style play and creative formations that were becoming increasingly popular across the South—including reverse plays, lateral passes, and flexible, faster-moving formations—and creating a speedier, more exciting game.

No matter what new formations and plays Ferguson had in mind, the bigger season story was his team was back on the move. This time, they were off to West Virginia, with a brief stop in Chicago to pose for photographs with the legendary University of Chicago coach Alonzo Stagg, plus a detour to Washington, where Ferguson had somehow arranged for a White House lawn photo op with President Herbert Hoover. Ferguson also worked in some side trips to Mount Vernon, Lexington, the Shenandoah Valley, and the Allegheny Mountains. This mixing of tourism, celebrity moments, and sports would prove an intoxicating experience for Ferguson, with unexpected consequences.

Wesleyan played two games in West Virginia, losing 61–0 to Davis & Elkins, a small Presbyterian school in Elkins, and New River State College, in Montgomery, which only months earlier changed its name from New River State School and became a four-year institution. New River defeated Ferguson's team, 32–0. The cheers were noticeably muted when the team returned to Mitchell. Things didn't improve much back in South Dakota—the season ended with two victories, six defeats, and one tie, a scoreless draw with hated Yankton that meant the season was not a total write-off.

Setting money, marital, and other problems aside, Ferguson once again led a basketball team that, in the 1931–1932 season, exceeded even the impressive record set the previous year. This one went undefeated in seventeen regular season games and won a third straight conference title, news that to Ferguson's surprise and disappointment appeared on page two of the student newspaper—the front-page story ran under the headline, "Wesleyan Wins State

Forensic Contest." It was a throwback to earlier years, when the literary and debating teams were sometimes regarded more highly than athletics. The basketball team returned to the front page when Wesleyan accepted another invitation to compete in the annual AAU tournament, where it reached the quarterfinal round before falling in overtime.

A revived Ferguson returned to Mitchell and accepted a challenge from the House of David, a talented band of touring bearded basketball players representing a Michigan-based fundamentalist religious sect. In a game that packed the Corn Palace, Wesleyan won 40–37. Mitchell's businessmen also successfully scheduled a game with the touring national AAU champions, the Wichita Henrys, jamming the Corn Palace one more time.

The standout basketball season may also have been the impetus for the not quite big-time coach to at least generate demand from some other colleges. Just before the exhibition contest with the AAU champs, Ferguson was invited to meet with Drake University's faculty advisor, who was in Minneapolis at the time, to discuss the recently vacated position of athletic director and head football coach. (Drake's former athletic head, the extremely popular Ossie Solem, had left to become the new head coach at Iowa.) Ferguson was one of thirty-two candidates to apply for the position, and one of only two to formally interview in Minneapolis. While not quite "big time," Drake, located in Des Moines, Iowa, was a definite step up from little Dakota Wesleyan and did boast football royalty on its regular schedule: Notre Dame. The job went to Evan Williams, a seasoned and highly respected football and basketball coach, who had spent the last thirteen years as athletic director at the same Minnesota high school that launched the career of Drake's prior man, Ossie Solem. Stewart Ferguson, in contrast, had logged only three years as Dakota Wesleyan's athletic director, but he was stuck.

CHAPTER 7

METHODIST MEAT

Stewart Ferguson's slide from the good graces of his Wesleyan Methodist brethren began after the close of the 1932 school year. He did not recruit any football players during the summer, confident that his celebrity would bring more than enough talent to campus. He even discouraged boosters—notably including university president Roadman, who insisted on winning teams as a means of luring students to Wesleyan—from promising too much to prospective players. There was grumbling, but Ferguson ignored it.

Once again, a big trip overshadowed the team's overall results. This season it was a train trip to Spokane, Washington, to face a strong Gonzaga University team, with Ferguson content to get some additional national exposure for the university. The lackluster fall finished up 3–5, the finale a disputed 2–0 loss to Yankton, in which Ferguson unsuccessfully protested Wesleyan's rival getting a fifth down on one of its fourth quarter possessions.

Although Ferguson suffered a second straight disappointing football season, the promise of another superb basketball team left him not overly concerned about his standing with the school. Led again by sensational junior center Jake Beier—who would go on to become the first thousand-point scorer in Dakota Wesleyan history—Ferguson's Tigers won a fourth consecutive conference title (though they did drop their first conference game in three years) before losing in the first round of Kansas City's Amateur Athletic Union tournament.

By the start of autumn, Fergie was feeling much less certain about his overall job security. The past successes, which included national attention for the three basketball teams Ferguson had coached to tournaments sponsored by the AAU, were celebrated with banner headlines and noisy rallies. But basketball was not football, and there, Ferguson had failed to field winners in the prior two seasons. He knew the knives were out, and he knew why. He also publicly expressed doubt that 1933 would turn his losing streak around.

At the first practice, on September 5, Ferguson told reporters that he was pessimistic about Wesleyan's prospects because there were so few talented candidates for the team. Making matters worse, President Roadman had an extra set of eyes on this Tigers team; his son Chuck, a freshman reserve the prior season, was trying out for the squad. When Ferguson asked him what position he wanted to play, Chuck said quarterback.

Two consecutive losing seasons—along with the weakened economic climate—had cost Wesleyan much fan support, and so just before the opening home game against Springfield's Southern Normal, Dakota Wesleyan announced it was lowering admission to thirty-five cents for adults and a quarter for children. Ferguson announced that President Roadman's son would start at quarterback. Southern won 14–0, continuing a disturbing streak for Ferguson—five seasons, five opening game defeats.

On top of the concerns around his team, Ferguson privately felt himself drifting from a coach's usual "whatever it takes to win" attitude. In fact, after a surprising and sudden comeback win the next week at Spearfish Normal—aided by a blocked punt and interception late in the game—he told reporters he was restricting scrimmage to "tag tackling" in a week of needed rest for his players, heading into a homecoming game against Huron. Years later, he reflected: "I was becoming a decent coach rather than the typical one."

He also felt he was increasingly becoming Methodist meat, and the knives were about to get sharper. President Roadman, representing Dakota Wesleyan at the forty-ninth annual five-day Methodist Episcopal church state conference in Vermillion—and scheduled to address conference members the next morning—was enjoying the festive Saturday night education banquet, when word reached him that Dakota Wesleyan had lost a football game.

It was October 14, and Wesleyan had dropped its homecoming tilt to Huron College, a small Presbyterian coeducational school that could (and did) rightly brag that it was the first college in Dakota Territory to award a degree, in 1887. Huron had narrowly won, 7–0, but the score was not what triggered the heated dinner conversations in Vermillion. Although there was an intense rivalry among the half dozen South Dakota schools affiliated with various Christian denominations, the loss by Wesleyan, the only Methodist college in the state, was not the main issue, either. The issue was Ferguson himself.

There had been talk about him for years, and according to Ferguson, it had intensified during the summer of 1931 when he and his wife Ione sued each other for divorce, including a "he said, she said" list of accusatory claims. To Methodists, divorce was a sin, and it was a safe bet that some pastor, somewhere, would assail it from the pulpit every Sunday. Even so, Ferguson might have survived the gossip and enmity if he had made even the slightest effort to disarm his enemies. Instead, he goaded them by his words and actions, which included his current flaunting of a relationship with a Mitchell divorcée.

Like many college coaches, especially those in small towns, Ferguson was constantly under scrutiny. At denominational colleges, this scrutiny went beyond final scores. It invariably included, sometimes unfairly, the example of Christian living that a coach was supposed to exemplify. His relationship with Dakota Wesleyan, along with much of the Mitchell business and social establishment so important to the college, continued to deteriorate and time was running short to mend fences.

The season lurched on, and the losses piled up. By early November, the Mitchell *Evening Republican* chimed in: "There's lots of skeptics in these parts, Mr. Ferguson." Heading into the final game against Yankton College, the team had won just one game and hadn't scored a point in over a month. The Yankton game remained by far the most important of the year; Yankton, a Congregational school, was more than just another denominational rival—it was an intense and long-running competition between two cities that claimed supremacy in South Dakota's southeast corner. In Ferguson's eyes, as he wrote later, "It was a game for my job."

A game tied 6–6 at halftime turned in the third quarter as Yankton's four-year all-conference fullback, Albert Postulka, took over, running for one score and passing for another, while Wesleyan's offense remained stagnant in a 19–6 defeat. Thinking about his overall situation, Ferguson figured that a couple of the college trustees would support him, but that the majority would judge him unfit to continue, and not just because the Dakota Wesleyan team had won only one game. "Because I was dating the most luscious blonde in the city, who had recently been divorced, it was natural that criticism of me as a coach would be further stimulated by jealousy," he wrote. It was vintage Ferguson, attributing his problems to sexual envy and hypocrisy, and to petty vendettas by ambitious and opportunistic colleagues.

After the disappointing loss to Yankton, Ferguson kept his skewed point of view private and focused on the basketball team, led by the conference's top player, senior Jake Beier. Ferguson prioritized "rigorous" daily conditioning and zeroed in on two new players to join Beier and two veterans for his most effective starting five. Toward the end of January—with his team still undefeated in the conference but showing a tendency for "nervous" play with the ball—he gathered reporters for a state of the team address, saying that "by February 5, I and everyone else will know whether I've got a basketball team worth hollering about."

He was referring to the upcoming home match-up with Augustana. When the date arrived, both teams were an identical 6–0 in conference play. In front of another packed, "frenzied" Corn Palace crowd, Beier fouled out with seven minutes left but Ferguson's crew hung in before a last-second game winner curled in and out of the basket. Wesleyan remained second in the conference the rest of the way, finishing out of the top spot for the first time in five years. The final dagger for Ferguson's coaching career at the school was just weeks away.

In a touch of cruel irony, it was track—a sport that five years earlier was mentioned as a needed growth area and another reason for Ferguson's hiring at Wesleyan—that finally pushed his simmering discontent to the surface. On April 27, 1934, one day before a home dual meet with Huron, the first track event of the season, the Athletic Committee notified Ferguson that most of his track and field team, twelve in total, had been declared scholastically ineligible. While there was no produced evidence of administrative foul play, Ferguson felt otherwise; he described later in his unpublished memoirs that this tactic "was the favorite Holy Inquisition of college [deans] and presidents" to accelerate the departures of coaches they were ready to cast aside. Enraged, he instantly decided to take this information to the *Evening Republican*, thinking it would make some hot reading for the local sports fans.

As soon as he read the story, however, Ferguson regretted it. The school's reaction was swift. President Roadman was away on a business trip but directed his administrative dean to call Ferguson into his office and tell him that unless the story was immediately retracted, he would be fired. Ferguson refused, rushed downtown to the *Republican* offices, and announced his resignation.

The news was reported on May 1 under an eight-column-wide headline. Roadman took the high road, mentioning Ferguson's "genius for producing winning teams and giving Wesleyan national prominence." The story also noted that Ferguson had met recently with the president of Arkansas State College about its open athletic director position—reported two weeks earlier to have occurred in Chicago—and that the coach's salary had been sharply decreased in the last two years, which was not really the case. Though Ferguson humorously failed in his earlier attempt for a salary bump, all Dakota Wesleyan teacher salaries had been reduced by 10 percent in the fall of 1932, part of the school's overall budgeting plan as the depression wore on.

The bottom line was that Ferguson had one foot dangling out Mitchell's door for a few years, and he finally forced his way through. As the school year wound down, the news came that Dakota Wesleyan had hired a new athletic director. He was Lester Belding, who had played fullback at the University of Iowa and was now coaching the high school team in Mason City, Iowa, which would one day become famous as the setting for *The Music Man*.

Roadman said he wanted Ferguson to attend the welcoming breakfast for Belding. Ferguson demurred on grounds that his presence might dampen the enthusiasm of the moment. Roadman insisted and suggested that Ferguson might need his help landing another position. "Naturally, I attended," Ferguson wrote later.

When the academic year ended, and with his contract officially expired, Ferguson turned his attention to finding a college that would appreciate a friendly, eccentric, combustible history buff with a thin skin and tendency to reject assorted authority types. To his surprise, he would shortly find one.

PART 2

FINDING FUN—AND FAME

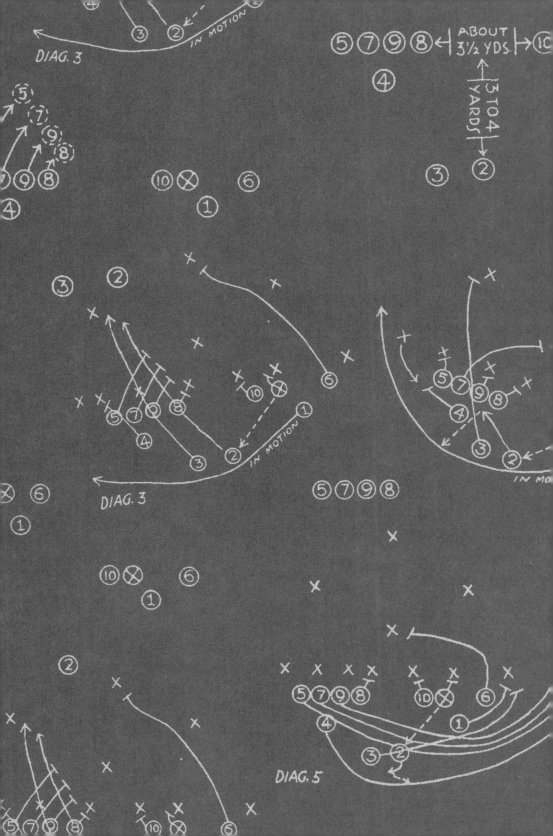

DIAG. 3

ABOUT 3½ YDS.

3 TO 4 YARDS

DIAG. 3

IN MOTION

IN MO

DIAG. 5

CHAPTER 8

DAMN YANKEE

Finding himself with neither a job nor any prospects for one but with a scheme for getting rich without breaking a sweat, Stewart Ferguson boarded a Chicago and North Western train and left Mitchell for Chicago, via Milwaukee, in early June 1934. The scheme involved a complicated horse racing system Ferguson had worked out. It was difficult even for him to explain in plain language, but the basic idea was to divide the weight of a horse, minus the weight of the jockey, saddle, and other gear, by the distance of the race to determine what he called the energy burn rate. Somehow, this would separate winners from losers. He had been working out the details for several months with make-believe bets that paid handsome dividends, and now he was anxious to try the real thing.

He arrived in Chicago with most of his life savings, withdrawn from a Mitchell bank account, and immediately made his way to the Arlington Heights racetrack, one of three in the Windy City. He bet two dollars on the first race and lost it. But in the second race, a long shot named Golden Sun returned $125, and Ferguson bet half his winnings on a nag named Venus De Milo. The horse lost, and before the day ended Ferguson had squandered all the money he brought to Chicago. It got worse.

"Then came the customary long string of losers," he wrote later. "Before the end of the week, I was playing the horses only to show." That is, to place third. It wasn't long before he spent almost all his savings. Disgusted, he abandoned his betting system, but not his love of horse racing, which he had come to enjoy in his youth while watching cowboys in Gregory, South Dakota race their mounts along Main Street for Saturday night saloon money. He returned to Mitchell for the rest of the summer. As the new school year drew near, he began thinking seriously about finding employment.

Before the summer, Ferguson had contacted an agency that specialized in placing teachers. He telephoned to see if there was any news. Yes, there was: Monticello Agriculture and Mechanical College, in rural Arkansas, was offering to reimburse travel expenses for anyone willing to travel there to interview for the job of athletic director. The reimbursement offer was good enough for him, so off he went.

Within two hours, Ferguson was aboard an Illinois Central train headed south. He got off after a sleepless night in Memphis, which he had imagined as a delight of majestic Mississippi River vistas, seductively hot blues tunes, and willing women. The reality, he said later, was that it was sweltering, dirty, and unwelcoming, and he resumed his trip, after a nap in a room rented by the hour, on a Missouri Pacific train bound for the Louisiana coast. It was a jolting, rocking ride on an unpadded seat in a day coach filled with what Ferguson described as unwashed bodies and snoring farmers. He felt disgusted enough to detrain at McGhee, Arkansas, about twenty-three miles from Monticello, and take a bus the rest of the way. It took him over a loose-gravel, chuck-holed roadway past some of the most dilapidated houses he had ever seen. The land looked exhausted, the inhabitants listless, dust everywhere. Ferguson wondered if he was smart to return to the South. At least in Louisiana he had found a kind of ethnic charm and wild beauty.

The bus pulled into Monticello, which to Ferguson looked depressingly uninviting. A farm and timber town of three thousand inhabitants, it was located in the deep southeastern corner of Arkansas near the borders with Louisiana and Mississippi. Downtown was a square with a new Drew County courthouse standing in its center. Arranged around the square, in one- and two-story wood or brick buildings, were businesses as diverse as an insurance agency, a barbershop, a ladies' wear emporium, and a pool hall. Along with the nearby rail and bus depots, two movie houses, and a couple of other shops, this was almost the entire Monticello business district. "Baptist architecture," Ferguson sneered, adding, "The paper-littered sidewalks . . . and the cook stove heat made it a nightmare for anybody who had seen any other cities." This first impression defined his feelings about Monticello for his entire stay.

There was no taxi service to the college, located about three miles away, and he didn't know there was a school bus shuttle; a sidewalk loiterer agreed to take Ferguson out to the campus. "Ain't never took anybody out there except for two dollars," he told Ferguson. Ferguson had only three dollars, but he handed the money over, threw his suitcase in the back seat, and climbed into the car. Later, he would learn that the usual standard fare was a quarter, and that, as happened often in his life, he had been taken like a rube.

The college was located about a mile off Highway 13, at the end of a long driveway lined with oak, crepe myrtle, chinaberry, magnolia, and pine trees. The car rattled over a cattle guard and for the second time, Ferguson wondered what he was getting himself into. He liked the flowers and shrubs; the college boasted that there were 108 varieties arranged on the campus, which was laid out on a hilly rise around a traffic circle. But architecturally, Monticello A & M looked like an unfinished public works project. A brick armory was located next to a dormitory, with the administration building behind a structure Ferguson couldn't identify. It reminded him, he said later, of a mildewed high school.

In fact, into the 1920s, A & M had been a high school called the Fourth District State Agricultural School, established in 1909 by the state legislature under pressure from the Arkansas Farmers' Educational and Cooperative Union, an influential lobbying group of the day. Its members, almost all cotton planters, saw that while they were selling cotton, they also were forced to go outside the state for almost everything they needed, from cattle feed to clothing. The answer, they decided, was agricultural diversification, and the key to that was better education in farming and homemaking. Not only that, but they wanted the politicians to place these schools amid big farms, the better for farmers to keep an eye on things. The Fourth District school, which provided learning from sixth through twelfth grades, covered seventeen counties in the southern tier of Arkansas. At the same time, three similar schools were established in Magnolia, Russellville, and Jonesboro, and, like the Fourth District school, one day they would also become colleges (and athletic rivals).

Through some hanky-panky involving financial pledges of help from Monticello's business and farming leaders, Monticello won out over Fordyce, which also wanted a special state school to teach "scientific agriculture" to its boys and girls. At the time, most schools in southern Arkansas, as almost everywhere else in the rural south, were one-room buildings that taught all classes at the same time, doubled as churches, and closed during the planting and harvesting seasons. The amount in the disputed pledges was only $200, but that was enough to sour relations between the campus and downtown factions. It would fester long enough to make Ferguson's life miserable.

Classes began in 1910, with 137 students sharing space in a downtown building that housed Hinemon University School, which offered a classical education that featured Greek, Latin, and French to the sons and daughters of well-to-do planters and merchants. The following fall, students of Fourth District, or SAS (for State Agriculture School), moved onto the new campus, with its unfinished administration building, small dining hall, Sorrells Hall dormitory for boys (named for a trustee), and part of Willard Hall for girls (named for a teacher). Each room was furnished with a mirror, a broom, an oil lamp, a wood stove, a barrel for water, and a wash pan. Outdoor toilets, segregated by sex, were near the dorms. The first meal was served the night before classes began, with boys and girls seated separately at seven tables. Frank Horsfall, who had just been hired to run the school, asked the girls present to serve the food. Only one volunteered. The girls, it seemed, had grown up on farms, planting, hoeing, and picking cotton, and undoubtedly figured that they had spent enough years in undignified labor. So Horsfall and his wife served the meal.

At the beginning, four courses were offered: sixth, seventh and eighth grade with emphasis on agriculture and domestic science; the same classes but at the high school level; A *Special Course for Farmers*; and A *Short Course for Farmers and Others*. Students were expected to devote half their time to carpentry, blacksmithing, sewing, cooking, and tending to the crops grown in the school's fields and gardens, or to the herds of Jersey and Holstein cows roaming over two hundred acres of grazing land. Tuition was free, and the school handbook estimated the cost of a full academic year at $90 for room and food, $12.50 for books, and a $5 registration fee.

Overseeing everything was one of the most remarkable and controversial men in Arkansas education. Frank Horsfall, the son of English immigrants, was principal, president, and founding father. He had been lured to Monticello in 1910 from Oklahoma, where he headed another agricultural school. At the University of Arkansas, he was the only member of the 1900 school of horticulture class, and he attained regional celebrity for his work in experimental fruit development. Now, in Monticello, he taught eight classes a day, kept all the administrative and financial records, managed the dorms, farm, and dairy, and hired and supervised student labor. Everybody called him "Chief." When she was not caring for their four children, his wife acted as dormitory matron and school nurse. But all did not go smoothly.

Horsfall was a strict disciplinarian who banned dancing, smoking by girls, and cars on campus, and made attendance mandatory at chapel services where he assailed modern morals. At one chapel talk, he said that "a person who danced, violated all of the Ten Commandments, danced for gratification only, and would go to hell." Girls were required to wear cotton stockings because he considered silk stockings unladylike. He was quick to confront rowdy students, sometimes threatening to punch them, and had once faced down a gang of Monticello toughs who planned to wreck the campus as a Halloween prank. When another gang invaded the girls' dorm on horseback, Horsfall brandished a shotgun and warned he would shoot if they did not get out. They got out.

There were serious crises of other kinds. The school almost went broke, and farmers complained that too much attention was paid to non-agricultural subjects, like music. Of the nine faculty members in 1915, three taught music. Horsfall battled everybody from governors to local merchants over everything from his decision to use student labor instead of local workers, to suspicious payments he made to trustees. He survived repeated investigations and demands for his resignation, however, one of them made by angry townspeople during a noisy, ugly meeting held at the county courthouse. Newspapers carried his various fights on page one for months at a time.

In 1923, with enrollment at 420, the school and the University of Arkansas entered into an agreement to offer two years of college courses. With that, the Fourth District Agriculture and Mechanical College, as it was renamed, became a junior college. That technically was the status when Ferguson arrived on campus, although by 1934, A & M was offering a four-year college program. In fact, it had held its first college graduation, with a class of eight, in the spring.

Ferguson knew nothing about the "Chief" or anything of the school's background. More important, he did know that 1934 was its most tumultuous year yet, with an all-out student revolt and a purge of faculty members who sided with them against Horsfall. Only a handful of students were on campus—most were still at home, helping their families with the harvest, or slaughtering, canning, and carrying out other season chores. Ferguson asked to see President Horsfall and was told the Chief was away and no one knew when he would return.

To pass the time, Ferguson walked through knee-high weeds growing around the football stadium, which had been equipped with lights for night games the previous year, making A & M the first school in southern Arkansas to play at night, a novelty that attracted more fans than the games themselves. The stands held two thousand spectators, and Ferguson took a seat on one of the wooden planks. A student joined him.

Ferguson said hello. "You're a student here?" he asked.

"Yeah," the student replied, "if you can call this goddamned place a school."

"What's wrong with it?"

"Everything," the student said.

To change the subject, Ferguson asked about the football team's prospects. The boy said he wasn't sure A & M would field a team. "Nobody ain't going to play on it," he said. Ferguson asked why. "Cause they can't fire Coach Hammons and get by with it," the boy replied.

This was something else Ferguson did not know. Foy Hammons had coached the football team for three seasons, winning thirteen games, losing nine, and tying five. This included a 7–2–1 record in 1931, the best record in the fourteen years since A & M had hired its first coach. Hammons was popular with students, even more so after he supported their demands that Horsfall relax some of his rigid, outdated campus rules. After the conflict with Horsfall and his allies turned incandescent, and students signed a petition calling for change, Hammons publicly approved the actions of the student body. Trustees struck back at a meeting in June by withholding contracts from Hammons and two other teachers. He beat them to the draw, though, by resigning. Not knowing any of this, Ferguson asked why Hammons had been fired, as the boy mistakenly told him. "To give some son-of-a-bitch from up north a job," the boy said. Apparently, word of Ferguson's imminent arrival—and the presumption that he was going to take the job—had spread around town.

Ferguson asked what was wrong with a coach from up north. The boy retorted, "What's right with any goddamned Yankee?" That was enough for Ferguson. He was going to leave Monticello and take his chances elsewhere, until he remembered that he didn't have enough money to go anywhere. He decided to stay until his traveling expenses were reimbursed. As he approached the administration building, a white coupe roared to a screeching stop. "That's the Chief," someone said.

Ferguson introduced himself and Horsfall invited him into his office, where he plucked a piece of paper from a pile on his desk. It was a contract, which trustees approved earlier in the summer, appointing Ferguson as a history teacher with the additional duties of coach.

"Sign it," Horsfall ordered.

"Well, I don't know," Ferguson began.

"Don't know what," Horsfall roared. "You've got what you came for, didn't you? Well, sign it and stop wasting my time."

Ferguson signed. After all, he reasoned, it was nearly September and most, if not all, teaching jobs had already been filled. Besides, he figured that his clashes at Dakota Wesleyan with fans, administrators, and the press had given him a skin thick enough to deal with anything he would find at Monticello. Wishful thinking.

CHAPTER 9

SOUTHERN SHOWDOWN

Stewart Ferguson sized up Monticello, Arkansas, in the days after signing his contract to coach the 1934 Monticello A & M football team. If he did not win, he was in trouble—the kind of trouble that got a man run out of town. Downtown, at the Monticello Drug Store where businessmen met once a week to talk sports, there was considerable speculation about Ferguson. He was a Yankee, and that was bad enough. But, by God, they said, if he was able to make winners out of these Aggie boys, they might forget where he came from.

Ferguson wasn't sure. He heard players were going to boycott him because his predecessor, the popular coach Foy Hammons, had been forced to quit despite his overall winning record in three seasons. Hammons's problems were political; he picked the wrong side in a struggle over the way President Frank Horsfall ran A & M.

The athletic budget was counted in nickels and dimes. There was no recruiting, and as far as Ferguson could tell, no great enthusiasm on campus for the football program. Before he quit, Hammons scheduled seven games, all with state rivals, starting with Henderson State Teachers College, an Arkadelphia school coached by Eugene ("Bo") Sherman, who at twenty-seven was the youngest head coach in Arkansas. His teams won often and by large scores and he was dogged by rumors that he used ineligible players, who were paid, to boot. Like Ferguson, he was the son of a Methodist minister.

Resigned to whatever might happen, Ferguson waited until September 10, the day classes began, to invite boys to try out for the team. Despite his fears of a boycott, more than twenty students turned up. Among them were four lettermen, including center Van Tuberville, team captain and a central figure in the student revolt against Horsfall, and quarterback Sonny Gordon, A & M's most dangerous offensive threat.

But there were too many small, slow, raw candidates. One day, Ferguson tested their speed by challenging the team to a fifty-yard race against him. He finished ahead of everybody and concluded that his team was in for a long, hard season. An overall malaise gripped the squad, and it was nothing new. Spring football practice had been abandoned because the players were too apathetic to exercise. Hammons partly blamed this on the increasingly irrational rules that Horsfall enforced to prevent even innocent contacts between boys and girls. The rules had long divided and roiled the campus and spread downtown, but Horsfall was unmovable.

Just four days before the start of the season, as part of the *Arkansas Democrat's* detailed check-in on all of the state's college teams, Ferguson tried his best to temper expectations and sell a potential one-win campaign: "Don't expect much from this season. . . . We'll bring the boys along slowly, taking the bumps as they come, and all the time we'll be pointing for that Thanksgiving Day game with Magnolia A & M. If we can beat the Muleriders on Turkey Day everyone hereabouts will consider it a successful season."

The team he was working into shape was known as the Boll Weevils, named after the cotton-eating beetle when President Horsfall, at a 1925 pep rally before a homecoming game against Magnolia A & M, declared, "The only gosh-darned thing that ever really licked the South was the boll weevil. Boll weevils! That's what you are—Boll Weevils!" To Ferguson's delighted surprise, his little Boll Weevils took the field for the first game in Conway, against sporadic opponent Hendrix College, looking like a real team. It played like one, too, holding Hendrix to a scoreless first half before losing 18–7.

That was pretty much the highlight of the season. In the following weeks, Monticello lost to Henderson State 63–0, College of the Ozarks 45–0, Arkansas State College 19–0, Arkansas Polytechnic Institute 53–0, Ouachita College 57–0, and finally, in the year's most important game, to archrival Magnolia A & M 7–6. Definitely not "successful." No Monticello squad had done so badly, and even before the season ended Ferguson was resigned to losing his job. The sniping started early, and from within the A & M family.

One day, Ferguson was summoned to a meeting with the faculty committee charged with determining player eligibility. The chairman got right to the point. "Did you pick up Spot Holmes and give him a ride back to campus on the team bus?" he asked.

"Yes," Ferguson replied. "What's wrong with that?"

"Evidently, you're not willing to follow rules and regulations set by this committee," they said. "You know there is a rule against picking up hitch-hikers." Ferguson explained that Holmes was a student. It made no difference; he had ordered the driver to stop and pick up a hitch-hiker.

"Will you ever pick up a hitch-hiker again?" someone asked Ferguson.

"I guess I will if it's someone like Spot," he replied.

"You've just made a most serious statement," the chairman said. "You are excused, Coach Ferguson."

Ferguson understood what had happened. He was the outsider—unconventional and difficult—and it was time to leave before he was fired. He packed his belongings, loaded them into the A & M bus that made regular trips downtown to the bus and train stations, and walked to the administration building to tell Horsfall that he was quitting.

"So, you are going to keep on picking up hitch-hikers, are you?" Horsfall began when Ferguson walked into his office.

Ferguson was starting to speak when Horsfall cut him off: "If you had told that bunch of sorry asses that you wouldn't pick up any more hitchhikers like Spot, *I'd* have fired you on the spot."

"Wouldn't make any difference," Ferguson said. "I'm quitting."

"Like hell you are!" Horsfall bellowed.

Ferguson stayed. Later, he said this was the moment he began learning how to fight for the things he believed in. Horsfall, who was fighting desperately to keep his own job, told Ferguson that he was the coach and everyone else could go to hell.

Reinvigorated by an impromptu pep talk from the school president, he focused on further developing and discussing a pet play that was transforming from an earlier "Louisiana Line Divide" name to something he was now identifying as a "Swinging Gate." He needed a way for his small, inexperienced team to maintain possession, thus limiting the number of scoring opportunities from stronger, more powerful Arkansas opponents.

As Ferguson explained to an enthusiastic *Arkansas Democrat* sportswriter, the setup would start from a typical unbalanced line— say with two players to the left of center and four to the right—but the linemen (guards, tackles, and ends) would shift before the ball was put into play, leaving only one lineman to the left of center and five to the right. After the shift, the left guard and center would remain lined up in tight formation, but the right guard would take a position about two yards from the center, leaving a gap in the line. The remaining linemen would take tight positions to the right of the right tackle and when the quarterback started the play, these four men would simply pivot, or as Ferguson described, "swing outward like a gate," opening the hole through which most of the strong side plays (with the now five linemen) would run. He added that various forward and lateral passes and weak side plays would increase the deceptiveness of the formation. Years later, Ferguson wrote that "the most noticeable defect" in his new pet play was that it seemed to produce only short gains; the 1934 version didn't quite slow down the weekly slew of opponent possessions—or touchdowns.

Upon the conclusion of the winless season, Ferguson took what he considered a logical and necessary step. He sent a not overly fresh round of resumés to more than one hundred colleges, even though he suspected his records at A & M and Dakota Wesleyan would not bring an avalanche of offers. The local "whispering criticism had swelled into demands for an immediate [coaching] change," but for a brief period, the downtown "wolves" shifted their attention to President Horsfall. After a reign that had lasted twenty-five years, from the first weeks of the school's founding, the embattled Monticello president was fighting not only for his job but for his reputation and his legacy.

Horsfall insisted that investigation after investigation had cleared him of the many charges of mismanagement, malfeasance, and unethical conduct. At crisis meeting after crisis meeting, trustees backed him. But in January 1935, he finally wilted. "Our enemies are not going to give up," he said, and just like that, he was gone. The trustees issued a last statement, saying they accepted his resignation with reluctance. Downtown, whoops of triumph greeted the news, and the *Pine Bluff Commercial*, the most widely circulated newspaper in Monticello, proclaimed the end of a "blue rule" administration that had, among other things, banned dancing, curtailed athletics, and locked dormitory doors at night.

A committee that included C. C. Smith, the A & M bursar, and Marvin Bankston, the head of the important Department of Agriculture, was appointed to run the school until Horsfall's successor was named. Tired of the long, bitter political row, the five-member board of trustees also quit. A new board appointed by the governor was expected to choose Bankston or another member of the faculty, but after three months of intense lobbying, they turned to an outsider.

Hugh Critz was a graduate of Mississippi A & M, thus fulfilling a requirement that Monticello's president hold a degree in agriculture, and was once president of Arkansas Polytechnic Institute, which satisfied a desire for administrative experience. Although only a handful of people on or off campus knew anything about Critz, he quickly became a celebrity by association: his son, also named Hugh, was a Major League Baseball second baseman—a defensive wiz—for the New York Giants and was briefly part of the so-called "million dollar infield" that included future Hall of Famers Billy Terry, Freddie Lindstrom, and Travis Jackson.

Only a few months before, in mid-September, Hughie, as he was known to fans, had figured in a widely publicized prank by Dizzy Dean, the St. Louis Cardinals' star pitcher. Before a game at the Polo Grounds, Dean put a black cat on a leash and walked it back and forth in front of the Giants' bench. The cat stopped in front of Critz. Dean pointed at him, mumbled a curse, and signed a hex. It didn't work. "Mr. Critz performed prodigiously at bat and afield," Lindstrom told the *New York Post* after the game. Indeed, Critz went three for four and played his usual stellar second base.

Ferguson knew about Hughie, and soon he would learn that Hughie's father was an enthusiastic supporter of football determined to make A & M a pigskin power in Arkansas. "He made football appear as the most glorious aim of American democracy," Ferguson wrote later. "He was the greatest promoter I ever met."

On his first day as president, Critz summoned every member of the A & M faculty into his office and asked him or her to stay on. To his surprise, Ferguson was included. He was embarrassed, too, because he was anxious to leave Monticello and waiting for responses to the many resumés that he sent to other colleges. Ferguson did not say yes or no but left Critz with the impression that he would return to coach in the fall of 1935. The next day, Critz met with a delegation of Monticello citizens, who told him they too wanted to see a championship football team, but that with Ferguson calling the shots, this was extremely unlikely. By now, Critz knew how bad the 1934 team was, and who townspeople and most students held responsible.

Several days later, Critz called Ferguson back into his office. "Ferguson," he said, beaming, "I've just learned that you're a crack history teacher." Ferguson said yes, he taught history. "I've always tremendously admired good history teachers," Critz said. "God knows we need more of them."

Ferguson suspected what was coming but decided he would not make it easy. "I just want to be a football coach," he said. Critz reeled back into his chair in mock surprise. "You mean," he sputtered, "I've found someone who would rather coach than teach history?"

"That's right," Ferguson said. He figured that since Critz had asked him only days before to stay on as coach, he would dictate what happened next. Critz was silent for a minute or so, then waved Ferguson out of the office.

Nothing happened for a few weeks, which Ferguson filled by drawing up a tentative schedule for the 1935 season and sizing up prospects during visits to high schools in the area. But as he made the rounds, he heard rumors that the citizens of Monticello, who always played an important part in college life, wanted to talk about the coming football season and had scheduled a meeting for that purpose at the Drew County courthouse.

Critz confirmed this and gave Ferguson a ride downtown on the night of the meeting, held in a second-floor courtroom used for important civic events. The room was buzzing as Ferguson and Critz walked in. It looked like a lynch mob, Ferguson said later, adding (not completely inaccurately) that in a town without Jews, Catholics, or Republicans, a losing football coach was considered a fitting substitute target for mob justice. Critz was introduced and, to respectful silence, delivered an unscripted address that praised the virtues of Monticello and the outstanding education that its boys and girls received at A & M. He also painted a rosy picture of the college's football prospects, predicting a winning record in 1935 that would raise Monticello's reputation, bring economic rewards to merchants, and create swelling community pride.

Ferguson wondered how Critz managed all this without a sarcastic sneer. Then, without warning, Critz asked, "Do you want a good football team?" Back came a thunderous yes, with booted feet stamping on the courtroom floor. Critz waited until the hubbub died down, and then asked, "Do you want the current football coach?" This time, the answer was a no—roared loud enough to shake the lights hanging overhead.

"You have answered my question," Critz said solemnly and sat down.

Ferguson walked out of the courthouse without saying a word. The next day, he was rushed to the hospital for an emergency appendectomy. As he recuperated, Ferguson weighed his options. He could quit A & M and seek a coaching position somewhere else, but with his record, he figured his chances weren't good. The same with teaching history; he did have a master's degree, but so did thousands of other teachers seeking jobs amid the still deep Depression. Or he could swallow his pride and accept Critz's offer to stay and teach history.

As soon as he left the hospital, he resigned as coach and agreed to teach history. Critz was pleased. In a way that surprised him, so was Ferguson. He realized that he didn't particularly care about football anymore—that it was stubborn pride that made him want to coach and that it was time to put it aside. It had caused him too much heartache, and, he said, caused too much harm to young men who were exploited by schools with false notions of what was important, and by fans whose values were twisted and debased by the brutality they saw. One day, he saw the pep squad practicing near the football stadium. He kept walking.

CHAPTER 10

A HERO'S WELCOME—FOR BO

Eugene ("Bo") Sherman was playing semi-professional baseball in Osceola, Arkansas, when Hugh Critz, the new president of Monticello A & M, offered him a chance to redeem his reputation and get involved again in college football. Critz wanted Sherman to coach A & M and make fans forget the awful 1934 record, the worst in school history. Sherman had turned out champions, but there was a certain amount of risk in hiring him—he was on probation for cheating. There had been nasty rumors about his teams at Henderson State Teachers College, at Arkadelphia, which had won the Arkansas Intercollegiate Conference championship and had rolled up impressive scores against several schools, including a 63–0 thrashing of the A & M Boll Weevils. There were the usual pay-for-play stories, but more damaging were stories that Sherman had knowingly fielded ineligible players. This was his downfall.

On November 17, 1934, Henderson defeated the College of the Ozarks, 6–0, in a game the conference said it would recognize for the state collegiate championship even though the Ozarks weren't AIC members. After the game, the president of the College of the Ozarks filed a formal complaint with the conference, accusing Sherman of using three players ruled ineligible by the AIC, two of them because they already had played for four years. (All three were starters in the rout of Monticello A & M.) Sherman argued that since Ozarks was not a member of the conference, his team was not obliged to honor its eligibility rules. College of the Ozarks then produced a contract, which committed Henderson to playing the game under AIC rules.

The conference, at its December annual meeting, suspended Sherman as an Arkansas college coach.

Then, on April 27, the conference lifted its suspension but put Sherman on probation indefinitely. Critz immediately telephoned Sherman, who was also rumored to have been offered a job on the University of Oregon football staff. Sherman drove to Monticello to sign a contract to coach football. It was the first faculty change made by Critz since he had officially joined the school as president on April 5. Stewart Ferguson, who had coached in 1934, had resigned the job under pressure by Critz and a majority of Monticello businessmen and citizens who lobbied for a winning football team to give their small, little-known town something to brag about.

The only thing Arkansans knew about Monticello, except for the fact it was the home of an unaccredited college for farmers, was that it grew tomatoes. Farmers shipped them to markets in neighboring states in crates marked "Monticello Ridge's Finest," and this led, in the summer of 1934, to a festival to promote and celebrate tomatoes.

It was simply called the Tomato Festival and merchants eagerly signed up to provide prizes, which they hoped would bring visitors from surrounding areas and establish their town as the official Tomato Capital of Arkansas. It was a one-day event, on a Saturday, the day when farmers went to town to shop, let the kids see a movie, get haircuts, take in the mule auctions, and catch up on town gossip.

Prizes of up to eight dollars were awarded to winners in such categories as best of one-half bushel pinks, one-half bushel ripes, and canned pickles and chow-chows. There was a fifty-dollar prize for the best float with a tomato theme, and ten dollars for the girl voted best out-of-town beauty. The winner of the Monticello bathing beauty competition received a season pass to the municipal swimming pool, while the queen of the festival was presented an evening gown by the McDaniel ladies' wear shop. The festival lasted until the outbreak of World War II, but by that time neighboring Bradley County had taken over as the state's number one tomato grower and had organized a rival festival.

While the town celebrated its tomatoes, the coaching transition at A & M picked up steam. Stewart Ferguson recuperated from his appendectomy while the town showered Sherman with a hero's welcome; it was immediately clear that whatever Sherman wanted, he would get. Critz kept the good times humming by passing word to the Chamber of Commerce that it could run the football program.

Almost everybody who followed sports to any degree knew about Sherman, just twenty-eight when he arrived in Monticello. He had played baseball and basketball at Henderson but was most famous for his football exploits; he had been elected to the all-Arkansas college team four times, twice as tackle and twice as quarterback. Upon graduation, he stayed on to serve as an assistant coach under Bo Rowland, the inspiration for Sherman's own nickname. Two years later, when Rowland became an assistant at the University of Oklahoma, Sherman was hired to coach the Henderson Reddies. During the three years he spent there, Henderson won two state college championships and lost only one game. Now, here he was and gearing up to transform the hapless, hopeless Boll Weevils.

Downtown supporters reckoned it would take money to guarantee a winning program, however. Merchants pledged support on lists circulated by the chamber of commerce, which then solicited funds from the A & M faculty. Given the environment that Critz encouraged, most professors coughed up. Ferguson was steaming, but for once, he kept his mouth shut. He promised to pay ten dollars a month, the same sum he gave to the First Methodist Church. It constituted a bit of a sacrifice because his salary was only $150 per month.

The reason for the slush fund was not advertised, but in his agreement with A & M, Sherman was promised $2,100 a year in salary or, in the words of his contract, "so much as may be collected and available." For "collected," Ferguson said when he learned of the deal, read "extorted." If he was miffed, there was a good economic reason—his own salary was $750 a year less.

Money to cover Sherman's salary was not the only thing that the Chamber of Commerce wanted. A bigger problem was rounding up enough big, fast, tough players to make Monticello A & M a competitive team. The answer came from a most unlikely source, a professor who suggested sending out a recruiting party—in a caravan of cars, pickup trucks and buses that would tour towns in southeastern Arkansas, talking up the football program.

Merchants quickly lined up about one hundred cars. A & M provided two buses, the college marching band, the girls' drum corps, and the faculty. They made three trips, all on Saturdays, when organizers could count on a crowd, to the biggest towns in the area—Warren, McGehee, Hamburg, Star City, Fordyce, El Dorado, and a dozen wide spots in the road along the way. The caravan set off just after breakfast from the A & M campus, led by cars decorated with slogans and flags, their horns blaring, and drivers and passengers waving and cheering at anyone along the road. The musicians, cheerleaders and marching girls rode in the buses. The faculty, equipped with little tin whistles, was assigned to ride in the front seats of the cars. Some professors deeply resented the whole exercise, but more feared losing their jobs. Ferguson thoroughly enjoyed it all. He rode in the fifth car, thus escaping most of the dust thrown up from the rutted, gravelly roads.

The length of the stop, and the grandeur of the presentation, depended on the size of the town. In some sleepy hamlets like Dermott, a railroad stop about ten miles from the Mississippi line, the show and the pitch for talent lasted no longer than fifteen minutes. In county seats, such as Hamburg or Warren, the music, marching, speeches, and appeals for bruisers lasted as long as forty-five minutes. In every case, though, the routine was pretty much the same.

The second vehicle in the procession was a truck, carrying a ready-to-assemble stage, loudspeakers, and other paraphernalia, and as soon as it rolled into the center of a town, Monticello volunteers quickly unloaded and set up. To draw a crowd, a loudspeaker in the first car blared music and calls for everybody to come along for the fun. It was the same technique employed by medicine show impresarios, hillbilly singers, and revival preachers. As soon as the platform was assembled, President Critz, Coach Sherman, a delegation from the chamber of commerce, and several members of the girls' drum corps climbed up and took their places. Critz would wave his hand to quiet the band, and roar out a greeting on behalf of A & M.

He always started with the same men's dressing room crack. He would look over the scantily clad girls standing along the front edge of the platform, dressed in close-fitting shorts that revealed their legs nearly to the hip; then, with a wink, he would turn to the crowd. "Friends," he would say, "I've been told that it takes legs to win football games." Whoops and hollers inevitably followed. Critz made his pitch, proclaiming the coming of football glory, then introduced one of the businessmen to speak of the economic benefits produced by winning teams. Between speeches, the band blared out martial airs and peppy popular tunes. Sherman always spoke last, and always said the same two sentences. "Just watch us," he said. "We'll take 'em all." With this, the band broke into music, the faculty blew their whistles, hats were waved, and when the stage was broken down and loaded back on the truck, Critz signaled the band director, Lee Wallick, to stop the music. A minute or so later, the caravan was racing off to its next stop.

The caravan paid off. About forty football players arrived on campus and were given rooms in Sorrells Hall, a dormitory previously used by all male students but now set exclusively aside for athletes. It was the first time that athletes at A & M had been given special attention. Ferguson was dubious. Most of the recruits were "tramps," he said, meaning athletes who went from school to school, playing only as long as they were given free food, lodging and spending money. The most talented player was a running back Ferguson and most other Arkansas sports fans knew well: Duke Wells, a three-year all-State force at Henderson State when Sherman was coach. Wells had run wild the previous season when Henderson demolished A & M.

His recruitment was somewhat unusual, even by the standards of the day. Three Monticello businessmen drove to Arkadelphia, a bumpy three-hour ride over back roads, and, in the middle of the night, packed Wells's belongings, spirited him out of his dormitory, and returned to Monticello before daylight. Exuberant supporters hailed it as the most successful athletic raid of the year. Unfortunately for A & M and Sherman, Wells fell ill within a week and was rushed to a Monticello hospital, where he underwent an emergency appendectomy. (No truth to the rumor Ferguson put a spell on him.) He was out for the season and ended up as a trusted coach of the backfield.

As for the rest of the recruits, Ferguson noted that some had not even graduated from the eighth grade, while others claiming to be transferring from other colleges could not produce any evidence that they attended classes there. Some instructors were tabbed to administer psychological testing for students aged twenty-one or older—apparently, a state law admitted such students under certain circumstances. In the case of football players, passing the test was a formality. One instructor later explained to Ferguson, "Football players aren't supposed to know anything." (At the end of the fall semester, Ferguson noted that several members of the team not only had not attended any classes, but they did not even know what classes they should have been attending.)

Critz knew, but when the issue was raised at faculty meetings, he made it clear that the football team's success was paramount. Anybody who objected, Ferguson said, was advised to start looking for alternative employment. Ferguson kept his thoughts to himself, but he told colleagues he admired Critz for not playing the hypocrite. Critz wanted a championship team, period.

Ferguson did his bit. Sherman registered almost the entire team in a freshman history class that Ferguson taught. He knew that Critz wanted them all given passing grades. "I smiled like Mona Lisa," he wrote later, "when the dean gave me admission cards for the players." Few of the players ever attended his class. Some came from time to time "out of curiosity." One was a regular because he had his eye on a striking "bayou belle." Another went because Ferguson's soothing voice helped the player sleep better. The same player once slept through a football practice and, according to Ferguson, Sherman told him to stop going to class because it apparently cost him shut-eye. Ferguson passed them all.

Sherman's biggest problem was keeping his players from attacking one another. Some of the roughest were bullies who picked on smaller players, most of them boys who had played on area high school teams. A few toughs kicked, punched, gouged, and even bit other players during scrimmages. One carried a knife to practice because, he said, he hankered for knife play. Ferguson thought he was a fit successor to Jim Bowie, who had designed his celebrated and extremely lethal knife in 1830 while working in Arkansas.

Fans who came out to watch practice approved of the rough stuff. They told Sherman it was toughening up the boys for the season ahead. "An ordinary schedule is too easy for this bunch," Sherman was told, prompting him to add two games to the schedule. After the 1934 fiasco under Ferguson, A & M had reduced the schedule to five games, all against traditional opponents. Now, with the promise of great success in the making, Sherman added his old school, Henderson State, and North East Louisiana College, in Monroe, which he decided would serve as the opening game of the season.

It was about ninety miles to Monroe, and as the A & M bus left the campus, just after breakfast, Ferguson stood among the crowd seeing the team off. Cheers rang out, and Sherman raised his arms in a victory salute. Ferguson wondered if Sherman would show any mercy to North East Louisiana, or any opponent. "He had a reputation for crushing hardness against any team he played," Ferguson wrote later. "He played for keeps."

CHAPTER 11

ROUGH BOYS

The telephone in the National Guard armory, where the Monticello A & M athletic office was located, rang shortly after four thirty on the afternoon of Saturday, September 28. The student clerk answered it, turned to Stewart Ferguson, who was doing some paperwork, and said, "Coach says they lost." Ferguson snorted in disbelief. The gang of aggressive toughs assembled by Coach Eugene ("Bo") Sherman with the help of downtown merchants and a not-so-secret slush fund couldn't have lost. Not to North East Louisiana College, in Monroe, a school added to A & M's schedule at the demand of football supporters impressed by what they saw in preseason workouts. It was the opening game of the 1935 season and expectations were soaring.

No, Ferguson said, Bo wanted to surprise everybody with an announcement of a great victory when the team bus returned to campus for a postgame celebration. That was something the boyish Sherman would do. The bus arrived just after seven thirty, rolling to a stop in front of the administrative building, where Ferguson, most other faculty members, and most of the four hundred plus students were waiting. Cheers rang out, and the A & M band struck up a lively tune. The doors opened and Sherman stepped out, followed by his team. The sight shocked Ferguson and stunned the crowd.

It was clear to Ferguson, and everyone else, that the Boll Weevils had taken a terrible beating. The faces of some were marked by nasty bruises and cuts. A couple had lost teeth, and one player needed help stepping down to the ground. Most of the team looked at the ground as Sherman, speaking in a subdued tone, reported the score. North East had won 31–0.

"The boys were learning that there were other tough boys in the world," Ferguson wrote later. But, like most other people who had seen Sherman's team in practice and heard stories about their brutal, pitiless style, Ferguson remained confident. "We said, 'Just wait until the next game.'" The following week, playing at home before more than two thousand fans, A & M was thrashed 34–0 by Hendrix College, a Methodist private school in Conway with a reputation based not on athletic prowess but academic excellence. Ferguson attributed the loss to low morale and bad luck. But after the third game, a 12–0 defeat by Henderson State, where only a year earlier Sherman had achieved such success, the mood on and off campus turned ominously sour. Downtown, in the courthouse square drugstore that served as the headquarters for the businessmen's group most actively involved in the football program, there was angry talk of wasted money on tramp athletes. Ferguson noted with malicious glee that some of his most severe critics had begun speaking to him again.

It was after the fourth game of the season, a 44–0 shellacking by the College of the Ozarks, that the rebellion erupted. The Boll Weevils had not only lost every game; they had not scored a single point. Some merchants stopped contributing to the slush fund, an option not available to A & M faculty members who suspected their jobs depended on their continued financial support. President Hugh Critz had made that plain. Ferguson continued his tribute, ten dollars per month.

A & M won its fifth game, 28–0, over Arkansas Polytechnic Institute, but it was too late to muffle the surging, angry chorus—and perhaps more dangerous, the increasing lack of any interest whatsoever in the Boll Weevils.

The season limped to a finish with three more defeats, two of them convincing shutouts. The last game, the Thanksgiving Day showdown against archrival Magnolia A & M, ended with a dispirited Monticello A & M going down meekly, 7–0. Sherman and his team finished 1–7, a bleak record second only to the 0–7 mark that cost Ferguson his job the previous season.

Abruptly, on December 27, Hugh Critz resigned. He had been A & M's president for only ten months. Despite the gossip, it was poor health, not Sherman's failure, that prompted his decision. Although he disapproved of the way Critz had ceded control of the A & M football program to downtown merchants and ignored the corrupt abuses that followed, Ferguson was sorry to see him go. For one thing, during his brief reign Critz had allowed dances on campus, the first in school history. Students could only attend if they produced letters from their parents giving them permission, but it still signaled that the school was moving away from the strict codes of morality imposed at colleges affiliated with religious denominations.

Importantly, Critz also increased spending on books for the library. The previous year, $2,421 was budgeted for books, but the library added just thirty-nine volumes. The lack of books and other research materials was the chief reason A & M had failed inspections by the agency that accredited colleges.

Before he left Monticello, Critz called Ferguson into his office for a farewell chat. Critz sighed that the performance of the 1935 football team was enough to make anybody sick. "Even though he made no attempt to integrate sports and education, he was honest," Ferguson said afterwards. "He wanted to win in football and was openly willing to use any means to do so." And if investigators came around asking about abuses, he added, Critz told them to go to hell. "He was something I like to call a human man."

Marvin Bankston, head of the important Department of Agriculture and, like Critz, a graduate of Mississippi A & M, was elected by trustees to succeed him. The student body greeted the late February news with tumultuous enthusiasm—the college dismissed classes for a parade and rally of support downtown. To the farm, timber, and cattle industries in southeastern Arkansas, Bankston's election sent a signal that agriculture and animal husbandry remained the school's highest priorities. Students saw a further easing of rigid rules of conduct on campus. As for football, Ferguson saw more of the same.

"Though Bankston disliked the manner in which football was being conducted," Ferguson wrote, "he had the common sense not to make an immediate issue of it." Ferguson noted that Bankston did not interfere with the work and plans of the downtown crowd and continued to feed and lodge players that Monticello merchants had recruited.

The players making their way to Sorrells Hall in the summer of 1936 seemed, to Ferguson, bigger and meaner than the previous season's crop. Downtown, the new reasoning was that merchants and other supporters of the team had not spent enough money last year. The remedy was an increase in the amounts donated by businessmen, some of them coerced to do so by the fear of boycotts and shunning. Bankston didn't say anything about the faculty's contributions, but Ferguson and the others continued to pony up.

On campus, there were whispers of doubt about some of the new recruits. Two of them, allegedly, were alcoholics whose addictions were offset by their vicious play. The business manager asked one recruit how he planned to pay student fees. According to Ferguson, he replied, "They done told me if you asked for any goddamned money, just to tell you all to go to hell."

The season itself was another debacle for Monticello fans and Sherman. The team lost five of seven games, but at least defeated Magnolia A & M. This time, businessmen voted with their wallets. As loss followed loss, so many stopped paying into the slush fund that it soon lacked enough money to cover the room, board, and pocket money given to players. Some players, in turn, threatened not to play their best if they weren't paid. Worse, as far as downtown contributors were concerned, was a rumor sweeping through town that some of the money for players had been diverted to other pockets. If this meant Sherman, as some alluded, it would not only disgrace the coach, but it would also cost the college dearly.

One merchant involved in the slush fund was so troubled that he called Bankston to ask if contributors could change the way they paid athletes. Instead, Bankston asked to see the pledge list used to set assessment. The merchant arrived with a bundle of cards listing contributors and amounts. Incensed, Bankston tore up the pledge cards and told the merchant to spread the word—henceforth, A & M would not permit any financial support to its athletic program, unless approved by him personally.

That ended the slush fund, but not the problem. Football players continued to stay in Sorrells Hall and eat at the dining hall, but without paying. Bankston did not evict them, because of uncertainties about the status of the school's legal obligations. Meanwhile, Ferguson came up with an idea. He suggested hiring the players, paying them from funds allocated for student labor. He was chairman of the committee on student labor, which employed students and paid them fifteen cents an hour, for jobs that ranged from cutting the grass to washing pots and pans. Ferguson suggested at a faculty meeting that he would consider giving athletes the easiest jobs. Committee members expressed doubt but gave the go-ahead.

Ferguson soon assembled the football players and made his proposal. Nobody accepted. One player insisted the school keep its promise to pay his expenses. Another said he wouldn't decide until he talked with downtown supporters. In the end, none of the players accepted any kind of job.

At the end of the 1936 academic year in May, Bankston asked Ferguson to inspect Sorrells Hall with him. Another one of Ferguson's positions was dean of men, which required him to make periodic inspections of boys' dormitories. However, he had never gone to the athletic dorm. "We were not welcome, and we knew it," he wrote later.

The dorm was in shambles. The hallway was littered with shattered whiskey bottles, smashed furniture, and other debris. Sinks were broken, doors knocked off their hinges. The walls were full of holes and covered with scrawled obscenities and pornographically altered photos of film stars and *Esquire* magazine models. Nailed to some walls were girls' panties, with names and dates written beneath. In the corner of one room, Ferguson and Bankston found a heap of condoms. "We soon stopped searching for more evidence in fear that the news might leak out that we had a veritable whorehouse on campus," Ferguson wrote. That was enough for Bankston. Sherman would stay, but his team would go.

Nobody thought about football until almost the day classes began. Any talk around downtown supporters helping out was hooted down—even by the merchants who still wanted to see a winning team. The squad Sherman assembled for the 1937 season was small and raw. A few boys turned up, seeking to play for pay, but were told that those days were over, and left. A few players returned because they liked and admired Sherman. By the time the season opened, on the road and once again against North East Louisiana, Sherman had scrounged together twenty-three players, backfilled with freshmen.

On the eve of the opener, Sherman told the *Monroe News-Star*, possibly in jest, "We will probably get beat 100–0." He nearly nailed it. The Boll Weevils were humiliated, 111–0, the most one-sided defeat in A & M history to this day. The season ended with six losses and one victory. The school had also suffered in another way: the Boll Weevils, frustrated by their inability to win, had resorted to dirty play. Their unnecessarily crude and brutal zeal disgusted most fans on and off campus and alienated most other colleges in the state.

Trustees, faculty, and Bankston decided it was time to consider dropping football altogether. Privately, Ferguson gloated. "I'll be truthful and frankly say that I kicked up my heels and chuckled far into the night," he wrote later. "Some revenge does have a sweet taste." Shortly after the school year, Ferguson made a decision of his own, opting to leave Monticello A & M.

CHAPTER 12

STRANGEST. CONTRACT. EVER.

During the spring of 1938, the debate over whether to abolish football at A & M raged on. Several influential professors, farmers, and other interested parties thought maybe it was time to disband the team. Coupled with the especially rough play, crowds the previous fall were so sparse that gate receipts did not even cover the fees paid to referees, umpires, and head linesmen, who received fifteen dollars each per game. In addition, A & M had won a total of four games the last four seasons, and the previous year's embarrassing 111–0 rout by North East Louisiana College disgusted even the most avid supporters.

But to the chamber of commerce—which included some of the college's trustees—football generated great free publicity for a town with few, if any, other attractions that might appeal to outsiders with money, and for that reason, members generally opposed abolishing the sport. Nor was President Bankston, with the game possibly remaining in his blood from past playing days at Mississippi A & M, ready to give up on football. Bankston decided to give the sport one more chance, and the question left was who would coach.

Sherman still had his supporters in town, helped undoubtedly by the fact that he had married a local girl. But Bankston was ready to move on from the ugly impact Sherman's recruits had on campus and on the playing field, and he set his sights on an ideal replacement—Stewart Ferguson.

Bankston did not promote Ferguson, though, because he knew very well that the man was detested by much of the downtown crowd. Why would he recycle a coach—a "goddamned Yankee" to boot—who had lasted but one year and posted a 0–7 record that stood as the worst in school history and led to Ferguson's humiliating dismissal after a raucous meeting in the county courthouse?

For one thing, appointing Ferguson would relieve everybody of the cost and bother of searching for a new coach. For another, Bankston reasoned that giving Ferguson the job would save the financially strapped college money; another hire meant another salary after all, and Ferguson might well agree to attach an additional title to his impressive portfolio. Finally, Ferguson already had coached one season and because he failed spectacularly, his pride might well inspire him to seize an opportunity to show he could produce winners.

Besides, Bankston was too heavily involved in agricultural programs and busy promoting several pet projects to devote much time to searching for a coach. During his years as head of the Department of Agriculture at A & M, he developed a special affection for cows. One of his first acts after his election as president was the establishment of a special dairy program, named the *Barnyard Battery*, to promote friendly feelings for cows. He even selected the titles for students who oversaw the project, starting with its leader, who was called "Pacifier General." "If the cows got more love and sympathy from our students, they would give more and better milk," Bankston said. It was an important point because the college depended on its sizable prize herd for not only the milk and butter consumed in the campus dining hall, but for the considerable income that sales to Monticello eateries and grocery stores produced.

When Ferguson got wind that Bankston was thinking of rehiring him as coach, he told Bankston there was absolutely no chance he would return to coaching, which he sneeringly dismissed as a calling for nitwits. Academic professors, he said, were not subject to the opinions of several thousand people whose one-dollar admission to games gave them the right to second guess the coach. Also, Ferguson noted, academics were rarely fired, and never because they failed to recruit an effective player or because a student suffered an injury that kept him out of class. That was why he wanted nothing more than to teach history, he said. It offered security, ease, respect, and the chance to meet experienced women.

"I was having too much fun in my job," he would write later. He meant jobs. In addition to teaching history, he wore several other hats in the spring of 1938: chairman of the Department of Physical Education and Health, supervisor of campus labor, dean of men, director of athletics, and lecturer of a course identified in the student handbook as PE 233: Foundations of Physical and Health Education, which met every weekday at 7:30 a.m. and was much favored by athletes who mostly slept through it.

In the classroom and around campus, he was universally called "Coach" (even though he hadn't had the job in four years) and, in sharp contrast with the downtown community, was known across the student body for his mild-mannered nature. A recent edition of the *Weevil Outlet*, the twice-a-month school paper, asked: "Can you imagine 'Coach' Ferguson being impolite?" And the latest A & M yearbook, in its *Familiar Expressions* section dubbed him "Gee gosh, that's swell" Ferguson. Overall, his A & M status quo was kind of swell. His salary, at $150 a month—a sum that had not changed in his five years on campus even with his growing number of hats—also wasn't a current issue. "There was just about enough time left to enjoy an abundance of recreational activities," he later wrote. "At the same time, there were several very desirable young ladies employed by the college who wanted the company of a bachelor, a most opportune time for plenty of good times."

A few days after classes ended, Ferguson set off in his 1934 LaSalle coupe for Baton Rouge, Louisiana, where he was spending a third straight summer working on his doctoral degree in Physical Education at LSU. He covered tuition and other costs by lecturing summer students. As he noted, there were also plenty of good looking "Frenchy" schoolteachers as eager for romance as for summer course credits. It was a welcome escape from any further talk of coaching high-pressure football.

Meanwhile, back in Monticello, Bankston was on a mission. He wrote Ferguson at LSU, sending a signed contract and urging him to take the job. Ferguson responded with a long letter rejecting the offer. But Bankston would not let up.

Getting nowhere with his de facto boss, Ferguson scrambled together a new plan—he decided to "eliminate further argument by obtaining another job." He wrote to his old friend S. M. Brame, who was about to begin his thirtieth year as principal at Bolton High School in Alexandria, Louisiana, where Ferguson had spent one of his happiest years as a teacher and coach and who once told Ferguson to contact him if he ever needed a job. Brame wrote back that it so happened there was an opening for a top assistant coaching position, and if Ferguson wanted the job, it was his. Elated, Ferguson immediately wired Brame, accepting the offer and expressing his appreciation and eagerness to start work.

Bankston, however, was not one to give up that easily. He called back to say that he was dispatching C. C. Smith, the college's business manager, to Baton Rouge to reason with him. This was a smart move. Smith had done several favors for Ferguson, most notably sending him money via Western Union when his funds were running low, as they often did during vacations. Ferguson was simply unable to stick to a budget, something that would later come to haunt him and Smith.

Smith arrived in Baton Rouge the next day, just in time for lunch. Over a casual bite, Smith said it was absurd to think Ferguson would coach again. The two men laughed at the very notion. Smith, a smooth talker, shrewdly waited until after lunch before making the pitch. They had been strolling around when Ferguson said he felt a little drowsy and wanted to rest; they plopped down on a concrete tier in an outdoor amphitheater on the edge of the LSU campus.

"Coach," said Smith, "we've decided to give you a raise of, shall we say, fifty dollars a month for the next year. Do you think that's enough?"

Ferguson was surprised and disarmed, but not enough to fall for any tricks. "Thanks very much," he replied, "but you can't pay me enough to coach."

"Who said anything about coaching?"

"Well, that's different," Ferguson said.

Smith, all smiles, said that he and President Bankston knew how Ferguson felt about coaching, and they respected his views. They also knew that Ferguson was the kind of fellow who was willing to help out in a pinch. "I'd like to see any damn job you can't handle," he said. Ferguson shrugged. "I just try to do my best."

Smith pounced. "Let's just say for fun we can't find a coach for next year. You would help out, I'm sure."

Ferguson wasn't biting. "You know damn well you can find a coach," he said, "and if you can't, I'll find one for you."

"Yes, we can find one," Smith said. "Some dumb bruiser who will ruin the boys and the college. I'd rather we didn't have any coach than one like that. Come to think of it, I don't think we should have a coach at all."

Smith quickly clarified that the football team would not need a coach, not if someone like Ferguson, who understood the proper place of football in college life and its role in building character, volunteered to give players advice from time to time.

"I damn sure won't do any coaching," Ferguson said.

Smith was shocked—shocked! —that Ferguson would think that was the plan. "I was thinking that maybe you, and President Bankston, and myself should sit on the bench during games to kind of keep the boys from fighting, and maybe go out and watch them practice once in a while. You wouldn't mind that, would you?"

"I guess not, but I won't do any coaching," Ferguson said. "I'll do what I can to help. I'll make out the schedules and even buy the equipment. You know I can save you some money there."

"That's the stuff," Smith exclaimed. "We knew we could depend on you."

Ferguson wasn't so sure. "Who," he wondered, "are the fans going to blame when we lose games?"

Smith said he and Bankston would not let anybody blame Ferguson, even if A & M lost every game during, say, the next three seasons. Ferguson was silent for a minute or so. "Put down all the stuff we've been talking about on paper and then sign it," he said, breaking the silence. This was what Smith was waiting for.

He pulled out an old envelope and wrote only three sentences. The first said that A & M was not paying Ferguson to coach. The second said no one formally associated with the college would hold Ferguson accountable for any losses during the next three years. The third said that Ferguson could do whatever he pleased with the athletic program, without hindrance or contradiction from anyone at A & M.

It was a blank check, and as Ferguson, without exaggeration, would later boast, it was surely the strangest contract in sports history. Smith signed it first, then Ferguson, and a few minutes later, after a handshake that sealed the deal—gentlemen's style—Smith left for the more than two-hundred-mile drive home to report success to Bankston. But as he sat in the amphitheater, Ferguson reviewed what happened and, as he later wrote, decided he had been bamboozled:

> It wasn't until after Mr. Smith left that I realized what a sucker I'd been. There wasn't much difference between giving ideas and helping the boys out and coaching itself as long as I attended practices and sat on the bench during games. It was depressingly clear that I'd been slickered back into coaching again, but then things like this have been happening to me all my life.

Still, as conflicted as he claimed to be, a part of Ferguson welcomed the opportunity to coach again, and this time on his terms.

CHAPTER 13

"GOING CRAZY"

When he was sulking, a characteristic lifelong reaction to doing something that he regretted but could not undo, Stewart Ferguson always blamed outside forces, never himself. In the early days of September 1938, back reluctantly in Monticello, Arkansas, Ferguson blamed the Arkansas A & M College football program for his own vanity and puny willpower that allowed his superiors to talk him into a contract to coach the team. His only consolation was that, technically he was not the coach. This, he felt, freed him from such activities as recruiting until forced to do so.

In the *Arkansas Democrat* season preview, Ferguson took a distinctly different spin from his comments four years earlier. Most tellingly, winning games was hardly foremost in his mind: "We are only undertaking the task of building a foundation for next year. . . . We are not making an effort to draw players here this year." Ferguson added that that no matter the results, their opponents will know that Arkansas A & M is still on the "map" and will continue to put a team on the field. The emphasis on the word *map* was an initial clue to where Ferguson was taking his Boll Weevils; his last words spoke to his conviction that the school would find a way to hold onto its football program.

He did nothing to prepare for the season until school opened on September 5. Ferguson justified his inaction by blaming the losing record of last year's team and a lack of money to bribe recruits. Registration day found him at his desk in the athletic building, waiting for young men who expressed interest in playing.

Thirty players showed up for the first practice; a few were re-turning lettermen from a team that won one game while losing six the previous season, including an 111–0 beating that embarrassed the school as well as the Monticello business community that not so secretly financed the team. As for the new candidates, Ferguson described them as light, scrawny boys from rural schools and small towns around Monticello. He had hoped that some of the bigger, brawnier graduates of Monticello High School, a regional magnet for athletic talent, would turn up. None did, but Ferguson breathed a sigh of relief when he saw Stanley Cheshier, a sophomore letter-man and former star of the Monticello Hillbillies high school team. Cheshier's presence, as a respected student and athlete, ensured that Ferguson would not face any whiff of anti-Yankee boycotts by play-ers, as he had when he first coached A & M.

Among those seeking a place on the roster was the Reverend James R. Sewell, a thirty-three-year-old Methodist minister from Possum Valley, a farming settlement near Monticello that had be-come a state joke because of its name. Sewell enrolled at A & M after suffering a career crisis and went on to play four different positions, appointed himself Boll Weevil chaplain, and later played a surpris-ingly different role in Ferguson's life.

Another candidate was J. P. Leveritt, a bodybuilder and gymnas-tics star who was working his way through A & M as an adagio dancer and whose talents reportedly included an ability to cure sick chick-ens by rubbing their feathers in a certain way. Leveritt would become an A & M legend and take on a most unlikely role at the White House during the final days of World War II.

Joining the hodgepodge of players was a delegation from the chamber of commerce. Ferguson knew well what they wanted: to continue the tradition of businessmen helping A & M recruit play-ers, often by openly paying them salaries. The relationship with the downtown crowd had already led to one ugly scandal that almost shut down the football program. Ferguson was not interested in re-newing the partnership, partly because of his genuine disdain for athletic mercenaries and partly because of his resentment of anyone who thought he was for sale. This went double for the Monticello business community, which spearheaded the campaign to get rid of him earlier.

The longer he inhaled the spew of the chamber delegation, the more Ferguson felt justified to tell them what he really thought, no matter the consequences. He proposed that the businessmen run A & M's football program while he managed their shops and added that after years of cheating poor Black residents and sharecroppers, their businesses could use some ethical improvement. The delegation stormed off, threatening retaliation.

While Ferguson was making an emphatic break with the downtown football crowd, on campus students and faculty were convinced the school planned to discontinue football and that Ferguson had been hired to oversee its dismantling. The team's returning players missed Coach Sherman (now coaching at Nashville High School in the western part of the state after getting word on summer vacation that his A & M contract had not been renewed, reportedly due to a lack of finances) and overall, the squad pegged Ferguson as just a history teacher. As a result, there was almost no interest in the Boll Weevils, which quite pleased Ferguson. This spared him the kind of heated exchanges on campus that wrecked his reputation off of it. He had his way of doing things and determined that nobody was going to change it.

"Quite deliberately," Ferguson wrote later, "I coach from a rather cool distance. I've heard enough of being willing to die for Coach So-and-So to make me more than a trifle sick to my stomach." The reason was simple: he believed cynical coaches had exploited the sensitivities and immaturity of young men to win at any and all cost, when it was a coach's duty to develop healthy character even if it meant losing games. Ferguson was slowly developing a coaching philosophy that would make him a national laughingstock in some eyes and a national hero in others.

In any case, his team was slow in getting ready for the season, with the first game scheduled for September 23 against Mississippi State Teachers College in Hattiesburg. As Ferguson looked over his twenty-one travelling players, he still wasn't sure who would play where. The only player he felt good about was Tom Curry, a husky end who had played the previous year for the Pine Bluff Zebras, winners of the Arkansas state high school championship. Ferguson decided to build his offense around Curry's talents as a pass receiver and was meeting with the team in a Hattiesburg hotel room to outline the game plan when a Western Union messenger knocked on the door and handed him a telegram. It read, "Tom Curry ineligible. Do not play him." It was signed by the A & M athletic committee, which had battled Ferguson so fiercely four years earlier over his picking up a student hitchhiker. Without Curry, Ferguson feared the worst for his team against the Mississippians, who scored within two minutes of play.

The final was 39–0, and not even the failure of the stadium's lighting system, which left both teams playing in near darkness, and finally flickered out for several minutes during the second quarter, slowed Mississippi State. More telling were the statistics; A & M gained just twenty-nine yards rushing while Mississippi State rung up 675.

A week later, in a game at Millsaps College in Jackson, Mississippi, Coach Ferguson charmed his way into a headline running across the top of the town's *Clarion-Ledger* sports page: "Millsaps Faces 'Swinging Gate' Formation Here Tonite." Although he hadn't coached football in some time, Ferguson continued to study, tweak, and promote his Swinging Gate play. In fact, he published an article two years earlier in the *Athletic Journal* magazine—titled "Inside The 10-Yard Line"—that presented its merits.

Knowing how difficult it was to score from close to the opponent's goal line—where "a good goal line defense works as a unity" and "becomes more compact" due to having significantly fewer yards to cover closer to the goal line—Ferguson made the case that countering with a split or divided line would eliminate that unity and cause defensive players to "think about their spacing in relation to one another; psychologically, we have given them a problem to keep in mind." His three key principles of the divided line and pivoting "swinging door" centered on relieving pressure on offensive linemen (due to no individual blocking assignments); instilling an advantage for ball carriers (stationed so close to the linemen, the defense would have less reaction time to shift into any developing holes); and forcing the running back to take a direct path, rather than any "fatal" hesitating or changing of decision within ten yards of the goal.

Of course, he also crowed wildly—and falsely—that "my teams have failed to score from inside the 10-yard line but three out of something more than 50 attempts in five years." Since he started dabbling with the play during the last few years at Dakota Wesleyan and in his first coaching round at A & M, it had hardly delivered a plethora of touchdowns; more likely it was a bewildering tangle of limbs and bodies that left hapless ball carriers at the mercy of opposing linemen. Ferguson also mentioned possible variations (such as lateraling to a back set in motion) and did admit the "unorthodox" aspects of the play, but encouraged coaches to try it. (Allegedly—and conceivably pushed by Ferguson—on October 23, 1937, CBS Radio broadcaster Ted Husing described the Swinging Gate on Ohio State's three-yard score to beat then-undefeated Northwestern.)

After the X's and O's tutorial, replete with step-by-step diagrams, Ferguson ended in his signature self-deprecating style: "Now, I shall appreciate having someone telling me how to get to the 10-yard line."

As for the current game with Millsaps, the opposition encountered no issues driving to A & M's ten-yard marker, but repeatedly bogged down near the goal (providing some new data points for Ferguson's research), while A & M could muster only two first downs in a 10–0 defeat. After the two trips to neighboring Mississippi, the team returned home for some more traditional local competition.

The Boll Weevils were members of a mini-conference called the Little Big Three, along with Arkansas State College and Magnolia A & M. Such small interstate conferences were fairly common. They fostered rivalries that heightened fan interest and, at a time when every penny counted, cost relatively little. One drawback, however, was that members sometimes dropped out for one reason or another, and this happened in 1937 to Magnolia, when the school's president abruptly called off the season the week before its opening game due to a lack of players.

It was an especially costly blow; historically, the Magnolia Mule Riders were A & M's most intense rival, and their games drew as many as 2,500 fans, by far the largest crowds of every season. Magnolia's withdrawal meant Hendrix College stayed on the schedule and served as the first home game of the season. A & M and Hendrix had played seven times before, with A & M losing every game. Hendrix made it eight-for-eight by defeating the Boll Weevils 13–0.

In the following week's edition of the *Weevil Outlet*, a headline read, "Aggies Lose to Pine Ridge University, 33–0." (Diehards still called them Aggies, the traditional nickname given all A & M schools.) The story described how Ferguson tried to turn the tide with the Swinging Gate but was baffled by Pine Ridge's trick plays, which included variations on the flying wedge and Statue of Liberty.

The story was a deadpan spoof. There was no Pine Ridge University. But so casual was the interest of most students that they put it down as just another loss. A column on the same page illustrated the point. "At the Hendrix football game the other night, there was the weakest, most pitiful excuse for pep that this eye has seen in many a year," the writer said. "It's doubtful that even the three hundred students [at the game] could be heard by the cheerleaders. We hope and pray that we'll be able to live it down."

After three shutouts, Ferguson was just praying to see his Boll Weevils score. In their fourth game, against Louisiana College, in Alexandria, Louisiana, his team failed again. The Louisianans won 14–0, but Ferguson was starting to think his small, inexperienced squad might gain by passing what it could not gain running. He installed a five-foot-seven freshman, James Scriber, at quarterback with instructions to mix passing with the Swinging Gate. Scriber forgot the Swinging Gate, but threw forty times, and completed thirteen for 175 yards. It was by far the highest number of passes A & M had ever thrown in a game, and Ferguson was so pleased he didn't care that Scriber had neglected his pet play.

An undefeated, powerful West Tennessee State Teachers squad won, 50–0, the following week, in the Boll Weevils' only Saturday game on the schedule. Finally, in its sixth game, at home against mini-conference foe Arkansas State, A & M scored. Ralph Baker, who was playing his first game at fullback, reached the end zone on a three-yard run. Arkansas State won 27–6 in a rough game, in which some of its players were ejected for slugging and two Boll Weevils were hospitalized. Ejections for slugging (striking opponents on the head, neck, or face) were included in expansive 1932 college football rule changes to "set up safeguards against hazards" of the game. As part of a first-time home and home series, the two teams played again the following week, in Jonesboro, and again A & M fell, 18–6.

Next up was Northeast Center College of Monroe, Louisiana, which one year earlier had humiliated A & M 111–0. After that historic whooping, word spread from the Monticello Recreation Parlor ("Games, Sports, Drinks, Tobaccos, Meet Your Friends Here")— downtown's beer hall and pool hall hangout for gamblers—that the Boll Weevils quit because they had not been paid before the game. To add to this year's drama, it was homecoming for A & M. Northeast won 19–0, which Ferguson declared a moral victory and promised the team a weekend in New Orleans as a reward. Before that, however, there was a season-ending Thanksgiving game against Southeastern Louisiana College, in Hammond, Louisiana, which defeated A & M 48–14.

They ended the season with no victories and nine defeats. How bad was it? It was the worst single season record in A & M history, surpassing even the 0–7 squad in 1934, which led to Ferguson's forced removal as coach. There was more. His team this year scored all of four touchdowns, was shut out in six games, and gave up 238 points. Under normal circumstances, there would have been loud cries for Ferguson's ouster. This time, however, there was only resignation. For one thing, his crazy contract protected him from any criticism, and gave him two additional years before any such accounting. For another, the indifference on and off campus spoke loud and clearly. Almost nobody cared about him or his inept Boll Weevils.

As promised, Ferguson treated his boys to a weekend in bawdy New Orleans. The Reverend James Sewell demurred, on grounds that he had been invited to preach on Sunday. In a way, it was a shame;

Sewell could have gathered enough anecdotes for a month of Sunday sermons.

As soon as the A & M bus left the campus, Ferguson told the boys all training rules were suspended. He lit up and passed around the cigarettes. At the first stop, in a joint called Joe's, the boys played cards, shot pool, drank beer, and pinched some souvenirs. The boys who could dance and remembered to take a jacket and tie were invited to a school soiree, where, to their surprise, they were "complimented as being good Arkansas dancers." The only awkward moment came when one of the Boll Weevils trespassed onto a woman's property and stole persimmons from a tree. But, to Ferguson's relief, the woman who owned the tree was talked out of calling the cops. The team spent the night in a motor inn outside of New Orleans.

The next day, as the team bus rolled across the Huey P. Long Bridge into the city, there was applause and cheers, and after checking them into the Jung Hotel, Ferguson told the boys they were on their own. He went to the racetrack. The boys scattered. By the end of the day, they had seen all the important sights, tried oysters, and downed an impressive amount of what one participant called "conversation soup." That night, back at the hotel, Ferguson introduced a few of them to the Tom Collins.

Early the next day, the team headed for Baton Rouge, where Ferguson leveraged his ongoing relationship with LSU to nab free tickets for the school's annual big-time game against Tulane. He regarded both colleges with great affection dating to his own earlier years as a coach of several Louisiana high school players who went on to star for the Bayou Bengals and Green Wave.

The team left for Monticello immediately after the game. When they arrived—cold, hungry, and dog tired—Ferguson said he hoped everybody eligible to play would return the following season. He said he had ambitious plans.

That was for sure. Between games that fall, Ferguson had contacted dozens of colleges, offering to play them in 1939. From the replies he received, he scheduled ten games, as far away as Philadelphia and Cleveland. Only two games were scheduled in Monticello, which he later wrote was an indication of his regard for Monticello's hometown fans. He also scheduled stops along the way that would allow his players to see sights that none of them ever thought they would see and that would satisfy his own nomadic ambitions. Besides, he was plotting something completely alien to college football. "Going crazy," he called it. Soon, to various degrees of bemusement or indignation, the rest of the country would wholeheartedly agree.

CHAPTER 14

"A DIZZY LIAR"

Before the looming "going crazy" schedule, Stewart Ferguson was busy overhauling the entire A & M health and physical education program and turning it into an integrated and formalized part of the college's overall educational structure. He had started in the fall of 1937, upon taking on the role of department chair, by instilling the most thorough male physical examination ever conducted in the school's history. Each boy saw at least five of Monticello's specialists—including radio and X-ray; eye, ear, nose, and throat; dentist; and general practitioner—with recommendations made for follow-up treatment as necessary.

Ferguson then focused on a redesign and major expansion of A & M's physical education department. He set up a new, robust full year intramural structure with six teams of boys (all football players participated!) playing round-robin tournaments in touch football, volleyball, track and field, and softball. A council, with a representative from each team and a faculty assistant who served as intramural chairman, governed the activities. An intramural program for girls was organized based on their campus residences. Introduced along with the improved intramurals were new physical education theory and teacher training courses, plus significantly expanded and enhanced activities, including the addition of co-recreation classes. Complementing the intramural program were activities such as folk dancing, fencing, tumbling, and archery; a group of sophomore girls proudly represented the school in the state's annual Folk Dance Festival up in Conway.

By the spring of 1939, as laid out in the local daily, the *Advance-Monticellonian,* Ferguson and his A & M health and physical education team were getting additional attention. The Southern Physical Education Association selected Coach Ferguson as one of the twenty-five leaders—one of just six college directors chosen and the only one from Arkansas—to help construct and illuminate physical education in the South. The regional association further honored Ferguson by electing him to the vice chairmanship of three of its divisions, along with asking him to speak about A & M's progressive program and its connection to new thinking in education at its March convention in Tulsa, Oklahoma, attended by one thousand or so delegates from fourteen southern states. He was a hit. The Tulsa papers said Ferguson's talk on A & M's new athletic program was the "most sensational and revolutionary idea advanced" in the four-day program. The Men's Athletic Section of the convention even asked him to describe his beloved Swinging Gate formation.

Upon Ferguson's return, the *Arkansas Democrat* ran a feature story in which he provided some further perspective on the philosophical changes he was aiming for, especially around football. Unlike the increasing number of small colleges who had "de-emphasized" football in the recent depression years, Ferguson described it as one of the games the college would treat as a laboratory, in which areas such as sportsmanship and building new relationships with other student bodies would mesh with removing the pressure to "win" for the players and coach.

Stewart Ferguson left for his summer of teaching and coursework at LSU feeling upbeat, filled with thoughts of a new positive era of athletics within A & M's overall academic structure. Upon his return, however, dread trumped desire. "The insane football schedule," as he later characterized it, was an imminent reality and he was on his own to get ready.

This year, the only thing he did before registration day was to order $1,000 worth of new uniforms. He selected bright yellow and green jerseys, with stripes in alternating colors, which caused some complaints because the college colors were green and white. One downtown wise guy suggested yellow reflected Ferguson's psychological makeup. Another said yellow would go nicely with the playing style of his Boll Weevils.

Ferguson passed the word around that football prospects should report on September 1, one week before class registration day. One showed up. He was J. P. Leveritt, who served as Ferguson's student assistant, doing everything from counting footballs used in practice to making sure everyone was on the bus at the start of every trip. He also ran the school's tumbling and wrestling teams. Ferguson was not surprised that nobody turned out. Farm work kept many boys busy until the start of classes. So, he rescheduled the first practice for September 8, eight days before A & M's first game in Ruston, Louisiana, against Louisiana Institute of Technology.

Louisiana Tech was coming off an extraordinary 1938 season, not for its performance on the field but for an inspirational decision by the team's coach, Eddie McLane. He had suffered serious injuries as a passenger in a head-on automobile accident the prior November, spent three months in a hospital, and although unable to walk, insisted on continuing to coach. He did so, after a fashion, situated in a wheelchair in the back seat of a car whose top was sliced off at a local garage, and installed with a loudspeaker to enable the coach to run practices. McLane attended all the home games, and his team ended the year with three victories, seven losses, and one tie. Shortly after the season, he was promoted to athletic director, and the school hired Ray Davis, a closely tied former player and assistant coach of McLane's, to take on the active coaching responsibilities.

Getting ready for Louisiana Tech and the following eight games posed a considerable challenge for Ferguson, given the indifference to the team by most students and residents of Monticello. A lot of people assumed that Arkansas A & M would not finish out the season.

The most visible result was that only a dozen or so boys bothered to show up for the rescheduled first practice. Most wanted to play in the backfield so they could carry or pass the ball. Ferguson looked over the sorry lot and announced that any boy, regardless of talent or experience, who wanted to travel to Ruston and beyond was guaranteed a place on the team. "This brought out several more boys but no football players," Ferguson wrote.

Yet, he was about to strike it lucky. As a bit of Arkansas backwoods wisdom put it, "Every now and then, even a blind hog finds an acorn," and for Ferguson, two acorns turned up unannounced and unexpected five days before the Louisiana Tech game. They had just arrived in Monticello from Little Rock and were looking for jobs as football players.

"One of the boys, Terry Field, was a young giant, over six feet tall with a handsome face and a body beautifully proportioned," Ferguson recalled later. "Annie Robinson, the other lad, stood about five feet five, weighed 130 pounds and looked more like a Kewpie doll than a football player."

Ferguson could not know it, but that Kewpie doll was an exceptional prize. He played a half-dozen sports, and excelled at all of them—from boxing, where he won several amateur tournaments, to baseball, where a scholarship to play third base for the University of Texas was rescinded because he didn't stick with the sport through high school. Field and Robinson were blunt—they would play football for money. Ferguson shook his head. Okay, the boys said, they would settle for free room, board, tuition, and laundry. Ferguson explained that A & M had abolished free rides for athletes. In fact, he said, all that he could offer them was travel. Field and Robinson were quiet for a moment, then Field spoke up. "Hey," he said, "I guess we'll stay."

Robinson asked if he and Field were required to practice that very day. Ferguson said no, happy to do anything that would encourage Field to stay. Robinson did not look like an athlete, but if he was Field's friend, that was enough for Ferguson. The next day, they returned for the two-hour afternoon workout and Ferguson almost drooled as he watched Field. "The boy was big and fast and smart," he wrote.

Robinson just fooled around until nearly the end of practice, when he asked Ferguson which position the coach wanted him to play. "The same as you played in Little Rock," Ferguson said. Robinson laughed. "I was a cheerleader," he said. Ferguson laughed, too, dismissing the skinny runt as a clown.

Ferguson realized there wasn't enough time to teach much more than the general rules and basic principles of football to his raw, mostly rookie, players. He also kept up his commitment to player safety, initially fostered towards the end of his Dakota Wesleyan days, teaching them how to best protect themselves from serious injuries.

On the morning of September 16, as Ferguson prepared for the bus ride to Ruston, he realized the new uniforms had not arrived. Worse, most of the old A & M equipment had been sold to neighboring high schools. There weren't enough shoulder pads, hip pads, or helmets to outfit even a starting eleven. Desperate, Ferguson called the Monticello High School coach and asked to borrow a few pieces of game equipment. As bad luck would have it, Monticello was playing a game on the same day, and could not spare anything.

Ferguson was considering what to do next when a member of the Athletic Committee, composed of faculty members charged with the responsibility of making sure that only eligible students played, arrived with worse news. The committee had declared most of his team ineligible. Ferguson, almost exploding in anger, raced to a men's room, flushed the toilet repeatedly to mask his outburst, and cursed the committee, the sporting goods company that had let him down, and everyone else who had landed him in this mess. Then, his temper under control, Ferguson went to President Marvin Bankston's office to tell him what had happened. He also explained that if A & M forfeited the game, as was likely, the college was liable for a sizable financial settlement. Now, he had Bankston's full attention. The president summoned the Athletic Committee into emergency session.

The committee quickly made the entire team eligible, explaining that its earlier action was prompted by the failure of the boys to fill out forms declaring they were competing in football. But, from the glares and murmurs of several members, Ferguson knew that once again he had created more enemies.

He herded his waiting team onto the creaking 1934 Chevrolet bus that would carry it to Ruston, about one hundred miles away, a trip that Ferguson was sure would end in humiliating defeat. At least, he thought, he was getting a guaranteed five-hundred-dollar payment.

Arriving in Ruston, Ferguson ordered the bus to stop outside the city's only sizable hotel and went inside to register his players for a few hours' rest and a meal before game time. The proprietor said sorry, but he never allowed football teams to stay. They caused too much damage, he said, and frightened other guests. Ferguson invited the man to step outside and see his team. "Why, they don't look at all like football players," he told Ferguson, who was thinking they didn't play like a football team, either. The boys were invited to register.

While the boys were eating, Ferguson called Coach Davis. Much embarrassed, he explained about the missing equipment and asked if he could borrow some of Louisiana Tech's pads, helmets, and jerseys. To the surprise of the home crowd, the Boll Weevils emerged from the visitor's dressing room wearing the same uniforms as the Bulldogs.

Ferguson had assembled his team at seven o'clock, about an hour before the kickoff, and after it dressed in Tech's hand-me-downs, he called for a moment of quiet. He knew they were nervous—for some, it was the first time they had ever played football. It was time for a pep talk, to rally their spirits and ease their doubts.

"I spewed out the ancient and trite appeal for the boys to give their all for the college, their parents, sisters, brothers and the girls they intended to marry," Ferguson wrote later. "I told them that the game was a crisis in their lives that would forever affect them." With a faked lump in his throat, he added, "I would give years of my life for a chance to play tonight."

Suddenly, the lights went out. A fierce lightning storm had swept Ruston, plunging part of the town into darkness, including most of the Louisiana Tech campus. Several hundred fans stayed in the stands—including dozens of black townspeople who paid a quarter apiece for seats in a remote, segregated end of the stadium—as electricians worked to repair a damaged relay station. A marching band entertained the crowd and Ferguson, waiting in the sweltering, gloomy dressing room, wondered what else could go wrong.

During the pregame rituals, he found out. Some Boll Weevils just stood along the sidelines, watching Tech going through its routines. Ferguson's heart sank. His players did not know what to do. Other players copied the same exercises as Tech players but performed so poorly that some fans thought A & M was engaged in a parody meant to mock their opponents.

Three plays after the kickoff, Tech scored. Before the first quarter ended, it was 13–0. The game ended 32–0. The only offense shown by A & M was the passing of Robinson, who explained to Ferguson after the game that he had mainly thrown the ball to keep the larger, faster Tech defenders from killing him.

Annie wasn't exaggerating by much. Three Tech players were ejected for slugging, and back in the dressing room, Ferguson counted up the toll on his players—"two broken noses, several sprained ankles, a badly twisted knee, and [plenty of] swollen bumps."

More depressing to Ferguson, though, was the look of disappointment and hurt in the eyes of the Boll Weevils. "I remembered their eager and spirited expressions as they left the dressing room for the game," he wrote later. "They had trusted a dizzy liar who told them they could win, and offered them no other satisfaction."

On the gloomy ride back to Monticello, Ferguson thought about what was to come in Pennsylvania, West Virginia, Texas, Ohio, and Missouri, where he would take his trusting, unsophisticated boys. Within the next two weeks alone, A & M would travel to Philadelphia and Charleston, cities where fans were used to real teams and real games. Not even the consolation of $1,500 in guarantees lifted Ferguson's spirits. What he needed was something that would transform his team—and himself. Somewhere just north of the Louisiana line, the answer came to him.

CHAPTER 15

EPIPHANY

As the son of a stern Methodist minister who had prayed his wayward boy would follow him into the pulpit, Stewart Ferguson easily and naturally identified with the conversion experience of Paul the Apostle, the relentless persecutor of early Christians who, in one blinding moment of divine revelation on the road leading to Damascus, became a tireless, influential champion of Jesus Christ.

Stewart Ferguson's own road to Damascus—with the same kind of transforming vision that led Paul to forsake his old faith for a new one—wound haphazardly through several states and over thousands of miles. In a way, Ferguson thought, he had been as blind as Paul, who spent three days and nights fasting and praying after losing his sight, not knowing what the future held, before he was miraculously healed to begin his new ministry. Ferguson knew it was not a calling that his colleagues would easily accept, understand, or appreciate, but like the true believer he had become, he was unmoved by their appeals to return to orthodoxy. It began on the campus of Monticello A & M on September 20, 1939. By God, he said, he was going to play football for fun, and that was that. His good fortune was that his own disciples, the young men on the A & M Boll Weevil team of 1939, were enthusiastic converts, too.

In the *Arkansas Democrat*'s last preview of 1939 Arkansas college football teams, Stewart Ferguson made it official. Expounding on his comments to the paper in the spring, Ferguson described the school's new gridiron program as "football for fun," explaining that the game was "given entirely back to the boys." He went on to define more of the framework:

Football is merely another course in the department of physical education. No boy is expected to report for football unless he really likes to play the game, attendance at practice is not compulsory, and there are no such things as rigid training rules, etc. With us football is just a game, and we intend to keep it that way.

Two days later, the team bus, christened the Green Dawg in a nod to the school colors and local Green Dog bus line, rattled off over the gravel main road that led east, toward Philadelphia, Pennsylvania, a city that none of the boys had ever seen but knew from Coach Ferguson's history classes as the cradle of American democracy. The game there with St. Joseph's College was incidental to the discoveries and adventures that lay ahead.

The first stop was fifty-five miles away, in Pine Bluff, an Arkansas farm and railroad town familiar to most of the boys. But after a brief stop, Ferguson ordered the Green Dawg's driver, senior Alvin Beverburg, to step on the gas. By lunch, the team was in Forrest City, where Ferguson insisted on a quick workout on the local high school athletic field before eating. This was to loosen up after sitting for hours in narrow, hard, upright seats, as well as to make at least a passable show of practicing.

On the road to Memphis, which Ferguson had never liked and called "the Sodom and Gomorrah of the delta," the team was promised a few hours to explore Beale Street and all the other sights they had heard about. While his team wandered the Memphis streets, Ferguson walked a bit, rethinking the schedule he had so meticulously drawn up. Originally, he planned to arrive in Nashville for dinner and to spend the night, but already hours behind schedule, he figured the team could not possibly get there until midnight. Wrestling with timetables, he said, usually gave him a headache, and he had one now. He also had a flash inspiration, one that would define everything else that he did as a college football coach.

"I decided to never again try to work out any problems connected with time and mileage—one of the few intelligent decisions

I ever reached," he wrote later. "This decision added much to our pleasure in traveling. We generally just started out in the general direction of our destination and let arrival time take care of itself. We ate and slept where meal and bedtime caught us. For we were traveling for fun."

Newly freed of the constraints and demands of timetables, Ferguson decided to stop for supper in Jackson, Tennessee where, as he often did in strange places, he asked around for the cheapest eats in town. The one he chose was divided into two rooms, one decorated with garish red and green neon lighting, with a detailed menu, and the other, behind a plain door, offering plain fare. Ferguson split the boys into two groups and sent them into the two rooms. This, he said, taught him another important lesson: the fancier the premises, the less food served for the money spent. "The appetite of the boys was the only atmosphere we ever needed," he said.

It didn't take much for Ferguson to put a town on his list of places to avoid on future trips, and Jackson was a case in point. After supper, the boys walked across the street to the bus station to use the toilets there. Ferguson was sitting on the bus when the station manager came over with an ultimatum. "By God," he yelled through the window, "you didn't eat our food and by God, you're not going to use our rest rooms." Happy to depart Jackson, Ferguson mellowed and began thinking of the boys sitting two by two behind him. He liked their refreshing eagerness, their openness, their willingness to try something new, and their individuality.

There was Coy Brown, a sleepy looking guard who, in Ferguson's opinion, worried most about where he could spit the chewing tobacco that inspired teammates to call him "Brown Mule," for the brand of plug he favored. The happy-go-lucky Brown, known across A & M's campus as "Feller," also happened to be team captain and editor of the school paper, and naturally fell into the role of Boll Weevils press agent.

There was Tunis ("Goldenlock") Bishop, an eighteen-year-old Little Rock high school wrestling champion (along with his twin brother and teammate, Buell), nicknamed for his resemblance to Flash

Gordon, who played in the backfield and always shared the seat with Brown. "He was anxious to startle the world about most anything," Ferguson wrote. Despite Bishop's habit of lashing out verbally at anything that upset him, Ferguson, likely seeing bits of himself, regarded him as a nice boy whose outbursts hid an essentially quiet nature.

Across the aisle from Brown and Bishop sat John Strange, a tackle who rarely was called by his first name because, in Ferguson's opinion, his surname described him so aptly. He had red hair, crossed eyes, and a squeaky voice, characteristics that made him the butt of many practical jokes. He was the most popular player on the bus. J. P. Leveritt, the lone student to show up at the first call for practice, was one of the most remarkable athletes Ferguson ever met. He played several positions and at times served as team manager. Leveritt was an acrobat, wrestler, bodybuilder, adagio dancer, and according to the college newspaper, the most handsome boy on campus. His physique, which Ferguson compared with Mr. America, inspired awe and attracted swarms of smitten coeds. Although easily the best player on the squad, Fergie didn't use him much because he disliked the rough aspects of the game.

There was also James R. Sewell, the thirty-four-year-old Methodist minister who played guard and enrolled at A & M a year earlier because he wanted to get involved in campus ministry. Naturally, everybody, including Ferguson, called him "Preacher," and he conducted weekly worship services on the Green Dawg. Then there was Collier Jordan, the center, a barber who hitchhiked to Monticello from Vernon, Alabama, and was working his way through school cutting hair.

There were several others, and all were asleep, twisted into awkward positions, when the bus rolled into Nashville sometime after midnight. Leveritt and Ferguson roused them and herded them into the city YMCA, where an unhelpful clerk made the crew wait nearly an hour before showing them the cots where they spent a short, restless night. It was enough to add Nashville to Ferguson's little list.

The bus was showing its age and hard usage. The transmission made grinding noises, the engine knocked, smoke curled from the exhaust, and the crawl up hills was so slow Ferguson feared the boys would have to get out and push. More worrying was that the Green Dawg might not last until Philadelphia, because among other things any repairs or a replacement would knock a devastating hole in Ferguson's budget.

The sluggishness and wheezing of the bus led to irritation and strain among the boys, in some cases resulting in profane shouting matches. Ferguson did not intervene, though, because he believed that boys could sort things out better on their own, and generally, they did. This bothered some parents and even some colleagues at A & M. But Ferguson was adamant about not curtailing individual expression.

"Everyone, except myself, was sure that I was too liberal a chaperone," he explained later. "It was seldom that I attempted the regulation of anything. We had no training rules, no restrictions on conduct, and but very few general suggestions on anything." Moreover, the boys were allowed to speak freely, "without compulsory regard to the possible sensitivity of Reverend Sewell or myself." Sometimes, he noted wryly, a boy would curse in one breath and break into a religious song the next. "Both were natural and expressed his feeling at the moment," Ferguson said approvingly.

The boys had grown up in homes where religion, mostly evangelical Christianity, was important. Ferguson felt that his own upbringing in a Methodist home enabled him to differentiate between true reverence and hypocritical piety. "When 'Preacher' Sewell held his weekly service for the boys, as the bus rolled along the highway, the refreshing fervor of the boys in song and prayer would really sanctify most churches and homes I have seen," he said later. "Hardened and routine purveyors of the gospel could well use some of the religious spirit of my boys."

The bus stopped in Cookeville, Tennessee, where Ferguson asked for permission to use the football field of Tennessee Polytechnic College to work out. Two of the school's coaches not only agreed but came out to watch.

"You mean to say this is a college team?" one asked, incredulous.

"Sure," Ferguson replied, "and we're playing ten tough teams this fall."

One Tech coach said A & M was smaller than the Cookeville High School team, adding, "I guess you've got a very fast team."

"Maybe we have," Ferguson said. "But, then, I never try to figure out just how we will win."

The coach snorted. "Win?" he said. "You think you're going to win in Philadelphia?"

Ferguson admitted his Weevils may lose that one.

"What kind of offense do you use?" the coach asked. Now Ferguson was really stumped. Consistent with his new "football for fun" and handing the game "back to the boys" mantra, he had not bothered to teach the Swinging Gate or any other offensive formations and systems with this crew. So, he lied, saying he was going to spring a surprise on St. Joseph's and would rather not share it with anyone before game time.

The Tech coach shook his head. "I must say you're covering up plenty," he said. "I haven't seen your team show a damn thing since they came on the field. If you've got anything at all, you sure as hell have me fooled."

Ferguson smiled. "That's how we fool 'em all," he said.

The struggling Green Dawg made it to Marion, Virginia, where Ferguson got lucky. He found a mechanic who was willing to work all night to put the bus back in running condition. Ferguson put the boys up at a roadside motor lodge. The next morning, the mechanic reported he had installed a new transmission, and the boys rolled away, cheering, with Ferguson whooping as loudly as anyone. The next stop was at Virginia Military Institute, at Lexington, where a special friend awaited.

Ferguson had met Russell T. ("Russ") Cohen when both were coaches in Louisiana. They hit it off so well that in 1930, when Ferguson coached little Dakota Wesleyan College, in Mitchell, South Dakota, Cohen—then coaching powerful Louisiana State University—arranged a game between the two mismatched teams in Baton Rouge as a favor to a friend. LSU won 76–0, but the score meant nothing to Ferguson, whose respect for Cohen bordered on hero worship.

Now, after coaching stints at the University of Cincinnati, Vanderbilt University, and Clemson University, Cohen was on the athletic staff of the Virginia Military Institute (VMI), and Ferguson was determined that his boys meet one of his idols. While his team loosened up on the VMI field, Ferguson told Cohen about his new philosophy—to play for fun. Cohen said he liked to win too much to subscribe to anything like that.

He was just a college teacher coaching without pay, Ferguson said, referring to his unusual contract with A & M. Bemused, Cohen said, "Why anyone who can talk like a college professor would coach is something I can't understand."

As he left Lexington, Ferguson impulsively told his team he wanted them to visit Charlottesville, home of the University of Virginia. Alvin Beverberg set off, but as the Green Dawg climbed the mountain separating Staunton and Charlottesville, the engine began clanking, the radiator boiled over, and the bus slowed to a shuddering, walking pace. Ferguson and the Boll Weevils got out and pushed, sweating, and swearing. They were straining to get the bus over the crest of the mountain when a sudden rainstorm swept the area and drenched everybody. It was still raining as they pushed the bus into Charlottesville. Ferguson spent a fruitless hour trying to find a cheap café and a helpful mechanic. When by some stroke of unexpected good fortune, he found the bus ready to roll without repairs, he and the boys hurriedly left town, and Charlottesville joined the list of places Ferguson swore he would never visit again.

There was still time to see more sights before the game, so Ferguson took the team into Washington, D.C., a city whose layout "seemed too artificial" and did not live up to his and the team's lofty expectations. However, it was the nation's capital, and he had talked about it enough in class. So, he ordered Beverberg to drive up and down Pennsylvania Avenue, a variation of an old-fashioned small-town tradition called "dragging Main Street," which involved driving back and forth on the main thoroughfare on weekends, eying girls, tooting horns, and playing radios at earsplitting levels. After an hour or so of sightseeing, the team checked into a motor lodge without heating but with a fine view of the Potomac. The next morning, sniffling and sneezing, the Boll Weevils set off to meet a Washington big shot.

Ferguson had written President Franklin D. Roosevelt, asking him for an audience with his team, "the sons of your supporters in Arkansas." He had not received a reply, but, as a backup plan, Ferguson also had written Postmaster General Jim Farley, who accepted the invitation and agreed to meet the Boll Weevils at his office. Farley was charming, telling political yarns, swapping sports stories, and posing for photographs. When the boys from A & M left an hour later, they told Farley that if he ran for any office, he had their votes. The experience redeemed Washington in Ferguson's eyes.

The next day, A & M was to play St. Joseph's, but it was a relatively short trip to Philadelphia. The boys arrived just before dark in good humor and so hungry that Ferguson skipped the usual search for a cheap eatery. He decided to spend a few extra dollars for the Friday night special at the Hotel Normandie, where they were staying. There was only one problem—the dining room had a strict jacket and tie policy for men. Five boys lacked jackets, so Ferguson ordered the five fastest eaters to go first, then return and lend their proper attire to waiting, less well-dressed teammates.

As he was eating, Ferguson mentioned to the player sitting next to him that the dinner cost $1.25. Instantly, the player shouted, "Eat everything you can. This stuff is costing us a buck and a quarter apiece." Ferguson, never at a loss for words, explained to the waiter that the boys were from Arkansas.

Back in his room, Ferguson's telephone rang. It was a *Philadelphia Enquirer* sportswriter who wanted to expand on some promotional material that Ferguson had written and mailed—something he did before every game.

The sportswriter asked why A & M played for fun, as Ferguson stated in the material he prepared. "To make people laugh," Ferguson replied. "Laugh at a football game?" the writer said. "Sure, you should see us," Ferguson bragged.

The sportswriter said he fully intended to do just that.

But now that he was on the record, Ferguson realized he had not thought exactly what his players should do to entertain the crowd. He called a team meeting and said he needed them to come up with some funny business. None of the boys were interested; they had just met Davey O'Brien, the All-American and Heisman Memorial trophy winning quarterback the previous season at Texas Christian University, and several of his pro Philadelphia Eagles teammates. This was the last thing Ferguson wanted to hear, the kind of thing that would inspire his boys to play as hard, and as seriously, as O'Brien and the Eagles.

The next day, arriving at the stadium for the game, Ferguson was approached by the same sportswriter, whose story in the morning paper promised spectators an amusing display of football. The story had added to Ferguson's dismay, and he tried to push past the writer, who said all he wanted was the starting lineup. Ferguson said he didn't know.

"Do you mean you let the players themselves decide who is to play where?" the writer asked. Ferguson nodded. "Yes," he said.

Thus was added, spontaneously and casually, another ingredient in the A & M fun 'n' games canon. From now on, Ferguson said, players would decide not only where they would line up but how long they would remain in the game. In fact, he thought players would do a better job of substituting than any coach.

His team showed plenty of common sense. Annie Robinson, the most gifted A & M athlete next to Leveritt, started at quarterback. The other players who filled spots on the line and in the backfield were logical choices, too. In one way, Ferguson was pleased. In another, he worried that his players would ignore his promise of fun football. It took the Weevils about one half to set his at mind at ease.

With the ball on A & M's own goal line, on fourth down, Robinson refused to punt, and instead threw a forty-yard completed pass. During a timeout, Ferguson asked why he passed on fourth down. Robinson said tracking the number of downs was "too much trouble." Thereafter, Robinson—eschewing any thought of a huddle—sang out plays with the "flair . . . of [an] opera star" and threw passes on virtually every down to almost everybody on the team, legal receivers or not. The Boll Weevils lined up in formations no coach had ever concocted, and on some plays, ran backwards before turning upfield. St. Joseph's won 40–13, but the reward for Ferguson came in the next day's sports pages.

The Boll Weevils' "unorthodox" style, featuring a "dazzling" array of passing, opined the same *Philadelphia Enquirer* reporter, to Ferguson's enormous satisfaction, "has not been seen outside the recreation periods of the state's insane asylum."

But, as so often happened, there also was bad news. This time, it involved money. The St. Joseph's athletic director said he could not give Ferguson the one thousand dollars he guaranteed because a sporting goods company was suing to claim it.

This was another legacy of the days when Monticello merchants tried to make A & M the best-known and most successful football program in Arkansas, if not the surrounding states. Part of their overhaul was new uniforms and equipment, which apparently no one ever paid for. Finally fed up, the company had gone to court.

Ferguson had left Monticello with three hundred dollars, which was long gone, along with whatever personal funds he carried in his pockets. There wasn't enough money for breakfast, but Ferguson had an idea. He wired C. C. Smith, the A & M business manager, asking for a fifty-dollar advance on his salary. Soon, he was at Western Union collecting it and all was well again.

The Monticello boys then quickly accepted an invitation by the Eagles to watch their professional football game Sunday with the Brooklyn Dodgers. Not only that, but the Eagles suggested the Boll Weevils join them on the team bus ride to the stadium, and then to top it off, invited the boys to sit on their bench during the game.

It was a real education, Ferguson recalled. For starters, Annie Robinson, watching the also pint-sized O'Brien pass, planned to crank up A & M's aerial game even further. His decision would give the Monticello squad one of America's most entertaining teams. Outside of the South—especially at Davey O'Brien's alma mater Texan Christian University, with Coach Dutch Meyer's standing "you may fire when ready" order to his quarterbacks—it was still largely a period for running attacks, but Annie changed all that fast for A & M.

Also, Dave Smuckler, the Eagles' fullback, taught all the boys a most impressive new trick. As he sat on the bench, he smoked a large cigar. Called to go into the game, he tucked it into his helmet, put the helmet on, and charged onto the field. Once back on the bench, Smuckler took off his helmet, removed the cigar, and resumed puffing.

Back on the bus, Ferguson noticed his boys practicing hide-the-cigar with lighted cigars, and if he had worried before about the Boll Weevils getting into the spirit of fun, he worried no longer. His boys were about to fulfill his craziest dreams.

CHAPTER 16

MARX BROTHERS OF FOOTBALL

A bit after noon on October 9, Stewart Ferguson walked into the Student Commons at Arkansas A & M for his cup of coffee, but today it wasn't just the commons' too weak caffeine fix he craved. After a whirlwind trip that continued up to New York for the World's Fair and then out to Charleston, West Virginia, for a game with Morris Harvey (known today as the University of Charleston), he was there to bask and gloat.

He knew he would find President Marvin Bankston in his customary place, seated on the middle stool at the soda fountain, nursing a glass of milk, chatting with other faculty members. Even before Ferguson took the stool next to him, Bankston shouted a greeting, and added, "It was sure nice getting the name of the college in the big city newspapers."

He meant the sports pages of the dailies in faraway Philadelphia, Pennsylvania, and Charleston, West Virginia, which had carried big stories about those crazy Boll Weevils from Monticello. In seasons past, A & M was accustomed to perfunctory summaries of their games in Arkansas papers, often limited to a few paragraphs that moved on the Associated Press or United Press wires. Now, finally, the Boll Weevils merited special attention.

"It was plenty of fun for us, too," Ferguson said.

Another professor spoke up. "I see," he said, "just having fun at the expense of the college." Ferguson bridled. This was another of his enemies, spreading a little poison.

Bankston jumped to Ferguson's defense. "Coach will probably make money on every game he plays this fall."

The professor brushed off Bankston's retort. "Tell me," the professor continued, "how is losing games all over the country going to help the college?"

Now it was Ferguson's turn. "Better than losing them in Arkansas, as you guys always did."

The only sour note on the first extended trip of the season was the conduct of two of his players, who had complained about everything from the food to the hard seats on the school bus. Ferguson figured they were homesick, but their attitudes harmed morale and Ferguson decided to dismiss both boys from the squad. He replaced them with two others, who were impressed by the new attention given the team by coeds and wanted to share in it. Then, after only two days at home, the boys were back on the bus, starting south on Highway 13 toward Odessa, Texas.

The game, against Daniel Baker College, located in Brownwood (over two hundred miles east of Odessa) but scheduled for a neutral field, was a lucrative deal for Ferguson. A group of service clubs—the Kiwanis, Lions and so on—were anxious to raise Odessa's athletic profile and had promised Ferguson a handsome financial guarantee. Odessa was an oil boomtown with plenty of new money, and Ferguson was looking forward to pocketing some of it.

Before crossing into the vast, open spaces of East Texas, which Ferguson knew would make his players restless and irritable, there was a prolonged meal stop in Shreveport, Louisiana, then a brief stop at a roadside gas station for soft drinks. The boys grabbed every bottle from an icebox, handed a fistful of nickels and dimes to the attendant, and jumped back on the bus for the long, sweltering ride to Fort Worth, where they would spend the night.

"The next day's travel [into West Texas] was just about as interesting as a trip to a country outhouse—something one had to do," he wrote later. The only break came in Abilene, where the team stopped for a fried chicken and fixings lunch and where, to Ferguson's delight, the waitresses sneaked extra portions to all the boys. He added Abilene to his "good" list of towns, worthy of future visits.

The team arrived in Odessa, and even before they registered at their hotel, Ferguson was raving about the hospitality and friendly reception, which included free movie tickets, coffee and soft drinks, tours of the city with pretty coeds as guides, and plenty of smiles all around. The welcome continued with a lighthearted Boll Weevils feature in Friday's *Odessa News-Times*, touting their lack of set offensive and defensive formations and freewheeling play, with a merry Ferguson chiming in that "those boys of mine think of the most unlikely things to do."

The "Saturday night lights" game was A & M's giveback. Daniel Baker won 33–13, but as far as Ferguson was concerned, the score wasn't important. His boys had fun and so did the crowd, which roared at some of the antics, a few of them accidental. In one play, Carlton Spears, the Boll Weevil halfback and team co-captain who also served as president of A & M's senior class, heard footsteps behind him as he ran with the ball. He lateraled it without looking, shouting, "I'm tired, you carry it for a while." To the referee. The laughs convinced the team to add the stunt to its developing repertoire.

The next day, A & M headed back to Monticello for its first home appearance of the season on Friday afternoon against Louisiana College. Ferguson worried his team would treat the contest seriously, depriving fans of the same fun that spectators elsewhere enjoyed. Not only that, but he pictured his team as the bull's-eye for its incoming opponent. Louisiana's new head coach, Jack Walker, had taken over the top spot after one year as an assistant, and was in a prickly mood after three straight "lickings." Just before leaving for Monticello, he had issued an ultimatum to his team: "bear down or turn in their suits."

Ferguson was right to worry. The Louisianans were all business, and in Ferguson's eye, needlessly and repeatedly "knocked most of my players flat on their backs." The final was 29–6, but Ferguson was more depressed by the reaction of his players. They angrily retaliated with fists and feet. The result was an ugly game, the last thing

Ferguson wanted. Little Annie Robinson was the only reason for fans to cheer. After every pass, he was knocked to the ground, but rose, grinning, to strut and taunt the visitors.

On November 2, after nearly three weeks at home, the Boll Weevils hit the road again. Ferguson planned to spend the night in Springfield, Missouri, one of his favorite towns, but snow began falling a bit south near Hollister, and Ferguson decided to get off the highway. He found a hotel and settled down for the night, while the boys lingered in the lobby, looking over the souvenirs and knickknacks. When Ferguson woke up the next morning, the proprietor was screaming that the boys had robbed him blind—ashtrays, painted rocks, postcards, dozens of cheap keepsakes were missing. Ferguson described the stuff as valuable as a "chastity belt in a whorehouse," but he spent an hour searching the bus and suitcases. In the end, he paid a few dollars for items the man insisted were still unaccounted for. The players felt so bad that for several weeks they wouldn't even pick up discarded newspapers.

A satisfying lunch in Springfield made up for Hollister. "Springfield, the best place in America to eat a meal, or spend a night," Ferguson wrote later. "It is the Palm Springs for poor people."

Rolla, the home of the Missouri School of Mines, the next A & M opponent, was a sharply different story. A cheerless, dismal place, in Ferguson's views: "It has more discouraged and drooping mouths per thousand population than any other city I ever saw." The same was true, he thought, of the Miners and their fans.

A small, fiery crowd, dominated by profanity-spewing drunks as far as Ferguson could tell, awaited the Boll Weevils, which gave the boys an idea. Several of these fans crowded around A & M's bench, shouting abuse. One, a whiskey bottle sticking out of his pocket, staggered onto the field during the pregame warm-up. The Boll Weevils greeted him warmly and one player shouted to the crowd that the drunk was going to show them how to play football. The crowd roared with laughter at the shenanigans that followed, the drunk lurching around and the A & M players pretending to keel over from his breath.

Ferguson got into the spirit of things, too. He invited the drunk to sit on the A & M bench and call plays. To Ferguson's amazement, his team scored a touchdown. As the crowd jeered, several A & M players rushed to the sidelines, hoisted the drunk onto their shoulders, and carried him around the field in celebration. When he returned to the bench, the drunk slumped in a stupor that lasted the rest of the game.

A & M did its wildest to entertain, and Ferguson wondered if his players had inhaled some of the fumes permeating the stadium. They refused to punt, passed from a dozen formations Ferguson had never seen, and topped it off with a loopy maneuver that involved seven laterals. The last one wound up in the hands of genial guard "Feller" Brown, who threw a long, complete pass—his first ever heave—to the Miners' ten-yard line. This was enough for Gale ("Gloomy") Bullman, the Miners' coach, a straight-talking football traditionalist, and playfully nicknamed as an assistant coach a few years back by Washington University's head man, Jimmy Conzelman. Bullman gathered the officials on the field and explained that the Boll Weevils weren't playing real football. When the officials laughed, he stormed off, muttering and cursing.

By the end of the game, which the School of Mines won 28–13, Bullman had become a convert. Maybe watching Annie Robinson sprinkle in some real football with two second half touchdown passes warmed him to the Boll Weevils. Whatever the reason, Bullman offered Ferguson a contract for a game the following season, but Ferguson, who already was making other travel plans for 1940, declined.

Immediately after the game, A & M set off for St. Louis and a Saturday night of fun. For some boys, this meant pool halls. For others, the pleasures were as simple as riding streetcars or dropping into church socials. For Ferguson, it meant a night of taking in the sights, strolling the busy downtown, his fedora rakishly tilted, eying the women.

He had just gone to bed when one of his boys rapped on his hotel door to say he had fallen in love. Ferguson, who had been there so many times, in so many towns, yawned and offered up some advice: "Why don't you . . . kiss her goodbye, and tell her we just have to leave?"

"I've already kissed her and hugged her and everything," the boy said. "I can't leave without talking things over with her."

Ferguson was a sucker for many things, and above all love. "One can travel anytime," he wrote. "So we stayed over Sunday in St. Louis, and the next fall, my football player began staying permanently in the city with one of the sweetest wives [a] man could desire."

Early on Monday, the team left St. Louis in a thick fog and headed for Chicago. Along the way, the boys spotted something new and strange. Snow fences, Ferguson explained, to keep snow off the highway. The boys laughed. They thought coach was kidding.

In Chicago, Ferguson and the boys amused themselves until bedtime. They headed to Colosimo's restaurant and the surrounding alleys to sneak a look at the gangsters but returned to the hotel disappointed. The storied haunts of the bootleggers, torpedoes, and molls was, as Ferguson put it, "as quiet as Star City after nine o'clock at night." This was quiet indeed. Star City, not far north of Monticello, was just a wide spot in the road with signs warning motorists to watch out for wandering pigs. In fact, in Ferguson's opinion, the toughest characters that the boys saw were staying at the Wabash Street YMCA, where Ferguson found rooms for three nights.

Among the sights the boys visited was the University of Chicago, where they ate in the dining room, practiced on the football field, and talked with its players, resigned to playing out their final season. The official announcement came six weeks later. President Robert Hutchins, with the backing of the board, decided to drop the sport because he thought it detracted from Chicago's academic life.

Ferguson was baffled and scornful. "I've often wondered why the University of Chicago, with its reputation as an intellectual giant, should have found its football program too difficult to solve," he later wrote. "It has solved problems more difficult and attempts tremendous research on questions not nearly as pressing in modern education as the conduct of intercollegiate football."

Hutchins, Ferguson fumed, had acted cowardly. "This withdrawal from intercollegiate competition smeared some of its intellectual bravery with yellow," and added that failure to continue football created doubt about its "practical courage" in dealing with "truly live problems." He wasn't finished: "The University of Chicago had an exceptional opportunity to guide the conduct of football toward more collegiate ideals. . . . It doesn't do much good for a sports nincompoop from Arkansas to offer himself as a football messiah, but a college like the University of Chicago would have saved football, I still believe."

Self-deprecation aside, Ferguson's ranting about Hutchins' decision years after the fact revealed what a dagger it was to his own developing views on optimizing the world of athletics within the overall collegiate experience. Even though his own obscure little college was unlikely to accomplish much in the way of football glory, he wrote, it never quit.

Ironically, if Ferguson had ever sat down with Hutchins, he would've found they had much in common. Born almost precisely one year apart and each the son of a serious-minded minister, they were both unorthodox innovators and rabble-rousers, unafraid of pushing their agendas to improve the overall education system. Though they clashed on a shared point of view concerning leisure and fun— "having fun, that was a wholly impertinent question for me," Hutchins remarked at the end of his life—Ferguson would have appreciated part of Hutchins's comments in a 1954 *Sports Illustrated* column on requirements for a university to maintain a football program, particularly that "students . . . have come to the college in the ordinary way, with no special inducements."

Yet, back in the fall of 1939, Ferguson did not have time to fret over Hutchins and the University of Chicago. He and his boys were on the go. The plan was to visit Notre Dame, and the next morning, the Boll Weevils left Chicago for "gridiron heaven" in South Bend, Indiana, where Ferguson hoped the Fighting Irish athletic department would let his team work out on the sacred soil associated with Knute Rockne, the Four Horsemen, and other immortals.

The Green Dawg slowed to a stop at the guarded gates, the main entrance to Notre Dame, but a security man, apparently thinking A & M was on official business, waved the bus onto the campus. Spotting a big boy a few yards away, Ferguson asked for directions to the athletic department. The reply was so courteous Ferguson thought even Methodists like him would find the Catholic university very much to his liking.

Once again, Ferguson got lucky. He was sitting in the athletic department's waiting room when Joe Boland walked in. Boland, a member of the Notre Dame athletic staff, immediately recognized Ferguson as the Dakota Wesleyan coach whose team had played St. Thomas College, in St. Paul, Minnesota, when Boland was the coach there. They chatted a few minutes before Boland took Ferguson to meet the coach of the Fighting Irish, Elmer Leyden.

As he shook Leyden's hand, Ferguson almost swooned.

"Many fans doubt that Rockne will ever be equaled as a coach at Notre Dame," he later wrote. "My personal doubts are just as strong that the university will ever find another coach with the courage, dash, and enthusiasm of Elmer Leyden. He is pure Notre Dame. He sweetened the smell of pigskin for all those who played under him."

Ferguson's effusive praise of Leyden was well warranted. The former All-American fullback in Knute Rockne's famed 1924 "Four Horsemen" backfield, Leyden returned to coach at his alma mater in 1933 and became known for his high energy yet reasoned approach on the sidelines.

After lunch with the Notre Dame coaches and players, Ferguson and the boys went to the Irish practice field to watch Leyden and his team in action. They were so captivated, they stayed until dark. Ferguson later wrote that all of the A & M boys liked Notre Dame, "even the Baptists." The Arkansas crew crashed for the night nearby and left the next morning for their scheduled overnight stay in what Ferguson called "drab, dirty, itchy Toledo."

Up early the next morning, Ferguson called the athletic department at the University of Toledo, seeking permission for his team to work out on its football field. After hours of waiting for a reply, he decided to move on to Ann Arbor and the University of Michigan. In his experience, larger colleges gave prompt approval while the small ones dilly-dallied, something he knew well from the languid pace at his own college back in Monticello.

The bus stopped outside the Michigan athletic department a little before noon and for a few moments, Ferguson sat looking in awe at the building. Nervous, he walked in and asked for Fielding Yost, the legendary Michigan athletic director and former longtime coach who had made his Wolverines a fearsome football machine.

Yost stood up and shook Ferguson's hand. Ferguson thought that Yost, sixty-eight years old at the time, looked old but kindly, with a genuine interest in Arkansas A & M, whatever and wherever that was. He walked outside to the bus, greeted the Boll Weevils, and invited them to use Michigan's athletic facilities. Ferguson was thrilled, and his boys were just starting to throw a ball around when Yost walked onto the field. He asked Ferguson if it was okay to teach the boys a few plays. Ferguson turned away, choked up, and nodded his approval.

For more than two hours, Yost drilled the A & M squad, teaching several plays and explaining what made them work. One was a fake kick play that Michigan used to beat Ohio State two weeks later. At one point, a Michigan assistant coach suggested it was time to end the workout. Yost waved him off. When the practice was over, Yost asked Ferguson if he thought his boys would like to eat in the Michigan Union, where his own team dined. Ferguson thought that the kitchen was closed. If it was, Yost replied, he would order it opened. It was open and as Ferguson and his team sat, waiting for their meals, Yost walked in and sat down to join them. He said he wanted to pass on a few more tips for playing winning football. It was one of the greatest days in Ferguson's life. He wrote later that he could see Yost in heaven coaching the greatest players who ever lived, and that he would gladly act as water boy.

A few minutes after leaving the Michigan campus, Ferguson and the boys caught a whiff of an overpowering smell. Collier Jordan, the Weevils center and resident barber, apparently had confused onions and garlic in the Michigan dining room and eaten an entire bowl of the "stinking rose" stuff. The smell was intolerable, and the boys were demanding he do something, but Ferguson was stumped. Tackle Terry Field, a crafty sort who once got two A & M blondes to wear their hair the same way to win his affection, suggested Collier stick his head out a window. For the rest of the trip, that's how Collier rode, with his head out one window and clothing stuffed around him to block any fumes coming back inside.

The Boll Weevils' next stop was Cleveland, where they had reserved rooms in the Allerton Hotel and were scheduled to play John Carroll College the following day. As soon as Ferguson reached his room, reporters and photographers began calling. The chain of events had actually started five days earlier when a sportswriter from the *Cleveland Plain-Dealer* had tracked down Ferguson in St. Louis and telegrammed him with a friendly request to forward his team's season record, since A & M's games never seemed to be included in the extensive weekly college football results reported in the Sunday papers. Ferguson did a bit more than that.

He immediately fired off a detailed letter describing his "playing for fun" football squad, mixing in some vintage Ferguson truth-stretching, like his proud yarn of last fall completing "42 passes in one game with Louisiana College without making a touchdown." He also emphasized that "we are one of the very few teams in the country 100 per cent pure with respect to subsidization." Ferguson wrapped it up with a gleeful rendition of last week's wild play that wound up as a double lateral and a first ever pass (and completion) by guard Coy Brown, along with a quite truthful reflection: "I realize that we sound like a goofy team and we probably are, but I am sure you will enjoy seeing us play."

That initial feature ran prominently in Tuesday's paper, and after the team was swarmed in the hotel lobby upon their Friday arrival, Ferguson told his boys they were becoming important. That evening, another local paper, the *Cleveland Press*, ran an article on the team that worked in some of the coach's advance promotional material and included Coy Brown, the cheeky captain, taking exception to a question on whether they were against winning. "We play for keeps, only the other fella's been doin' the keepin'." Apparently, Brown was just warming up; he had some fun with another reporter, intercepting a call intended for Ferguson: "Yes . . . I'm with the Arkansas team, but Mr. Ferguson is not the coach. Mr. Spears is. And you'll probably find out more about it if you call Mr. Bishop."

The team woke up Saturday morning to see their photos splashed across the *Plain-Dealer's* sports section, from a bunch of them playing cards in the lobby to one with a face full of shaving cream, ahead of a possible night out on Cleveland's Euclid Avenue. Years later, Ferguson said, "It was like riding a Cadillac on the road to fame."

The game itself, played in freezing conditions and mud, was no contest. At halftime, John Carroll, which would lose only once all season, led A & M, 49–0. Co-captain Carlton Spears told Ferguson in the dressing room that the game wasn't fun. Ferguson agreed but said that didn't mean they should quit, and they didn't. A & M held John Carroll scoreless in the second half, scored a touchdown, and found their fun.

The account of the game in Sunday's *Plain-Dealer*, from the same sportswriter who telegrammed Ferguson a week earlier, could not have pleased the coach more: "Not only did the visitors hold the Carroll team scoreless after the intermission, they unmasked one of the wildest, razzle-dazzle attacks ever seen on a Cleveland gridiron to score one touchdown and carry them 78 yards to the threshold of another."

Little Annie Robinson completed fourteen of seventeen passes in the second half, including five straight that took the ball to the Carroll four-yard line when the final gun went off.

After taking in the action, another Cleveland sportswriter coined the A & M boys the "Marx Brothers of Football."

NEA Service Sports Editor Harry Grayson, based in New York and one of the most popular sportswriters of the time, also attended the affair. As part of an overall A & M feature—including a snazzy, smiling photo of Coach Ferguson—he said it "was refreshing to see college kids playing for fun." Over the next several days, Grayson's article was picked up by papers across the country, further spreading the story of Ferguson and his band of Boll Weevils.

After the game, Ferguson, who often allowed his emotions to trump perspective, said that it was the greatest comeback he had ever seen in a football game. He celebrated by splurging on a huge turkey dinner for the team. They could have stayed another night in Cleveland, but the boys were anxious to return home. It was a twenty-four-hour drive, with brief stops in Columbus, Ohio, and Sikeston, Missouri, but Ferguson gave the go-ahead. "We wanted to hear a cow moo and a mockingbird laugh at us," he said. They heard the cows, for sure, and mockingbirds they never expected.

CHAPTER 17

BUSOLOGY 101:
THE WANDERING WEEVILS

Stewart Ferguson subscribed to a newspaper clipping service that mailed him all available articles about the Boll Weevils. He promptly tacked them on bulletin boards in A & M dormitories, the library, and other buildings. Soon, the boards were completely covered and Ferguson, who was in charge of student labor among his several A & M hats, was ordering more built.

Faculty and students caught up on the team's exploits. "We were laughed at, admired, condemned and even cheered wildly," Ferguson wrote later. Initial reactions from the newspapers were light and supportive, with one describing the Weevils as "stupendous, hilariously ridiculous, and the screwiest football set-up in the country," and another stating that while no Boll Weevils would be christened All-Americans, "somebody ought to set aside an even higher honor for them," and "we could use a lot more Boll Weevils from coast to coast." Letters, too, began streaming in from scattered college presidents and coaches praising Ferguson and his Weevils for introducing a new and better era in football.

Out of all this came a nickname, bestowed on A & M's traveling troupe by a radio reporter. He called them the "Wandering Boll Weevils," which, over time, was shortened to "Wandering Weevils."

Finally, a brand name catchy enough and commercial enough to promote. Yet it never occurred to Ferguson or anyone else at A & M to trademark the term and turn it into a bonanza. As the Chicago Cubs faithful demonstrated for years, there is value in lovable losers, and the Wandering Weevils were naturals.

So far, they had played seven games, six of them far from Monticello, and lost every one. Now, in mid-November, they were home to face Northwest Mississippi, an unaccredited two-year college in Senatobia, an area so poor and hard hit by the depression that students were allowed to pay tuition in garden and farm produce.

Students who had ignored the team now turned up along the sidelines to watch what Ferguson called practice. Mostly, they played touch football. They lined up in formations that used ten men on the line, or with some linemen facing their own backfield, or with only the center, Collier Jordan, on the line. Ferguson often joined in the laughter.

Most of the downtown business community was definitely not amused. Above all, it feared ridicule. And unorthodoxy, in all things, was the dangerous slippery slope that led to derision and mockery. At the Monticello Drug Store, Ferguson was scorned by one town dentist as "a damn crazy Yankee who should be playing tiddly-winks in the state hospital for nuts."

It was the homecoming game, and like many colleges, Arkansas A & M tried to book weaker teams to guarantee the hometown fans a victory. Ferguson had done this, but then heard from a coaching colleague that the Mississippians, in addition to receiving free room, board, tuition and laundry, were paid cash bonuses for victories. This was something he decided to keep to himself, and for what he considered a very good reason—a double cross.

He went back downtown on Thursday purposely to draw his critics into speculation about the next day's game. Sure enough, a couple of businessmen who regularly bet on football games stopped Ferguson and asked for some inside information on the Mississippians.

"What are your chances?" one asked.

Ferguson considered the question for a moment or two before answering carefully, "Well, I can't say, but I do know Mississippi hasn't lost a game this season. Their boys will greatly outweigh us, and some pretty good Arkansas boys are playing on the team." Ferguson added that if he were a betting man, he would give the Mississippians forty points—that is, he expected the visitors to outscore his boys by forty or so points. That was good enough for the gamblers, who quickly wagered accordingly with the bookie at the Monticello Recreation Parlor, which included a blackboard for posting up-to-date sports scores carried by ticker tape.

In seasons past, homecoming games were not sure bets to attract large crowds, but this year a huge turnout filled the wooden bleachers and standing room along the sidelines an hour before kickoff. Most of what Ferguson sneeringly dismissed as the Monticello Board of Football Strategy stood behind the A & M bench, shouting instructions to the team.

Initially, the Boll Weevils played it pretty straight and scored within minutes on a five-yard off-tackle run by Tunis Bishop. Shortly after a Mississippi score, A & M started to open things up, and a deep Annie aerial to Stanley Cheshier connected, putting the Weevils back on top. By halftime it was 18–6, and although fans were cheering, the team sensed they also were disappointed at not seeing the antics and foolery that amused spectators elsewhere.

As they came out for the second half, the Weevils danced onto the field in a conga line, played leapfrog, marched stiffly like toy soldiers, and pretended they were skipping rope. They sang nursery songs between plays and snapped the ball to the cadences of nonsense rhymes. Years later, Ferguson remembered one of them:

> Here we come, you son-of-a guns,
> you better lay 'cause we're makin' hay.

Little Annie Robinson even told the Mississippians where the ball was going on several plays. Ferguson figured his team could score as often as it wanted, but his Weevils were enjoying themselves too much to push or pass the ball over their opponent's goal line. The final score was 26–6. Everybody but the gamblers loved it. The next weekend, A & M went to Conway, north of Little Rock, to play Hendrix College. Annie put on a show winging the ball for an eye-popping 283 yards, a personal best, as the Weevils clowned their way to another defeat.

The season ended with a Thanksgiving Day game against Missouri State Teachers College, in Springfield, a city Ferguson clearly loved and visited as often as he could arrange a game or stopover there. The night before the Green Dawg's departure, he went to bed thinking of the pleasures Springfield might provide. When he awoke the next morning, Ferguson learned that five players had violated a team rule by attending a campus dance. He did not impose many rules, but one was early bedtime on the night before a trip. Normally, he would overlook the violations, but Ferguson—who still regularly kept a lookout for other coaching openings—was eying a job with Missouri State, and he desperately wanted to impress the folks there by winning.

He was uncharacteristically upset with the group, and when he stepped on the bus, told the offenders to decide their own punishment. All five, among them team co-captain Carleton Spears, stepped off the bus.

Though Ferguson felt like a "heel" for leaving the players behind, he and his short-handed Weevils headed north to Springfield in a steady rain that continued through the following afternoon's game. The field was so spongy that it made running an adventure. Ferguson told the boys not to leave the dressing room until five minutes before kickoff. He and captain "Feller" Brown went outside for the coin flipping ceremony and any last-minute instructions from officials. The handful of spectators huddled under the stands or umbrellas. Suddenly, Ferguson heard a commotion coming from the Boll Weevil dressing room.

His football team was waddling onto the field, flapping their arms, and quacking like ducks. A few belly-flopped onto the field, sending up sprays of water. Ferguson guessed they got the idea from Joe Penner, a hugely successful vaudeville star of the day known for his catch phrase, "Wanna buy a duck?" They kept it going during the game, with Robinson calling plays in quacking cadences, and players using borrowed umbrellas as props. An intercepted pass led to the only score of the game, which Missouri won 7–0. It ended another dismal season for the Weevils. One win, nine defeats.

Back in Monticello, Ferguson spent the next several days thinking and making notes. He was committed to fun football, but for all the publicity and attention, he did not think of it in any larger, more ambitious context. "Neither the college nor myself rated enough importance to begin glorifying ourselves as reformers," he wrote. Nor, he realized, was his philosophy likely to attract talented recruits to A & M. Not even the Monticello High School coaches liked the way Ferguson ran the program, and since he flatly rejected any suggestion of supporting athletes by paying their expenses, he could not buy a team.

"Unable to offer financial rewards to the boys who played for us, we had to give them something for which to play," Ferguson recalled. "So we gave them fun."

Ferguson also thought through the overall financial impact of A & M football. Before his football for fun experiment, the college simply could not afford the sport. Some home games did not draw enough fans to cover the fees paid to the officials, small in-state away game guarantees did not cover expenses, and A & M no longer charged students an athletic fee. In addition, the recent years of paying to recruit, house, and feed Bo Sherman's "tramp" athletes had crippled the school's athletic budget. Now, driven by the larger out-of-state game guarantees, Ferguson reported that the 1939 football program had cleared $1,700, marking the first time A & M football ever turned a profit.

Further nagging Ferguson was whether the willy-nilly, football for fun program had pushed common sense too far, and if the excessive number of days away from campus was "hurting more than helping the boys' education." As the season was winding down, he addressed the issue across the overall campus community. Ferguson decided to pen an article in the *Weevil Outlet*, framed with a catchy headline: "Busology—New Subject In Education—Gains In Popularity." He opened directly: "Are the Bollweevils being educated?" With that, he argued that the best way to learn is a "modern" method that leaves the formal classroom behind and takes advantage of all five senses. Describing visits including Fort Knox, the tobacco country, Independence Hall, and Wall Street, he laid out the multifaceted geography, history, English, and economics lessons undertaken by his barnstorming boys. Ferguson summed up crisply: "I'm sure Mr. and Mrs. Faculty that if you weigh the facts of our trips you will agree that busology is a great course."

Ferguson did not mention that he supervised classes in physical education and history and arranged for other professors to provide work for the students while away from campus.

He also didn't touch on the added bonus of Reverend Sewell's weekly sermons; in a recent one—titled *What is light?*—Sewell quoted the Golden Rule and added it's "just a rule of sportsmanship. Yes, that simple."

"Busology" did not sway the opinions of various members of "Mr. and Mrs. Faculty." They demanded a vote to decide A & M's football's future.

A meeting was held after the season, and President Bankston—who, with a big boost from his persuasive college business manager, C. C. Smith, had roped Ferguson back into coaching duties—counseled the faculty to state what was wrong with the new program and to argue solely on an educational basis. One faculty member jumped in and reiterated that the team spent too much time away from class. Ferguson followed with a long-winded discussion highlighting the benefits of the new football program and added that the football team's grade point average was on par with the general overall A & M student body. It was true.

The faculty voted to keep football.

Within two weeks, Ferguson scheduled games that would take the 1940 Wandering Weevils to schools on both the Atlantic and Pacific oceans and several cities between.

He also publicized a list of principles that he, Bankston, and Smith had recently cobbled together over Lucky Strikes at a free-flowing, smoky dormitory summit. By the start of the 1940 season, Ferguson was promoting the ten-point list as a manifesto for A & M football. Its language was deceptively simple:

1. Football is conducted according to the best principles and theory of both general education and physical education.
2. The game is played for the fun of it.
3. All high pressure policies and procedures are eliminated.
4. Football is made more educational through experimental approaches, player responsibility, and travel.
5. Intersectional schedules are played for the promotion of a wide range of contacts with other teams and student bodies.
6. Original, unique, and non-standardized formations, plays, and tactics are used to emphasize player thinking and initiative.
7. Liberal and democratic policies are used with as much responsibility as possible placed upon the players.
8. No players are subsidized.
9. Clean, courteous and sportsmanlike play is stressed constantly.
10. The attitudes, welfare, and interests of the players are always placed above the outcome of the game.

With something of an A & M mandate, it was time to put the explicit list to the test.

CHAPTER 18

HERSHEY KISSES

Seduced by fantasies of national celebrity and financial bonanzas, Stewart Ferguson weeded through offers from more than fifty schools anxious to schedule his Wandering Weevils football team in the autumn of 1940. By early spring, he finalized his plans and announced that he had chosen eleven colleges in ten states as far and wide as New York and California. The lone Arkansas opponent was Hendrix College, which he put on the schedule partly because it was a Methodist institution and he was, whatever his flaws, a faithful Methodist.

It was the most ambitious schedule in Arkansas A & M history. Before Ferguson and his clowning ensemble ended their tumultuous, meandering season, it would bring the school more publicity—good and bad—than even Ferguson thought possible.

This should have been the big news in the *Weevil Outlet* school newspaper that week, but Ferguson was upstaged by a cherished annual tradition—the campus scavenger hunt, with teams from fraternities, sororities, other college organizations, and even an anti-aircraft battery from the local National Guard racing to find hidden plows, live frogs, decorated corn cobs and other objects. It was typical Ferguson timing, but his mind was elsewhere.

An indefatigable promoter, he had mailed out a blizzard of press releases, announcing that he expected A & M to clear $10,000 for the season, a breathtaking bit of hyperbole, considering the college had just completed its first football season in the black. Hoping that talented athletes would find their way to Monticello to play for him, despite a refusal to give them athletic scholarships, Ferguson ordered thirty new garish gold-and-green striped uniforms. As he had done the previous fall, Ferguson sauntered around campus a day or so before classes started, stopping at bulletin boards to add another typed notice to the announcements clutter. His notice simply said that any boy who wanted to see America should see him—and that was, once again, the extent of his recruiting of athletes.

By that early September day, he knew that big, strong, fast, experienced athletes were not coming. Instead, the opening day of practice found him with a collection of forty mostly green, slight, scrawny candidates. Scattered among the loads of newcomers were six returning starters, including newly minted captain and honor roll student Stanley Cheshier, who Ferguson also tabbed as an assistant coach as part of a new plan for the season.

The season opened September 16 in Pineville, Louisiana, against Louisiana College, a school Ferguson had been steadily scheduling and which he knew well from over a decade prior when he taught and coached at Bolton High School, just across the river in Alexandria. Ferguson figured the 1940 Louisiana outfit was too talented for his boys, and he was right. A & M lost 28-0 and gained three yards rushing. However, for Louisiana College, there was more to celebrate than a victory—over 1,800 fans, the largest home crowd in four years, paid to see the crazy Arkansans that they had read and heard so much about. For Ferguson, there was a five-hundred-dollar check, the guarantee that the Louisianans had contracted to pay A & M.

The Weevils returned home immediately, and a week later Ferguson was in for a wonderful surprise. At about midnight the evening before the Weevils were scheduled to leave for their game with East Kentucky State Teachers College in Richmond, Ferguson was awakened by a knock on the door of his office, where he usually slept the night before departures. He opened it and discovered to his shock, delight, and relief, Annie Robinson standing there with a sheepish grin.

Robinson, the passing-demon star of the 1939 Wandering Weevils, with a playful streak that made Ferguson laugh as loud as anybody, had not been around for a while. A few weeks after the football season ended, Robinson left campus. It was a mystery to most students, but not to Ferguson.

What happened was that Robinson, who like Ferguson loved to bet on horses, asked his coach to lend him two dollars to bet on a race at the nearby Hot Springs track. He had a hot tip, Robinson said. Not until later did Ferguson learn that his star had spent the money on a license to marry his high school sweetheart. Robinson had written Ferguson during the summer to say his football playing days were over because his wife and mother-in-law insisted he get a job.

Now, here he was. Annie said he had sneaked away from home because he wanted to travel around the country again and had read about the Wandering Weevils' plans for this season. Ferguson immediately woke up the A & M registrar to re-admit him. By breakfast, Ferguson had alerted several teachers to enroll Robinson in classes. During the frenzied early morning, Ferguson tried to explain some new plays he had drawn up. "I don't need any plays," Robinson replied. "Just give me the ball."

Eastern Kentucky was a tough and talented team, coached by Rome Rankin, a no-nonsense type who, as Ferguson sourly noted, ordered his players to carry a football with them everywhere, even to bed, if they fumbled it during a game. This was a punishment imposed by many coaches, to Ferguson's disgust. "I think it's just as sensible for these same coaches to carry the news of their latest defeat on big signs strapped to their front and back," he wrote.

Eastern Kentucky would end the 1940 season undefeated, with eight victories that included drubbing the Wandering Weevils 39–0. There were a few laughs. With the ball on the Kentuckians' two yard line—inside the ten! —Ferguson expected his team to use his beloved Swinging Gate. What followed confounded even Ferguson. The ball was passed among three A & M backs and then sent backwards in a series of laterals by three more players before Robinson hurled the ball far downfield, where it was intercepted beyond the Kentucky goal line and returned to near midfield. Asked why he didn't use the Swinging Gate, Annie said, "Well, coach, I just had to fool you, [too]."

For many of the boys, the next game against Lebanon Valley College in Annville, Pennsylvania, was a special treat. The reason was that the game was scheduled not in Annville, a dull little town, but in Hershey, the chocolate capital of the United States. The boys were promised they would receive special gift boxes of candy.

For Ferguson, it was a treat too. The game contract included all expenses, including rooms and meals in the popular Community Inn, located at the intersection of Chocolate and Cocoa Avenues and owned by the Hershey Estate, which managed the hotel and a half-dozen related enterprises. A & M players were assigned double rooms that cost $4.50 per night. Hospitality extended even to the Hershey Cinema, where the Weevils were treated to a screening of *Those Were the Days*, a football movie set at the fictional Siwash College and featuring William Holden and Ezra Stone (of the *Aldrich Family*, a wildly popular radio comedy of the time). The Boll Weevils loved everything they saw, right down to the streetlamps along Chocolate Avenue shaped like Hershey Kisses.

As for Ralph Stegall, an end on the team, it was truly a life transforming moment. He and several teammates were waiting for a streetcar outside the hotel when a group of girls walked past. One of the Boll Weevils shouted out a greeting. The girls stopped to chat, and one of them, Sarah Boyer, caught Stegall's eye. He caught hers, too. When they went their separate ways, Stegall asked if she wanted to see him play. She said no, she didn't like football. But they promised to write each other, and they did, all through the war that took him overseas. When the war ended, and after visiting his family, Stegall hitchhiked from Monticello to Hershey, married his Sarah and settled down to a life in the chocolate capital.

The contractual deal signed by Ferguson split the total gate receipts equally among Lebanon Valley, A & M, and the Hershey Estate; to Ferguson this was a wonderful chance to show off his promotional talents and build up the crowd. During a team layover, he stopped in at the offices of the *Harrisburg Telegraph*, where the "friendly little professor" talked up his boys and A & M's overall "football for fun" program. On the day of the game, the *Harrisburg Evening News* opened its final preview by highlighting A & M's "unusual formations, gayly colored uniforms, spectacular forward passers, and sensational gridiron antics," and added that "Coach Ferguson has established himself the reputation of being one of the biggest showmen in college gridiron circles." The only trouble, as far as Ferguson was concerned, was the earnest young school spokesman for Lebanon Valley, who insisted that the game was serious business. Ferguson groaned that his emphasis on "blood and thunder" would dampen enthusiasm for the game and discourage people who wanted a good time.

During the hoopla, Ferguson received a telephone call from New York. An editor at *Collier's* magazine, one of the country's largest circulation general weeklies, wanted to put a photographer on the A & M bus for a week or so for an article. Ferguson agreed, but later confessed he was as jittery as "a woman with two dates on the same evening."

The photographer, Hans Groenhoff, arrived in Hershey before the game, introduced himself, and with his friendly professionalism set Ferguson's mind at ease. He walked along the sidelines during the game, taking pictures, getting the players used to seeing him. One of the pictures appeared in the November 23 edition of *Collier's*, showing a dozen Boll Weevils genuflecting and cheering on the sidelines after (to their surprise) A & M scored. Orion Gates, a substitute end, had scooped up a fumble and ran eighty yards for a touchdown, the first points of A & M's season. No one at A & M knew Gates was ineligible to play—only a few months earlier, he signed a contract to play professional baseball.

Lebanon Valley won the game, 28–6, but Ferguson was counting noses, not points. The game drew around three thousand spectators. His cut of the gate was about $1,000. Ferguson was in no hurry the next morning to leave what he later called "the natural courtesy of these really sweet chocolate people." After the team eventually left town, Groenhoff rode along as they detoured through Washington, D.C., via Gettysburg, where the boys stopped to look over the battlefield and where, as he often did, Ferguson grew melancholy thinking of General Robert E. Lee's defeat. It was not that he was a racist,

Dixie diehard. It was that by nature, Ferguson admired lost causes and their doomed leaders.

By the time the team bus reached Roanoke, Virginia, it was nearly midnight. Ferguson decided to call it a day and negotiated prices in the first hotel he saw. Only when the boys were in their rooms, as he walked along a hallway, making sure that they were all accounted for, did he realize where they were. "It was a whorehouse," he recalled later.

One of the boys told Ferguson he never met such friendly girls. He put it down to the famous southern hospitality that Virginia advertised. Later that night, another boy asked Ferguson to loan him two dollars. This prompted Ferguson to spend the night watching the hallways and lobby for hanky-panky. He was red-eyed and exhausted when the bus pulled away the next morning.

Ferguson had spent almost all of his expense money on hotels, food, and the sights in Washington and elsewhere, so by the time the team reached Nashville, which did not exactly win over Ferguson a year earlier but served as a kind of crossroads for traveling teams, he was looking for a rock-bottom bargain. He found a place that charged just $18.75 to put up the entire team. Ferguson counted his bankroll. He figured he could afford a couple of fifty-cent meals on the way back to Monticello. He felt in one vest pocket for the coins that he always set aside for Lucky Strike cigarettes. There was only a dime, not enough for an entire pack. He deliberated on buying a sack of roll-your-own Bull Durham tobacco but opted to hold on to the precious dime in case of emergency. The money, the boys, and Ferguson barely lasted until they rolled onto the Monticello campus just before midnight.

CHAPTER 19

CALIFORNIA DREAMIN'

Stewart Ferguson's ambitious fall football schedule called for a quick turnaround, but this time his prized slinger—and top Weevil attraction—was officially calling it quits. Several times in the last couple weeks away from home, Annie Robinson received telegrams that left him too depressed to concentrate on football. They were sent by his wife, who demanded he come back and get a job. Finally, he confessed to the coach. Ferguson, driven all his life by nomadic impulse, understood how his star quarterback felt, and figured Annie would leave the Wandering Weevils upon the team's return to Monticello. Robinson did just that, departing Arkansas A & M without attending a single fall class and leaving a huge hole for Ferguson to fill.

Finding a new quarterback wasn't the only thing worrying Ferguson. The team bus was falling apart and needed urgent repairs. Ferguson also needed to catch up on classroom assignments, which he left for other instructors to carry out. His other jobs, as dean of men and supervisor of campus labor, meant handling a ton of paperwork. Finally, he wanted to prepare and send out more publicity releases promoting his crazy football team. He had about forty-eight hours to do all this, because in two days, he and the boys were setting off again, this time on a trip lasting thirty-one days, about one-third of the fall semester.

By staying awake an entire night, he accomplished all his administrative chores. The bus was repaired, and at noon on Thursday, October 10, the Weevils boarded the Green Dawg. The Phi Sigma Chi fraternity gifted Ferguson with a carton of Lucky Strikes and gave all the players a sack lunch. The cheerleaders sent up a boisterous good-bye and the bus pulled away, headed first for Denton, Texas, about three hundred and fifty miles away, for a game less than eighteen hours later with North Texas State Teachers College. Verl Gill, one of the six Monticello-born and raised Weevils, handled documenting all of the team's exploits for the big trip. Gill was an excellent choice to chart the goings-on of a big group—he was one of ten siblings, eight of them boys.

The team stopped for supper in Mount Pleasant, Texas, after Ferguson saw a sign outside the Hillbilly Café advertising soup, meat, vegetables, dessert and either a soft drink or coffee for forty-five cents. By then, several players were so tired and irritable that the driver, senior Joe Coker, had threatened several times to stop and fight his two chief tormentors, Frank Carson and Ralph Stegall, who sometimes acted as relief drivers.

There were moments of levity. One involved a boy who felt so uncomfortable with nudity that he could not urinate in front of any-one else. His embarrassment became painful at the stops Ferguson ordered by a convenient clump of bushes or a patch of trees. This was an alternative to long lines formed at gas stations, which, Ferguson fumed, played havoc during the times he didn't have the luxury of his more favored lax schedule on the road. Coker even poured warm water from the radiator into the boy's hand, the folklore remedy for reluctant bladders. When this did not work, several teammates forcibly removed the boy's pants, leaving him nude below the waist. Two hours later, at the team's next outdoor toilet break, his embarrassment apparently was gone. "Lo," Ferguson said later, "the boy accomplished his mission [in] the bushes first of all."

The Weevils were anxious to see Denton, but not for the usual tourist reasons. The city was the birthplace of film star Ann Sheridan. She was a thousand miles away and Denton, as far as anyone knew, did not celebrate her earlier citizenship in any way. To the boys from A & M, this was not important. They were star struck enough to settle for walking on the same streets Miss Sheridan had once graced. By a coincidence, her latest movie, *City of Conquest*, co-starring James

Cagney, was showing at one cinema and the Weevils were given tickets to see it.

The team stayed at the Southern Hotel, where Ferguson once more found himself haggling in the middle of the night with a manager who flatly refused to rent rooms to football players, on grounds they vandalized or stole property and scared other guests. One sight of the Weevils, small and nonthreatening, convinced another manager to make an exception. The boys, even those who grew up in homes where chickens roamed kitchens and living rooms, generally behaved in a civilized manner. In fact, the hotel knocked off a chunk of the overall bill and sent a letter to Coach Ferguson saying how nice the players were.

The game was a joke. North Texas—in the midst of three straight Lone Star Conference titles—won 79–0. But, the big crowd, about ten thousand, was greatly entertained. The Weevils pretended they were directing traffic, waving Texas backs toward their goal line. They blindfolded the head linesman at one point, to keep him from spotting players who were offside, and on one play substituted the football with a miniature that they tossed around in a game of keep-away that ended when a Texas player snatched it and ran across the A & M goal line. The referee ruled that it counted as a touchdown.

After the game, two North Texas teachers went to the Weevils' dressing room to congratulate them on their fine play. More surprising to Ferguson, two North Texas players went to the hotel and asked if they could play for A & M, starting right away. Ferguson politely turned them down, on grounds there was no room on the bus. The next morning, the boys awoke early, urging Ferguson to hurry. The next stop was Hollywood.

Over fourteen broiling hours later, the Green Dawg reached Tucumcari, New Mexico, which intrigued Ferguson. He decided to stop for the night. Luckily for him, he found cheap rooms at the Hotel Randle. In the morning, only one place called the Flag Ranch was open for breakfast. Ferguson felt quick compassion for the hungover owner, exasperated by her needy boyfriend. He asked for a menu. "Menu, hell!" she snorted. "It's cakes and coffee or get the hell out." Ferguson said cakes and coffee sounded about right.

All day the bus pushed westward, the boys and Ferguson gawking at the sights and scenes they identified with cowboy movies: Albuquerque, Gallup, adobe villages and cliff dwellers, the Continental Divide, and the Painted Desert ("disappointing," Ferguson said). Magically, recalled Ferguson, a fifty-cent apiece "banquet" served by some sort of "feminine Christ" just outside of Winslow, Arizona, was such a fine sight to see.

After staying overnight, the team made a brief stop in Flagstaff, Arizona, where Ferguson got permission for a practice session on the local college football field. Then, to the grumbles of his team, anxious to get to Hollywood, it was off to the Grand Canyon. Ferguson said that he always wanted to see it; enough said. The great canyon left the boys in awe.

It also provided an irresistible temptation. "Some of the boys stole some souvenirs," Verl Gill wrote in his diary. "We got arrested by park guards and had to give them back." In fact, police stopped the bus and searched it for an hour before they were satisfied all the missing items were recovered.

There was a thirty-minute detour, at midnight, to see the Boulder Dam (in 1947, Congress would change the name back to the Hoover Dam). A few weeks later—as part of a sprawling *Advance-Monticellonian* feature on the six local Wandering Weevils—Paul Stegall, Ralph's brother, nicely summed up both experiences: "I saw ... the Grand Canyon—truly nature's masterpiece" and "the Boulder Dam—a man's masterpiece . . . which gave us a good comparison between man and nature."

Ferguson hurried his boys back onto the bus. They were out instantly. After failing to find any bargain lodgings along the highway, Ferguson told Coker drive to Las Vegas to crash for the night. As soon as they were assigned rooms in the Overland Hotel, with its green and red welcome signs blinking, the team revived and hit the streets. In one casino, they gazed open-mouthed as film star—and native Arkansan—Slim Summerfield rolled the dice. Finally, Ferguson herded his fading team back to the hotel for a few hours' sleep before resuming the trip to Hollywood.

It was eight o'clock and the night was just beginning when the Weevils breezed into Los Angeles. They weren't even hungry—a few miles outside the city, Ferguson saw a roadside sign reading, "All you can drink orange juice, 10 cents." Perfect timing since the team had just snuck in a little practice session at Valley College in San Bernardino. He stopped the bus, distributed dimes, and watched his boys drain every drop in the owner's jugs. They found two more of these stands nearby and did the same thing.

Ferguson had budgeted two days in Los Angeles. That would take them to October 17, two days before the next game in Reno against the University of Nevada. The boys intended to make the most of the time, starting with a tour of the Warner Brothers motion picture lot. Ferguson wasn't sure if it was pity or pure goodness on the part of the studio heads, but the guide told the boys they were the only football team invited to see the stars and sets.

Next up was a date with the best-known hillbilly in Los Angeles—and nationally—Bob Burns, a radio star from Arkansas. Known fondly as "The Arkansas Traveler," he and his trusty bazooka (an instrument he invented and named years back, crafted from "spare gas fittings and a whiskey funnel" that sounded like a "wounded moose") entertained audiences on NBC's national *Kraft Music Hall* radio program. Ferguson had sent him a telegram before leaving Monticello asking for a visit to the Burns spread in the San Fernando Valley. An invitation was waiting for Ferguson at the team hotel.

The bus arrived at the high iron gates guarding the Burns estate, which Ferguson could see several hundred yards away. As he was looking for a latch to open the gate, a woman's voice boomed out asking for identification. Ferguson ignored it and asked Coker to toot the bus horn. Again, the disembodied voice asked what he wanted. Ferguson was wondering who was speaking when the voice said, "I guess you're from Arkansas." The gate swung open and the boys cracked up at their dumfounded leader.

A maid invited them into a reception room where Burns waited. He grinned, greeted the Weevils, and introduced his wife, who looked as if she had seen enough of Arkansas and its inhabitants to last a lifetime. Burns walked with them around his six-hundred-acre farm, posed for photos with a mule that had appeared in a film with him, and signed photos of himself playing a bazooka. Back on the bus, someone said, "He's just like us, he's even got dandruff."

One of Ferguson's colleagues at A & M, Marcel Durand, helped set up the next part of the LA swing. Durand suggested that Ferguson look up his brother-in-law, Sidney Johnson, the business manager for the *Los Angeles Times* and father of four daughters who had cameoed in several motion pictures. Johnson thought the Arkansas boys might like to meet some Hollywood girls. He called several UCLA coeds and asked them to serve as chaperones. After a tour of Sunset Boulevard, Johnson took the boys to their hotel and told them the girls, including two of his daughters, would show them the town. The boys were outnumbered, and some of the Weevils were so shy they refused to leave their rooms. Ferguson finally talked the stragglers down into the lobby and gave them the bus to use for the evening.

Late that night, they returned bursting with reports about their adventures. The boys went to Grauman's Chinese Theater and looked at the handprints and signatures of the stars preserved there in cement. They ended up at Hollywood's hip Hawaiian Hut. Knowing that some of the boys lacked money even for necessities, Ferguson wondered how they managed to pay for meals, drinks, and cover charges. The boys said the club was so honored by their presence they refused any payment. Ferguson never told them what he learned later—that the girls had paid for everything and told the cashiers to let the boys from Arkansas think it was on the house.

Ferguson had his own thrills. He was waiting for a table at the Bar of Music café when he noticed a blonde nearby. It was Betty Grable. Ferguson almost swooned. On their last night in Los Angeles, the boys were guests of Bob Burns's big radio show and took part in a cornball football skit. The special guest that night was actress Dorothy Lamour, known for her striking, long brown hair and trademark sarong; her informality impressed Ferguson and won over his team.

There was one thrill left. After the broadcast, Ferguson treated the team to dinner at Eaton's Rancho, a popular eatery on Ventura

Boulevard. Because of the cost of sitting down to eat, Ferguson told his boys to sit on the stools, where food was cheaper. A waitress heard him. Ferguson heard her tell another waitress, "Tell the chef to make the servings plenty big, and if the boss doesn't like it, tell him to take it out of my pay." It was an act of spontaneous generosity that moved Ferguson to tell his boys later that if they wanted to marry well, marry a waitress.

While they were eating, Roy Rogers arrived in a fancy cowboy suit. The boys, who had seen him dozens of times on Saturday afternoons at the Amuse-U movie house in Monticello, were ecstatic. A few minutes later, when Coach Ferguson heard Jeannette McDonald, the singing partner of Nelson Eddy, was in the main dining room, one of the waitresses said he and the boys could have a look. One by one, they quietly approached to stare wordlessly for a moment before returning to their stools.

"I was so dizzy with aesthetic ecstasy when I returned that I could hardly sit on my stool," Ferguson said later. "One of the waitresses said, 'What did I tell you? She's the swellest one in the whole bunch.'"

By the end of their unforgettable meal at the Rancho, it was after ten o'clock. Ferguson corralled his team and left for Reno, and a game that would still make Ferguson seethe years later. It also would pose a great dilemma for the team.

CHAPTER 20

"PAID IN FULL"

Stewart Ferguson and his Wandering Weevils left their Hollywood adventures behind and headed north toward Reno, where A & M was scheduled to play the University of Nevada on Saturday afternoon. After they slept for a few hours in Bakersfield, the bus wheezed on a mountainous climb, its radiator overheating, and the motor knocked with noises of distress. Ferguson had hoped to give the boys a full night's rest, but the Green Dawg didn't pull into Reno's Golden Hotel until after two in the morning, less than twelve hours before kickoff. The game was promoted not only as the Nevada homecoming game but also as a chance to see the increasingly renowned Wandering Weevils. The latest coverage was an AP feature currently running in many daily papers across the country, touting the "we-don't-care" boys from Monticello A & M as "giving high pressure football another kick in the pants this fall," along with a headshot of Coach Ferguson and a whimsical comic sketch including four players intently studying a coaching diagram on a chalkboard—of a map of the United States.

Ferguson and his boys did not have to wait long to get a look at their opponent. Upon entering the lobby the following morning, they saw the entire Nevada squad—the Wolf Pack—lounging on chairs and sofas. Ferguson figured the impromptu welcome committee, sculpted and "vicious" appearing, was likely a calculated scare tactic by their coach, Jim Atkins. Among the group was one surprise, Marion Motley, whose presence might have upset other hotel guests—he was Black.

Motley, a fullback who was born in Georgia and raised in Ohio, would become a star for the Cleveland Browns after World War II and pioneer the campaign to desegregate pro football. He was elected to the National Football League's Hall of Fame in 1968. In 1940, he was Nevada's greatest offensive threat. Although ineligible, for academic reasons, to play in conference games, he was the chief reason Nevada averaged more than forty points per game. He was a fearsome runner and blocker.

For A & M, Motley posed a serious problem. It had never played against a Black player. Rigid segregation laws made it impossible in the Deep South. Several Black collegians were playing at universities in other parts of the United States, and a few—notably Kenny Washington and Jackie Robinson of UCLA—were outstanding athletes. As talented as they were, however, they were unwelcome on Dixie campuses. Generally, southern teams playing colleges with integrated squads asked—sometimes diplomatically, sometimes not—that they bench Black players. In most cases, the opposing coach quietly agreed. Ferguson did not ask that Motley not play, but his players were upset about the likelihood that he would.

"Most of my players were real southerners of long heritage," Ferguson said later. "To them, the idea of playing against a Negro just wasn't cricket. Regardless of whether the boys were right or wrong in their attitude, it was not unusual collegiate courtesy to ask opposing teams their attitude in this regard."

Ferguson added that people who have never lived in the South might not understand the reluctance of his players—or any white athletes below the Mason-Dixon line—to face Black opponents. Further, he observed, the North was hardly innocent in its racial attitudes. In his own South Dakota, he had witnessed terrible discrimination against what he called the "quite noble" Sioux peoples.

In any case, Motley was allowed to play, no matter what the Weevils thought. His presence was promised in the advance stories of the game. In addition, Coach Atkins gave a stern warning to his team in the *Nevada State Journal's* final preview: "Anybody who lets down will be jerked from the game." As he boarded the bus for the ride to the stadium, Ferguson compared the Green Dawg with a cart carrying French aristocrats to the guillotine.

Motley ran wild, and the Wolf Pack won 79–0. While the first two Nevada home games had drawn only about three thousand fans each, this one packed the stadium with an estimated 4,500 spectators and they clearly did not appreciate the few antics the Weevils attempted. "The razzle-dazzle turned into a fizzle," the United Press reported. "The invaders found no opportunity to pull any of their screwball plays in the face of the massive, hard-charging Nevada forward wall which swept down the Arkansas linemen." A & M's longest gain was four yards. Nevada intercepted eight Arkansas passes and the Wolf Pack second and third strings played most of the game.

Motley was unstoppable. The first time he touched the ball, he faked a reverse and rumbled thirty-six yards for a touchdown. The second time, he sprinted forty-five yards for another score. The UP recap added, "Motley turned in a nice play when he faded back 20 yards to pass and was seized by four tacklers. The big halfback dodged and jumped around as their hands slipped off him, then plowed straight ahead for 22 yards before six men brought him down."

For Ferguson, worse was to come. He and his battered boys were changing into their street clothes when a messenger arrived in the dressing room with a $500 check. Ferguson usually put checks into his pocket without looking, but, this time, he said, something made him peek. Across the bottom, in tiny writing, were the words "Paid in full." Ferguson gave the check back to the messenger.

The Nevada agreement was a guarantee of $500 with an option to share gate receipts equally. With the paid attendance of about 4,500, however, Ferguson figured he was owed a sizable chunk more. He walked over to the office of the athletic manager, who assured Ferguson that the $500 was a partial payment. The college would pay the remainder, he said, when it had finished counting up the expenses to determine A & M's share.

Assured, Ferguson left. After several inquiries over the next several months, he finally received a financial statement that said when expenses were subtracted, A & M's share of the gate was less than

$500, but that Nevada would honor the contract and let him keep that amount. Ferguson exploded. He noted that expenses included rent for the A & M dressing room, fees for doctors on duty in case they were needed, team trainers that Ferguson never saw, the cost of the footballs used in the game, and, most outrageous, hotel expenses for the Nevada team. A & M had paid its own hotel bills.

"I will always wonder why it was necessary to pay a hotel bill for a team living only a few feet from the gridiron while refusing one for the team coming two thousand miles," he fumed. He wrote a letter to Nevada's president, who said that as far as he was concerned, A & M was paid the proper sum. For years after, whenever Ferguson talked about Nevada—and he did, often—he compared its administration with chiselers and con artists.

As much as he detested his treatment by the college, Ferguson loved Reno. Everyone was friendly, the atmosphere exotic, and meals and accommodations affordable even on a shoestring budget. "The biggest little city in the world," Reno called itself—proudly displayed in neon across its arch over Virginia Street—a declaration that Ferguson interpreted to mean most tolerant about gambling, prostitution, and divorce. He set about warning his boys to avoid temptation in all its seductive guises. "As for myself," he confessed later, "I've never been able to resist taking as many peeps as possible at all the sin I can find."

After dinner, Ferguson slipped out of the hotel. With hat pulled down over his eyes, he walked in a circuitous route to the notorious Stockade, then one of the country's most celebrated legal brothels. He did not go in but continued a slow perambulation taking him past several other bordellos. On a second passing, he heard a woman call, "Here comes that cheap guy again." Someone behind him snickered. Ferguson turned around and saw about half of his Weevil team.

His boys caught him gambling, too. In his sermon on the evils of gambling earlier that evening, Ferguson stressed the need to stay away from slot machines, 'one-armed bandits' certain to take all their money. "Of course, I mentally excepted myself and immediately began planning some way to beat them," he said later.

The way to do it, he determined, was to drop a dime into each machine that failed to pay off on its last play and then move onto the next machine and repeat. On this night, Ferguson's system hit. Lights flashed, bells rang, and a cascade of dimes poured out. As he fished the coins out, he heard a grunt of disapproval. It was J. P. Leveritt, who could now add coach watchdog to his regular role as Ferguson's loyal right-hand man. Ferguson smiled sheepishly. He had won twelve dollars and decided that more than offset Leveritt's silent rebuke. Shortly, he would need every dime of his winnings.

CHAPTER 21

HANDSPRINGS, BACKFLIPS, AND A "W"

When the Wandering Weevils weren't eating, they were thinking of their next meal. When Stewart Ferguson wasn't thinking about the amount of money already spent, he was counting and worrying: counting the money that they had left and worrying that it would not last until he and the boys were home again in Monticello.

All the talk about making $10,000 that he encouraged before the season started was now clearly out of the question. A & M was literally living from game to game, paying its way with the guarantees it received after each game—$500 was the usual amount. Some days, Ferguson and the boys ate high on the hog and slept beneath soft, clean sheets. Other days, they ate roadside snacks and napped in the Green Dawg. As they departed Reno and its expensive, dissipative charms and headed for their next game in Arcata, California, the boys left the feast behind and prepared for the famine. Ferguson ordered driver Joe Coker to slow down if he saw a sign along the highway that promised bargain meals and beds. Just before noon on October 21, outside Westwood, Ferguson spotted something even better—a sign pointing to a lumber camp. He told Coker to exit there.

Lumber camps provided their cutters, trimmers, and other workers generous fare at reasonable prices and for the boys from Arkansas A & M, offered another attraction. Having grown up in the timber country of southeast Arkansas, the boys were captivated by the miles of tall redwoods and the machinery that turned them into logs. They wandered around the sawmill while Ferguson negotiated for lunch. Back on the bus, sated but still recovering from their late nights in Reno, the boys dozed for most of the afternoon.

At the town of Weaverville during a snack stop, Ferguson announced that Arcata was only one hundred or so miles away. It took more than twelve harrowing hours to drive it, though, because Ferguson had not counted on a narrow and twisting road through the Sierra Nevada Mountains overlooking a deep chasm. After only a dozen miles, Ferguson wanted Coker to turn around, but there was no place to turn. On and off during the night, the Green Dawg was forced to pull into a niche to allow oncoming cars to pass. Everyone was too scared to sleep. The sun was rising when the bus rolled into Arcata, home of the Humboldt State College Lumberjacks, and by breakfast the boys were registering at the nearby Eureka Inn. Ferguson did not even ask about the room rates. He and the boys had earned a long, comfortable rest.

A drenching rain settled in for the next two days, so Ferguson cancelled workouts scheduled on the Arcata stadium field. The weather upset him for another, mercenary, reason—the rain might reduce the number of spectators and leave A & M with only its guarantee instead of the option of a split of the gate receipts. It didn't help that the game was scheduled for a Wednesday night.

But the boys loved Eureka, even the breakfast at the Greyhound bus station. They were given tickets to movies and a tour of a large factory that converted redwood logs into lumber. A drug store owner served huge, hot meals and charged a fraction of the prices listed on the menu. The only sour note was the relentless rain.

Ferguson "rewarded" the last eleven boys to suit up by announcing them as the starters. The group wisely opted to skip warmups, while Ferguson and the rest of the team headed to the stands under a makeshift tent made from parkas. On the field, the Weevils took their cue from the weather and found some fun. They played barefooted, splashed up and down in puddles, made steamboat whistle sounds for signals, and greeted opposing players by yelling, "Ship ahoy!" One A & M back stripped to his jockstrap and slid whenever he carried the ball. Officials didn't object, the few fans were entertained, Humboldt's coach went along with the gags, and there was a nice final ironic touch. Humboldt won 13–0 and both touchdowns were scored by a player with a perfectly picturesque name for the A & M boys—Forrest Waters.

The crowd was not large enough to cover the officials' fees, but Humboldt promptly paid the $500 guarantee and apologized that it was not more. The school's athletic department said that it would add a few dollars if Ferguson needed it. He did, but Ferguson refused the offer because, he said, he was dealing with honest men, not the type he found at the University of Nevada. "There," he wrote later, "we might have had to pay for the mud and water we collected on our uniforms."

A & M was on its way before six the next morning. The team had to cover 1,700 miles in four days, and Ferguson was anxious to get going. The reason? He was going home to South Dakota, which he left with such anger and disappointment six years earlier. He wanted redemption and revenge, and above all, respect. For this game, at Rapid City, he wasn't sure he wanted his boys to play the clowns.

An exhilarating drive down the coast left its mark on Pete Cheshier, Stanley's younger brother and a Weevil soon to take on more of a leading role. A few weeks later (in the same local Wandering Weevils feature with his fellow Monticello brethren), he noted that "the giant Redwoods of California [were] the most interesting living thing which we saw." After turning east and grabbing a quick bite at a café outside of Lake Tahoe, the Weevils returned to Reno, but this time, Ferguson and the boys did not check into the Golden Hotel and stayed clear of the casinos. They found a cheap boarding house that allowed the boys to sleep four and six to a room. Ferguson still had three long days of travel before the next game and finding enough money for food was the priority.

Most of the following day was spent slogging through Nevada. Just before sunset, the Green Dawg crossed into Utah, and for hours, the boys stared listlessly out the window at the state's celebrated but inhospitable salt flats. About ten o'clock, the Weevils pulled into Salt Lake City, which Ferguson later depicted as the "cold virgin among American cities" driven by his distaste for its wide streets and spread out buildings. The next morning, Ferguson counted and recounted his shrinking bankroll. He needed to spend less than fifty cents a head for breakfast and found a generous café owner ready to bargain. He loaded the boys up with scrambled eggs, toast, and coffee, and to Ferguson, it was just another example of the generosity and charity that he found so often, so unexpectedly, under the most unlikely circumstances.

A second straight day of extended travel, across Wyoming, landed the Weevils for a supper in Rawlins, which Ferguson later dubbed "the westest city in the West." The boys saw real cowboys and heard more cussing than back at the Monticello pool hall. Ferguson quickly got into the mood himself. As he paid for supper, he said to the woman cashier, "A hellish carload of damn thanks." She merely nodded. Ferguson said she probably thought he was one of the locals.

The team reached a bustling Casper at eleven o'clock. It was Saturday night and Ferguson and the boys walked from café to café on Center Street, gulping coffee and taking in the sights. Finally, Ferguson herded everybody into another cheap hotel for a few hours' sleep. He liked it when his team did not get much sleep. It made them more likely to doze on the bus the next day and less likely to think about food and the hard, narrow seats where they spent so many hours.

Still, there was a lot of griping on the Green Dawg as the Weevils and their coach pushed on toward South Dakota. "We had been eating lightly," Ferguson said later, "and empty bellies make sour minds." Maybe a bit of exercise would lighten the mood. The bus pulled off the highway just before entering South Dakota. Spotting a "deceptively smooth cow pasture," Ferguson let everyone out to toss the ball around. A few minutes later, several returned to the bus, their hands covered with cactus needles. "To hell with Wyoming," one said. Everybody climbed back onto the bus and Coker drove on to Hot Springs, South Dakota, for lunch at Edith's Home Café, which Ferguson noticed provided plentiful, inexpensive food.

Edith charged $15 and change to feed the team chicken and all the trimmings, and a grateful Ferguson gave her every cent he had left as a tip. Ferguson had stumbled upon a find; the owner was also a regular host of the town's monthly chamber of commerce luncheons.

Ferguson and his frazzled Weevils finally reached Rapid City and the Alex Johnson Hotel a few hours later. The Alex Johnson billed itself as the "Wonder Hotel of the World," guaranteed that it was fireproof, and offered exotic cocktails in its widely advertised Indian Room. The Dinosaur Park Pickup, at thirty-five cents, was a house specialty and honored the nearby tourist attraction of seven dinosaur sculptures (located along a ridge once home to dinosaurs of the Late Jurassic and Early Cretaceous eras) built in 1936 for tourists visiting the Black Hills to see the ongoing construction of Mount Rushmore National Monument. Most of the boys grew up in Baptist homes with stern edicts against drinking, dancing, and other transgressions, but they sometimes surrendered to temptation and sampled the Devil's brews. However, with no money, they couldn't even buy the Indian Room's twenty-cent beer. Nor could Ferguson, but he could charge meals pending payment of the money that his Weevils would receive for their game the next day against the South Dakota School of Mines.

Coming home left Ferguson terribly conflicted. He had not spent much time in Rapid City, which was best known for the great granite carvings a short drive south; Theodore Roosevelt's visage had debuted a year earlier and the awe-inspiring monument, designed and led by American sculptor Gutzon Borglum, was increasingly becoming known as "The Shrine of Democracy." (Although Mount Rushmore was still a year away from opening to the public, the Wandering Weevils did get to soak up its brilliance on their ride into town.)

Ferguson's clearest memories concerned football—he had coached Dakota Wesleyan when it played the Hard Rockers, as the School of Mines called its athletes, in the early 1930s. Dakota Wesleyan had won two of three games, but his endearment to Rapid City was inspired more by its hospitality than its athletic prowess. Everywhere they went, the Weevils heard applause and cheers and were given free tickets to movies. Waitresses served platefuls of extra helpings of food. At the end of the season, the Weevils voted Rapid City as the friendliest city they visited.

Monday was a busy day, starting with Ferguson's search for a laundry that would clean the uniforms his team wore in the monsoon weather in northern California. The Weevils had packed their uniforms sopping wet and they were still soaked. He took them to three laundries before one agreed to dry them.

While waiting for the uniforms, Ferguson took several players to the Cosmopolitan Club, one of the town's many civic service organizations, for radio and newspaper interviews. The *Rapid City Daily Journal* had already been hyping the game and "the Arkansas grid shenanigans" squad for nearly a week, while another paper published a story headlined: "Little Fergy (Remember Him?) Preaches Fun Football." Ferguson gave a short talk about the "eccentricities" of his team and said that he did not think his team could win, a prediction greeted with skepticism. A typical coach's reverse psychology. Besides, they already expected a bunch of clowns and the prediction sounded like part of his promotional routine.

In reality, Ferguson was worried that he would look like a fool no matter what happened. He wanted to look good before spectators who remembered him and in several cases played football for him. But he knew his players were not prepared, physically or emotionally. They had lost all six games, scoring just six points; opponents had scored an astonishing 263. The Weevils had practiced only once during the past five days, a workout in Wyoming abbreviated by cactus barbs. Wearied by the constant travel, they seemed dispirited and disinterested.

The boys dressed slowly. Ferguson turned off the lights and went outside. Fifteen minutes later, the team emerged from the dressing room, ran through a few exercises, then lined up for the kickoff. A & M received the ball and years later, a still amazed Ferguson vividly recalled what happened next:

Little Pete Cheshier received the ball from the center and J. P. Leveritt at right end sprinted away with an unusually fast start. Pete threw a high and looping pass down the sideline. It was obvious that the pass would fall short of the speeding Leveritt, and three Mines players came in for the interception. Suddenly in scarcely more than a stride, Leveritt stopped and started coming back for the ball. He came with a rush to leap high in the air and take the ball from the outstretched Miners' hands. They tried to tackle him but he twisted away from all of them but one whom he dragged several yards before shaking [him] off. Other Mines players tried to cut off the racing Leveritt but he quickly reversed the field, then sprinted for the goal line. Upon approaching it, he startled officials, players and fans by turning handsprings across the white stripes. It was the greatest play I've ever seen in football.

The crowd remained in stunned silence until Ferguson signaled Leveritt to come off the field. Then it erupted in a roaring salute that lasted until Leveritt, the expert gymnast, repeated his handsprings and backflips along the sidelines.

Cheshier, invoking his best Annie Robinson impression, continued to wow the crowd. He threw forty-one times—completing twenty—and spearheaded the team to a 26–0 halftime lead. Ferguson called off any more scoring; there was some clowning around, but the Wandering Weevils played it mostly straight, and won, 26–6, their first victory of the season. The day left a lasting imprint with Ferguson. The overall play, and the victory—led by a group that were anything but football 'tramps'—filled him with an enormous sense of pride and spiritual purity. Ferguson later reflected: "I would rather win a glorious game like that than buy a national championship."

With a fresh $500 check and his financial problems temporarily over, Ferguson loaded his boys onto the Green Dawg early the next morning and set off on the 1,200-mile trip back to Arkansas, and their first contest of the season before the home folks in Monticello. First, though, was a detour to Mitchell and the ghosts of Ferguson's past.

W. T. Ferguson

Stewart's father, Reverend William T. Ferguson, pictured here around 1910, was a strict patriarch who viewed football as a morally damaging, frivolous, and dangerous game. He hoped in vain that his son would follow him to the Methodist pulpit instead. *Gregory Methodist Church*

Partly because so many players had gone into the Armed Services, seventeen-year-old Ferguson made the 1917 Dakota Wesleyan University football team despite being physically small and still in high school. *Dakota Wesleyan University Archives*

Stewart Ferguson's playing days were defined by his tenacity and roughness. In this 1923 DWU team photo, he appears in the middle row, sixth from the left. *Dakota Wesleyan University Archives*

Dakota Wesleyan University president Earl A. Roadman, seen here in a 1929 yearbook photograph, ominously described Ferguson's new job as the school's athletic director and football coach as "a challenge." *Dakota Wesleyan University Archives*

The 1931 DWU football team poses on the White House lawn during a visit to Washington, D.C. Ferguson (front row, sixth from the left) stands on President Herbert Hoover's right. *Dakota Wesleyan University Archives*

The 1933 DWU yearbook, *The Tumbleweed*, described Ferguson as "one of the best qualified collegiate athletic directors in the North-west." *Dakota Wesleyan University Archives*

Arkansas A & M's founding father and first president, Frank Horsfall, was a stubborn disciplinarian who alienated students and Monticello citizens alike. Ferguson, however, admired him for standing up for what he believed in. *UAM Special Collections*

Arkansas A & M's business manager, C. C. Smith, photographed here in 1939, duped Ferguson into signing the strangest coaching contract in sports history—on an old napkin. He also wired money to Ferguson during the team's cross-country odysseys. *UAM Special Collections*

On the grid or in a hotel meeting, the Boll Weevils act plumb looney

For a 1941 photoshoot with *Newsweek*, Ferguson and a handful of Wandering Weevils obligingly acted "goofy." Team captain Paul Stegall (far right) played the straight man. *Newsweek*

From 1939 to 1941, Ferguson's Wandering Weevils traveled from coast to coast across 33 states, lost 30 games, and sang a smashing rendition of "You are My Sunshine" from the press box at Bradley Tech. *UAM Special Collections*

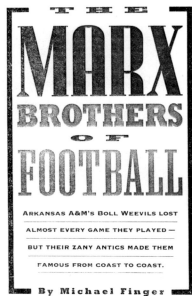

THE MARX BROTHERS OF FOOTBALL

ARKANSAS A&M'S BOLL WEEVILS LOST

ALMOST EVERY GAME THEY PLAYED —

BUT THEIR ZANY ANTICS MADE THEM

FAMOUS FROM COAST TO COAST.

By Michael Finger

"*Welcome, everyone, to the second quarter of today's great game between the Bradley Braves and the Boll Weevils from Arkansas A&M. It looks like we're ready to play now, and the Weevils have possession on their own 43-yard line. Uh oh . . . wait a minute, folks, wait a minute! All the Arkansas boys have suddenly turned around, and now they've got their backs to the other team. Why, our fellows don't know what to make of this . . . they're standing up and laughing and—there's the snap. Holy cow! The Weevil quarterback has taken the ball and now he's turned around! He's running the wrong way with it—he's racing back towards his own goal line! He's at the 30, the 20, the 10, and—Great Caesar's Ghost!—he's been tackled at the 5 by—can you believe it?—one of his own players!! Boy oh boy, what a crazy play! They don't call this nutty Arkansas team the Marx Brothers of Football for nothing, no sirree!*"

HALF A CENTURY AGO, ARKANSAS A&M COLLEGE IN Monticello put together a motley squad of football players who made headlines wherever they went—and they went just about everywhere. A Nevada newspaper called Arkansas A&M "the most unusual team playing football in the United States today," and a Georgia reporter said a match-up with them "was like lightning striking a rainbow." Fans jammed stadiums to see the Boll Weevils play—not in hopes of seeing a victory, because there were only three of those during the entire 1939, 1940, and 1941 seasons. No—what they came to see were the bizarre antics and crazy formations of a football team that played the game for the sheer fun of it, and to catch a glimpse of the quiet little coach from South Dakota who brought the Weevils to life.

Reprinted in a November 1999 edition of *Memphis Flyer*, this comic played on the Wandering Weevils' reputation as "the Marx Brothers of Football" by depicting the players as quacking caricatures of comedian Groucho Marx. *Memphis Magazine*

Stewart Ferguson wore many hats at Arkansas A&M College (now called the University of Arkansas at Monticello) during the late 1930s and early '40s. He was the school's dean of men, athletic director, and instructor in physical education, psychology, biology, and medieval history. Back home in South Dakota, he had played and later coached football for Dakota Wesleyan University, becoming the winningest coach in the history of that school. After earning a master's degree from Louisiana State University, he came to Arkansas A&M and was invited to coach the Boll Weevils.

His first season, in 1935, was a coach's nightmare; he lost every game. The school annual that year, ever cheerful, actually pointed to a *loss* as a highlight of the season: "The Boll Weevils played their best game in the annual Thanksgiving Day classic with Magnolia by holding the Muleriders to a 7-6 victory." At the end of the year, the school president held a public meeting and asked the good citizens of Monticello if they wanted to keep the present football coach. The resounding reply was NO, according to a manuscript written by Ferguson and filed in the college archives: "I was disgustingly through with the game of football," he wrote. "The game had given me . . . the most intense worry and discouragement of my life. Despite working harder, and I believe coaching better, I could not have had poorer success in any occupation." He continued, "Just thinking about football in the spring of 1935 bored me. That fall the sound of a kicked football gave me a headache, and the smell of pigskin was putrid."

Ferguson resumed his teaching and administrative jobs at the school, and a new coach was hired, who didn't fare much better. After heavy losses in the 1936, '37, and '38 seasons, A&M decided to abolish the football program rather than dump more funds into it. But Ferguson had a better idea. Hire me back as the football coach, he told the school president, and I'll get our program back on track. There are just three stipulations, he said: 1) I will get no pay for coaching, 2) I'm not required to win a single game, and 3) I can coach any way I wish. They gave him the job.

Ferguson wasn't as crazy as everyone thought; he just wanted to make football a game again, instead of a business. "I wanted no part of this new kind of football that was developing," he wrote. "Football was no longer a sport in most of our colleges; it was a racket that gambled with the bodies and spirit of our young men."

THAT AUTUMN, FERGUSON POSTED A TYPED NOTICE ON BULletin boards around the campus; it said simply that any boy who wanted to travel from New York to California should join the football team. As one might expect, the advertisement attracted a rather unusual group of athletes, including a 38-year-old Methodist preacher (who earned the nickname "El Preacho"), the town barber, and a former cheerleader who ultimately became one of the team's best passers. Gymnasts and acrobats also joined the team, but very few bona-fide football players from local high schools signed up.

While such a line-up—or lack of one—might dismay other coaches, it didn't faze Ferguson. A sportswriter for the *Arkansas Democrat* said that posting that notice pretty much ended Ferguson's duties anyway, since "this quiet little upsetter of pigskin traditions doesn't bother much with coaching." That's not quite true. He taught the team basic rules and fundamentals, and even offered some handy inside tips, like this one: "As for blocking, the best way in the world to block is to step on the other guy's toes." The rest of it was up to them; Ferguson admitted, "I have lost

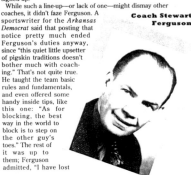

Coach Stewart Ferguson

With the United States' entry into World War II, Ferguson served his country as head instructor of a flight school for the Civilian Pilot Training Program (CPTP), despite having no aviation experience. In this 1941 photo by John Vachon, an instructor lectures CPTP students in Rockville, Maryland. *Library of Congress*

The enormously profitable Homestake Gold Mine, seen here in a 1910 photo by William Richard Cross, was the foundation of the town of Lead—and underpinned much of the town's rivalry with neighboring Deadwood. *South Dakota State Archives*

FOOTBALL
TONIGHT

FRIDAY, SEPT. 22—7:45 p. m.

DEADWOOD AMUSEMENT PARK

Deadwood High School

—VS.—

Custer High School

Don't miss this first game of the season, under lights!

—ADMISSION PRICES—
Season Tickets will be
available at the gate
Adults—60c
D.H.S. Students—25c
Grades—15c
Other HS Students—50c
Federal tax included

Ferguson's 1944 Deadwood Bears were crushed in their opening home game against Custer High School, an ad for which is seen here. It was an inauspicious start to what proved to be a winless season, but to Ferguson's surprise, in no way did this wear out his welcome in Deadwood. *Deadwood Pioneer-Times*

Ferguson's 1952 Bears qualified for the state championship basketball tournament hosted at "The World's Only Corn Palace" in Mitchell, South Dakota, seen here. Constructed in 1892 to showcase the state's agricultural potential, in 1946 the theme of its famous murals was "America the Beautiful." *South Dakota State Archives*

Stewart, Edna, and Freddie Ferguson pose for a family photo, circa 1953. *Courtesy of Jill Tiffany*

Ferguson, far left, was happy to be back on the field with the 1955 Deadwood Bears after spending much of the previous year recovering from a life-threatening surgery. *Courtesy of Jill Tiffany*

Edna Ferguson speaks at the dedication of Ferguson Field in Deadwood on September 21, 1956. *Courtesy of Jill Tiffany*

For his achievements as a coach, Ferguson was inducted into the South Dakota Sports Hall of Fame in 1994. *The South Dakota Sports Hall of Fame*

CHAPTER 22

DETOUR

Whatever he thought about the people he blamed for losing his coaching job six years earlier, Stewart Ferguson remembered his native South Dakota with great fondness and wanted to share its attractions with his Wandering Weevils football squad. He also was anxious to rediscover his past, mine his memories, resolve the conflicts that ate at him, and, just maybe, absolve himself of fault for things going so wrong before.

In three days, on November 1, Arkansas A & M was scheduled to play its first home game of the 1940 season against Hendrix College, which was becoming something of a rival. It was the only Arkansas college on the schedule, and Ferguson knew that defeating Hendrix would alleviate the disappointment and anger at him and his team for their miserable record so far.

But he also knew that he might not get a chance to return to South Dakota anytime soon. Nostalgia and absolution won out: at sunrise on October 29, Ferguson herded his boys aboard the team bus and began the 1,200-mile journey home with a detour to Mitchell, the scene of his earlier rise and fall.

As the bus left Rapid City, traveling along the flat, straight highway that would take the team all the way across South Dakota to Mitchell, Ferguson pointed out the obscure farm hamlets and railroad stops he recalled so clearly. Kadoka, a pioneer's misspelled anagram for Dakota. Belvidere. Murdo, where his father once preached to a tiny Methodist flock. Vivian. Presho. Kennebec. And across the

Missouri River to Chamberlain, where the Green Dawg's brakes suddenly locked up. Joe Coker managed to pull into a garage, and while mechanics installed new brake linings, Ferguson walked up and down Main Street, thinking—and hoping—somebody might recognize him as Preacher Ferguson's oldest son. Nobody did.

The repairs took so long that the team did not arrive in Mitchell until about two in the morning. Ferguson checked his boys into a hotel but was too agitated and excited to sleep. He walked around downtown. Mitchell seemed smaller, its buildings less impressive, and his memories of its citizens grew sharper. "Time improves wine, rots eggs and does both to people," he said later.

He passed a clothing store where the owner once defended him, and a few doors away, a café where his supporters had turned critics. Behind a door a few steps farther along was a woman he once dated, "a violet odored bit of heaven," and on a nearby street was the man who bought him a cup of coffee after he had resigned from Dakota Wesleyan, a "true friend" when he really needed one.

Ferguson glanced at his wristwatch and to his surprise, found that he had walked for most of the night. It was almost breakfast time. He roused his players and led them to a favorite restaurant, the Navin Café, before a bus tour that included the college campus and the more fabulous than ever Corn Palace (with the addition of Moorish-designed minarets, turrets, and domes to further resemble a true palace).

Still sorting out his time in Mitchell, Ferguson stopped for a quick chat with a sportswriter from the *Daily Argus Leader* in Sioux Falls. The reporter noted that "little Fergie wore the same grin with which he used to greet rivals" during his dominant early thirties Dakota Wesleyan basketball run. Little Fergie began by sizing up Monday's victory at Rapid City. "The boys can play quite a bit of football when they want to, but we're principally concerned in having fun and giving the spectators a good show."

The reporter also observed that Fergie "talked with the same apologetic whisper, while fidgeting with nicotine-stained fingers that hardly seem to fit with a football coach 'without a worry.'" Like many sportswriters around the country, he didn't understand that the coach with the crazy, doesn't have to win a game three-year contract worried constantly—more than anything, about the overall health of his boys.

Back on the bus, Ferguson and his Weevils crossed the James River and headed due south to Arkansas. A train engineer recognized the Green Dawg, covered with patches and slogans, and saluted it with a long blast on his whistle.

The team stopped for lunch in Sioux City, Iowa. Ferguson wanted to buy extra copies of the prior Sunday's *Sioux City Tribune*, which had given him prominent play in a story about his return home.

"Look out, South Dakota, Stewart A. Ferguson is coming back and what a comeback. The former coach of the Dakota Wesleyan Tigers now travels with the screwiest, most unorthodox football aggregation in the land, the Arkansas A & M Boll Weevils. And to top it off, Fergie is probably the most envied man in the grid coaching fraternity." Ferguson bought twenty copies and piled them under his seat on the bus.

The team traveled all day, with a few brief stops, before reaching Nevada, Missouri, where Ferguson woke up the proprietor of a roadside hotel and found rooms for everybody but himself. Early the next morning, they rode on through the fog for the last leg of the trip home.

Ferguson had often lamented that there was no radio on board the bus. It would have provided entertainment that undoubtedly would have kept the boys in a better mood. In the absence of a radio, they often broke out some harmonicas and sang popular hits of the day or old gospel favorites. "Three Little Fishies," a novelty song that dominated the airwaves for months, was a favorite. So were the current hillbilly hits by Gene Autry and others. As the bus traveled homeward, the team sang lustily with J. P. Leveritt acting as conductor, waving his arms and calling out lyrics.

And so it went, until drowsiness won out as the bus passed through Little Rock, Pine Bluff, and then Star City, where Coker deftly maneuvered around hogs sleeping on the highway. Less than an hour later, and after a month of roaming, the Wandering Weevils were home. At ten o'clock at night, the bus rolled to a stop outside the campus home of President Bankston, and the boys piled out.

The Weevils held a "bull" session on their recent escapades until one in the morning. About twelve hours later, they ran onto Aggie Field, as the college stadium was still called, where a crowd of two thousand or so waited to see the team they had followed through the newspapers and on the radio. Hendrix College was not an ideal opponent for a team hoping to win fans by clowning around. Because of its excellent reputation for clean, honest competition, and its dig-nified approach to athletics in general, opposing teams measured their own performances against the lofty ideals set by Hendrix. "A victory made any season a splendid success," Ferguson said. Besides, he added, victory gave Baptists, who dominated Monticello's civic and social life, "a nice chew of Methodist meat."

The teams battled to a scoreless draw, with the Weevils playing it straight, until just two minutes before the final whistle when A & M committed its only strategic blunder. Tunis Bishop, who had begun the season as a lineman but was now playing in the backfield, inter-cepted a Hendrix pass on his own five-yard line and was immediately tackled. For some reason, A & M punted on the next play, and Hen-drix ran the ball back to the Weevils' twenty. Two plays later, Hen-drix scored on a pass play, added the extra point on another pass, and ended with a 7–0 victory, only its second win of the season. For the Weevils, it was a seventh defeat in eight games.

"It was a rather nice kind of defeat for us, though," Ferguson said later. His "little, soft, green" Weevils played good, clean football despite continuous travel with little sleep, skimpy meals, and limited workouts along the way, and held their own in a game against a tough rival with plenty of rest, good food, and rigorous practice.

The 1940 season was far from over, though. Ferguson had booked three more games in New York, Missouri, and, wrapping up the schedule, in Monticello against Northwest Mississippi, an un-accredited junior college that Ferguson believed would serve quite nicely as a homecoming patsy.

The Weevils would not leave Monticello again for nine days, giving the players an opportunity in some cases to attend their first classes of the fall semester. Or, in other cases, to quit school altogether to join the military or go to work.

Ferguson called a team meeting the night before their scheduled departure for the East, and said he decided to take it easy, traveling leisurely to give everybody plenty of time to admire some of the country's great tourist attractions. Ferguson, as avid a tourist as any of his boys, studied the brochures and planned a schedule that included Civil War battle sites, historic monuments, famous universities, and other landmarks.

As it turned out, the plans covered everything but the emergencies that left Ferguson scrambling to save the season.

CHAPTER 23

DITCHING THE GREEN DAWG

The honor society made forty cheese and cold cut sandwiches for the Boll Weevils to eat on the first leg of their formidable trip to the East Coast. Lee Wallick and the A & M marching band blared out some military airs, the pep squad sent up a rousing cheer, and the bus pulled away from outside President Marvin Bankston's campus residence as Stewart Ferguson and his Weevils waved from their windows. The boys were off on the barnstorming adventure of a lifetime.

Over the next six days, the Green Dawg—now garishly decorated with the team's schedule for 1940, decals from tourist sites already visited, and signs declaring "THE WANDERING BOLL WEEVILS TRAVELING FROM COAST TO COAST" painted along each side—would cover a meandering 1,600 miles to New York via Mississippi, Alabama, Georgia, South Carolina, Delaware, North Carolina, Virginia, Washington, D.C., Maryland, and Pennsylvania. The final destination was Hempstead, Long Island, where the Weevils were scheduled to play Hofstra College on November 16.

Along the way, Ferguson would point out the sights he considered important, often based on his previous visits. By now, the boys greeted most of his opinions with some skepticism. Ferguson wasn't very good at hiding his prejudices, and nothing illustrated this more than Greenville, Mississippi, the first sizable town on the route.

Until six weeks earlier, the only way to cross the Mississippi River from Arkansas to Greenville was on a ferryboat. But now, motorists driving along U.S. Highway 82 could cross the new steel bridge. As the Weevils crossed over, admiring the engineering, they expected Ferguson to order a break in Greenville to answer nature's call and buy soft drinks, especially since Mississippi required all incoming motorists to declare plants, fruits and vegetables, an attempt, ironically, to prevent the spread of boll weevils and other crop destroying pests. Ferguson, however, ordered driver Joe Coker to keep moving. He did not like Greenville.

"Once upon a time," he wrote, "I applied there for a coaching position." He recalled how during his interview with the governing board of Greenville High School he noted that there were things he considered more important than winning. "That's all I mentioned before becoming a leper in the superintendent's office and being hurried toward an open door." Thereafter, Greenville joined his lengthy list of cities forever damned for one reason or another.

As Coker drove across mile after mile of rich black delta soil, the engine began coughing "like a consumptive rat terrier," Ferguson remembered. A bad spark plug, Coker said. He stopped in Greenwood for a replacement while Ferguson found a café advertising cheap lunches. An hour later, it was back on the bus and the road, passing clusters of shacks and woebegone farmers.

The first night's stop was Tuscaloosa, Alabama, home of one of the country's most successful college football teams—the Crimson Tide of the University of Alabama, which was especially well known to the Weevils because it celebrated two famous athletes from the same southeast Arkansas region as Monticello. One was Paul ("Bear") Bryant, who had grown up in neighboring Cleveland County and would become a coaching legend. The other was Don Hutson from Pine Bluff, about an hour's drive north of Monticello, an All-American end and later a star Green Bay Packers receiver. The Green Dawg circled the Alabama campus a few times to give the Boll Weevils a good look. During one loop, Ferguson spotted a café just off campus. He went inside to haggle with the proprietor for supper and, to his surprise, found several diners speaking in unmistakable northern accents. It was a hangout for students from the northeast—bargain hunting, "goddam Yankees" according to the ornery local student waiter. The Boll Weevils ate quickly and quietly.

Next, Ferguson began looking for a place to spend the night but found only "No Vacancy" signs across the state. Defense plant workers were apparently renting every available room. Coker drove all the way to Atlanta before Ferguson found an affordable hotel. Its owner used part of the upstairs to store onions, and the bedsheets in Ferguson's room were so dirty he spread newspapers on a chair and snoozed in it instead. He wondered how General Sherman overlooked the hotel when he burned Atlanta.

The next day, he was gung-ho to finally see the University of Georgia. Upon arriving in Athens, Georgia, he asked university officials for permission to use its athletic facilities for a team workout. The answer was a blunt, chilly no, a surprising response considering the hospitality Ferguson was used to receiving at large schools. Add another city to his bad list: "When I see Athens again," he wrote, "it will be in Greece, not Georgia."

In some ways, Ferguson was as innocent as any of his players, and he often chose to visit a city based on his own drummed up romantic notions. One of the cities that he was determined to explore on this trip was Charleston, South Carolina. He was almost always disappointed by the reality of a city his imagination made glamorous and exciting, however, and Charleston was no exception. For one thing, the whole city seemed to reek of fish, even the Charleston Hotel where the team stayed. More important, it wasn't at all glamorous or exciting. Not like, say, New Orleans, which he found naughty and highly entertaining. He could imagine New Orleans in French lace panties, he said, but not Charleston, "an old, limping, blue nosed woman."

On they went to Wilmington, North Carolina, where Ferguson found an eight-five-cent turkey dinner at a drug store and was tempted to stay because of the bargain prices. Finally, though, he decided to press on to Norfolk, Virginia, to spend the night. It was raining, with patches of fog cutting visibility to a few yards. Ferguson told Coker to slow down and play it safe, then stretched out on the front seat to sleep.

He was awakened by screeching brakes. A bump threw him from his seat. The bus almost turned over, then fell back on its four tires. The boys scrambled to push out the jammed door, and as they passed Ferguson, assuring him that they were okay, he felt a lump in his throat slowly dissolve. He exited last, stepping into a pool of water. One by one, he called out names. Everybody was accounted for. One of them said, "Poor bus," and players whooped with relieved laughter. Ferguson joined in and, on a whim, plunked down on his rump into a water-filled ditch.

A motorist took Ferguson and Coker to Plymouth, the nearest North Carolina town. Coker went to a doctor's office and received several stitches over one eye. Ferguson reported the accident to the police. A few minutes later, a state patrolman arrived, accompanied by a trembling, elderly Black man. The Green Dawg had collided with his stalled pick-up truck. Loaded with scrap lumber and missing lights, it was left in the highway while its owner went for gasoline.

One of the men at the police station identified himself as a judge and asked Ferguson how much he wanted in damages. "This n—r ain't got a dime," he told Ferguson, "but I'll give you a judgment against him, or lock him up, whichever you say."

Ferguson said forget it. The police shrugged. The old man walked away.

Plymouth didn't have any hotels large enough for his team, but several families volunteered to put up his players for the night, a helping hand that would greet Ferguson—with a different travelling team—down the road.

Ferguson assigned his players according to some wicked whim that sent the most profane Weevil to the home of a woman who radiated propriety, and J. P. Leveritt, the most religiously devout boy on the team, to the home of a family with two teenaged daughters who smoked and kept a clothesline of drying panties. Ferguson himself chose to stay with a widow whose reputation for morality, he said, was exceeded only by her reputation for good deeds. It was late, but the boys were hungry. Ferguson walked them to the only café in town, and the boys lucked into scrambled eggs, the one thing the owner said he could prepare that late at night.

As the boys ate, Ferguson telephoned C. C. Smith, who reported that the bus was not insured. This wasn't Ferguson's fault—while he wore a lot of hats, managing the college's insurance policies was not one of them. He and Smith agreed to leave Coker in Plymouth until the bus was repaired, while Ferguson and the team made other plans to get to New York. Ferguson figured he could just cover the costs of going by bus, but only the initial leg on a chartered outfit. He and the team, and all their equipment, would then go Greyhound.

The team chartered into Norfolk the next morning and squeezed onto a Greyhound bound for Washington, D.C. During a two-hour layover, Ferguson herded the Weevils into a café. The owner tried to shortchange him. Ferguson, his nerves already frayed, got into a noisy cussing match that amused the boys. In the middle of the heated exchange, the waitress chimed in, calling Ferguson a tightwad for leaving too small a tip. Ferguson signaled to the physically imposing Terry Field for some "toughie" support. Field left his seat and stalked toward the cash register. The owner said, "Okay, okay, here it is," and handed over the change. Ferguson's good mood returned, but only briefly.

Back at the Greyhound terminal, the bus driver to New York refused to allow the Weevils to get on board with all their gear. He said there wasn't enough room. Ferguson hustled back to the ticket office. "I've got tickets and I've got to get my boys to New York," Ferguson shouted. "We've got a game tomorrow." A definite fib—the game at Hofstra College was three days away—but the coach was desperate. The station manager joined in, agreeing with his driver. Ferguson and the team volunteered to stand all the way. The answer was still no. Enough with the little fibbing; Ferguson circled back from the station and said the manager had instructed for the driver to let them on, which sent the huffy driver looking for answers. Ferguson pushed his team on board. The driver returned and shouted to them to get off. The Weevils just grinned, while other passengers laughed and told the driver to give it up and get going.

It was a cold and rainy dawn as the Weevils stepped off the bus in New York City. Ferguson was too exhausted to resist when a tour guide suggested checking into the Hotel Times Square, which Ferguson liked for the location but not the price. He had barely stretched out on a bed when he heard heavy pounding on the door, and voices shouting, "Coach, coach, we're in *Collier's*."

Ferguson shot up, any thought of sleep gone, and realized that he and the Wandering Weevils were officially famous.

CHAPTER 24

COLLIER'S

The *Collier's* feature, written by Kyle Crichton, began: "At a time when the world is pretty strange at best, we get the Arkansas Aggies in addition. We have had football teams that did this and football teams that did that, but this is the first one that considers the season a wreck if it wins a game." The story described the Wandering Weevils as one of the best attractions in football, erroneously called them "fabulous gentlemen from the Ozarks"—the Ozark mountains are nowhere near Monticello—and made Ferguson sound like a revolutionary genius. Making it into *Collier's*—with its two million readers and rivalry with the *Saturday Evening Post* to be the day's most popular mass market weekly—marked a turning point for the Arkansas A & M Boll Weevils and Stewart Ferguson, who had worked so long and so energetically in promoting his hapless little football team. He could not have paid for better advertising or for a more sympathetic hearing.

Under the headline "Football is for Fun," the magazine introduced a band of innocent goofballs and their wily coach, and admiringly suggested that they just might restore some sanity to a sport increasingly corrupted by commercial pressures and influences. In Monticello, the article stirred mixed feelings of pride and embarrassment, but Ferguson knew he and his boys had achieved something extraordinary. In a realm ruled by Notre Dame, Michigan, Yale, and the other big schools, Arkansas A & M had squeezed into the sun for a rare moment's reflected glory.

Ferguson imagined that everybody in New York now knew about his team, and to a certain extent, he was right. Football fans whose interests went beyond the Ivy League, the Fighting Irish, Fordham, and other East Coast favorites would have seen or heard about the Wandering Weevils, whose crazy exploits were carried by the AP and UP wire services and mentioned on radio sports programs.

In addition, over the last few days, almost all of the local New York papers had run a Weevils story celebrating the team's arrival into the area and "play for fun" system. The *New York Post* said that each game finds the Weevils "surprising Stew Ferguson, their coach, with plays he's never seen before, even in nightmares." And the *Nassau Daily Review-Star* took things to an entirely different level, with Ferguson in the spotlight: "Our interest lies chiefly in Coach Ferguson, whose philosophy will probably go down in history as the most unique contribution, ever made to college football." (The *New York Times* had also given Ferguson and his travelling band of Weevils some play a few weeks earlier.)

"We were really something," Ferguson said later. If anyone disagreed, he took the copy of *Collier's* magazine he kept rolled up in one pocket, ready for display, to prove the Wandering Weevils really *were* something.

Before leaving Monticello, he promised the boys a couple of days in New York, experiencing and exploring a city portrayed in their hometown pulpits as a sinkhole of sin and vice and lauded in almost every other way as a smorgasbord of irresistible possibilities. Now, as they ate breakfast in the hotel's coffee shop, Ferguson told them they were free to go anywhere and do anything, as long as everybody was back by ten that night. He wanted the team to get a full night's sleep before leaving early the next morning for Hempstead, on Long Island, where they were scheduled to play Hofstra College on Saturday.

The Weevils scattered. A few went to see Broadway shows, with *Tobacco Road*, about a quaint Georgia backwoods community, and *Hellz-a-poppin*, a long-running slapstick romp, the favorites. Tickets cost only $1.10, making Broadway an affordable experience. Some roamed Chinatown or Central Park. A couple ventured up to Harlem, which the Arkansans knew only from the wildly popular *Amos 'n' Andy* radio show. The RKO Palace, near the hotel, provided free passes to visiting teams and some of the Weevils went to see *Down Argentine Way*, starring Don Ameche and Betty Grable, plus a Donald Duck cartoon and selected shorts. Halfback Teddy McKinney and two teammates went to the Lower East Side, where they found themselves in a delicatessen and saw their first rye bread. A lifetime later, McKinney recalled that it was "the best ham sandwich I ever ate."

Ferguson was running so low on money that he decided the team would travel to Hempstead by subway and the Long Island Railroad. After breakfast, the Weevils set off lugging suitcases, duffel bags with uniforms and other game gear, and various bags and sacks. In addition to his suitcase and a medicine kit, Ferguson draped a necklace of footballs around his neck. New Yorkers had seen many strange sights, and this ranked right up there. The team trudged to the Times Square station, became confused by the tangle of signs directing riders to various lines, and finally found the platform for the Jamaica Express, on the No. 7 subway line that would carry the Weevils—really wandering now—to the LIRR connecting train.

A No. 7 train roared into the station but stopped only long enough for about half the Weevils to make their way onboard, stranding the rest in a confused cluster. "The boys left behind had their first lesson," Ferguson wrote later. "Arkansas speed doesn't get things done in New York City."

Ferguson and the players who managed to board the subway got off at the next stop, took a returning No. 7 back to Times Square, rejoined everybody else and started over. This time, Ferguson ordered the boys to space themselves along the platform and jump aboard when the train stopped. They all got on board, but Ferguson, to his chagrin, got left behind. He took the next train and caught up with his waiting Weevils at the end of the line. The esteemed Groucho Marx would have been proud to call this travelling troupe family.

Eventually, the team found its way to the Hempstead station, and took a bus to the nearby Garden City Hotel, where Ferguson had made reservations. The hotel billed itself as one of the country's classiest. Famous aviator Charles Lindbergh stayed there the night before making his historic flight across the Atlantic. In fact, the desk clerk and one of the bellboys confided to Ferguson that he was occupying the very same room as Lindbergh, something Ferguson suspected they told some gullible sap every night.

Once registered, Ferguson called room service and ordered dinner for the team. His budget did not allow for anything fancy, so Ferguson ordered simple meals and then, casually, asked the price. The answer shocked him; the total was more than he usually spent for an entire day's meals. He quickly cancelled the dinner order, saying that the team would order separately. As soon as he hung up, he left the hotel and scouted out restaurants downtown. He settled on a café located in a refitted streetcar, so small the team ate in relays.

As Ferguson and the team returned to the hotel, they were met by a group of Hofstra students standing outside the entrance and serenading the visitors with peppy college songs. The hotel manager did not approve of Hofstra's impromptu concert and ordered Ferguson to end the noise. Ferguson said he couldn't do that, sending the manager into a shouting rant that subsided only as an elderly, fashionably gowned woman entered the hotel. The manager greeted her in an obsequious manner, which she ignored, and Ferguson guessed she was one of the hotel's classy customers. She asked Ferguson what was going on. He said he was sorry if the singing disturbed anyone, but that he wasn't going to stop it.

"Who wants it stopped?" she asked.

Ferguson nodded toward the manager.

"Are you actually the coach?"

Ferguson nodded again.

"Then, if you're the coach," she said, pointing to the manager, "why don't you tell this lousy bastard to go to hell?"

"She is what I like to call a woman," Ferguson wrote later.

The next afternoon the Weevils rode out to Hofstra Field. A cold, damp wind was blowing, and the weather was so cold Ferguson told his team to warm up in the dressing room. The boys trotted onto the field just a minute before kickoff. A & M jumped ahead early in the first quarter, after recovering a fumble on Hofstra's sixteen-yard line, on a run by little freshman Benny Gaston. But a few minutes later, Pete Cheshier, the Weevils' only effective passer, dislocated his shoulder. The game was effectively over for A & M; Hofstra, in its sixth year of existence and its fourth playing intercollegiate football, won 32–14, and impressed Ferguson with its crisp, advanced offensive arsenal.

"Hofstra was the show," Ferguson said. "We were just a bunch of frozen clowns."

Hofstra arranged for Cheshier to go to the nearest hospital. Ferguson asked J. P. Leveritt to help Cheshier check out and gave him fifty dollars, all he thought he could spare. That was only a token payment, said Ferguson, telling Leveritt to let the hospital and doctor know the college would pay the rest of the bill as soon as it received one. A few hours later, Leveritt returned with Cheshier and the fifty dollars. Hofstra had told the hospital to forward the bill. When Ferguson called Hofstra, he was told the college wanted to extend a courtesy to A & M by paying the bill. Once again, Ferguson was reminded of the opposite treatment he received from the University of Nevada, which, he griped, had charged him for doctors he never saw.

There was more hospitality as a sorority sponsored a postgame sock hop to honor the Weevils. The trip back to New York City after the dance was another tiring test on the LIRR, which carried the boys to Pennsylvania Station, a dozen blocks south of Times Square. Loaded down with equipment and baggage, the team plodded all the way to their hotel. Several people shouted out greetings, recognition that Ferguson attributed to *Collier's*.

Some of his players went to bed and others rallied for another look at the bright lights. Ferguson went to Harlem to see the celebrated chorus girls at the Paradise nightclub. (The Paradise, along with the Cotton Club and Connie's Inn, was considered one of the big nightclubs in Harlem in the late 1920s and early 1930s, and unlike the other two, had not since moved downtown or closed. The club was distinct for another reason: it was the only one of the three where Black patrons were welcome.)

On Sunday, the team attended a professional football game at the Polo Grounds and saw the New York Giants—who shared the venerable upper Manhattan ballpark with the baseball club of the same name—beat Arkansas's Don Hutson and his Green Bay Packers, 7–3. Ferguson went looking for a bus; the Green Dawg the Weevils had ridden for thousands of miles was still in North Carolina, where driver Joe Coker was waiting for a new motor and chassis. Ferguson found one he could afford, bought tickets for Springfield, Missouri, the site of the next A & M game, then divided all the remaining money among the boys for food along the way.

Checkout time at the Times Square Hotel was five o'clock, but when the manager learned the Weevils weren't going to leave the city until ten, he told Ferguson to relax and give the boys a little more rest time. Ferguson would cite this as another example of New York's generosity and hospitality.

There was a surprise when A & M left the hotel. Crowds clapped and shouted as the team walked several blocks to where the bus waited. "No city has such bold and open curiosity as New York," Ferguson noted. Spotting the stenciled Arkansas A & M College lettering on the team's duffle bags, people instantly identified them as the wacky team from *Collier's* and surged around the Boll Weevils. Ferguson beamed. He was brought back down to earth when he heard somebody call out, "They call this bunch of kids a college football team? Looks more like grade school stuff to me."

The team traveled all night and the next day before finally reaching St. Louis at eight o'clock on Tuesday morning, stiff, tired, and "hungry enough to beg." There was no money left for food, so Ferguson resorted to his emergency play. He telegrammed his A & M money man, C. C. Smith, and asked for an advance on expenses. A few hours later, the money arrived via Western Union. The team took a day to rest and resumed the trip to Springfield on Wednesday morning. As the bus rolled along, Ferguson began wondering what his Weevils could do to earn the $500 guarantee that he was promised. Pete Cheshier's injury deprived him of his only effective passer, and he sensed that the team did not feel up to any silly pranks.

During a stop at a roadside café, John ("Bud") Cubage—who had tossed a few balls after Cheshire left the Hofstra game—volunteered to take over the reins at quarterback. Why not? Cubage would start at quarterback in the Thanksgiving Day game against unbeaten Southwest Missouri State Teachers College.

For Ferguson, Springfield was clearly worthy of a second consecutive Thanksgiving visit. Beyond his calling the city the best place in America to eat a meal or spend the night, the fans were appreciative and Southwest Missouri played hard but fair. Although Cubage completed several passes, A & M did not offer its hosts much competition; Springfield won 34–0, its ninth victory and eighth shutout of the season.

A & M sent a replacement bus to Springfield to take the Boll Weevils home to Monticello and a season-ending game against Northwest Mississippi, a junior college that Ferguson scheduled for a second straight year and one with little chance of defeating even a team as feeble as his A & M crew.

It was also the homecoming game, held unusually late because the Weevils were on the road for most of October. Still, a sizable crowd turned out to see A & M win 28–0, its second win of the season. To the delight of the spectators, and Ferguson's pleased surprise, Cubage passed for two touchdowns.

Another treat greeted Ferguson in the mail that had piled up during his absence: offers from fifty-two colleges to play his Wandering Weevils in 1941. The only obstacle was the real, some said inevitable, likelihood of American involvement in the war raging across most of Europe and Asia. In that case, A & M, like so many other small, struggling colleges, would most likely drop football for the duration. Ferguson hated to think about it. He had even bigger plans in store.

CHAPTER 25

FORK IN THE ROAD

Bad news for Stewart Ferguson and whatever fantasies he entertained for the 1941 football season was announced January 6, when the Department of War called to active duty all 124 members of Battery B of the 206th Coast Artillery Anti-Aircraft Battalion, an Arkansas National Guard unit stationed at Arkansas A & M College. Among its members were twelve returning players, including the 1940 Wandering Weevils team scribe, Verl Gill. The unit was sent to Texas for a few weeks of training and then shipped to a remote temporary base in Alaska, where the greatest danger was bear attacks.

Their induction into the U.S. Army left Ferguson with only four lettermen, but that wasn't his only problem—with American entry into the war seeming increasingly imminent, there was talk of putting a pause on football. While publicly denigrating what he saw as the excesses of big-time college football and the overheated emphasis placed on it by fans, Ferguson quietly and intensely campaigned to block any action by A & M to abandon the sport. He liked the freedom it gave him to roam America with his screwball squad, and the publicity that turned him from a losing nobody into a crusading somebody with a suitcase full of clippings to prove it.

Besides, he had something left to prove—his cockeyed campaign to purge the college game of commercialism attracted national attention during the 1940 season, and now, he saw a splendid chance to persuade a multitude of holdout skeptics that he was serious. Sometimes it was difficult to believe he really meant all the bombast and bravado, and there were times when Ferguson spoke with his tongue firmly lodged in one cheek. Still, war clouds or not, he pressed on.

From the now fifty-six "bona fide" colleges that had contacted him seeking games with his Wandering Weevils, he selected twelve, located as far from little Monticello in distance and imagination as Newark, New Jersey, and Fort Worth, Texas. Ferguson laid out his plans in a January newspaper interview with the *Arkansas Gazette* and also proudly stated that his "arch-enemy" in logged mileage, St. Mary's, a small Catholic college in San Antonio, Texas, "didn't even come close" with their ten thousand miles the prior season. (He also would have likely brushed off the later reported twelve thousand miles figure.) "We traveled 14,000 and I'm taking miles out for our bus break down in Virginia." Ferguson, not surprisingly, did not comment on St. Mary's colorful coach, J. C. ("Mose") Simms.

Like Ferguson, Simms was a rabid promoter who, for instance, ignored St. Mary's official school colors of blue and gold and instead went with a flashy red, white, and blue uniform, sprinkled with stars. In just about every other way, however, the two men could not have been more different. Unlike Ferguson, Simms was big and loud and more importantly, ran his football program—which he had essentially bought from the school with his own oil money back in 1934—like a professional outfit. For starters, the team traveled in style in a huge double-decker Pullman bus stocked with electric razors, air conditioning, a bathroom, and sleeping quarters. As for the players, Simms explained on the road during the prior fall that "every one of the 33 boys . . . was recruited. . . . Every one of them is getting tuition, room, board, and books for nothing." By April, St. Mary's had had enough of Simms and his brazenly professional ways; the school president announced that they were cutting all ties with their coach in order to take "full control of the details of its athletic program."

Ferguson, meanwhile, pumped out a blizzard of promotional material to major U.S. newspapers and magazines. Only one appearance was scheduled in Monticello, a homecoming game on November 27 against traditional antagonist Magnolia A & M, which was returning to football for the first time in five years. Ferguson continued to prefer playing far from Monticello both for personal and financial reasons. His relationship with downtown businessmen who had insisted on helping run the football program still rankled him. Besides, A & M would earn more money playing on the road.

While prepping for his most wandering season yet, Ferguson was also adapting to a still new—and quite personal—situation on campus. For the second time, Stewart Ferguson was a married man. No, not to a waitress, but to a member of A & M's current student body, junior Edna McAdams.

A fellow South Dakotan, from the Hot Springs area in the southern Black Hills, Edna McAdams had chosen the remote Monticello school because it was inexpensive. In the summer of 1938, she received Coach Ferguson's contact information from a mutual connection and wrote him asking for a job upon her arrival on the A & M campus. Ferguson and junior James ("Doorknob") Clark, a short assistant football trainer and grader of student papers for Ferguson, who had earned his nickname after a freshman hair cutting initiation left him as bald as a doorknob, met McAdams at the bus station and helped get her settled.

Ferguson hired the freshman as a secretary to run his office while he was away with the Weevils. Soon "Yankee" McAdams, as the school paper's gossip column affectionately dubbed A & M's only South Dakota student, and "Doorknob" were an item. McAdams dated Doorknob into her sophomore year. As she recounted years later, she and Ferguson then "started a romance, which we kept very quiet." Edna, a carefully coiffed brunette, was an active member of the fine arts focused Bohemian Club and a top student; she would be selected the following year into the school's Lamda Sigma honor society for junior and senior women who were "outstanding in scholarship and leadership."

The couple exchanged vows on June 6, 1940, in the home of C. C. Smith, who also posted a one hundred dollar bond that was to be forfeited to the county if the marriage was not officially recorded within one week. Fewer than a dozen witnesses, including A & M president Marvin Bankston and his wife, were present. The most unusual touch was supplied by the Reverend James Sewell, the thirty-five-year-old Methodist minister and senior whose weekly inspirational sermons added to the education of his fellow Wandering Weevils "Roads Scholars." Sewell, who had just received the honor of delivering the commencement address to A & M's 1940 graduating class, performed Ferguson's nuptials. Thereafter, Ferguson claimed he was the only coach in the country who was married by one of his own players.

With the 1941 season quickly approaching, Ferguson once again refused to recruit players during the summer, preferring to wait until registration of classes began. During the first assembly of the new school year, he issued an invitation to boys to try out for the team and offered the same enticement as last season—a chance to see America and have fun.

At the first football practice—held twelve days before a second straight opening game at Louisiana College—he was greeted by the four remaining lettermen: Benny Gaston, Frank ("Buddy") Carson, John Scritchfield, and Paul Stegall, who was elected captain after the 1940 season. Ferguson's call to adventure and fun had attracted another ten boys, mostly freshmen with little if any athletic experience. For an additional boost, Ferguson popped into one of J. P. Leveritt's gym classes. Leveritt had graduated in the spring but stayed on as a physical education instructor (and assistant dean of men), and he had an intriguing prospect, freshman Homa ("Bix") Stillwell. Stillwell had never touched a football, but his acrobatic skills and clownish behavior would make him a Wandering Weevils star.

"Statistically," Ferguson wrote later, "my Boll Weevil team resembled high school cheerleaders more than football players." No problem there; after Annie Robinson's stunning Weevils stint, Coach Ferguson could certainly find room for former cheerleaders. Ferguson added that "the boys averaged 163 pounds in weight and were but a month over eighteen in age. The Monticello High School team in our hometown was heavier, more experienced and, I suspect, older."

He put his team through a few practices before loading them on the resuscitated Green Dawg for Alexandria, where he was to face a

Louisiana College team with a rookie coach and a young squad—several players had departed for the Army's National Guard—not predicted for much success.

No matter. Louisiana College won 60–0 and played second and third stringers for more than half the game. Ferguson, though, was pleased with his overmatched boys, especially Lawrence ("The Stork") Lavender, a skinny end whose nickname came from his awkward gait. Lavender had gotten so carried away he tackled everybody, including game officials and opposing linemen. He explained that tackling was so much fun he couldn't resist.

Ferguson returned to Monticello, cheerfully predicting that this team might well lose all twelve games, and, for good measure, might not score a single point all season. This was not happy news to people who disliked the idea of Arkansas A & M becoming a national joke, including team captain Paul Stegall, a highly skilled tackle who was all about football, not funny business. Over the next month, the argument over the direction the Boll Weevils should take—quit the clowning or double down on the laughs—would boil over and leave Ferguson questioning his insistence on playing for fun.

CHAPTER 26

HAMBURGER & BANANAS

The telephone rang in Stewart Ferguson's hotel room while he was still unpacking his suitcase. It was a sportswriter for Asheville, North Carolina's *Citizen-Times*, and he wanted to interview Ferguson. The Boll Weevils, who had just arrived after a meandering two-day trip from Monticello, were scheduled to play the local Mars Hill Junior College Lions the next day, and Ferguson was anxious to promote the game and his play-for-fun philosophy. He went down to the hotel lobby, shook hands with the reporter, and went into his spiel.

Ferguson spent an hour with the writer, telling him about his small, inexperienced, and short-on-talent team. He expounded on his notions about letting the boys do what they liked on the field as long as they played fairly and enjoyed the game for its own sake. He reviewed the past two days to demonstrate how the team traveled.

The team had left campus headed for Asheville after a Tuesday morning sendoff. The boys worked out on the high school football field in Forrest City, Arkansas, spent the night in Nashville, practiced again on Wednesday in Cookeville, Tennessee (the home of Tennessee Polytechnic Institute), and arrived in Asheville about half past ten that night.

It was almost midnight when Ferguson went back to his room, feeling that he had found an ally who understood and supported him, and would say so in his account of the game. A good bet, as earlier in the week the paper happily pushed the A & M buzz for Thursday night's game—"one of the best attractions in college football" and "a rollicking, fun-making, gridiron show"—and reached deep (seemingly without a map) to add that the Weevils sported "some of the outstanding small college players in the Midwest."

Ferguson's good mood lasted until breakfast Friday when he read the game recap in the *Citizen-Times* after Mars Hill won, 19–0. The story called the Boll Weevils "almost as funny as a rubber crutch," said they disappointed the one thousand spectators, failed to provide the entertainment that Ferguson promised, and added: "It was the consensus of opinion that the Aggies would do better if they would stick to real football and quit trying to please the fans with comedy."

Ferguson was livid. For one thing, the paper did not mention that the fans in fact laughed and applauded at his team's goofy antics, odd formations, and nutty business during timeouts and halftime. The reporter, he bristled, was one of those purists who obviously preferred football rough and cheerless. In addition, the writer probably did not know that the Mars Hill athletic director invited Ferguson to return the next year, "and for a higher guarantee."

"It was the most viciously mean criticism we ever received," Ferguson later groused. The thin-skinned Ferguson apparently tuned out the writer's later comments that the Aggies "displayed several fine players" with a defense that was "well staged."

The next game was scheduled only two days away, in Boone, North Carolina, with Appalachian State Teachers College, and Ferguson hurried to get there—out of Asheville, in any case. Little Benny Gaston, a fun-loving sophomore halfback, had taken on team scribe duties and marveled at the "beautiful Great Smokies" that followed them the whole way, reinforcing Ferguson's strong stance that his boys appreciated the natural and manmade wonders of the United States and learned more about American history by observation than most students did by reading books.

Ferguson had arranged for the team to sleep in a big Appalachian bunk room, but he had not realized the heat was turned off at the end of the day. The Weevils were shivering by the time they unpacked, but the reception they received more than made up for it. They were invited to a two-hour pep rally in their honor, with the Boll Weevils high kicking alongside the Appalachian cheerleaders and Bix

Stillwell, a gifted drummer, banging out a wild solo with the Appalachian marching band. Afterward, Ferguson and the boys were invited to join Appalachian coaches and players for dinner in the college's dining hall. All in all, Ferguson thought the reception might have made his boys forget the "stinking typewriter" back in Asheville.

What they would always remember was the bathroom. In the visitors' dressing room, the Weevils found a bit of doggerel scrawled over the only toilet. Buddy Carson recited it fifty years later: "Ain't no use to stand on the seat, mountain goats can jump forty feet." Nobody knew what it meant, but the Arkansans repeated it to each other all during the game.

"The game was a flop," a still sour Ferguson said afterward, with Appalachian State winning 67–0. "I was ashamed to take the $500 guarantee." A & M had halfheartedly clowned around, just enough to give the two thousand spectators a taste of the funny stuff that fans had heard about. Although Ferguson did not know it, it was the last time the Boll Weevils would play more or less orthodox football.

Ferguson was sitting in the dressing room, waiting for his boys to change back into street clothes and get on the bus for the next leg of their trip when a dignified, elderly man knocked on the door and asked to see the coach. Ferguson stepped outside.

"I wish I were president of a college that turned out football teams like yours," the visitor told Ferguson.

"But we played so rotten," Ferguson replied, "and did you read what they said about us in Asheville?"

"Of course," the old man said. "That's one of the reasons I came down here to see you. Your boys have taken two bad punches, but they are still the kind of boys I would like to see at our college."

The dignified gentleman was Dr. B. B. Dougherty, co-founder and cherished president of Appalachian. A local legend in college education, he served from 1899 until his retirement in 1955.

The Boll Weevils spent the night in Bristol, a town split down Main Street between Virginia and Tennessee. Ferguson was too tired to ask which state they were in. Besides, he was too busy medicating his boys, who were sneezing and coughing from colds they caught in their Appalachian bunk room. After doling out pills and syrups, he went to the lobby to think—three games coming up and a sick team. Collecting any additional guarantees felt like a Ferguson fraud.

He looked up. Two of his boys stood there. "We've been worrying about your cold, coach, so we bought something that we're sure will help you," one said. One boy pulled a brown pint bottle from his pocket. "Daddy says it always helps colds and makes you feel better. It may smell a little like liquor, but that's just the way it smells." In his room, a misty, appreciative Ferguson took a swig.

The next day, the Green Dawg and its sniffling passengers headed for Cincinnati, passing through Virginia, Tennessee, and Kentucky, with a rejuvenated Ferguson pointing out scenic sights, scouting for cheap eats, and encouraging his boys to think about the coming adventures. Up early the next morning, the team traveled to Dayton, Ohio, where Ferguson had arranged to practice at the University of Dayton and discovered to his joyous surprise that a group of newspapermen and photographers were waiting to see them work out and take pictures. On the spur of the moment, Ferguson decided to take the team to Detroit. It was far out of the way to their next destination, Peoria, Illinois, where they were going to play Bradley Technological Institute, but he wanted his boys, and himself, to step foot in Canada, just across the Detroit River separating the motor city from Windsor, Ontario. He thought the boys one day would like to say they had visited a foreign country.

"We spent quite a while writing postcards to friends back home and chatting with native Canadians," Benny Gaston wrote in his journal, which the campus newspaper later published. "We returned to the U.S.A. by going back through the Detroit tunnel. The customs officials there made sure that all of us were born in the United States."

The next day, Gaston said, was the one that the Weevils found most engaging. For football fans, it was a fantasy come true. The team left Detroit early in the morning for Chicago but stopped in Ann Arbor for a workout at the University of Michigan. Once again, the Weevils fooled around for photographers while Ferguson held court for reporters and chatted with curious bystanders. They stuck around to watch Coach Fritz Crisler, recently also appointed Michigan's director of athletics, drill his Wolverines before Ferguson eagerly led his latest batch of Weevils to South Bend and the hallowed grounds of Notre Dame.

Ferguson, an unabashed Fighting Irish fan, wanted his boys to share the deep emotional pull he felt whenever he visited Knute Rockne's grave and walked on the grass of its famous football stadium. He and his 1939 team had made the same pilgrimage, eating in the dining hall with Coach Layden, his staff, and all the players, and staying into the night to take in the Fighting Irish stars' entrancing practice. Since only captain Paul Stegall and J. P. Leveritt had made the earlier stop, this was an exciting new adventure for most of the Weevils. A visit with Frank Leahy, who had replaced Layden, a tour of the campus, and supper in the dining hall left the A & M squad in awe.

The Green Dawg, its engine wheezing, did not pull into Chicago until midnight. The bus traveled so slowly along the highway, holding up traffic, that motorists shouted out profanities and insults when they finally passed by, scanning the large "WANDERING WEEVILS" identification spelled out in bold, gold letters. Ferguson did not really care what angry, impatient drivers thought. As he wrote later, "We were becoming known to many thousands, so what the hell."

Ferguson's adventures in Chicago several years earlier, including his patronage of its racetracks, made the Windy City one of his favorite destinations, and this time he decided to stay for a couple of days before continuing on to Peoria. He told the team to forget practice and see the sights. The baseball fans lucked into a treat, a game at Wrigley Field between the Cubs and White Sox as part of Chicago's long-standing and fiercely contested City Series, while others went to the movies. There were rides on the El around the Loop and walks along the shores of Lake Michigan. As usual, Ferguson's only instructions were to return to their hotel in time for dinner.

The following day, Thursday, Ferguson accompanied his team to the University of Chicago for a tour, and although he deplored the fact the university—a onetime national football power—had dropped the sport, he ran his team through a leisurely workout on a field now used only for intramural games.

On the ride down to Peoria, which Ferguson admired for its bargains and a citizenry devoted to the good life, the Green Dawg ran into rain. It was still raining when the team arrived about noon. Ferguson called off a planned workout, to the disappointment of a photographer who wanted pictures for the local paper. He came up with another solution, encouraging the Weevils to clown around with a football in the hotel lobby as the photographer snapped away. In a radio interview that afternoon, part of his campaign to boost the gate, Ferguson cheerily guaranteed Bradley fans that his pitiful and puny boys posed no threat to any team anywhere anytime.

The team woke up Saturday to find it pouring. The rain fell all day, and just an hour before the scheduled kickoff the Bradley coach, A. J. Robertson, called to ask Ferguson to agree to a cancellation. He explained the new grass surface in the Bradley stadium made it dangerous to play. To make up for Ferguson's disappointment, Robertson handed over a check for $500, the full amount the two men negotiated months before. Ferguson refused it, saying that he would return later in the season and earn the money fair and square. They settled on Monday, October 27.

The skies started to clear the following morning when A & M left for Mobile, Alabama, and a game against Spring Hill College. It was a long, boring ride, and when some of his boys began squabbling, Ferguson quieted them by promising a movie after they checked into a hotel in Memphis, where they planned to stay overnight. The movie, to the team's delight, was *Sergeant York*, with Gary Cooper in the title role. Cooper was one of the most popular film stars in the South, and Alvin York, the modest backwoods Tennessee war hero Cooper portrayed, was a revered figure in the old Confederacy.

The Boll Weevils boarded the bus early the next morning, ready to roll, when Eldon Roark, who wrote an extremely popular daily column for the *Memphis Press-Scimitar*, "STROLLING with ELDON ROARK," stopped Ferguson and asked for an interview. Roark's page one feature the next day thrilled Ferguson:

The country's most traveled and in many respects its most famous football team passed through Memphis yesterday—the Wandering Boll Weevils of Arkansas A & M College of Monticello, Arkansas.

The Boll Weevils are a new idea in football. They play the game just for the fun of it, and it makes little difference to them whether they win or lose.

They travel so much they have but little time to practice. They have no training rules. They never use a standard formation. Most plays are made on the spur of the moment as they go into their huddle.

Coach Stewart A. Ferguson's one rule—and the only one he will get tough over—is that a player must leave the field the moment he ceases to enjoy it. His philosophy is that the team that has the most fun wins.

Today, they are one of the most drawing teams in America because they are unique. People go to see the amazing spectacle of boys playing the game, not for glory and dear old A & M, but for fun.

Ferguson couldn't have said it better. "That's the kind of reporter I like," he wrote later. Being tracked down by Eldon Roark was not the only unexpected delight of the day. Sharing space on the funny pages across the country with the likes of Popeye and Mickey Mouse were the "Screw-Boll-Weevils" (a new moniker and one that would stick) as depicted in John Hix's daily syndicated cartoon, *Strange as It Seems*.

The team spent most of the day sweeping through Mississippi. Around two o'clock, A & M arrived in Mobile, a city that Ferguson fancifully associated with a long-ago pop song. "Because I grew up under the influence of a song about Mobile Bay," he wrote later, "I was curious to the point of quivering to see that piece of water. I asked the [Green Dawg] driver to take us there as quickly as possible.

But the bay was just greasy, dirty water." Another romantic Ferguson illusion exposed by reality.

It was the only thing about Mobile that disappointed him. The game was scheduled for Wednesday night, giving the Weevils two days to relax and sightsee. "A county fair," Ferguson called the city. His players were strolling near the Spring Hill campus when they saw a small lake. Several stripped to their underwear and leaped in. They spent a couple of hours the next day counting ships in the Mobile docks.

The *Mobile Register* had been pumping the game for two days and said that "regardless of the outcome, the Arkansans and their screwball attack should provide thrills throughout." The visitors did not disappoint, as the Wandering Weevils circus did indeed come to town.

Spring Hill's victory, 37–0, was an incidental note in the hometown newspaper account, which focused on the wild, wild Weevils. Lester ("Yank") Corwin—a mysterious character who grew up on New York's Long Island and spent just enough time in Monticello to appear in two Weevils games—and halfback Floyd Reid entered and left the game doing handsprings and back flips. Other Boll Weevils rushed on and off riding a borrowed bicycle. On one play, the entire A & M line, except the center, faced its own backfield, showing its rumps to the Spring Hill players, and on the snap, rushed into its own backfield to grab the ball; the first player to touch the ball ran with it. Spectators laughed and cheered, while the Spring Hill coach, Earle Smith, dismissed the silly antics.

Ferguson couldn't dawdle after the game. He had scheduled the Weevils to play in Denton, Texas, about seven hundred miles away, in just under forty-eight hours. Tight schedule or not, Ferguson insisted on stopping for a leisurely lunch in New Orleans, a favorite haunt, before pushing on to Baton Rouge to tour and show off LSU, his long-cherished summer escape. Back on the road, Ferguson and his team managed to remain awake until they reached Shreveport, Louisiana, where they fell into hotel beds for a few hours' sleep.

Shortly after an early departure, the bus ran out of gas. A passing motorist was flagged down and talked into taking one of the boys to the nearest gas station and bringing him back. The delay caused

A & M to arrive in Denton only four hours before its game against North Texas State Teachers College, which precisely one year earlier thumped the Monticello boys 79–0; this time, Jack Cisco, the North Texas coach, announced he did not intend to run up the score.

The *Fort Worth Star-Telegram* began its review of the game:

> Old Arkansas A & M took it on the chin again. The 23 zanies who form A & M's football team gleefully absorbed a 60–0 whipping at the hands of the North Texas State Eagles.

Following the game, Arkansas A & M's coach, Stewart (Fergie) Ferguson made the following statement:

> "I have been coaching the Boll Weevils for four seasons, and I can safely say this is my worst team."

It was perhaps the craziest exhibition the Wandering Weevils ever gave. The lead North Texas cheerleader's boyfriend was seized before the kickoff by the Weevils, who put an A & M jersey on him and made him their kickoff man. Other cheerleaders sat on the Monticello bench. On one play, the entire A & M team took off its helmets and stood respectfully at attention as a North Texas player raced by for a score. It got worse. The entire A & M team tackled its own quarterback, Benny Gaston, on the Weevils' own goal line. Players sat on the bench eating bananas.

In later years, sportswriters recalled the game for another reason. At halftime, Ferguson left the game and disappeared. He returned late in the third quarter and explained that he had gone into town for a hamburger and coffee. For the rest of the game, he sat on the A & M bench, shelling and eating peanuts. Coach Sisco expressed his disgust and sent his entire team, except for the practice squad, to the dressing room in the third quarter. But spectators spent most of the game doubled up with laughter.

After the game, a man identifying himself as a North Texas professor burst into the Weevil dressing room, shouting that Ferguson was the greatest coach in the country and suggested that someone build a monument to him. Later, when Ferguson told this story to C.

C. Smith, the business manager wryly replied, "Coach, there already are appropriate monuments to you in every cow and horse pasture in the country."

The Boll Weevils had been gone for seventeen days. Homesick and sore, players took turns driving and the team was back in Monticello in time for supper. They would not stay long. "We stopped to pick up a couple clean shirts and headed east," Ferguson wrote. Usually, the team's comings and goings rated a lot of attention, but this time, the bemused Boll Weevils found themselves playing second fiddle to a blue-ribbon bull named Oscar.

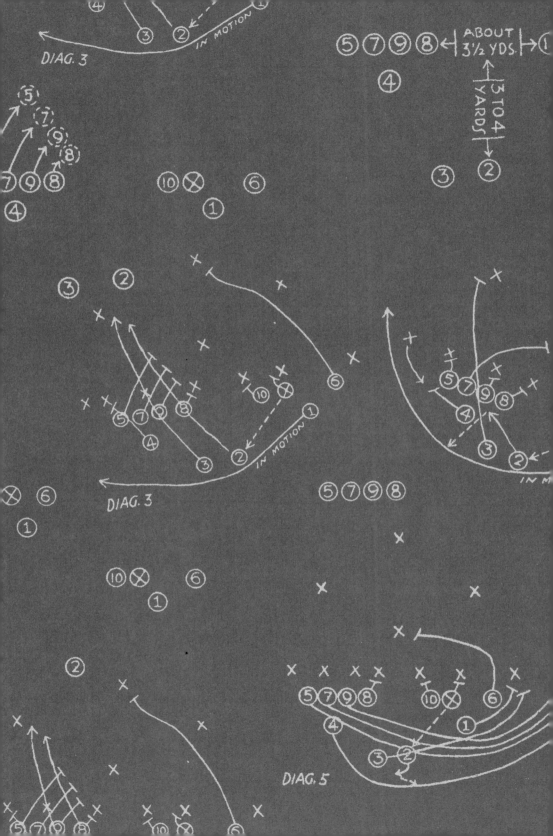

DIAG. 3

IN MOTION

ABOUT 3½ YDS.

3 TO 4 YARDS

DIAG. 3

IN M

IN MOTION

DIAG. 5

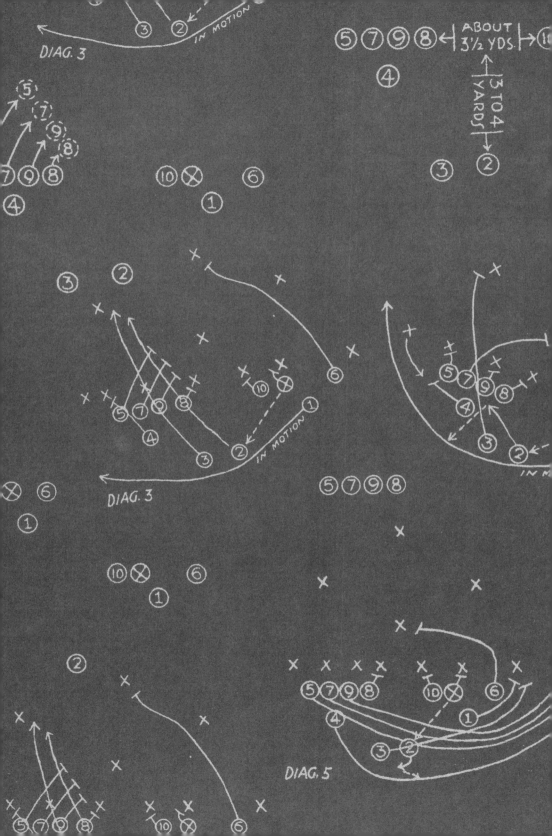

DIAG. 3

IN MOTION

⑤ ⑦ ⑨ ⑧ ← ABOUT 3½ YDS. → ⑪

④

3 TO 4 YARDS

③ ②

⑩ ⊗   ⑥
      ①

⑤
⑦
⑨
⑧
⑦ ⑨ ⑧
④

③   ②

⑩ ⊗
    ①
IN MOTION

⑤ ⑦ ⑨ ⑧
④
   ③
⑥ ②

⑤ ⑦ ⑨ ⑧
④
③ ②
IN M

⊗ ⑥
①

⑩ ⊗   ⑥
    ①

⑤ ⑦ ⑨ ⑧

②

DIAG. 3

⑤ ⑦ ⑨ ⑧
④
⑩ ⊗   ⑥
③ ②   ①

DIAG. 5

⑤ ⑦ ⑨ ⑧   ⑩ ⊗   ⑥

CHAPTER 27

DRUNKEN RAINBOWS

Just before six o'clock on the chilly Monday evening of October 27, 1941, Stewart Ferguson unfastened the strap around a large suitcase in the visitor's dressing room at Bradley Tech's football stadium, threw the case open, and invited his players to select any jersey they wanted. His players laughed and then began grabbing. One donned a bright pink jersey because it reminded him of a girlfriend back in Arkansas. Oscar Dove, a baby-faced seventeen-year-old, chose a black one because it made him look more sinister. Most players picked their old high school colors, and Lawrence ("The Stork") Lavender found a purple number that came closest to his last name. Ferguson sat on a chair in a corner, stubbed out a cigarette and clapped his hands in approval.

The jerseys were salesmen's samples that he had accumulated over the past couple years, "mostly silk or rayon, in black, purple, blue, red, white, green, orange, yellow, gold, or brown, as flashy as a drunken rainbow," he said later. Thus arrayed, the Wandering Weevils of Arkansas A & M College raced into the stadium for the sixth game of their nutty season against unbeaten Bradley Polytechnic Institute in Peoria, Illinois. It was the makeup game that Ferguson had promised after torrential rain washed out their originally scheduled exhibition, and a crowd of three thousand waited to see if the Arkansans were as crazy as the newspapers and radio said.

Ferguson had promised plenty of fun in interviews and A. J. Robertson, the Bradley coach, told his team to go along with whatever gags were coming. Officials agreed to ignore most infractions of the rules. It was a sensible decision, given the horseplay that began even before the kickoff.

The next morning's edition of the *Peoria Journal-Transcript* summed it up: "For the sake of the record, the score was 67–0. For the sake of the readers, we will just skip the touchdown details." Instead, sportswriter Russell Perry ran down a list of the goofier stuff, starting with the pregame warm-up when the Weevils used a baseball bat to drive footballs into the stands, played leapfrog, and marched onto the field chanting military commands to turn left, right, and present arms. There were some proven crowd pleasers: on the opening kickoff, Bill Bowers, the A & M left guard and designated kicker, raced from his own end zone to the thirty-yard line and deliberately flopped face down, as teammate Buddy Carson squibbed the ball a dozen yards or so up field. Weevil substitutes rode on and off the field on bicycles. Every time Bradley scored, the Arkansans tied a balloon to the crossbars over their goalposts. On extra point attempts by Bradley, the entire Weevil team cued up their London Bridge maneuver and fell to the ground. Benny Gaston, at quarterback, tooted on a trumpet instead of calling signals. But there were a few new wrinkles, too. Lavender entered the game wearing a top hat, tails, and monocle, and was spattered by mud balls thrown by his teammates. As Bradley players ran with the ball, they were waltzed by Boll Weevils. When Ferguson vanished from the A & M bench, his players went into the stands, searching and calling for him. And as the delighted spectators exited, several Boll Weevils stormed the press box, seized the microphone, and serenaded them with "You are My Sunshine."

After the game, the Boll Weevils were invited to a dance, and the party lasted until five in the morning. Ferguson told his boys they could sleep on the bus and decided to head out after breakfast.

The team was used to long days in padded seats on the road. By now, on this trip, the team had already spent four days traveling, highlighted by a visit to Abraham Lincoln's historic home in Springfield, Illinois. Ferguson had taken the team back on the road the previous Thursday after a stay on campus that gave his boys a chance to visit their classrooms, catch up on their romances, see their families, and even spend a day at the annual Drew County Fair, the town's biggest event of the year. A & M, with its exhibits of livestock and vegetables, always played a prominent role at the fair, but this year an uncharacteristic dispute had disrupted the schedule.

The problem revolved around Oscar, the college's prize blue-ribbon Holstein bull. A & M sent Oscar to county fairs all over southeast Arkansas with one proviso: he could go nowhere unless accompanied by the A & M marching band. The band, horns blaring, drums banging, escorted the decorated truck that carried Oscar to personal appearances. This year, however, there was a conflict. The band was scheduled to perform in nearby Hamburg at the same hour advertised for Oscar's arrival at the Drew County Fair. C. C. Smith, who embraced his bull responsibilities within his overall job of business manager, and Lee Wallick, the band director, spent hours negotiating with fair officials and finally settled on a compromise. The band would keep its concert date in Hamburg in the afternoon but would take Oscar to the fairgrounds an hour or so before it opened and then, after Hamburg, would return to Monticello to play fanfares and tributes to Oscar.

Oscar was important, but Wallick arguably was the most important figure at A & M. He was a creative treasure, with a reputation that had spread to neighboring Mississippi and Louisiana, where he was known as *The Music Man* for the same reason as Harold Hill, the fictional larger-than-life protagonist of Meredith Willson's hit musical.

While C. C. Smith had deftly resolved the Oscar matter, Stewart Ferguson was finalizing plans for the Boll Weevils' final trip of the season, promising his boys the usual mixture of sightseeing and adventure. The trip to Peoria included stops in St. Louis, a Ferguson favorite, and Springfield, Missouri, which he liked almost as much as New Orleans. Along the way, the Green Dawg slipped into a ditch during a driving rain. Instead of waiting for help, Ferguson and his boys easily lifted the bus back on the highway.

Now, A & M had to hustle to make their scheduled Thursday night game against Moravian College in Bethlehem, Pennsylvania, and for one of the few times in the Wandering Weevil era, Ferguson did not stop to admire any of the sights. The bus pushed through

Illinois, Indiana, and most of Ohio before stopping for the night in Canton, the future home of the professional football Hall of Fame. Another six hundred miles or so followed on Wednesday before the Weevils finally arrived in Bethlehem about midnight.

More than four thousand spectators turned out to see the game, which, to nobody's surprise, the Moravian Greyhounds won, 33–0. Ferguson figured the fifty-five-cents general admission and one-dollar reserved seats was money well spent for fans who wanted their football funny.

Before the game, Moravian officials told Ferguson not to worry if spectators left before the finish. "Everybody works for Bethlehem Steel," they explained, "and the next shift starts at 9:45." To speed things up, the teams did not huddle, the game did not stop on incomplete passes, and timeouts were abbreviated. As predicted, fans began leaving in the middle of the fourth quarter. Still, there were enough overly excited fans left at the end and several cut pieces off the Boll Weevil jerseys as keepsakes. "I stood around for some time, waiting for someone to cut my shirttail off, but no one seemed interested," Ferguson lamented later.

Seated in the stands, watching the circus on the field, was Bob Meyer, the coach of Upsala College in East Orange, New Jersey. A & M was scheduled to play his team in two days in Montclair, and Meyer had driven to Bethlehem to scout the Weevils and to appeal to Ferguson. According to a widely circulated AP item, the first-year college coach "invaded" the Weevils locker room after the game for a pep talk. He mentioned his team had not won a game and wanted to win his first one legitimately. Reportedly, Meyer pleaded for the Weevils "to get in there and fight against us. Play to win as you've never played before." Ferguson got rid of him only by promising to play seriously.

It was raining so hard in East Orange when the Green Dawg arrived that Ferguson offered Upsala the same deal he had offered Bradley: to return later when the weather was better, along with the prospects of a larger crowd. Upsala insisted on playing, and Ferguson wondered if Upsala would dare pull a Nevada and shortchange him.

The game, braved by a few hundred soaked fans, was played in torrents of rain with thick fog cutting visibility to a few yards and ankle-deep mud on the field. Upsala won 19–6, its first victory of the season, but the big news was that after giving up 343 points in seven games, the Wandering Weevils at long last scored their first points of the season on a thirty-four-yard pass from Benny Gaston to Bix Stillwell, an achievement that the *Newark Star-Ledger* bungled by noting that it was A & M's "daffiness boys" first score in three years.

As soon as he could get his boys back in street clothes, Ferguson took them out for dinner and promised them a full night's sleep. After all, the Weevils had played three times in five days and between games had traveled 1,300 miles in an uncomfortable bus. But the players told Ferguson no; they were invited to an Upsala dance party given for the football players and wanted to go. He shrugged but consented.

Ferguson was still sound asleep the next morning when the boys banged on his door and reminded him that he had promised they would start a three-day visit to New York by noon. The boys were cheering when the bus passed through the Lincoln Tunnel and revealed the skyscrapers of Manhattan. Ferguson was elated, too. New York was, just as Gershwin and Porter and Berlin and all the other tunesmiths put it, the greatest.

"I obtained rooms for the boys, gave each enough food money to last for three days, and said goodbye," Ferguson wrote later. "This was the last time I saw them together before collecting them three days later."

The adventures would stay with the boys forever.

CHAPTER 28

(ALMOST) CALLING IT QUITS

Hitting the Big Apple for the second consecutive year, Ferguson's loyal sidekick J. P. Leveritt was a young man on a mission. Devoted to bodybuilding for as long as he could remember, Leveritt, at twenty-two, was the closest thing in Monticello, Arkansas, to the sculpted musclemen he so admired and tried to emulate with homemade barbells and weights fashioned from cement blocks. He avidly read and collected bodybuilding magazines, followed their advice, and set a goal that one day he would meet some of his idols. That day had finally arrived.

A gymnasium located just off Times Square and operated by Sigmund Klein, an influential promoter of what he called a sport and others called an exhibition, was a popular hangout for bodybuilders. Shortly after Leveritt and his teammates checked into the Hotel Langwell, located almost in the heart of Times Square, he walked over to Klein's gym. With him was Bix Stillwell, whose curiosity was piqued more by Leveritt's enthusiasm than any interest in bare-chested men with bulging muscles and a talent for lifting hundreds of pounds of iron equipment.

Like their Weevil teammates, Leveritt and Stillwell had been each given thirty dollars for food and other expenses by Coach Ferguson, who told them that it should last until the team left in three days for their next game in Johnstown, Pennsylvania. Ferguson figured that ten dollars a day was a realistic budget in New York.

Leveritt and Stillwell introduced themselves to the gymnasium manager, who invited them to work out. He may have known about

the Wandering Weevils because some local newspapers had published stories about their game with Upsala College in Montclair,
New Jersey, the night before, and the *New York Post* had printed a
special blurb about the Arkansas boys:

> Like a fresh breeze blowing away the clouds of commercial
> claptrap that obscure the original purpose of an essentially
> simple sport involving the carrying and throwing of a wind-
> bag, the Arkansans sweep across the country every fall with
> no other pretensions than the desire to have a good time and
> pick up some spare change. They satirize the so-called 'sys-
> tems' with which the coaches kid the public into believing they
> are master minds, by making up plays as they go along; they
> do their own cheerleading, thereby exposing the silliness of
> trumped-up enthusiasm.

A bit florid, perhaps, but music to the eyes and ears of Ferguson,
frolicking elsewhere.

Leveritt was trying out some of the latest equipment when a
stranger, who had been sitting on a bench, stood and asked him if he
was Bert Goodrich. Leveritt was so shocked he could only shake his
head. Goodrich was not only one of his idols, but also was the ideal
of every boy who had ever dreamed of a perfect physique; already a
top Hollywood stuntman and famed vaudeville performer, he was
the first Mr. America, a title created in 1939 by the Amateur Athletic
Union, which sponsored the competition. The judges were especially
taken with Goodrich's "exceptional symmetry" and the title quickly
led to magazine covers and an overall celebrity status.

The stranger apologized for the mistake and said that he heard
Goodrich often worked out at Klein's gymnasium. This was true, the
manager said, explaining that Leveritt was only a football player from
Arkansas. At this, the stranger introduced himself as a talent scout
for a Madison Avenue advertising agency and said he had hoped to
recruit Goodrich as a model for a men's underwear ad campaign.
Given the amount of money Goodrich was likely to charge for posing

for commercials, and the fact that Goodrich was exceptionally well known, the stranger's story seemed implausible.

The stranger sized up Leveritt and suggested he would make an admirable model for the ads. Leveritt, a devout Presbyterian and officer of the A & M campus Presbyterian Club, was wary of anyone wanting to pay him for posing in men's briefs. But, when he was assured that the thirty-dollar offer was on the up-and-up, Leveritt agreed, and suggested Stillwell might also pose. The stranger thought it was a good idea. The two athletes went to a downtown studio later that day and spent a couple of hours shooting. "The advertisements ran in some magazine a few months later, without our names," Leveritt said later. "I don't know if anybody at home knew, but there wasn't anything embarrassing about it."

When Leveritt and Stillwell told Ferguson about their impromptu photo shoot, he thought it a wonderful adventure. Stories he heard from the other boys were less profitable, but as interesting in their own way. One showed the coach a wristwatch that he bought for $7.50 from a man on a sidewalk who said it was worth $100 but that he would sell it for just enough for bus fare to see his sick mother. Several boys went to Minsky's, the burlesque house on 42nd Street, near Times Square, to see the bumpers, the grinders, the slapstick, and the bawdy horseplay. It was the fading twilight for the genre—Minsky's would close the next year, with the theater becoming a movie house and then a pornography palace. Some boys toured the New York Public Library, at 42nd and Fifth Avenue, and posed for photos standing beside Patience and Fortitude, the sculpted lions who guarded the front steps and owed their names to Mayor Fiorello LaGuardia for the qualities he felt New Yorkers would need to survive the Great Depression.

Ferguson also rounded up a few boys for a scheduled photo shoot. *Newsweek* magazine was going to run a feature about the Boll Weevils in a couple of weeks, and said it wanted something goofy, so Ferguson sat under a huge black umbrella, pretending to draw up a play while four of his Weevils hammed it up around him and a resigned Paul Stegall, football in hand, just rolled his eyes.

As Ferguson suspected, the boys had spent most of their expense money on everything but food. He began counting his remaining funds carefully. The money would have to last until A & M's next game, on November 8, four days away.

The game was with St. Francis College, located in Loretto, Pennsylvania. But the college arranged to play the Wandering Weevils in Johnstown, about thirty miles south, where it anticipated a larger crowd. With plenty of time to reach Johnstown, Ferguson announced, his boys could afford another day of sightseeing. On an impulse, he decided to take them to see Yale University, in New Haven, Connecticut.

After a lunch stop along Route 1, the team arrived at Yale. While his boys toured the campus, Ferguson asked permission to use the practice field. Emerson ("Spike") Nelson, the Eli coach obliged and then invited the Weevils to watch his own squad workout. It had been a bad year for Yale, which won its first game before losing four straight by early November. They went on to drop three more, including back-to-back defeats by Princeton and Harvard to complete a 1–7 record, which would cost Nelson his job after only one season.

Ferguson was not terribly impressed. "The boys all seemed too scatter-brained, as did most of the students we saw in New Haven," he wrote later. "Of all the colleges I've ever seen, Yale offers the most promising nut factory for producing crazy football, and I have often wondered why it didn't beat me to the idea."

Ferguson splurged on dinner, and when he counted what was left of the money he had earned in Peoria, Bethlehem, and Montclair, he deemed it necessary to start economizing. The first thing was to find a cheap roadside hotel. He stuck to back roads, where less expensive lodgings were likely. Hours later, lost in a fog on a road he could not find on his map, Ferguson changed his mind and decided it was worth whatever money was left to find a decent place to sleep. He found it in Pottsville, Pennsylvania, which happened to be the birthplace of one Reverend William T. Ferguson. According to the coach, Pottsville was a hospitable place worth a return visit because of its generous, cheap eats. Once again, he was reminded of the rewards of serendipitous discoveries.

"On our travels," he said, "we found so many unadvertised but delightful places, and were disappointed so often in the advertised ones that I began instantly fighting travel literature on sight. The blind pointing of a finger on the map of the United States for a weekend or vacation is probably as good a choice as any."

The next stop was Edenburg, Pennsylvania, where the team stayed for two nights because the owner of a hotel there, a supporter of St. Francis, offered steep discounts to opposing teams. Ferguson felt marooned and would have moved along if he had enough money to do so.

The day before the game, Ferguson met "Big Jim" Leonard, coach of the unbeaten St. Francis team (on an overall twelve-game undefeated streak stretching to early the prior season) and told him he knew his own little Weevils could not compete; he suggested they cooperate in giving the crowd a good time. Leonard, an acclaimed former collegiate and professional fullback, agreed and even suggested that the Boll Weevils "borrow" some of his players during the game. After Leonard was gone, Ferguson told his team that St. Francis was going to play along with their antics. After the Upsala experience in serious play, it was clown time again.

St. Francis invited the Arkansans to eat in its cafeteria, where Buddy Carson—who had amusingly revealed in a recent *Weevil Outlet* "Profile" that he liked "Poetry and (Eloise)," disliked "Nosy People," and planned "to become an aviator"—recalled many years later that the Boll Weevils found carafes of wine on their table. This was another first, and a harbinger of the fun that lay ahead. Or so the Weevils thought.

For some reason, Leonard did not keep his word and within minutes after the kickoff, Ferguson's team was taking a terrific beating and he was complaining about the clipping, slugging, and piling on. After two of his Weevils were carried off the field, Ferguson told the team to avoid St. Francis players even if it meant throwing away the ball. At one point, he walked onto the field and announced he was taking his crew out of the game. But he relented when officials said they would maintain tighter control. After the game, on his way to the dressing room, Ferguson was elbowed and pushed by two St. Francis players. "This was the most deliberately brutal game we ever played and gave us more injuries than we had received in three seasons," Ferguson said later. "The boys took it without a whimper." The final score was 59–6, completing St. Francis' first unbeaten season.

Anxious to leave Johnstown, Ferguson didn't even bother showing his team the sights associated with the great flood there in 1889. The battered Boll Weevils traveled the next day to Philadelphia. Ferguson liked for his teams to visit the city where the U.S. Constitution was written and where he could take the boys to see the Liberty Bell. Invariably, one or more of them would put their fingers in its famous crack while someone took a photo. Finding the hotels filled with conventioneers, Ferguson negotiated space in the ballroom of one, with his boys spending the night on cots.

The physical beating by St. Francis had left Ferguson woefully short of healthy players. Money and morale were running low. It had been a long, draining season and three games remained, the first one in six days in Elkins, West Virginia. Ferguson was ready to call off the rest of the games and go home. "But, I knew the boys wouldn't stand for any of that kind of chicken heartedness," he said later. So, he took them to the sites associated with the birth of the United States, and at Independence Hall, while the guide was away, encouraged them to take turns sitting in George Washington's chair.

He also went looking for a doctor to treat Fuzzy Watts's leg. Watts, a short and stocky guard who had just sent a report back to A & M on the Bradley and Upsala games along with newspaper clippings, had suffered a badly crushed leg in childhood but insisted on playing football despite the risk of injury. Now it was bleeding. Unable to find an immediately available doctor near their hotel, Ferguson called around until he located a German doctor who worked from his home. He and Watts went to see him. The doctor did not have a nurse, so he asked Ferguson to help, and for an hour or so, the doctor stitched and bandaged Watts' leg. The charge was just three dollars, but Ferguson insisted he accept ten total; he gratefully added the doctor to his list of humane people.

The next night, the Boll Weevils stayed in a hotel so downscale that Ferguson thought it was another bordello. He warned the proprietor that almost all his players were underage and that if any of the women in the lobby propositioned them, he would call the cops. The night, he later noted, passed quietly.

For the third year in a row, Ferguson shepherded his team to Washington, D.C., and soaked up its history and sites over the next two days. There were tours of Congress. For Ferguson, there was another special reason for the excursion. He wanted a couple of the boys to meet Representative Francis Case, a friend from his days at Dakota Wesleyan. "I hoped my boys might hear him call me by my first name," Ferguson said. "He did, along with enough cordial conversation to puff me up as big as a bureaucrat."

Then, it was off to Elkins, West Virginia where the Weevils were scheduled to play Davis & Elkins College, whose 206 students—the fewest of any college A & M played during its three wandering years—already had suffered through nine lopsided defeats. Once in their hotel, the team found passes to the town's only movie house to see a double feature. Ferguson joined; there was nothing else in town to see or do. Between pictures, Ferguson was invited to say a few words. He climbed onstage and guaranteed the audience that his team would lose the next day. To cheers, he went back to his seat. Sure enough, his team lost, 41–0.

Only one game remained before A & M returned home to play Magnolia A & M, in the Boll Weevils' only appearance of the season in Monticello. The game was six days away, in Evansville, Indiana, giving Ferguson plenty of time to show his boys more of the country's historic and tourist sights.

At least that's what he said the next morning, a Sunday, when the Green Dawg left Elkins. The bus rolled through Clarksburg and stopped in Parkersburg, one of the coach's favorite towns for a bite, on account of the tasty, cheap eats and friendly waitresses. After a leisurely lunch, the Weevils headed for Portsmouth, Ohio, where he announced they were staying for three days. This was not the grand adventure that they were promised, but the town—rebuilt after a devastating 1937 flood destroyed sixty percent of the homes—was so congenial Ferguson couldn't resist. The Weevils even practiced a couple of times on the high school field.

After a couple of brief stopovers, they pulled into Evansville. The game, in Ferguson's words, was a "roaring slapstick." The AP account that appeared in many subscriber newspapers put it a bit more formally: "Football reached the heights of idiocy in Evansville today as the Evansville College Purple Aces, in between guffaws, downed the droll, screw-Boll Weevils from Arkansas A & M 26–6."

The report went on to say the game, played in a drenching rain, featured "a thousand" funny stunts. For openers, the Weevils entered the stadium, dressed in their rainbow array of jerseys, by climbing over the fence around the field. There were the usual pranks with umbrellas, bicycles, mud balls and balloons, and Lawrence Lavender—outfitted in a suit, top hat, white gloves, and cane—wowed the crowd when he took the snap from center and plunged into the line. Ferguson sat in the stands, flanked by coeds.

Early in the first quarter, a drunk weaved over to the A & M bench and sat down. One of the Weevils shouted to the crowd that it was the coach and invited him into a huddle. At this, Ferguson went to the press box to announce over the public address system that *he* was the coach, and that the drunk was an imposter. Police took the man away and explained they did not act sooner because they did not want to lock up the Arkansans' coach.

Ferguson and the boys had been gone from Monticello for thirty days and were weary, tired of travel, and worn out from the six games that had taken them thousands of miles from Texas to New Jersey, with stops in Illinois, Pennsylvania, West Virginia, and now, finally, Indiana. Everyone was ready to go home.

The team left immediately after the game and drove straight to Monticello for the final game the Wandering Weevils would ever play, against Magnolia A & M, an old rival, in the presence of a homecoming crowd with decidedly mixed feelings about the team.

Adding to the final festivities was the prize awarded the winning team. For years, the winner was presented a goat. A real, live milk goat that had been passed back and forth, according to the outcome of the annual game. The Weevils had won the last one, five years earlier, and with it, ownership of the goat. That alone was enough to bring sportswriters from Little Rock, Memphis, and elsewhere. That and a chance to write the Wandering Weevils' eulogy.

CHAPTER 29

FIRESIDE FOOL

The Wandering Weevils' homecoming game was scheduled for November 26, 1941, the twelfth game of a season that made them national celebrities to some and a national laughingstock to others. The contest against Magnolia A & M was the first one played that season in Monticello, and some of the boys were preparing to enter the military immediately after the final whistle.

For most of the previous three months, the team traveled around the country in a school bus covered with decals and slogans, playing college teams in nine states, acting like fools, and losing by lopsided scores. Everywhere they went, Coach Stewart Ferguson boasted that his was the worst football team in the country and no one disputed his claim. Now they had come home, virtual strangers on campus. Some of their professors didn't know who they were. One mother did not know her son had been touring the country playing football—she told neighbors he had joined the army. At a welcome home pep rally, cheerleaders did not know the names of some members of the team.

The winless wanderers had two days to prepare for the game with the Magnolia A & M Muleriders, a rivalry dating back to 1923 when both teams used the name Aggies. It was a long, spirited relationship, interrupted when Magnolia's president, Charles Overstreet, abruptly canceled football just before the start of the 1937 season. Ironically, it was likely Hendrix's big decision in early January 1941 to drop football—the school said "we simply couldn't undertake fully subsidized football and anything short of that would not produce the desired victories"—that opened up the final slot for Magnolia's return to the

Weevils schedule. (Interestingly, Ferguson never made a peep about the Methodist school—which he felt a certain draw to—dropping the sport, unlike his later critique of the University of Chicago's similar decision to abandon the game.)

But now that the game was scheduled for the day before Thanksgiving, it was a big deal, and not just because it reignited the old rivalry or because it gave students and Monticello supporters the chance, finally, to see what all the national fuss was about. The victor was to be presented an unusual prize.

M-Aggie was a nanny goat of uncertain age, tended and owned by the winner of the Monticello-Magnolia game, and changed hands every year according to which team won. Originally, Arkansas State College also took part in the "Old Goat" games. All three colleges were part of a mini-conference called "The Little Three," organized by the presidents of each institution to focus attention on their athletic programs and increase fan interest and revenue. But after a couple of years, Arkansas State said it was no longer interested in playing for the goat because it was not an agricultural school.

Monticello had won its last meeting with Magnolia in 1936 and regained possession of M-Aggie. Part of the tradition was that the goat's name changed every time it changed owners. The temporary name was always a pun on the name of the president of the losing school. Unlike Marvin Bankston, who considered the goat's name an honor, Charles Overstreet, president of Magnolia A & M objected to its current name, Charlene Overstreet, on grounds that it was unbecoming and disrespectful.

Ferguson was indifferent about the goat and, more importantly, about how his team would conduct itself on the field, whether they played it straight or continued the clowning that reaped so much national publicity. If anything, over the last several months, as it became increasingly clear his crazy football experiment was in its last act, he was already getting nostalgic. Heading into the season—picked up by some sportswriters during the fall (and by others many years later)—he weighed what it all meant:

Most of all, I want to be remembered by my players as a sort of fireside fool when they tell their children about the places they've seen … and the things they learned when they played football for Arkansas A & M. I want them to say, 'That Coach Ferguson was sort of a damn fool—didn't care much whether we won or lost. But boy!—the times we had and the things we saw.'

Ferguson shared a brief warning with his Weevils heading into the Magnolia game. He believed the Muleriders had been recruited and were paid by downtown Magnolia merchants, in the same way that the Boll Weevils were rounded up and subsidized a few seasons earlier. As the Magnolia bus rolled to a stop outside the gym, Ferguson went outside to welcome the visitors. "It was about the meanest looking busload of humans that I ever saw in Arkansas," he recalled later.

Their manners weren't much better. Before the game, Ferguson said, he went to the Magnolia dressing room under the stadium and asked if there was anything the Muleriders needed or wanted. One of them replied, "Yeah, you can get the hell out." Ferguson apologized, saying he was sorry he had mistaken the visitors for humans and promised to provide cages for them the next time they came. "They laughed," Ferguson said. "They thought I was complimenting them, and maybe I was."

Up in the press box sat sportswriters representing a wide range of outfits: the *Arkansas Gazette* and the *Arkansas Democrat*, newspapers with statewide circulation; the Associated Press; newspapers from Pine Bluff; Monroe, Louisiana; the neighboring *Ashley County Weekly*; and, using a campus correspondent, the *Memphis Commercial-Appeal*.

Though the kickoff was scheduled for two o'clock, a ring of cars was parked in a circle around the playing field with their headlights on, a tradition dating back several years. Buddy Carson's mother, like other mothers, sat in the front seat and shouted encouragement while his father joined other fathers pacing the sideline behind the Monticello bench. Neither had any clue what their son was about to do. About two thousand spectators turned out, but only thirty or so were from Magnolia because classes there did not end until four o'clock, and President Overstreet had warned that anyone who skipped classes for the game faced severe punishment. Among the spectators were a dozen Monticello players who were already on active military duty, among them Paul's twin brother Ralph Stegall and Ensign Carlton Spears, who had been assigned to Hawaii, where within days he would witness the Japanese surprise attack on the U.S. naval base at Pearl Harbor.

There was the usual small college homecoming rituals and hoopla. The Phi Phi Phi sorority sold pipe cleaners decorated with a photo of Paul Stegall. The Sigma Tau Gamma fraternity displayed a mule skeleton decorated with Magnolia A & M colors. A concession stand offered "mule chops" and "mule burgers" for a dime apiece. The marching band and drum corps strutted in new red uniforms; there was a football queen and court, and as the clock struck two, a wild entrance by the Boll Weevils, wearing the multicolored jerseys that Ferguson had been given by sporting goods salesmen. Some players wore hunting caps, others ski caps, and one, smoking a cigar, wore a derby tilted low over one eye. One was barefooted. Some of them rowed a small boat across the pond next to the stadium. Three others arrived in a cart drawn by a mule, and Bill Bowers, the son of a Methodist minister, ran onto the field bare-chested. As the crowd howled, he opened a suitcase, removed a bright orange jersey, and pulled it on. The pregame warm-up involved square dancing and some leapfrog, plus the usual assortment of tumbling and walking like ducks.

What followed was the kind of slapstick bedlam that had delighted fans from Texas, Alabama, New Jersey, and points in between. It began with an old, familiar gag—Bowers running full speed from his own goal line to kick-off, sprawling face down as he approached the ball, and letting a teammate squib the ball a few yards forward. Formations included the farcical "Swinging Gate," a Ferguson creation that looked like a melee. Substitutes rode bicycles on and off the field or entered and left under umbrellas held by teammates. Lawrence ("The Stork") Lavender, dressed as always in a purple jersey, pretended he was injured and was dragged off the field, covered with a sheet of canvas, and left there for the rest of the game. When players called for water, a sub ran onto the field with a brown jug marked "XXX."

Magnolia did not join in the spirit of things, but this was alright with Ferguson, who liked it when one team acted as straight man for the routines by his crazy Boll Weevils. As always, however, he grew angry when other teams took out their frustrations in ways he deemed unsportsmanlike. The officials, who generally ignored infractions by Monticello, called a dozen penalties for rough play and ejected two Magnolia players.

The surprise was that the Boll Weevils scored, on a two-yard run by Benny Gaston in the first quarter. It was only A & M's fourth touchdown all season. Carson kicked the extra point, and that was it for the Weevils. Magnolia won the game, and the return of M-Aggie, 25–7.

On the final play of the game, Buddy Carson intercepted a pass and kept running, right off the field and into the stands, where he grabbed his girlfriend, Eloise Groves, and ran with her to Benny Gaston's car. Gaston drove them to McGehee, his hometown, to the home of a Methodist minister who agreed to marry them then and there. Benny served as best man.

Eleven days later, on December 7, the Japanese struck at Pearl Harbor. The next day, America was officially at war and Stewart Ferguson, soon enough, was back on the move.

PART 3

HOME

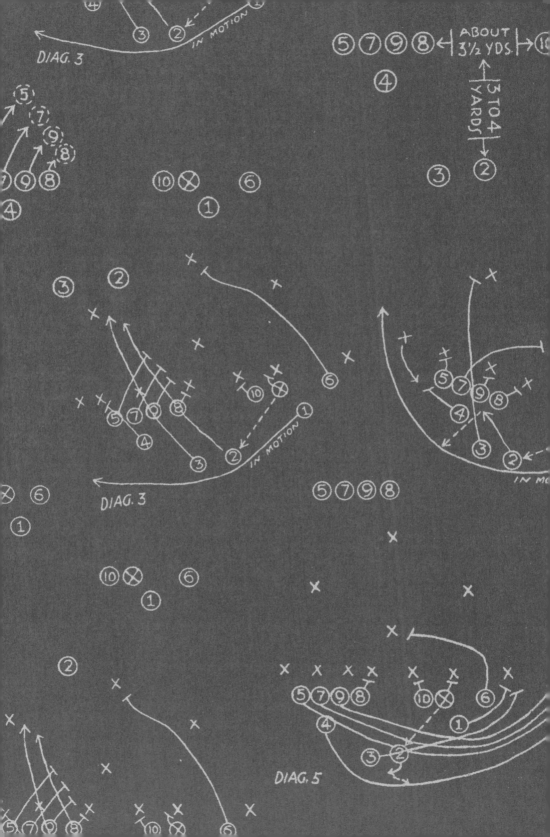

DIAG. 3

IN MOTION

ABOUT 3½ YDS.

3 TO 4 YARDS

DIAG. 3

IN MOTION

IN MO

DIAG. 5

CHAPTER 30

BACK TO (FLIGHT) SCHOOL

For Coach Stewart Ferguson, the impending end of his Wandering Weevils run initiated the path to a new beginning that would lead him home to South Dakota. By August 1942, with World War II raging in Europe, North Africa, Asia, and the Pacific and accelerating player shortages and travel restrictions, there was growing uncertainty if any Arkansas college football would occur in the fall. By mid-September, it was official: all Arkansas colleges, except the large state university in Fayetteville, canceled football for the duration of the war.

With no football on the horizon, Coach Ferguson shifted gears; he studied wartime subjects and applied for jobs. On December 17, in the small river port city of Natchitoches, Louisiana, a double-take sort of headline appeared in the Louisiana Normal *Current Sauce*, the local college's weekly newspaper: "C.P.T. Program on Campus Has New Instructor—Stewart A. Ferguson Becomes Head of Flying School Here This Week."

The Civilian Pilot Training Program (CPTP), then comprised of men in the army reserves and active-duty navy cadets, was introduced by President Franklin D. Roosevelt on December 27, 1938, and had its roots in similar 1930s European programs. The CPTP was the country's first full-scale, federally funded aviation education program, and its purpose was to create an additional pool of potential military pilots beyond the quickly growing number of fliers the army could train on its own. Five days after the December 7, 1941, Japanese attack on Pearl Harbor, President Roosevelt signed Executive Order 8974, turning the CPTP into a wartime program under the

War Training Service (WTS). All WTS graduates were now required to sign a contract agreeing to enter the military following graduation.

The program spread across the classrooms of over a thousand educational institutions (public schools, colleges, and universities) and the facilities of nearly fifteen hundred flight schools. Due to necessary construction work, the Natchitoches CPTP had been recently discontinued at the local airport connected to campus. The December enrollees constituted fifteen navy and five army flyers who would receive eight weeks of basic training, covering 240 hours of ground school and thirty to forty hours of flight time.

Ferguson's courses included mathematics, meteorology, physics, navigation, civil aviation regulations, and physical education. Outside of his longtime experience teaching and studying physical education, this range of subjects was completely new. Years later, his wife Edna reflected on her husband's accomplishment in a telling, matter of fact manner: "He was a smart man and he qualified himself in various subjects connected with that." Edna confirmed that he had no prior involvement in aeronautics, and added, "that was just what developed." While Ferguson was somehow head instructor of the flying school, Edna worked as secretary for the resident naval officer.

As Stewart settled into his expansive teaching responsibilities, the country was adjusting to being a nation at war. At many state colleges, as intercollegiate sports continued to be canceled, a different kind of football for the 1943 season popped up. At Arkansas A & M, a contingent of Navy V-12 trainees replaced Ferguson's traveling band of Boll Weevils, and Ferguson found himself drawn back into A & M's football fray.

The situation kicked off in October with an AP article that made its rounds in local papers across the country, including Arkansas, South Dakota, and Louisiana. Alexandria, Louisiana, a significant stop during Ferguson's sole year teaching and coaching at Bolton High School, was about sixty miles from his current home in Natchitoches and its October 14 *Town Talk* newspaper ran a notable headline in the middle of the sports page: "MONTICELLO FLABBERGASTED WITH GRIDDERS."

The article provided a quick overview of A & M's Wandering Weevils squads under Stewart Ferguson and went on to explain that A & M's football team was now a mix of navy-marine trainees and had just beaten Arkansas University. The update added that along with "transferred football talent from Southern Methodist, Texas Aggies, Oklahoma A. & M., Arkansas University, and other schools, there's a suspicion of some kind of coaching going on." A & M's President Marvin Bankston, Ferguson's erstwhile friend and ally, characterized how his school had unequivocally moved on from the Wandering Weevils days.

"Things seem to be mighty changed around here now," said Bankston, "but I can't tell you much about it because it's a military secret." By mid-November, the now loaded Boll Weevils were suddenly considered a big-time football outfit and were headed to Shreveport's Louisiana State Fair stadium to be the marquee team in a match-up against a college squad from Georgetown, Texas. In his "Raspberries and Cream" sports column, the *Shreveport Times'* Joe R. Carter spat out much of the same broad Wandering Weevil material from the October AP story and concluded with the tale that "once in New Jersey an opposing coach felt sorry for the Monticello team and gave it a pep talk before the game." That was enough for Coach Ferguson, and he immediately responded.

Never mistaken as thick-skinned, Ferguson unloaded in a four page, single-spaced typewritten letter:

> The wandering Bollweevil era may be over, for winning some-
> times does strange things to principles, ethics, and profes-
> sional pride, but I know from our experiment at A & M that
> college athletics can be worthy of the name. Financially, we
> were [far] ahead of the previous three years conduct of sports;
> educationally, our football squads averaged better grades than
> those for the student body [this one was a stretch, though
> the team's grades were on par with the overall male student
> body], and both the coaches and players are still not ashamed
> to hold up their heads even with the memory of 60-0 defeats.

We believed in what we did and had plenty of fun doing it.

That's why we will never be ashamed of our record in football.

Ferguson especially wanted to clarify the "false as hell" story, circulated two years earlier, that a rival coach in New Jersey gave the Boll Weevils a pep talk; it was time to set the record straight. Ferguson said former Upsala Coach Bob Meyer scouted the Weevils in a game against Moravian in Bethlehem, Pennsylvania and on Meyer's return to Newark gave out the information that he had pleaded with Monticello A & M to play serious football in their upcoming game. Ferguson remembered it differently:

> During the half, a number of people came to the dressing room and begged of us to become serious long enough to defeat Moravian. But, as I explained to Coach Meyer, if we became serious to a team that outweighed us by about 40 pounds a man, and [was a] much better football team, the game would quickly become a tragedy. Our only hope, as it was during all the season, was in comedy.

In his letter, Ferguson added that "his players listened to enough people that day to become serious in the second half and were quickly smothered under a 33–0 score." He closed by saying that he would be in attendance to cheer for the Boll Weevils in Saturday's game.

The following spring of 1944, Coach Ferguson read the news that Louisiana Normal's Navy Flight School, along with the thirteen others spread across U.S. colleges and universities, would be discontinued around July 1. It was time for another change, and for the first time since he opted to head south twenty years earlier, Coach Ferguson would not make a big life decision on his own.

CHAPTER 31

WELCOME MAT

Stewart Ferguson spent the better part of twenty years in the South. But it was never home. In the spring of 1944, many signs seemed to be lining up for Coach Ferguson's life journey to come full circle with a return north to South Dakota. The first indication was a healthy amount of wartime teacher turnover occurring in schools.

Ferguson learned of an opening as athletic coach and physical education instructor at Deadwood High School in the northern Black Hills of South Dakota. The town, lying in a canyon formed by White-wood Creek, with narrow streets and crowded corners, reminded him of the French Quarter of New Orleans and was an enticing fit. "The fascinating little city of sin," as Ferguson later wrote, gave off a comfortable frontier feel reminiscent of his treasured days growing up in Gregory. He also got the chance to stay for a night in Deadwood before a 1930 Dakota Wesleyan football game in nearby Spearfish, and a warm memory of "the sound of a mountain stream running around the foundation of the hotel" stuck with him throughout the years. Beyond the natural lure of Deadwood was Ferguson's overall affinity for the Black Hills, where the coach visited several times for Dakota Wesleyan athletics and, not coincidentally, scheduled a stay for his 1940 Wandering Weevils.

Then there was Edna. She grew up not far from Deadwood on a family ranch in Custer, in the southern Black Hills. Edna's aunt Fannie raised Edna and kept her apart as a baby from her two older brothers, who were sick with scarlet fever. Fannie still lived in the region. The stars continued to align a couple months later when a second position for an English teacher and school librarian opened up at Deadwood High School. As Edna reflected years later, Stewart wanted to make sure she felt comfortable before they considered a move. "He sent me to Deadwood . . . to see if I wanted to live in that area." On the school side, the decision maker was Superintendent Harry Stone Berger. Throughout the years, locals knew H. S. Berger—who had arrived in Deadwood in 1928 for his new job as superintendent—as an outstanding educator, outdoorsman, and a careful selector of teachers who traveled to universities in five states to personally interview candidates.

Coach Stewart Ferguson and his wife Edna—young, but quite literary—were a compelling pair. On July 17, 1944, the Deadwood Board of Education made things official. The Fergusons left the South behind, ready to start anew in South Dakota. In the Sunday, August 20 edition of the *Deadwood Pioneer-Times*, just below the page one lead on the Red Army's advance into East Prussia, was the paper's (and town's) welcome mat: "Former Wesleyan Coach Accepts Deadwood Post." The boastful biography set the tone on several fronts for Stewart A. Ferguson's new chapter.

The article led with Ferguson's five-year period as athletic director and coach at Dakota Wesleyan University and his overall thirteen years of experience coaching college athletics, plus another five coaching high school. It went on to highlight Ferguson's several summers as a visiting professor at Louisiana State University teaching physical education and noted his extensive educational background, including his 1923 nomination for the Rhodes scholarship as a student at Dakota Wesleyan. And similar to the announcement of Ferguson's return to his alma mater fifteen years earlier, the paper took literary license when naming his football mentors. For instance, the decision to highlight Notre Dame's legendary Coach Knute Rockne likely reflected Ferguson's forever pull to the aura of South Bend's Fighting Irish. The article closed with a brief mention that Ferguson also developed an athletic program at Arkansas A & M that attained national attention and publicity, which perhaps gave Ferguson some helpful breathing room for his new responsibilities.

As coach of athletics and boys' physical education, Ferguson was hired at a salary of $2,600—the same as his official salary at Dakota Wesleyan during the Great Depression—while Edna earned $1,700 for her new role as English instructor and librarian. Amid the recent, heavy turnover of teachers, Coach Ferguson became the third Deadwood athletics coach in the last three years, and he immediately dove into his new gig.

One day after the opening of the 1944 Deadwood school year, he handed out uniforms and ran his first football practice. Twenty-four boys suited up, and they were on the younger side as only six of the twenty-three seniors were boys and just one of them went out for the team. Two weeks later, on the bottom of the local paper's fourth and final page, an ad promoted the first game of the season: "FOOTBALL TONIGHT" at 7:45 p.m. under the lights at the Deadwood Amusement Park. The opponent was Edna's hometown Custer Wildcats, though she went to high school in nearby Hot Springs.

Coach Ferguson's first game in his Deadwood coaching career ended in a familiar fashion: a convincing loss. Tucked in among the latest front-page news of the Allied heavy offensive across Europe, a headline read "BEARS LOSE OPFNER to CUSTER, 39–0." It was an amusing oops by the editors, but an unpleasant start for Coach Ferguson. There was more of the same the following week when the Bears visited nearby Spearfish, located at the mouth of picturesque Spearfish Canyon. This time the game ran so late that Deadwood's *Pioneer-Times*, in a brief page one recap, could only report that Spearfish led 56–0 after three quarters.

Though Coach Ferguson's Bears suffered a third straight trouncing to the Rapid City Cobblers, the perennial Black Hills conference powerhouse, it was clear that the town's vibe was unlike anything from his prior stops. In a 55–6 homecoming defeat, the subhead read "Bears Show Improvement," and the beefier write-up highlighted strong work by several Deadwood players, along with details on their first scoring drive of the season. In addition, sitting at the wrong end of a 187–6-point differential (including the later confirmed 67–0 loss against Spearfish) to start his first season did not lead members to revoke Coach Ferguson's invitation as the featured guest at Deadwood's weekly Rotary Club meeting at the Wagner Café. The Bears' new skipper plainly told the group that his small, slow, inexperienced squad was improving each game. Coach Ferguson also touched on his coaching experiences at Arkansas A & M and Dakota Wesleyan, but it was clear he was singularly focused on the Bears.

With only two games left in a trial-by-fire first season, it was also clear Coach Ferguson was reprogramming himself as an actual coach. The relaxed Rotary Club meeting seemed to soothe Ferguson, and he started talking football to the local reporters ahead of Friday's game, a homecoming day trip to Sturgis, on the eastern edge of the Black Hills. He was particularly excited about some fresh offensive formations that he had concocted: "It is original and peculiar and won't be of interest until we do something with it, which I hope may be soon."

Ferguson tinkered with positions, and the Bears played with some spark after getting blanked in the first half. Junior Leland Hoseman found a throwing rhythm and a receiving partner in fellow junior Lowell Lang. The Bears fought back from a 25–0 deficit, and more than tripled their scoring output to date in their first competitive loss of the season, 31–19.

The Hoseman–Lang duo stayed hot as Deadwood returned home to face the tough Belle Fourche (pronounced bel-FOOSH) Broncs. French for "beautiful fork," Belle Fouche sat at the northern edge of the Black Hills near the confluence of what is known today as the Belle Fourche and Redwater Rivers and the Hay Creek. The Broncs had lost only one game to date and were still vying for the conference title. Hoseman and Lang connected for a couple of touchdowns, and the Bears' best overall defensive effort of the year had them locked in a 12–12 game with seven minutes left. A critical Deadwood penalty helped Belle Fourche take the lead and the Broncs added another score in a 26–12 final.

More improvement for Ferguson's Bears, but there was still one game left, against Lead. No matter the records going in, this game pretty much meant everything for these twin cities.

The deep-seated feelings between the neighboring towns were complex and could be traced back to the massive mine perched high above the town of Deadwood. During the 1876 gold rush, placer claims—discoverer grants of valuable materials near the surface—were staked throughout the Black Hills. Deadwood Creek, near the camp with the same name (within a gulch full of dead trees and giving rise to the town of Deadwood), was especially profitable. As the gold placers depleted, folks switched to hardrock mining. Two prospectors, brothers Moses and Fred Manuel, uncovered an encouraging vein of ore called a lead (pronounced "leed") at the Homestake Ledge. They staked their claim, built their mill, and mined $5,000 worth of gold. Activity ramped up; town lots were laid, a telegraph service started, and the growing town of Lead (named for the initial ore discovery) was officially incorporated in 1877.

The Manuel brothers sold their four-and-a-half acre Homestake claim to George Hearst, a self-made millionaire and mining expert, for $70,000, enabling a major expansion of the mine and accelerated growth for Lead. By 1900, Lead's population had swelled to over six thousand—with more than 1,800 workers on Homestake Mine's payroll—and over the years would remain more than double that of Deadwood. Along with the town's population spike, Hearst's wife, Phoebe, tapped the family's wealth to provide significant support. She established a free public library and kindergarten, donated to Lead's churches, and provided college scholarships to the kids of the miners and mill workers. She also planned and funded the Homestake Opera House and Recreation Building for the community.

Lead's local stature was growing. On March 7, 1903, the town's newspaper, the *Lead Daily Call*, happy to do its part, opened with a recent article from South Dakota's leading eastern newspaper, the *Sioux Falls Argus-Leader*, boldly headlined: "THE METROPOLIS OF THE BLACK HILLS." An excerpt from the article poured it on thick: "When the little mining camp was located here among the rich hills of Lawrence County, little did its pioneer founders suppose they were founding such an important and progressive city, that would grow into a metropolis and mining center of 9,000 population in such a short period of time. . . . In commercial, financial, and social ways, Lead is probably without a peer in this entire region."

As time went on, resentment about all the money in Lead festered among the Deadwood faithful. The fact that Deadwood—still embracing its wild, western roots—developed into the business center of the Black Hills region further complicated the dynamic between the towns. Most of the retail stores and all of the car dealerships in the region sprung up across Main Street in Deadwood. With Homestake's operation continuing to bulge, the employees came down with their weekly paychecks and spent, supporting Deadwood's merchants.

Meanwhile, a little bit of football fired up between the two neighboring gulches. The earliest games comprised town teams arranged by player-managers in the late 1890s, and by 1900, Deadwood and Lead high schools began their gridiron battles. These initial contests spotlighted the fierce loyalty and simmering tensions between Deadwood and Lead. On one occasion, responding to a Lead man's alternative interpretation of the rules that would have reversed a recent Deadwood win against Spearfish, Deadwood's daily paper, the *Pioneer-Times*, spouted vitriol:

> We as a committee wish to state on behalf of our football team, that when we want H.L Lord (the Lead City Idiot) to explain the rules and decide our games for us, we will inform him of our wants. This Lord is the same rattle headed idiot who tried to referee the Lead City-Deadwood game here some weeks ago. His refereeing was simply rank, and he showed to those who attended . . . his knowledge of football was lacking on every point, for every decision made by him had to be reversed.

More kindle was lit after a 1908 Deadwood loss at Lead City's baseball park. The *Pioneer-Times* recap stated that the "hotly contested" 0–0 game turned in the middle of the second half when Deadwood's talented left end was "disqualified by the Lead umpire on account of alleged slugging, which the boy certainly was not guilty of." A few pages later, the paper declared a challenge to Lead: "The football team of the Deadwood high school hereby challenges the football team of the Lead City high school to a football game to be played on any park of regulation size and all officials for the game to be from outside towns."

Though for a few years Deadwood didn't field a team because of a shortage of varsity players or had to cancel a season early, after the school disqualified too many athletes for failing to maintain the required number of classes, the rivalry continued to heat up. Starting in 1922, there were three straight years of two games, alternating between home sites, with the second occurring on November 11, Armistice Day.

The down gulch Deadwood boys had won only two games, and not since 1912, in the years since the 0–0 tie in 1903 that served as the official inaugural game of the rivalry. Drawing from its much larger population, the Lead teams—often dubbed the Mill City boys—were generally bigger and stronger, with many of the players children of Homestake miners. The Mill City boys piled up another four wins, but on the eve of the 1924 battle at Deadwood's Amusement Park (a sprawling layout on the northern edge of town that encompassed a baseball field and an area that housed horse racing, rodeo events, plus motorcycle and auto races), the Deadwood school oozed with pep. A snake dance spread across town and stopped all traffic, followed by a big bonfire, fireworks, cheer leaders, and songs, setting the stage for the grand finale, as cleverly captured by the local paper: "Lead was drawn through the streets in the dead wagon, and apparently there were no mourners."

Alas, Deadwood's immense school celebration did not produce a victory. A short five weeks later, Deadwood's feelings about the rivalry finally boiled over on the field. Lead was host for the Armistice Day game, and the town's *Daily Call* chronicled the day's events, including a huge community parade featuring Lead's local military unit and an American Legion dance in the evening. In between was the featured event, and the paper noted that Lead's players were confident of a victory. On the other side, Deadwood's *Pioneer-Times* talked up the team, encouraged folks to attend the game, and added an emphatic end, twenty-seven in all, to each news story spanning the front page: —BEAT LEAD—.

The man currently in charge of beating Lead was Clarence Shedd, who had joined Deadwood's staff the prior school year as an instructor in science and athletics. He had previously taught at a high school in Minnesota but originally hailed from Lead. Needing no local pigskin history lesson, Shedd was still looking for his first rivalry win and saw his team getting thoroughly outplayed, down 31–0 late in the third quarter, with one of his players tossed earlier in the game for slugging. A thirty-five-yard Lead gain by halfback Walter Johnson brought them close to another score, and Deadwood fullback Clarence Watson was ejected for kicking Johnson after assisting on the tackle. Coach Shedd had had enough.

He pulled his team from the field, thereby forfeiting the game. The next morning Shedd explained his actions but did not quell the situation: "The reason I jerked my team was primarily because I would not send in some little second-string men and take chances on them getting hurt. I wouldn't take chances on any criminal action. Furthermore, we have decided we won't have any more athletic relations with Lead high school. This is due to the action of the crowd, not the attitude of the players or referee."

Shedd, however, was not speaking for the Deadwood school. At a meeting later that evening between representatives of the local school boards, Deadwood's superintendent dismissed Shedd's statement and said that as far as his school was concerned, athletic relations between the schools would not be discontinued. Cooler heads prevailed and after a follow-up meeting with Deadwood and Lead city officials, the continuation of athletics between Deadwood and Lead was confirmed.

The 1924 season would be the last that the schools played two games, which meant more time for Deadwood to stew between annual losses. The now commonly acknowledged "ancient rivals" also soon took on new monikers—the Deadwood Bears and the Lead Gold Diggers—but the battle cry to "BEAT LEAD" marched on. For the first time in sixteen years, on Sunday, October 28, 1928, the *Pioneer-Times* proudly planted "Deadwood Bears 7, Lead Gold Diggers 0" in big bold letters across the entire top of its front page.

Order, however, was quickly restored and it took another fourteen years for the Bears to do it again. This apparently did not sit right with the Golddiggers (who had changed their name to one word during the 1930–1931 school year); on the eve of Coach Ferguson's arrival, Lead handed Deadwood its worst defeat in the rivalry's history, 63–0, reminding the Bears of which town was tops on the field.

As for Ferguson's first tussle with Lead, the Bears were hardly expected to hang with 1944's Golddiggers squad. Lead had won its first five games by a combined 110–23, while Deadwood had been outscored 217–37 to date. Lead also had seven returning lettermen from its 1943 5–0–1 conference championship team, its fourth title in the last six years. In charge was Coach Joe Dunmire, the prominent head of Lead's athletics since 1927.

The *Rapid City Journal* said the "Golddiggers may make this game look like a track meet," while the *Deadwood Pioneer-Times* reported that "despite the rapid improvement of the Bears, they will be outclassed by one of the best teams ever turned out in the Black Hills Conference." The local paper did add that the "spirited play of the Bears, however, will make the game an interesting one to watch." The prognosticators proved correct. Lead blitzed the Bears with three scores in the first quarter and never looked back, as they clinched another Black Hills football conference championship with an easy 38–7 victory.

Coach Stewart Ferguson's first season at the helm for the Deadwood Bears concluded with his team firmly in the basement, having lost all six games while being outscored by a comical 211 points. Yet, the sun rose on schedule Saturday morning and no "Coach Must Go" signs were posted in front of the Fergusons' downtown apartment. This time, the coach had no inkling whatsoever that he should start packing his bags.

CHAPTER 32

LOVEFEASTS

The feeling out process continued for Coach Ferguson during basketball season. The Bears managed two wins against Custer to avoid last place in the conference and bowed out immediately in districts to Spearfish, thumped 52–27. Lead, meanwhile, followed up its championship football season with a dominant 15–0 year in basketball, winning the conference and getting to the semis in the Class A state tournament, for larger schools, before falling to Huron.

Over the next few months, Coach Ferguson further ingrained himself into the Deadwood community. First, there was R. G. Cartwright's annual Juvenile Basketball Tournament, in which Ferguson would direct four groups of younger kids separated by weight classes. Cartwright, Lead's long time physical education director, ran the large event—leveraging both of Lead's gymnasiums—to promote fun athletic competition with a heavy focus on good sportsmanship. A few weeks later, Ferguson got to show off his own passion for physical education, co-leading the grade school's annual evening program with the girls' director. Finally, there was the high school's end of year awards program, where Coach Ferguson handed out athletic awards to a group of football and basketball players and cheerleaders.

Not yet fully grounded in Deadwood, Stewart Ferguson and his wife Edna left for the entire summer, spending time in the South and East. While they were away, a buzz began building in the Black Hills. It started in May with the announcement of the official surrender of Germany to the Allies. Shortly after the welcome news from Europe, Albro Ayers, the chairman of the mining committee of the

Deadwood Chamber of Commerce, stated the reopening of the gold mines was the largest problem facing the northern Black Hills. He pushed for immediate action by every member of the community to help rescind order L-208, which had closed the mines back in October 1942. Apart from maintenance and other war production jobs, the U.S. War Production Board had labeled gold mining as a nonessential industry and sought to conserve machinery and supplies for the more urgently needed war metals lead, zinc, and copper.

Ayers urged each citizen to write or wire South Dakota's congressional representatives—Senators Harlan J. Bushfield and Chan Gurney, Representatives Francis Case and Karl Mundt—and Julius A. Krug, chairman of the War Production Board (WPB). In addition, thirty-one western congressmen sent a letter to Krug to rescind the order, asserting that no other industry had been "subjected to such hardships as gold mining." Five days later, a WPB response said the lifting of the ban was under consideration. And on Monday, June 18, the news so many people had been hoping for finally arrived, spanning the front page of both local papers: Homestake was set to resume operations on July 2. By the time the Fergusons returned to Deadwood in August, the mine was staffing up, with preferences given to former employees and war veterans, and daily ore production gradually increasing.

The good news continued with Japan's surrender. On Wednesday, August 15, the massive headline, "WORLD WAR II ENDS" soared above the *Deadwood Pioneer-Times* masthead. The official word came in at five in the afternoon on Tuesday. Instantly in Deadwood, bells rang and the fire siren blew. Flags were raised on the streets, people banged on their car horns, and there were staccato bursts of firecrackers on the hills above the city. Mayor Andrew B. Mattley declared Wednesday a city holiday. Everything in Deadwood was closed and the day was observed with a parade, under the direction of the Deadwood American Legion Post, followed by a memorial service held in the Deadwood theater.

Football was right around the corner, and a prior winless season did not diminish the spirit of Ferguson's 1945 Bears team. Twenty-eight boys signed up to play, including every member of the 1944 crew except for the one graduating senior. Deadwood opened against Custer, and Coach Ferguson selected twenty-two boys to make a trip down to the southern Black Hills. Before departing, he told the paper his boys had been working hard and were in good shape for the game. Coach Ferguson was right, and the *Deadwood Pioneer-Times* was happy to oblige with a big, bolded page one headline: "Deadwood Upsets Custer In First Game Of Season." Junior Ronnie Burrington, the nephew of one of Coach Ferguson's players at Dakota Wesleyan, joined Leland Hoseman as another promising passer in a comfortable 18–6 win, Coach Ferguson's first victory since his Wandering Weevils decided to play it straight at home to finish up their 1940 campaign.

The win also spurred the paper's editor, Camille Yuill, into action. In her daily column, the "Backlog," Yuill served as the town's positive pulse, mixing in community news, fun local anecdotes, and sometimes important directives, all in the spirit of championing Deadwood and the surrounding Black Hills. In Sunday's musings, Yuill led with the Bears: "Congratulations, the Deadwood Bears and Coach Ferguson, [on] your victory over Custer. Even our severest critic, a Custer high school alumnus, says it was a good game. Now just for fun, let's take a few more of them. Anything can happen. Look what happened to Lead on its own field." As Yuill often did, she closed with a joke: "Stalemate—a spouse you are tired of."

For the second straight year, the Rotary Club invited Coach Ferguson to speak at its weekly luncheon, this time held at the Black Hills Power and Light offices. The Bears coach was in his element, explaining several football plays and tactics. Later that week, he told the paper the Bears would be significantly outweighed in Friday's home game against Spearfish, and their chances depended on stopping a beefy Spartans backfield. Mission accomplished: the Bears' "light but scrappy" line held tough, and the Burrington to Lang combo connected for three scoring strikes as Deadwood raced to a 31–0 lead after three quarters. Ferguson played his substitutes for the entire fourth quarter, and the suddenly 2–0 Bears—with more points scored than in their entire 1944 season—were off to face the Rapid City Cobblers.

Rapid City, voted as the "friendliest" stop by Ferguson's Wandering Weevils, was by far the biggest city in the Black Hills region, and at the time housed only one high school, where the 1945–1946 senior class alone contained more students than all of Deadwood High School. The disproportionate number of Rapid City kids generally resulted in strong sports teams, and over the years Deadwood–Rapid football matchups were David and Goliath affairs. Deadwood had three wins over the last forty years or so and had lost the last four games by an overall count of 155–13.

The *Rapid City Journal* billed the 1945 tilt against the "revamped" Bears as "passes" versus "power." Beyond the always herculean opponent, the football gods intervened. First, the team bus (channeling its inner A & M Green Dawg) broke down along the way, forcing the Bears to hitchhike their way to Rapid City. For good measure, a stiff wind sprang up just before kickoff and persisted for the entire game. Still, the Bears held the Cobblers to one touchdown in the first half before Rapid's power running game wore down the pass-happy Bears after halftime. Under the whipping wind, the Bears were undone by five interceptions and a few other near misses.

Though Coach Ferguson's Bears lost 20–0, the team's gritty play hardly went unnoticed. An ex-reporter for the *Deadwood Pioneer-Times* attended the game and called in his recap to the paper, which made its way into Yuill's Sunday "Backlog." "The best coached team was defeated by the power of the steam roller," he said. "Every time Deadwood got the ball, you'd hear the comment up and down the sidelines from Rapid City as well as other fans: 'Now we'll see some real football.'" He added that "the power of the Cobblers was too much for them, with the added handicap of a heavy wind against their aerial passing. But it didn't daunt their spirit and sportsmanship any. And Deadwood needn't offer any apologies for the kind of game Coach Ferguson's boys are playing this season, win or lose."

Though a tad hyperbolic, the summary showed that Coach Ferguson was molding a team that clearly possessed character.

The following Friday marked the full return of Bear Day, the high school's festive homecoming celebration, and the first one since the beginning of the war. After an afternoon assembly in the auditorium, the parade took center stage. The football team, with a spiffy Coach Ferguson parked upfront, followed the band ahead of a large procession of floats and a swarm of Deadwood grade-schoolers riding bikes decorated in orange and black. The jubilant group headed down Main Street, turned around at the Standard Oil service station, and looped around town before making a right at the courthouse and finishing back at school.

After the parade, Bear Day football captain Harry Adams crowned Shirley Ellis all-school queen, Adams and Coach Ferguson gave short talks, and the junior class won three dollars for their first-place float. The festivities concluded with the Deadwood Bears hosting the Sturgis Scoopers under the lights. A strong Sturgis line hurt the Bears on both sides of the ball and led the Scoopers to a 12–0 victory. The next week the Bears ran into the undefeated Belle Fourche Broncs, who cruised to a 32–0 win (and later a conference championship).

With three straight shutout defeats, Coach Ferguson and his Bears were reeling and still had to face their archrival Lead, the defending Black Hills conference champion.

In Coach Ferguson's first taste of the rivalry, big brother pounded little brother up the hill in Lead. Round two was at home, and this time it was a tight game. Timely tackling starred in the first half, as both teams stiffened on defense near their end zone. The first half remained scoreless, but the game quickly changed in the third quarter. The Bears recovered a Golddiggers fumble, and after two consecutive completed passes and an off-tackle burst by Hoseman, Deadwood sat three yards from Lead's goal line. The Golddiggers pushed the Bears back on a run into the line. It was time for a touch of Ferguson razzle-dazzle.

Fullback Ronnie Burrington tossed a short pass to tight end Lowell Lang, who lateraled to oncoming quarterback Hoseman, who sped across the goal line for the game's first points. Over time, the play would become known as the "hook and ladder" (arguably erroneously since no one in the sports world can confirm the origin of the name; the more literal "hook and lateral" never caught on). As teams throughout the Black Hills would soon find out, Ferguson loved his laterals, though unlike the Swinging Gate, he could not claim to have invented them. Though the point-after attempt failed, the Bears intercepted a Golddiggers pass a couple of possessions later and were driving for another score when the final gun went off.

For only the third time since the rivalry kicked off in 1903, Deadwood had beaten Lead and the town was ready to soak it in.

Yuill led her Sunday column with a playful toast to the Bears. "Congratulations, Bears and Coach Ferguson. That was nice going Friday night. As one guy put it, 'All is forgiven.'" She even used her reporter sense to witness Deadwood's touchdown, popping out for a fifteen-minute break from attempting to meet her deadlines.

The following Thursday, Deadwood's athletic association held a banquet for the team's entire thirty-man roster at the town's Methodist church, where the Fergusons and Superintendent Berger were regular members. Berger played toastmaster and was joined by the president of the board of education, the high school principal, and some of the faculty. A local resident hosted another team celebration two weeks later. So, after Coach Ferguson completed his second football season with a 3–3 record, two things were clear: the Deadwood community loved its Bears and particularly loved beating Lead.

For the first time since 1940, the town also embraced its first peacetime holiday season. Downtown stores were brightly lit and bustled with activity. Christmas carols burst through loudspeakers, and on the hilltop above the town, the Christmas tree gleamed after four years of darkness.

The Fergusons followed Thanksgiving at Aunt Fannie's in Custer with a trip to Carthage, Missouri, over Christmas to visit Stewart's mom, Edith. Twenty years apart in age, Stewart and Edna were finding their way as a married couple in a town that was feeling more and more like home.

CHAPTER 33

NEW ADDITIONS

As the world started the new year, 1946, in peace, Stewart and Edna
fell into a daily rhythm in Deadwood. They lived in a simple apartment
on Main Street. The big news that Safeway had finally opened downtown (purchasing the Cope Marketeria and adding to its sister stores
in Belle Fourche and Rapid City) did not impact the couple's typical meal routine. As Edna recalled years later, she had never cooked
a meal until she moved to Deadwood. "Never lived in a place with a
kitchen," she said. "'Coach' would say, Don't experiment on me with
cooking." Most of their meals, as a result, were eaten outside or picked
up at Pop's Grab It N' Growl, a narrow, one-counter gem of a café run
by "Mom" and "Pop" Collins where burger patties cost ten cents and
weather forecasts, health tips, plant advice, and political discussions
were on the house. Fittingly, the Fergusons preferred the stew.

Stewart was a member of the Elks Club, which ran a variety of
fun family and adult events throughout the year, along with its strong
charitable work, especially in support of the troops. He enjoyed the
camaraderie, and he and Edna both loved the slot machines. Ferguson was finally free from being caught with a sheepish grin by his
watchful A & M lieutenant, J. P. Leveritt who was now an actual army
lieutenant and, through an improbable series of events, President
Harry S. Truman's physical trainer. The town was currently in the
tail end of a post-Prohibition gambling boom; a massive raid the following year, ordered by South Dakota's attorney general, aimed to
permanently shut down Deadwood's abundant gambling establish-
ments but ended up just pushing them underground.

Edna joined the Methodist church's Women's Society of Christian Service, which organized community events, supported missionary work around the world, and served as a warm monthly social gathering that helped members develop and grow friendships in town. She and Stewart were regulars at Sunday services, as the coach remained connected to the Methodist church. The couple also shared a love of reading, the art of debate (Edna led the high school's "Declam" department), and a keen sense of style; Edna, in particular, always presented herself well.

Stewart and Edna's more comfortable footing in their second full year in Deadwood may have led to a significant change from their prior year's summer schedule. On May 20 came the announcement that Stewart Ferguson had accepted a position teaching a social science class at Black Hills Teachers College (BHTC) in nearby Spearfish for the first summer session. Four days later came word that Ferguson was also Deadwood's new high school social science teacher, filling the recently vacated position.

BHTC, which Ferguson knew well from his Dakota Wesleyan days, was founded in 1883 as the Dakota Territorial Normal School. From its inception, the institution was committed to the "instruction of persons both male and female in the art of teaching" and offered a range of teacher education classes across age groups. After a dip in enrollment during the war, its numbers were swelling, aided by the benefits of the Servicemen's Readjustment Act of 1944, more commonly known as the G.I. Bill. The news in July that Coach Ferguson would also teach the second session planted the Fergusons home for the summer, giving them a chance to slow down and take in the some of the magic of the Black Hills.

The region's magic and mystique dated back to the arrival of the Arikara tribe around the year 1500. The Cheyenne, Crow, Kiowa, and Pawnee tribes followed, before the Lakotas arrived in the eighteenth century, driving out the others. The Lakotas regarded these lands, which they named *Paha Sapa* or "hills that are black," as sacred. A mix of huge green pines, wildflowers, and prairie grasses gave the hills a spectrum of colors; but the thick ponderosa pine forests, rounded hilltops, and deep valleys have always made the isolated mountain range appear black from a distance, and the name stuck.

The Black Hills' awing topography was formed ages ago by a combination of intense winds, erosion, and volcanic activity. Spearfish Canyon, with its tree covered slopes and springs and streams cascading into brilliant waterfalls, along with the town's special summer events to celebrate its role in the building of the West, made the area a go-to vacation spot, beyond the usual stopover at Mount Rushmore. The region even attracted the respected *National Geographic* magazine, which had recently sent an assistant editor and photographer to work on an upcoming all-encompassing South Dakota feature.

While the *National Geographic* team was travelling throughout the Black Hills, the Deadwood and Lead papers had their own pieces of major summer news. Presented as part of an overall plan to cut production costs, realize efficiencies in printing, and provide the northern Black Hills "with an improved modern daily newspaper," the owners of the *Deadwood Pioneer-Times* sold and consolidated the paper with Lead's *Daily Call*. Mechanical production and printing would be handled in the *Daily Call* plant, and paper enhancements were to include a fully leased United Press wire service along with a complete NEA feature service. Hence, one merged newspaper.

Not quite. A few days prior to the August 1 transfer in ownership, the publishers of the *Pioneer-Times* decided—smartly, the down gulch faithful thought—that the paper would keep on churning, with a "completely staffed news gathering and business office" led by Camille Yuill, and no decrease in payroll. In fact, on August 1, the big change for the community of Deadwood was having to wait until the afternoon to read the paper and adjust to the *Daily Call*'s more sober font. The two papers were almost identical, laid out with the exact same headlines and articles; the only real differences were local merchant ads and theater listings.

As part of its first day post-merger, the *Deadwood Pioneer-Times*, now a heftier paper including a separate sports page, was ready to start talking football and reached out to Stewart Ferguson and Lead's Joe Dunmire to get their initial thoughts on the upcoming 1946 season.

Without any semblance of coach speak, Ferguson anticipated a challenging season due to the graduation of six of his starters. After last year's improved 3–3 record, he had decided to run a six-week training program in the spring. Ronnie Burrington's uncle, a Deadwood native and former Ferguson player at Dakota Wesleyan, along with physical education instructor and assistant coach Melvin M. Minton, both recently returned from the services, helped Ferguson out.

Minton joined Deadwood High School in 1930, a few months after graduating with a degree in physical education from the University of Wisconsin. He was hired to run the boys' physical education department, including all the basketball "weight" teams, and settled in as an assistant coach for the athletic teams after handling head coaching responsibilities for the first few seasons. By the summer of 1942, the outdoorsman and ace league bowler was a steady presence within the school. That June, the army called. He and twenty-nine other men from Lawrence County were drafted, and after passing his physical examination, Minton was assigned to Camp Grant, Illinois, for basic training. Two more training stops followed before he was scheduled for overseas duty and moved to Camp Ord, California.

Before he shipped out, however, Minton was reassigned to Atlantic City, New Jersey, in November 1943 to serve as a physical trainer and athletic instructor at a reconditioning facility for wounded veterans. After several months, now-Sergeant Minton led thirty-five instructors, working with eight companies of men, as the noncommissioned officer (NCO) in charge of the physical reconditioning program at the army's beachfront England General and Convalescent hospital. The following October, the *Deadwood Pioneer-Times* ran an article on Minton's work and the sergeant explained the program, which ranged from simple hand exercises to intense sports activities: "We take wounded American soldiers and make them exercise not because they like to but because it's the surest and fastest way to recovery." After one more remedial exercises assignment at Long Island's Camp Upton, Minton was honorably discharged and returned to Deadwood to renew his job as physical education instructor and assistant coach.

At the training program, Coach Ferguson ran a mix of individual drills and modified scrimmages, and the paper highlighted a handful of new players, including Fred North, Norman Oestreich, and Cecil Stoner, for their development during the program. All three boys would soon make a strong impact on Ferguson.

Ferguson estimated that twenty players would show up at the first practice on September 2 but had already alerted his potential crew to begin physical preparation: "There is definitely a job to getting in shape for football, and I've told my boys to do a lot of running if possible to build up their legs and wind." Football practice, however, would have to wait. Four cases of polio had recently been reported in Lawrence County, with one in Lead, and as a precaution, health officials recommended a two-week delay to the start of the school year. For Coach Ferguson, polio scares would always bring back the frightening days of years past when the disease struck his youngest brother Paul.

When practice finally got under way, Coach Ferguson happily focused on the positives for his new squad. "The boys have made more progress in the four days we have been practicing than they did during the first two weeks last season," he told the paper. Ferguson added that though the passing had been "just ordinary," the boys were learning fast and, above all, showed a lot of enthusiasm.

Heading into the home opener against Custer, the Bears coach remained pleased, as he shared with the paper on the morning of the game. "The team has been strengthened considerably during the past few days of practice. Our line plunging is much better and our passing has been good." Ferguson planned to trigger the offense through his favored unbalanced line, and on defense hoped to handle Custer's offensive combination of speedy backs and a tricky passing attack heavy on the laterals—a mix that had him looking in the mirror. In a tight, surprisingly run-heavy game, the Bears and Wildcats battled to a 6–6 tie.

The rest of the 1946 season confirmed Ferguson's initial fears as Deadwood lost its remaining five games. Amid the defeats, which included three games in eight days due to a rescheduled rainout,

Ferguson tinkered with the lineup, uncovering a new receiving threat in freshman Fred North, and kept up the positive energy. After the season concluded with an 18–0 loss at Lead, Coach Ferguson's second winless football record in three years, he could be forgiven for thinking that even in this different kind of town, he may have worn out his welcome.

Yet three nights later, Ferguson, Minton, and all the players were honored with a team banquet in the welcoming surroundings of the Methodist church. Tables were decked out in school colors, with small "Bear" pennant candy cups spread out as party favors. When it was Coach Ferguson's turn to speak, he was full of gratitude and pride.

On behalf of Minton and all his players, he started with a sincere thanks to the school board and the faculty for their support throughout the season despite the poor results. Though the team had been hurt by its late start to practice, Ferguson praised his crew for their competitive play and their consistent spirit: "The season was a success from this standpoint. There is another football season coming next year and with the same cooperation which was shown this year, Deadwood can have a winning team and perhaps a championship."

Feeling at ease in his surroundings, the coach's passion for the game had never been greater, and a last-minute replacement as the featured speaker for Lead's football banquet offered him a chance to talk more football. He reflected on his prior coaching journey to capture the characteristics of a great player: "courage, sportsmanship, the desire to play the game under handicaps, and determination." He concluded with a love letter to the sport. "There never has and never will be another game like football. All of us like to win, but it is the truly great players and teams that play football for the game itself."

As Stewart Ferguson readily acknowledged in his unpublished memoirs, basketball did not arouse the same passion in him. Yet he tirelessly ran Deadwood's A and B teams (comparable to today's varsity and junior varsity squads) and kept up with the strategies of the evolving game. After a second straight 4–8 regular season, Ferguson's three-year record in basketball stood at 10–26. Spearfish had bounced his team out of the District 32 Class B tournament (for

South Dakota's smaller schools) the last two seasons, and they were set for a third consecutive match-up in 1947. The third time was the charm as the Bears turned back the Spartans 38–31. Then they beat Buffalo to win the district championship, and the suddenly streaking Bears knocked off Wall and White River the following weekend to win the regional eight tournament, sending them to the Class B state tournament for the first time since 1940, when they had won their second consecutive state title.

Coach Ferguson was invited to the weekly chamber of commerce luncheon and promised a good showing. Forty-eight students, about 30 percent of the high school, were excused from Friday classes and traveled across the state to Aberdeen to attend the first-round game against the Miller Rustlers, a state tourney team for the third year in a row that many considered one of the year's favorites. The students were about to see history.

Trailing by six after three quarters, with three minutes left the Bears finally pulled even on a put back from a missed free throw. The Rustlers pulled ahead again, but with two seconds left, Bears junior forward Jack Mee was fouled on a shot. After a timeout, Mee nailed both free throws, and the game went into overtime. After the allotted three minutes, thanks to two baskets by Bears junior Fred North, the game was tied at forty-three and the coaches agreed to play a "sudden death" second overtime: the first team to score wins. Miller won the tip off, but the Bears snared a rebound and senior guard Gene Palmer pulled in a long pass, stopped, and sank a game-winner.

Upon winning the longest South Dakota high school state tournament game on record (forty-three seconds into a second overtime), the Bears were back on the court a few hours later to face the defending Class B state champions, the Webster Bearcats. Through support from Deadwood's local businessmen, the game was broadcast over the telephone at Deadwood's high school gym. The Bears hung tight through two quarters but were overwhelmed in the second half in a 51–28 defeat. With stalwart center Larry Kilty now out with a fever of 102, the Bears lost a consolation heartbreaker on Saturday night,

35–34, before heading home on Sunday and attending the chamber of commerce's weekly luncheon as special guests.

The last couple of weeks had been an unexpectedly enjoyable run. As the school year wound down, good news continued for Stewart, Edna, and the entire community. For starters, a $250 salary increase (on top of an increased cost of living driven bump four months earlier) for all Deadwood faculty was approved for the following school year due to a state legislature announcement of a higher mill levy need "to operate and maintain" the public school in the year ahead. Business in Deadwood was also at a record high and substantially above prewar levels, and retail stores were expanding their hours. Plus, the townspeople were getting creative on new ways to have fun.

As promoted in the local papers, "Let the ladies have their flower gardens, bird's nests, and off-the-face animal kingdoms, men it's straws on top Saturday." Officially proclaimed by the mayors of Deadwood and Lead—in conjunction with local straw hat merchants—Saturday, May 23 was declared Straw Hat Day across the twin cities. Both papers preached everyone to "come to town Saturday and draw straws."

Further, heading into the Black Hills' rapidly expanding summer tourist season was May's highly anticipated *National Geographic* illustrated feature on the state: "South Dakota Keeps Its West Wild." In a six-column page-one spread, Camille Yuill celebrated the article and shared the local highlights. Well-traveled *National Geographic* staff member Frederick Simpich wrote of the town, "There's Deadwood: Prowling the night spots of this once gambling, gun-fighting gold camp brings a vicarious fling of sporting life to many." A full page black-and-white photo of Lead illustrated "the hill-top town . . . the richest gold hole in the Western Hemisphere."

In June, Stewart Ferguson was back for another summer teaching at BHTC, adding education to his social sciences classes. Still another summer addition was the biggest news yet. On July 25, Stewart and Edna welcomed the arrival of Stewart Alford Ferguson II. The once gallivanting ladies' man was now a husband and a father.

CHAPTER 34

PAPA BEAR

While the town of Deadwood feverishly prepared for its big annual blowout—the Days of '76, now in its twenty-third year, celebrating Deadwood's first pioneers with two parades and three daily rodeos—Stewart Ferguson Jr. entered the world, turning his dad into a full-fledged family man. But, as Coach Ferguson was taking in the joy of becoming a father, word soon came that his mother Edith had fallen gravely ill.

He immediately left for Carthage, Missouri, where he was born and where Edith had been living with her sister for the past seven years. She passed before Stewart arrived. Throughout her adult life, Edith had battled health issues and suffered several tragedies—losing her daughter, her first child, to a mysterious illness in her crib and her husband in 1917 to pneumonia. No matter the pain she carried with her, she raised four sons and found solace in a lifelong devotion to the Methodist church.

Stewart knew the disappointment his always serious-minded mother felt about her eldest son not pursuing a life behind the pulpit. Yet, he was full of gratitude for her inner strength that held the family together in the months and years after his father passed, enabling Stewart to eventually graduate and begin his wild journey.

Shortly after Ferguson returned from Carthage, the flag was raised for another Deadwood school year. Over the summer, the school building had been "completely renovated," highlighted by new desks and a new sidewalk in front; still, the building remained cramped, with limited lavatories, a small gym, and no lunchroom. A week before school, Coach Ferguson returned to the practice field with another inexperienced, undersized football squad. Only three regulars returning from the 1946 team likely meant more of a developmental season for his Bears.

The Bears bussed down for another opener against Custer and fell short in an 18–13 final. Possibly invigorated by quarterback and team captain Freddie North leading the Bears in an organized pregame set of calisthenics (decked out in new, flashy, Ferguson-issued uniforms, striped along the shoulder), the pass-happy Bears bounced back for a surprising 33–12 triumph over Spearfish. Over the next few weeks, however, a mix of injuries, illnesses, and matchups with the top three conference teams led to three straight losses.

By the eve of the annual "game of the year" against Lead, Ferguson and assistant coach Minton scrambled to prep a completely reworked line, while the Deadwood maintenance staff scrambled to ready its home field during some stormy late October weather. Like its twin city rival, Lead also came into the game with an inexperienced group, featuring three returning lettermen, but unlike Deadwood, the Golddiggers had played tight games against the top conference teams.

As a brutally honest Coach Ferguson put it, "We're going to have to play our best ball to win." And as the *Deadwood Pioneer-Times* noted in its game recap, they did just that: "Through mud, rain, sleet, and snow, a rejuvenated Deadwood Bear crew Friday night on its home ground, passed and ran over and through a favored Lead team 18–7." A large crowd shrugged off the nasty conditions, and as often would occur in Deadwood versus Lead football, a star was born. Junior halfback Norman Oestreich had himself a game. After hauling in a first quarter pass through a downpour and racing about fifty yards to set up Deadwood's first score, Oestreich took off in the fourth quarter for a run around the right end and iced the game with a sixty-yard touchdown. Overall, Deadwood somehow completed ten of eighteen passes, with a dose of Ferguson's trademark laterals, and the coach dialed up a defense featuring five down linemen to crowd the line of scrimmage and bottle up Lead's power running game.

Afterwards, the paper caught up with the coach and asked for a reaction. "Boy, I sure am tickled," responded Ferguson, "Oh boy, I sure am." Though spirit and sportsmanship was the foundation of Coach ("Gee Gosh") Ferguson football—and would remain a higher priority than results on the scoreboard—he was not anti-winning. Wandering Weevils antics aside, he was a shrewd strategist that relentlessly bunkered down in his school office designing plays and crafting new formations. Overall, though, the outcome of winning games ran a clear second to his fun-first brand of play.

The team wrapped up the 1947 season with a banquet at the somewhat upscale Rocky Cove Supper Club, just outside of town, and a giddy Coach Ferguson called it the "best banquet we've had since I've been here." Two weeks later, Stewart and Edna Ferguson celebrated the baptism of Stewart Jr. at the Methodist church. Ferguson was riding high and even got some needed coaching relief when Coach Minton took on the B squad for the coming basketball season. There was more: his prior football fame was once again featured news.

Norman Thomas, head of the BHTC social sciences department and a summer instructor colleague of Ferguson, caught wind of a book, *Football Madness,* focusing on the escapades of the Wandering Weevils and its ringmaster, that Ferguson wrote and expected to publish in the spring. In a January article picked up by the heavily circulated *Sioux Falls Argus-Leader* and *Rapid City Journal*, along with Coach Ferguson's hometown newspaper, the *Mitchell Daily Republic*, Thomas touched on Ferguson's earlier days coaching high school in Louisiana and his return to coach at his alma mater, Dakota Wesleyan before a leisurely walk-through—a healthy portion of it true—of his mad, football-for-fun Wandering Weevils days. While it is uncertain how the article came about and to what degree Ferguson and Thomas may have been in cahoots, Ferguson was undoubtedly becoming a fixture in the community.

In the spring, Coach Ferguson continued to build a connection with his boys. As part of Deadwood's citywide "Paint-up, Clean-up, Fix-up Campaign," Ferguson and Minton led twenty of their players in a complete playground cleanup. There was another round of

off-season football practice, with a pronounced increase in partici-
pation from the prior year. And especially revealing was Ferguson's
further guidance in support of track.

Due to a lack of sufficient indoor facilities, coupled with typically
nasty spring weather that impeded practice conditions at the rodeo
grounds, Deadwood track consistently struggled to develop athletes
and construct a competitive team. Still, harkening back to his days as
a Louisiana high school track coach, Ferguson enjoyed the sport and
kept a look out for kids he could offer some support.

The prior year, he had driven a senior across the state to Sioux
Falls so that the boy could compete in the state finals after winning
regionals in the broad jump. This season, a scrawny senior named
Sheldon Jacobs was ready to run. A clarinet player for the high school
band and a member of glee club and chorus, Jacobs was better known
as a musician than an athlete. He did play in the high school intramural basketball league known then as "weight" clubs, however, and
made "one magnificent basket" during his four-year career. As a senior, Jacobs thought he was finally big enough to go out for football.

He didn't make the team but practiced daily and made an impression on Ferguson as a dutiful manager throughout the season—plus,
his coach, now universally known as "Fergie" across the Deadwood
community, naturally gravitated to fellow little guys. Towards the
end of the season, Ferguson called his number and sent him in. A
lifetime later, a laughing Jacobs still remembered the day: "He put
me in for one or two plays. It was just an act of kindness you know so
I could say, 'Yeah, I played football for Deadwood.'"

In the spring, Jacobs showed up for track and received a critical lift from Ferguson. "The thing that sticks in my mind was a very
important thing in my life," recalled Jacobs. "He taught me how to
'psych up.' . . . Basically, it's mental conditioning. Part of it is convincing yourself you can win. And I learned that, and I practiced it,
and in some respects it [has] been with me my entire life."

Jacobs ran the 100- and 220-yard dashes, and with Ferguson's
positive presence at his side, qualified for the 1948 state meet with a
first in the 220 and a second in the 100. He went on to place fourth in

both events in the state championships at Rapid City, scoring all of Deadwood's points and giving the school its best results since 1931.

By the end of August, having survived his first full summer as a dad, Coach Ferguson comically bemoaned after his team's first practice that his crew was "too few and too little." This year, however, the wily coach may have stretched the truth to remove any pressure for the coming season. Ferguson did have seven returning lettermen, four of whom had seen regular action. In particular, husky sophomore Denny Dyvig was back to anchor a more experienced line and veteran Norman Oestreich was becoming a running and receiving force in the backfield.

A bus trip to Wyoming's Gillette Camels—a nonconference, rural opponent with heftier kids—served as a new start to the season, and Ferguson planned to use all twenty-two of his travelling Bears in different combinations to start learning about his new team. What he learned most in a solid 12–0 win was that Denny Dyvig was also a determined fullback. A 19–7 home win against Custer followed in which Norman Oestreich dazzled with three first half scores, two on shifty runs and the other when he grabbed a sideline lateral after a pass and scampered eighteen yards for the touchdown.

Heading into a trip to Spearfish, Ferguson was looking to win three games in a row for the first time in his five-year Deadwood career. He and line coach Minton, however, scrambled to replace their two starting tackles and center who were out with a mix of injuries and illnesses. Nevertheless, the stopgap line dominated on both sides of the ball, while Oestreich and Dyvig consistently pounded out yards on the ground in an unexpectedly one sided 13–0 triumph. Ferguson even threw in a fake handoff-turned-quarterback sneak for some touchdown trickery. Coach Ferguson's undefeated Deadwood Bears were in unchartered territory; suddenly, the following week's battle against Rapid City was a big game.

The *Deadwood Pioneer-Times*, now with a mostly daily sports column by circulation manager Jack Cannon dubbed "The Black Hills Sports Scene," was talking Bears—on a Tuesday. After four straight losses to Rapid by a combined 131 to 20, Coach Ferguson tried something new at Monday's practice. To familiarize his Bears with Rapid's deceptive, run-heavy T-formation, Ferguson asked several former Bears who had played the T for their respective college teams to run plays against his boys.

Coming into the game, the undefeated Rapid City Cobblers were by far the class of the conference, spearheaded by a fast and powerful backfield and a defense that had not yet yielded any points. Ferguson's Bears held the Cobblers scoreless through the first half, before coming undone in the second half with three interceptions that each led to a Rapid City touchdown. The final was 26–0, but the net yardage was close, 153 to 129, and the Bears had two more first downs. They competed well against the Cobblers, who went on to sweep their remaining opponents and win the conference, but the Bears would need to quickly turn the page with last year's conference champs, the Sturgis Scoopers, on deck.

Although Sturgis was uncharacteristically weak after losing the majority of their 1947 starters, Coach Ferguson was 0–4 against them and two more starters in his front wall were out, one with a broken finger and the other academically ineligible. In many ways, this played right into Ferguson's hands.

A rare Thursday night home game cost Ferguson a precious day of preparation, but by the opening whistle he had his chess pieces ready to move around the board. He backfilled reserve backs into the line and moved Alvin Oestreich, Norman's younger brother, out of his guard spot and into quarterback. The Bears shifted positions seamlessly and executed a more run-heavy game plan, shutting out Sturgis 28–0. The elder Oestreich paved the way with another two scores, one receiving and one on the ground, and Ferguson was especially impressed with his "kids," as he tenderly called the Bear reserves.

One of those former "kids" that always stood out was starting senior end Maurice Etem. During the prior season, the imposing Etem began as a second-string center but when the team was hit with a rash of colds, he decided to start catching passes during practice sessions. Etem's work ethic impressed his coach and he was rewarded with some halfback reps during the latter stretch of the season. In the current school year, Etem was also the president of the senior class, as he amusingly recalled years later. "Well, I was kind of put up to it. My buddies said, 'let's get a guy for President.' We all agreed on it. So they decided on me!"

For the upcoming homecoming contest against Belle Fourche, Coach Ferguson surprised Etem by naming him team captain for the game. Years later, a pensive Etem fondly reminisced about his old coach: "I always thought of Fergie as one of the best teachers. . . . It was the way he explained things. He would go into details, more than you'd ever ask. And that's why we'd listen. . . . He would speak before and after [practice]. He would give us his philosophy, what we should be thinking."

Heading into the game against a tough and favored Broncs squad, Ferguson was thinking his team had practiced poorly all week, hurt by some of them missing time due to homecoming responsibilities. What played out was an extremely physical battle that was still score-less with less than two minutes left. On a fourth-and-nine play, junior quarterback Cecil Stoner faded back from the Broncs forty-five-yard line and hit half back Pete Becker, who cut through defenders at the ten and went in for the deciding score. With the Bears' fifth win, Coach Ferguson had just reached the total number of victories in his first four Deadwood seasons and the team had a chance to equal the school's best-ever record. They just had to beat Lead, which had gone through two significant changes over the last year.

First was the prior summer's announcement that Lead head coach Joe Dunmire—after twenty years leading athletics for the high school—was taking over as Homestake Mining Company's director of recreational programming. Bob Tegt joined Lead as head coach for the current season after longtime assistant Doug Bell handled the reins during the prior year.

There was also the welcomed news that Lead's Mountaintop football field had undergone a complete renovation, costing $30,000 (over $357,000 in today's dollars), courtesy of Homestake. The rock and gravel playing surface was replaced with sod accompanied by a new underground water system. The field was repositioned to run across the baseball outfield rather than the infield dirt, and space was provided for both permanent and temporary bleachers. Future plans called for the purchase of floodlights so that Lead could join most of the other cities of the state with night football.

As for game prep, Ferguson opted for a week of light workouts with limited tackling; the Bears had a number of recent injuries and were coming out of the particularly physical game against the Broncs. Lead also had some key injuries throughout the season, which contributed to a lackluster 1–3–1 overall record with two of its losses out of conference. Expecting the Bears to air it out, Coach Tegt focused on pass defense in his practices leading up the game. He did not have to remind his crew that Lead had lost two of the last three games to Ferguson's Bears. The prospect of two straight losses was inconceivable.

Big brother could rest easy. Although the Golddiggers didn't score until converting on a long drive to open the third quarter, they controlled the play, outgaining the Bears 234–76 and holding them to only two first downs. Yet, the defeat could not diminish the progress made on the field—Ferguson's first winning season with the Bears. A 5–2 overall record and third place in the Black Hills conference was something to build on, starting an unprecedented streak for the small school.

By the time May's school award ceremony came around, Ferguson had logged enough time to coach a few players for their entire Deadwood High School career. He was especially proud to congratulate senior Norman Oestreich, who capped a wonderful four years as the only student to letter in the trifecta of football, basketball, and track. After the school year, the coach smoothly fell into his summer routine of BHTC instructor and doting dad for two-year-old Stewart Jr. As summer wound down, Ferguson and his Bears hit the practice field for a fresh season. Just days later, tragedy struck the family of Deadwood.

CHAPTER 35

WINNING, ACTUALLY

The August 30 *Deadwood Pioneer-Times* led with the news of Norman Oestreich's fatal accident early that morning while at work for the Black Hills Power and Light Company. Norman had recently started full-time at the company, where his dad was a general construction superintendent, after having worked summers there during high school. Grouped with a crew on Hill City's Main Street, about forty miles south of Deadwood, Norman was on a thirty-foot pole stringing a power line when a semi-trailer caught part of the wire, causing the accident. A service was held a few days later in the St. Ambrose Catholic Church, and many of Norman's former teammates led the escort for his interment in Deadwood's Mount Moriah cemetery.

Conversations with Coach Ferguson helped Norman's younger brother, Alvin, better known as Al and now a senior and starter in the Bears backfield, get through this awful time. They helped Ferguson, too. A couple of years later while Al, who joined the U.S. Navy following graduation, was docked in Pearl Harbor on his return from a tour of duty in Japan and Korea, he received and immediately responded to a letter from his coach. Ferguson wanted to thank Al for cheering him up when Norm died, while also catching him up on Bears football. As Al wrote, the mutual feelings came flooding back:

> I was ready to quit football that day he died but after I had come up [to the house] and talked to you, it was just like Norm urging me on. . . . I said to myself, 'If it would have been me, what would I want him to do? The answer I got was, if it meant

football or going around moping all the time then I would much rather have him play football and keep my spirit alive rather than let it go with the rest of me.' That's what I did coach, but I haven't let up missing Norm for one minute. I don't think there are many athletes that can say their coach has done as much for them as you have for me. I don't know how I can ever thank you for it. . . . I can tell my troubles and things to you just as freely as if I were talking to Norm. . . . I just can't put into words the gratitude and thanks I owe you coach.

As the 1949 Deadwood football season unfolded and the team fought through its deep loss, Norman Oestreich's presence could be constantly felt through his younger brother. At Deadwood's Amusement Park, Al contributed to another opening nonconference win against Gillette with a seventeen-yard scoring scamper and was back in the thick of things in a 19–0 win in Custer the following Friday. He scored twice—once on a ten-yard cutback run and again after racing twenty-two yards on a double lateral—and set up Deadwood's third and final touchdown with an interception in Custer territory. The younger Oestreich picked off another pass the following week in a 26–7 home victory over Spearfish. Bear Day was up next and Coach Ferguson tabbed Al as team captain for the homecoming contest against Sturgis.

So far, the 1949 results had mirrored the prior season: three straight wins against Gillette, Custer, and Spearfish. Heading into the Sturgis game, another senior had cemented himself in Ferguson's lineup, one the coach had had a feeling about before they even met.

Years later Cecil Stoner vividly remembered the moment. "I was in the eighth grade and the bell rung. We were at lunch time and went back into class, and I had a note that Coach Stewart Ferguson wanted me to come down to his office, to see him after school." Stoner had just played his usual post lunch round of touch football and had no idea what the high school football coach wanted with him, but he went down to see him at the end of the day. "'You stole the football really well,' he said. And I says, 'Well, I'm just playing touch football.'" The coach wasn't done. "'No, the way you throw the ball, you stay here through high school, you'll be my quarterback.' And I thought that's a pretty big thing for a coach to say to an eighth grader, but it's something that you never forget."

By junior year—after already becoming the first freshman to letter in football under Ferguson—Cecil had indeed become the lead quarterback and signal caller. Now, Cecil and his teammates were trying to remain undefeated and beat Sturgis for a second straight year. It was a wet, snowy night, but Coach Ferguson sensed his team, and the large homecoming crowd, was ready for some fun. In the first quarter, up 7–0 after forcing and capitalizing on a Sturgis fumble near its own goal line, the Bears started a new possession with junior fullback Denny Dyvig replacing Cecil Stoner at quarterback. In his "Black Hills Sports Scene" column, Jack Cannon depicted what happened next:

> The most disgusted man we have seen in a long while was
> Coach Buell Woodle of the Sturgis Scoopers when just before
> the half . . . the Bears pulled a sleeper play right under the nose
> of the Scooper coaching staff and the bench. With the ball
> approximately at midfield, Cecil Stoner, Deadwood quarter-
> back, came close to the sidelines right in front of the Scooper
> bench. The members of the Scooper team who were not in the
> game and the Scoopers coaches and supporters immediately
> began to call to the Sturgis halfback in the secondary to watch
> for the sleeper play. Apparently, the halfback thought they were
> cheering him because he did not pay any attention to the shouts
> which were so loud they were picked up by the radio mike and
> heard by the listeners.

The Dyvig to Stoner sleeper—with Stoner finally downed at the Scoopers twelve-yard line—led to a second score, but Ferguson was hardly finished unleashing the tricks in this one. Dyvig and Stoner somehow converted another sleeper, Al Oestreich galloped for twenty-five yards from a kick formation (and was stopped on a later attempt), and the fourth-quarter capper was a new wrinkle on one of the coach's ol' goodies, the Swinging Gate. Stoner, back behind center, fired a pass to Oestreich for a fifteen-yard completion that set up a first down at the Scooper two-yard line. On the next play, Deadwood smoothly shifted its entire line to the right, leaving center Norm Lee matched up on the left end. Rather than the usual run behind the unbalanced line, Stoner took the ball from Lee and then passed it to him for Deadwood's third score, and an insurmountable 21–7 cushion.

Ferguson's litany of tricks that night—and in future Sturgis battles—left some painful scars with the Scoopers coach, Buell Woodle. Later, as head football coach at Deadwood, Stoner remembered coming across Woodle one time when the conversation turned to Ferguson. "I'll never forget," said Stoner. "He said, 'Cecil, I hated that guy.'"

The resounding win against Sturgis had the team rolling, but any notion that this emotional Bears season could lead to a championship one was dashed the following week. In front of Belle Fourche's homecoming crowd, the Broncs' fleet halfback Don Freemole took the opening kickoff ninety-one yards for a touchdown. Though the Bears kept pace in yardage, they never quite bounced back from the early hole and fell 26–0. Ferguson and his Bears still had a chance, however, to post their best season to date, and even better, it was Lead week.

Wintry weather challenged practice sessions for both squads, and the Deadwood city crews deployed a snow loader and trucks to remove the heaviest amounts of snow on the Amusement Park field as Friday night's game approached. Like the previous year, Lead came in with just one win, but Lead's *Goldenlobe* yearbook frankly stated the importance of the annual rivalry game: "The defeat of the Deadwood Bears makes any season a good one."

On a partially snow-covered playing surface, the Deadwood crews marked the field with coal dust to help the officials and fans delineate the yard markers and sidelines. The game was tight, and the snowy field froze on a cold, windy Friday night. Halfway into the last quarter, the Bears clung to a 7–6 lead. Suddenly, Lead halfback and co-captain Owen Plymell broke loose on an end around run and headed down the right sideline, coal dust mostly worn off and flanked with fans. Deadwood players pursued but stopped efforts to tackle Plymell when they heard a whistle, signaling that the Diggers back was out of bounds and they thought, the end of the play. Plymell smartly kept running; he went all the way for the go ahead and, ultimately, winning score.

After the game, Ferguson told the paper that one of the referees, Spearfish athletic director Joe Rygg, said he wasn't sure Plymell went out of bounds, so he couldn't call the play back to a specific spot. Inadvertent whistle or not, Ferguson—as had become his norm years earlier—did not contest the controversial play. The Bears had their chances, including a final possession quickly thwarted by an interception; they fell short and that was that.

The team was feted the following week with a ravioli dinner. About a month later, they received a much-needed lift. The Norman Oestreich Memorial Award Trophy was presented to the school by George Katchuba, a loyal Deadwood school supporter, conference athletic official, and overall sportsman. Honoring Norman's memory, the members of Deadwood's "D" Club (the group of male lettermen) would annually select the outstanding senior athlete of the high school based on "athletic ability, team play, and good fellowship" and inscribe his name on the trophy. A warm photo highlighted in the paper captured Al Oestreich and the other twenty-five members of the current lettermen club huddled around the new trophy.

A few months later, after the end of basketball season, the Deadwood School Board continued the celebration, hosting a special sports evening. The Rocky Cove Supper Club was the setting for a banquet honoring Deadwood's football and basketball teams, and the Bears did their namesake proud, each putting away a large T-bone steak, several servings of french fries, rolls, salad, milk, and topped it all off with ice cream. Local reporter Jack Cannon was an appreciative guest, recording all the festivities and key highlights.

For Cecil Stoner, it was the crown to an acclaimed high school sports career. He received his fourth letter in football, third in basketball, and was the first person to have his name inscribed on the Norman Oestreich Memorial Award Trophy. Also enjoying the evening was assistant coach Melvin M. Minton, who had grown into Ferguson's vital partner and good friend.

Fergie and Minton—though opposites in many ways—built a strong bond. Physically, the two of them were quite the contrast: Ferguson a scrawny five foot seven and Minton a strapping six feet. On the practice field, the two Deadwood mentors developed a coaching rhythm. The soft voiced, genial Ferguson focused on overall strategy, formations, and how to run specific plays, while the louder, more straitlaced but friendly Minton hammered home correct techniques and kept players in line. Cecil Stoner recalled that Minton was "a real hard worker" who "absolutely did not like any horseplay." Maurice Etem remembered him as "kind of a hard guy . . . but he was a good guy. . . . Everybody liked [him]."

Also connecting Ferguson and Minton was their mutual passion for physical education. Even better, Minton knew how to throw in the fun. As boys' director of the school's physical education department, he stressed developing a "normal and healthy" individual, and that meant a diverse program that also developed grace and coordination. Minton would show up one day with a record player for a group dancing lesson and arrive the next time rod in hand to teach fly fishing.

In his words at the spring banquet, Ferguson flipped the script from his regular crowing about losses during his Wandering Weevil days. Now, he was puffing his chest on how a good season next year could establish the best three-year record in Bears history. He closed by asking the boys to "play harder, train harder, and to sacrifice something that would make them better athletes." Often described as a master motivator, Ferguson seemed to have a feeling about the kids coming up.

But before he geared up for a new season, Ferguson expanded his summer teaching repertoire. He took a break from history and taught courses in educational psychology and trends in modern education. Change was also on tap at home as Stewart and Edna, after a few years of downtown apartment living, had moved into a modest house directly up the hill from the Methodist church. The best part was a backyard where Stewart and his three-year-old son—now nicknamed Freddie after 1948 Deadwood High School graduate Fred North—had ample space to play.

As football practice resumed, optimism reigned about Ferguson's Bears, fueled by eleven returning lettermen (though just three starters) and the energy and skill the team displayed early on. A more intensive B squad football program in both Deadwood and Lead, marked by a slate of scheduled games that had taken shape over the last couple of years, also helped. In the now regular nonconference opener against Gillette, the Bears combined a "sparky running attack and a clicking passing offense" for a dominant 28–7 victory. The game also featured a glimpse of speedy freshman halfback Billy Jones, who "showed promise of making good in the Deadwood backfield," according to columnist Jack Cannon.

Over the next three weeks, Ferguson's Bears kept finding ways to win. In a 19–0 home shutout over Custer, Jones was officially indoctrinated to Ferguson's featured sleeper play when senior fullback Denny Dyvig hit the all-alone freshman in stride along the left sideline; Jones went untouched for a thirty-four-yard score. The Bears struggled for much of the following week's game at Spearfish as the Spartans controlled the line of scrimmage behind an effective running attack. But Dyvig and Jones teamed up again to awaken the Bears on two huge plays. The first was another Dyvig to Jones sleeper strike that covered seventy-three yards with Jones grabbing the ball around midfield and outrunning defenders the rest of the way. Later in the first half, Dyvig was bottled up on a short plunge into the line, but craftily lateraled to Jones, who broke free from the pile and sprinted eighty yards for his second touchdown in a 19–12 win.

After a week off, Ferguson, who couldn't help getting inside the head of Sturgis coach Buell Woodle, took his play-calling mind games to a new level in front of the Scoopers' homecoming crowd. Ferguson put his aerial game on ice, used the sleeper play as a decoy, and stuck to a run-heavy game plan with Denny Dyvig leading the way. Behind a strong push from the Deadwood line, Dyvig carried twenty-one times for 117 yards and two touchdowns. The Bears scored in every quarter, building a 26–0 lead before two late Sturgis scores against several of Ferguson's reserves.

Like the prior season against the same schools, the Bears started 4–0 and were tied with the undefeated, defending two-time conference champ Rapid City Cobblers for first place in the Black Hills Conference standings. Once again, the Belle Fourche Broncs stood in their way. The Broncs entered Deadwood's Bear Day game with only one loss, to the Cobblers. The day before the game, Ferguson was concerned about his line; he reported to the paper that one guard was likely out due to injured ribs from the Sturgis game and that the other guard, Bob Hudson, a defensive star against Sturgis, would also miss the game due to injuring his knee and wrist in a playground accident earlier in the week. Ferguson's fears proved well founded. While his Bears fought hard and stayed even in the first half with the bigger and stronger Broncs—both in yardage and on the scoreboard—they were eventually whipped in the trenches and held scoreless after halftime. The Broncs ended with a commanding 343 yards on the ground in a 27–13 final.

His Bears were pounded, but Ferguson had to quickly regroup and prepare for Lead. The one game that both teams were desperate to win, no matter the standings, had only grown in importance since Ferguson's arrival in Deadwood. Further, the Bears had lost two straight to Lead. This year, it was the Golddiggers' turn to host on the Mountaintop. The teams locked into a third consecutive tight, low-scoring battle. Freshman Billy Jones—echoing some of the magic on display earlier in the season—formally introduced himself into the rivalry with two plays that made the difference.

With the Bears trailing 7–0 in the second quarter, an about-to-go-down Denny Dyvig tossed a lateral to Jones, who spun away from a cluster of Golddiggers and sprinted sixty-three yards for a touchdown. Dyvig's plunge for the tying point was ruled just short, and the Bears remained behind 7–6 as the game entered the fourth quarter. On the Bears' next possession, Jones went in motion to the right from his own thirty-nine-yard line and took off down the sideline, flying past the Golddiggers secondary. Dyvig stepped back and heaved a pass that Jones snared and ran another thirty yards to put the Bears out front. After the teams traded punts, the Deadwood line dropped Lead's halfback and co-captain Rod Meader for two losses on attempted passes, and Billy Jones had the final say, deflecting another pass as Deadwood took over before time ran out.

Ferguson and his Bears were literally and figuratively back on top of the mountain, but for the first time since 1928, the Bears actually had another game to play, out of conference, against the Tigers of Lusk, Wyoming. Understandably, the week's practices felt anticlimactic. While Ferguson tweaked lineups to stop Lusk's power single-wing attack, he sensed a letdown coming. In a sluggish game at Deadwood's Amusement Park—slowed by turnovers and penalties—Denny Dyvig's first quarter rush from inside the one and leap over the line for the point after was just enough to give the Bears a 7–6 win and their greatest season in school history to date.

After the Lead game, Jack Cannon congratulated the Bears on their "best conference season in the history of the school." With a research assist from Coach Ferguson, Cannon reported that the year's 4–1 Black Hills conference record (6–1 overall) bettered the previous school best of one loss and one tie. Some former Bear players wrote to the paper and disputed the claim, however, arguing that during the season in question, 1938, the Bears played tougher overall competition, including a win over Rapid City. But those players conveniently forgot to mention their season-ending loss to Lead.

By the annual football banquet a week later, the best team ever debate had passed, and the Deadwood boys—sixty in all with both the A and B teams in attendance—focused on their healthy quantities of fried chicken and french fries. It was a festive night, and one when Coach Ferguson had something more he wanted to say. In the public setting, Ferguson praised Minton's work—stating that he was far from an assistant; he was a co-coach. It may not have seemed like much, but Fergie understood he had a real partner in Minton, and he wanted the close-knit Deadwood community to know it.

CHAPTER 36

CUE THE CORN PALACE

Ferguson and his Bears followed up the school's (arguably) best football season in history with a satisfying one on the hardwood. In January, they hosted a nonconference benefit game against the Provo Rattlers, a team about a hundred miles due south, to raise money for the West River Children's Hospital and Polio Center in Hot Springs. The funds were critical since the disease was spreading throughout South Dakota and would peak the following year in a national epidemic. Dr. Jonas Salk's breakthrough polio vaccine was still a few years away.

In league play, the Bears beat Lead in both games, thrilled their fans in a close loss to conference champ Sturgis, and after a 10–5 regular season, finally fell to Spearfish in the district final. Though Ferguson's team finished a game short of the Class B state basketball tournament, the folks in Deadwood soon showed off their true community spirit.

The Sturgis Scoopers went on to win the state's Class A basketball championship for the second time, and the town of Deadwood wanted to toast their Black Hills cohorts. Organized by the chamber of commerce, almost one hundred people packed the Franklin Hotel's main dining room to celebrate the Scoopers. Coach Woodle of Sturgis graciously thanked the Deadwood community for the honor and congratulated Coach Ferguson and the Bears on their strong season—this was not an evening for Woodle to "hate that guy." Ferguson followed with warm praise, calling this Sturgis team the best in the state in "some time."

In mid-August, with Ferguson turning the attention back to his Bears, the *Deadwood Pioneer-Times* previewed the start of football practice with the headline, "Outstanding Material Will Greet Deadwood Coach Stewart Ferguson." The Bears candidates drew their equipment on August 23 and launched into training drills the following day, the earliest allowed across the state due to enhanced safety rules of the South Dakota High School Athletic Association. After their second workout, Coach Ferguson lent some credence to the paper's initial take. "Our prospects are just a little better than fair," he said.

It didn't take long, however, for Ferguson to throw some cold water on his unusual preseason praise. After the final practice before travelling for the team's first game at Gillette, he stated, "You can say that both Mr. Minton and I were very disappointed at the way the team looked." He added that only about fifteen Deadwood players were "big"—the rest of team were young underclassmen, making it almost impossible to run scrimmages between two teams picked from the squad. The audacious football scientist finished in signature deadpan form: "All of our experimenting will have to be done right on the playing field."

Ferguson did not have to delve deep into his gridiron lab in a win over Gillette, but he and Coach Minton did get into some chalkboard sketching—designing and discussing X's and O's—upon their return as special guests at a meeting of the Deadwood Jaycees, a local junior chamber of commerce chapter, with an "action" mandate "for the betterment of the community." Though the victories continued, it was a bumpy couple of weeks until a surprisingly easy 26–0 win over Hot Springs, ignited by another set of brothers. Billy Jones shared the backfield with his older brother Delbert, who ran for two scores on the day. But before turning to a tough matchup against also un-beaten Belle Fourche, Ferguson's new hobby almost cost him.

Ferguson had taken on stone fronting (or facing, as it is better known today). Years later an amused Edna recalled her husband's process. "He got a book, studied it, collected stones, wheeled them back . . . and mounted [the stones] on chicken wire." Amazing, Edna thought, since he couldn't even drive a nail. The operation was hardly foolproof. The weekend after the Hot Springs game, the self-taught mason slipped off his garage roof and landed on the concrete pavement, luckily suffering nothing worse than some injured ribs. On to a home game against the Broncs, who had spanked an undefeated Bears team the prior season.

A downpour just before the game encased the field in mud; the Bears slogged through to a 7–0 win, keeping Deadwood alive for its first ever Black Hills conference championship. In a scheduling quirk, the win set up a homecoming matchup against also undefeated Lead. The odd scheduling stemmed from the prior fall, when Rapid City High School and the conference mutually decided to release Rapid from the Black Hills football conference and allow it to schedule games against larger schools in South Dakota and neighboring states.

The Golddiggers' new head coach, Wendell Handley, was quite familiar throughout the conference as he had spent the last five years leading the Hot Springs Bison. Both coaches spewed typical pregame gloom, citing concerns that Thursday's poor weather—a messy rain and snow mix—could hurt their attacks. Ferguson also worried that several colds could impact the condition of his players. In front of another packed crowd for the two rivals, Lead controlled the play, but the game was scoreless until a sudden sixty-three-yard burst around right end from Lead's multisport star Jim Christensen in the third quarter. The Bears deflected the extra point pass attempt, but a bit later Billy Jones was wrapped up behind Deadwood's goal line for a safety. They didn't threaten again in the 8–0 loss to the eventual conference champion Golddiggers.

It was appropriate that the defeat against Lead was the last game played for the 1951 Bears; the scheduled home game against Sturgis two weeks later was canceled due to dangerous subzero weather and icy winds.

Even if Ferguson had a tinge of regret after another near miss at Deadwood's first conference title in football, at the hands of Lead no less, it didn't matter. He still needed to change gears and jump into basketball. It was one of Deadwood's tallest teams in years, but with half the lettermen gone, Ferguson downplayed their prospects for the season, saying the Bears "look just about ordinary." A 5–9 conference record was marked by working in lots of younger talent, along with filling in for the late January loss of starting guard Irwin Burtzlaff to an ankle injury. Deadwood also found itself competing in South Dakota's Class A division for the first time in school history.

The prior April, the state's high school athletic association announced a new "practical arrangement" for basketball, increasing the number of A schools from sixteen to thirty-two and redistricting into eight regions as appropriate. Based on the enrollment data, Deadwood just made the A cutoff and joined Lead, Belle Fourche, and Spearfish in one of the two new Black Hills regions for basketball. Lead hosted the new four-team section eight Class A tourney and was the clear favorite to advance.

Deadwood opened with a twenty-point win over Belle Fourche, helped in part by the Broncs playing without their starting center, Earl Norlin. Earlier in the evening, Spearfish held on to upset Lead 39–38, setting up a finals matchup with Deadwood. Ferguson's Bears broke open a close game in the third quarter, beating the Spartans 54–45. And just like that, the Deadwood Bears would represent the northern Black Hills as the smallest South Dakota school in the state's Class A basketball tournament. Sturgis, section seven winner and defending state champs, joined Deadwood as the other Black Hills representative. Deadwood's latest enrollment figure, in fact, would have reclassified it as a B school. Size aside, the locale for this year's state tourney was almost too good to be true for Ferguson: it would be played in Mitchell. Rather than a side visit to exercise past personal demons, however, this trip was solely about his Bears.

After a winning weekend, Camille Yuill, in her "Backlog" column, captured the essence of Ferguson and his Bear teams:

> The unpredictable Deadwood Bears, and their coach, Stewart Ferguson, have done it again. You just never know what these boys will pull out of the hat. We are mighty proud they are going to the state tournament and like everyone else, we will be rooting for them to bring home the title. But win or lose, we are sure

they will continue the same sportsmanship they have shown at home and play the game for the fun that is in it.

After a chamber of commerce breakfast at which Bears supporters turned out to wish them success, the team left for Mitchell. In his Wednesday "Black Hills Sports Scene" piece, Marv Kebschull, who had taken over as the local papers' sports editor, set the scene: "Next stop, Mitchell. Yup, that's where the Deadwood Bears will hold forth this weekend. It's no sightseeing tour—It's the state Class A basketball tournament."

Even Ferguson, the former traveling man, would have to agree, though maybe it was lucky they were on a tight schedule to prevent any possible detours along the way. The opponent was the Brookings Bobcats, the Eastern South Dakota Conference champs who went 17–1 during the regular season before dominating in sectionals. Prior to departing, Coach Ferguson said his team had been working hard to score an upset and to maintain the attitude that helped them earn both victories in the sectional tournament.

It was Ferguson's first trip to a state tournament since his 1947 Bears opened the Class B championship by knocking out heavily favored Miller in a historic second-overtime thriller. As for the familiar venue, Coach Ferguson said he was "quite happy" the tournament was at the famous Corn Palace. While not superstitious, he admitted he'd had good fortune there, losing only three times on his home court during his five years coaching at Dakota Wesleyan. The plan was to arrive in Mitchell in the afternoon before a light one-hour workout scheduled for the team at six that evening. But the plan quickly changed.

A late-winter blizzard buried South Dakota, closing the roads and stranding a caravan of the team and about one hundred and fifty of its fans, including Edna and young Freddie. The Deadwood contingent made it as far as Kadoka, less than halfway to their destination, and scrambled for accommodations in hotels, motels, and private rooms. The stranded fans swamped the governor and highway department officials with phone calls all evening, pleading with them to quickly reopen the roads. But heavy, whipping snow and accumulating drifts impeded any progress.

After shoveling and pushing their way free, the team and its fans were finally back on their way at half past six Thursday morning, following the snowplows along Highway 16. With five of the eight teams still slogging east toward Mitchell, the tournament committee pushed back the afternoon schedule by half an hour. The committee talked about a potential Deadwood forfeit but waited out the Bears' arrival until the last possible minute, moving the start time—originally scheduled for three o'clock—back another half hour. Just ahead of the re-rescheduled four o'clock start, the team pulled up to the Corn Palace, changed, and hit the floor.

The "stiff and weary" Bears quickly fell behind by ten points to the top-seeded Bobcats—eventual Class A state champions—but hung tough throughout in a 57–43 defeat. Coach Ferguson's crew rebounded with a consolation victory over the aptly named Mitchell Kernels on Friday before falling handily to the Watertown Arrows, another eastern squad, in a Saturday consolation finale. The final tally was a sixth-place finish in the eight-team tournament, but the Deadwood community welcomed back its Bears when the team returned home on Sunday afternoon.

The fire department, the one police car, friends, and supporters met the team upon arrival and escorted them to the school. On Monday, the Bears were dinner guests of the Black Hills Post 5969 Veterans of Foreign Wars at the Wagner Café. Mayor R. L. Ewing commended the team for its "spirit and sportsmanship" after a draining trip across the state. At its regular Thursday luncheon, the Rotarians honored the Bears, and a proud Coach Ferguson gave a short talk. He spoke of the strong team play despite its difficult trip, and said this 1951–1952 squad showed more courage than any team he had ever coached.

What the coach left out was that he and his Bears were the media darlings of the tournament. The *Argus-Leader* and Mitchell's *Daily Republic* both grabbed some time with the Deadwood mentor for feature stories. Ferguson reminisced about the antics of his Wandering

Weevils teams and made sure to highlight that other than ditching the yuks, his football philosophy hadn't changed. "We have the same ideas at Deadwood, but we don't play like clowns. We insist on a boy's best—no more. We strive to have a good time and it works to our advantage in many ways."

As Ferguson resumed his spring schedule of teaching and coaching track, Easter Sunday soon approached, an important family day for the Fergusons. Edna, Freddie, and Edna's aunt, Fannie, returned from a Saturday of shopping in Rapid City and Ferguson hosted Easter, highlighted by Freddie's egg hunt in the backyard. Summer meant more teaching at BHTC and some family traveling; life was good.

But with football season around the corner, some unexpected news arrived: Coach Minton announced his resignation from the Deadwood faculty.

CHAPTER 37

TRANSITION

The news that Melvin M. Minton had accepted a position at Rapid City High School as a science instructor and coach of the school's B football team was a gut shot felt throughout the Deadwood school, but especially by Coach Stewart Ferguson. Over the span of seven years, the two contrasting coaches had gelled into a trusted team.

On the football field, they collaborated to teach the game in a way that resonated with a variety of players. Coach Minton always impressed Ferguson with his ability to understand the skill sets of each student. As Ferguson told the *Rapid City Journal*, "Minton knew thoroughly the capabilities of every boy in town." More personally, the brotherly kinship that they established would be sorely missed.

While Ferguson moved on without his partner, much uncertainty surrounded the 1952 Bears squad. Only one other 1951 starter joined junior halfback Billy Jones as practice got underway a week before the start of school. Ferguson would have to mold a crew from a handful of returning lettermen, other returnees who had not lettered, some B team players, and others with no prior experience. Inexperience combined with little size prompted a popular Ferguson refrain: he planned to play "a wide-open game to compensate for the lack of power."

Ferguson had a team full of questions, but he did not have to wait long for Minton's replacement. As school opened, it was announced that Glenn Burgess had accepted the position of physical education instructor and assistant athletic coach. A 1948 graduate of BHTC and member of the football, basketball, and track teams there, Burgess had since been coaching and teaching physical education in rural Gregory, the once wild and still treasured town of Ferguson's youth. Considering all the change surrounding Ferguson's Bears, the start to the season, not surprisingly, proved difficult.

For the first time, they lost the opener to the Gillette Camels when an end zone interception in the final two minutes halted a Bears go-ahead scoring chance. They bounced back to beat Hot Springs in a sloppy, fumble-heavy game. The following week, the bigger, stronger Belle Fourche Broncs, who only bothered to pass once the entire evening, pasted the Bears by a score of 32–7.

On a night when the Bears were trounced in front of their hometown fans, Ferguson lingered after the game and led new assistant coach Burgess to the Broncs bus. The Bears coach congratulated the entire Belle Fourche staff on a well-earned victory and the officials on a strongly officiated game. Ferguson's sportsmanship-first approach also carried over to his handling of star tailback Billy Jones.

During a recent fat-chewing session among the Black Hills coaches, much of the conversation centered on Billy. The sentiment was clear: the triple-threat back (running, passing, and kicking) was the most naturally talented player in the conference. Billy's phenomenal talent aside, since his freshman debut, he had earned a reputation as a hothead and had been ejected from a chunk of games for mouthing off at officials and other players. No matter the score of the game, Ferguson never questioned when Billy got tossed. Instead, Ferguson simply reinforced to his gifted tailback that he was much more valuable to his team on the field than seething on the bench.

Heading into this season, Billy seemed to have gotten the message. He had not been ejected through three games and boasted an improved attitude overall, as noted by officials working Deadwood games. His change in demeanor was on full display in the past week's whipping by the Broncs, as one of the officials commented after the game. "Why he even reached down and helped one of the Belle players up after he was tackled," the official said, as if he couldn't believe that Billy was the same kid.

As the season continued, it was clear the 1952 Bears were a team in transition. A hot Spearfish Spartans crew took control in

the second half and beat the Bears 27–13. The next week, the undefeated, conference leading Sturgis Scoopers shook off a resilient
Bears team in the third quarter, piling up nearly four hundred yards
on the ground and coasting to a 45–12 victory. After the loss, Billy
Jones showcased his evolving maturity in his effusive comments on
the Scoopers' speedy running back, Wayne Simons: "Gee, that Simons is terrific. Generally when I get in the clear, I can go all the
way. But tonight, every time I thought I was loose I would hear the
pitter-pat, pitter-pat of Simons' feet and he would haul me down."

Ferguson's boys bounced back from the Sturgis game with a solid
32–13 win over Custer on Bear Day. After the final whistle, it was
officially Lead week. The defending Blacks Hills Conference champ
Golddiggers entered the game with just one loss, to still undefeated
Sturgis, and remained alive in the title race. Big brother had stood
tall against Deadwood three of the last four years, and the scheduled
Thursday night game challenged both coaches with a short practice
week that became shorter when a cold rain and snow mix—eerily
similar to the previous year's Lead week weather—moved in Monday
afternoon and worsened on Tuesday. For Coach Handley, it meant
fewer reps to determine how best to replace recently injured starting
fullback Chuck Trentz, a vital position in Lead's single-wing formation; for Ferguson, it meant less time to shore up a leaky defensive
line that had missed several tackles against Custer. By game time, the
weather had cleared, and a fierce sibling battle ensued.

Behind several solid runs from senior co-captain Bob Roesler,
Lead started fast with Roesler's two-yard touchdown bulge capping
the opening drive. Fellow co-captain and star guard Jim Kornmann
booted the extra point to put the Golddiggers up 7–0. Early in the second quarter, a strong Bears defensive stand—following a potentially
costly Billy Jones fumble on Deadwood's own twenty-seven-yard
line—seemed to spark Ferguson's crew. After a few short gains from
Jones, a holding penalty nullified a completed first down pass from
Jones to senior backfield mate Paul Synder. Two plays later, Ferguson spread out the formation, stacked to the right, and a nearly gobbled up Jones tossed across the field to a wide-open Synder.

Snyder sprinted fifty-one yards to the Golddiggers' eleven-yard line, and two runs by Jones put the Bears on the board. A fake placement rush attempt found Jones trapped by defenders, but he spotted fellow junior "Big" Ed Morris open in the end zone for the tying point. The game remained 7–7 into the third quarter when Lead's Roesler broke through the right side of Deadwood's line, shed some tackles, and went sixteen yards for the go-ahead score, his second touchdown of the day. Another successful Kornmann kick put the Golddiggers up 14–7.

That remained the score early in the fourth quarter when Kornmann fumbled an attempted punt, giving Deadwood new life. Three plays after taking over from their own thirty-nine, the Bears sat at midfield and their lethal short pass and lateral out of the spread formation clicked for a sudden score—the junior trio of Jones to Morris to Reece Palmer doing the honors. One problem. A penalty for illegal use of the hands wiped out all but eight yards of the play. No problem; a short run by Jones gave the Bears a fresh set of downs, and on the next play, Ferguson went right back to the lateral. This time, rising talent John Smiley snatched the Jones toss and fed it to Palmer, who motored to the end zone. Jones was stopped on the extra point attempt, leaving the Bears down 14–13.

Palmer, who teamed with Jones as a starting guard in basketball, wasn't done. With four minutes to go—on a third and twelve from their own thirty-one—Lead tried to trick Deadwood with a fake run followed by a jump pass from the fullback to the wingback, but Palmer intercepted the ball on the Golddiggers' thirty-five and ran another eighteen yards before he was brought down. Two Billy Jones runs moved Deadwood within three yards of the goal line, but an offsides penalty pushed them back to the eight with under a minute left. Two plays later, Jones faded back and found a wide-open Palmer in the end zone, putting Deadwood in front with thirty seconds to go. The Bears couldn't convert the extra point, but time quickly ran out for Lead.

After the game, Jack Cannon made a point to highlight the "gold star" sportsmanship shown from both sides in the hotly contested battle. The two coaches could be proud as players consistently helped up opposing kids after a tackle and extended compliments after good runs. Deadwood versus Lead was as intense as ever, but respect over roughhousing now ruled the day.

Though more change was on the horizon, the wild win over Lead drifted into a fulfilling winter for Ferguson as he enjoyed molding a young basketball team with an all-junior starting lineup. The season tipped off with an opening week home thriller against defending conference champs Rapid City, in which the clock went out to start the second quarter and the assistant coaches (including Melvin Minton) had to keep the remaining time on stopwatches as the delirious Deadwood faithful watched their Bears fall just short in a frenzied final minute. Immediately after, Coach Ferguson commended the officials on their terrific work, knowing well the challenge of refereeing on the gymnasium's small court.

During the Christmas holiday break and before meeting up with his family in Denver, Ferguson made one last trip to Carthage, Missouri, and returned with the old photo of his Dakota Wesleyan football team with President Hoover on the White House lawn in 1931. In the first game back, in Rapid City after a nearly one-month layoff, Ferguson hoped again to give the undefeated Cobblers "a little" trouble.

The Bears did more than that. They led nearly the entire game and held off the Cobblers in another helter-skelter final minute, securing a 54–52 upset win. The *Pioneer-Times* recap emphasized that two Ferguson tactics helped provide the winning edge. One at the outset was moving "Big" Ed Morris, the rapidly improving—and still-growing—junior center, from a corner slot on offense into the middle, in front of the key. Morris's teammates fed him several passes that he converted into layups and short shots; the new man in the middle also forced Rapid's skilled center Neil Doeden into tough looks. Ferguson's other move was switching to a half-court press on defense in the third quarter, which rattled Rapid into a few turnovers.

Two weeks later, the young Bears ran cold up at Spearfish and were outplayed by a Spartans team that leaped them in the conference standings. Afterward, a candid and gracious Ferguson told the paper that "we didn't get up far enough for this one and Spearfish played wonderful ball." On tap was an out-of-conference early February weekend trip two-hundred-miles northwest to face Miles City, Montana, which had already knocked off the top three teams in the Black Hills Conference. Emitting a full Wandering Weevils ethos, Ferguson conveyed his plan to the local paper: "We're going on this trip for a little relaxation and fun and to play a little basketball."

Once again, Ferguson's Bears played more than a "little" ball and were down just four points before Miles City pulled away in the final three minutes. The good times continued three nights later when Deadwood upset conference leader Sturgis in one more frenetic finish. With under twenty seconds left and the game tied, Billy Jones took his accustomed football hero role to the hard court. He forced a turnover underneath the Sturgis basket, scooped up the loose ball, and scored the winning hoop.

The fun season with Ferguson's core group of talented juniors marched on. Until Tuesday, March 10, that is, when a page five *Deadwood Pioneer-Times* article about the resignation of a longtime school maintenance man and an updated teacher salary schedule carried some additional information. As part of a regular session meeting of the Deadwood Board of Education the prior evening, teacher contracts were extended for the 1953–1954 school year along with the following assignment change: Stewart Ferguson was appointed head football coach and assistant basketball and track coach, and Glenn Burgess was appointed head basketball and track coach and assistant football coach. Just a one sentence update and not exactly breaking news; yet it felt sudden.

The next day, the paper's local sports section was heavy with buzz previewing the wide-open Black Hills Section Eight Class A basketball tournament, with opening Thursday evening matchups of Spearfish versus Lead and Deadwood versus Belle Fourche. Jack Cannon opened his *Pioneer-Times* "Cannon Reports" column casting a light on Stewart Ferguson: "If sentiment can do anything, the Deadwood Bears are going to have to be installed as favorites in the Section Eight basketball tournament which opens at Lead Thursday night." Cannon thought it would be a nice bow for Ferguson to take one more Bears team to a state tournament, but that was not a big deal for the coach. As much as Ferguson loved and sought the limelight over the years—climaxing with his Wandering Weevils escapades—his focus always centered on the experience of his players. As for the school board's decision to split the A football and basketball coaching going forward, that structure had already become more common in the conference; Lead made the shift a few years prior. Cannon asked Ferguson for his thoughts on the change, and the coach replied, presumably truthfully, that he was "quite happy" with the revised structure, explaining that "coaching both football and basketball is too much a strain for anyone."

In fact, Ferguson was stretched thin. Beyond all his coaching work, he was also teaching history and civics, along with newly offered college credit classes in the evenings. Though Ferguson still enjoyed studying the game of basketball, devising strategies, and staying on top of changing rules, he was never shy about his true love. It was always football.

Sophomore Hank Frawley—who was truly neck and neck with "Big" Ed Morris for bragging rights as the tallest Bear and spent some time playing on the A team that season—perfectly captured his former coach years later, with a hand from longtime friend and former Deadwood classmate, Janet ("Chyba") Thoresen. A chuckling Hank led off: "We'd get into class and start talking about history or civics and we'd end up reliving the last football game." Janet added, "Yeah, us girls would always get you guys to talk about the game last night because we were behind in our shorthand or something and we were doing that while you guys were playing the game all over again." Even if the girls were to blame for getting him off topic in class, Ferguson's passion for teaching the sport was as ingrained and obvious to Deadwood players and students as it was years ago when his jaw dropped as Louisiana's Beauregard Parish superintendent informed him that Dry Creek didn't have a football team.

For now, Ferguson still had a basketball team to coach, so he quickly moved on and prepped his Bears for a tough match-up with Belle Fourche, which had battled Sturgis for the conference title for much of the season and had crushed the Bears one month earlier. This time, triggered by a fourth-quarter press, Ferguson's crew cut an eight-point deficit down to one with fifty-five seconds left before missed free throws and other miscues resulted in a 41–38 defeat. The season aptly ended with one more furious finish as Spearfish edged out Deadwood 57–55 in the consolation game, scoring the deciding basket with five seconds to go.

Coaches Ferguson and Burgess shared the responsibility for track in the spring. Ferguson handed out the awards for both basketball and track at the annual overall school ceremony in May. A school year that began with the unexpected departure of Coach Minton and finished with an imminent transition in Deadwood basketball was coming to a close. While Ferguson shrugged off the reduced upcoming coaching workload, it was fair to wonder if he felt any morsel of extra motivation heading into football season in the fall.

CHAPTER 38

A SPECIAL SEASON

"Toss A Coin For Black Hills High School Champ This Fall." So led the *Rapid City Journal*'s comprehensive 1953 football season preview, in which many of the conference coaches sung the usual lament of replacing lost lettermen. Deadwood Bears coach Stewart Ferguson, however, did not play any of his underdog cards. He spoke about growing his "gambling" game, favoring touchdowns over yardage. Throwing no cold water on his team's chances heading into the season seemed to indicate one thing: Ferguson felt quietly confident that his now senior-led squad could be special.

Fresh from an August trip to California with Edna and Freddie, Ferguson kicked off practice on the first day of school registration, a week before the start of classes. Eleven lettermen and seventeen others competed daily as the September 4 opener at Gillette approached. While Ferguson planned, as usual, to use the first game to experiment with several combinations in the backfield and line, one anchor was tailback Billy Jones, who opened his senior season with a resounding statement, scoring all four of Deadwood's touchdowns in a 24–7 victory. Ferguson used every one of the twenty-three players selected for the trip and was able to assess multiple aspects of his new Bears squad.

A trip to Hot Springs kicked off the conference schedule the following week, where new coach Stan Marshall pegged his Bison as hard workers, but with limited speed in the line and inexperience in the backfield. He offered a modest "improvement in each game is our goal" in his pre-season remarks. The team was coming off an

0-7 season, but Hot Springs totaled eleven lettermen, centered on seven returning linemen. And as portrayed by *Pioneer-Times* reporter Joe Langston, now on the paper's sports beat, the Bison hardly resembled a winless squad: "Like a rabbit pulling a magician out of a top hat, an astonished crowd watched Hot Springs uncoil a team of unsuspected strength against Deadwood here Friday night."

Behind 13–7 in the closing minutes, the Bison drove down to the Bears eight-yard line, with the crowd on its feet. Bison halfback Pat Serry had provided the big play when he broke through the Bears line, changed direction, and ran twenty-three yards before he was finally tackled. Three tough Bison runs got it down to the one, forcing a fourth and goal with seconds left. Bison quarterback Jim Strain headed wide to the right on a keep play but Bears tackle Larry DiSanto broke in behind the Bison blockers and pulled Strain down two yards short of the goal line right before the final gun. Phew. Next up was a Belle Fourche squad that had just been soundly beaten by Sturgis.

After a full week of practice, Coach Ferguson said he was playing the games one at a time in an attempt for a clean record, a fitting cliché as Ferguson had never managed a perfect record at Deadwood. He added some good news that the State Board of Control cleared Jerry Sternad, a recent in-state transfer from Faith, to join the team. The six-foot, 185-pound Sternad would provide a needed jolt to the line, replacing starter George Clark, who was out for the season with a broken arm.

For the matchup with the Broncs, Ferguson thought it best to stick with his favored wide-open formation and target big play touchdowns, rather than slog it out with the typically heavy Broncs. Although his Bears struggled to get going and were down 7–6 at half-time, Deadwood came out firing to start the third quarter. They rolled to a 33–7 win behind a little razzle-dazzle, a couple of highlight grabs by Reece Palmer, power rushes by John Smiley, the booming foot of "Big" Ed Morris (including nailing Deadwood's first extra point kick attempt of the season), plus a helpful heap of triple-threat Billy Jones.

Returning to Deadwood for their first home game of the season against Spearfish, the Bears were locked in a first-place tie with defending conference champs Sturgis. Spearfish was coming off an unexpected rout of Hot Springs, a team that came within a yard of stunning Deadwood only two weeks earlier. It was an all-around entertaining but frustrating first three quarters as both teams moved the ball well but couldn't manage any points. The game turned late in the third quarter when Bears guard Bill Beshara recovered a Spartan fumble on the Bears forty. As the Bears offense ran onto the field, Ferguson decided to change things up and feature Billy Jones in a single-wing formation, looking to take advantage of Spearfish's smaller and less experienced line.

It worked. Billy ("The Most" or "Bullet Billy") Jones, as he was now known respectively by the Deadwood and Rapid City papers, started to do his thing. With strong blocking support from fellow backfield mates Palmer, Smiley, and Gene Whitelock, Jones played the starring role in Deadwood's surprise performance of power football. Through a series of off-tackle and over-guard plays, he carried the ball again and again, scoring twice in the fourth quarter to provide the game's only points. On the first touchdown, from Spearfish's seventeen, Jones "broke off left tackle and swivel-hipped through the secondary to score standing up." His capper was a bulge from the three, in which he hit the line twice and powered across the goal. Ferguson's Bears posted an eye-popping 234 yards on the ground and only thirty-four through the air, giving next up (and undefeated) Sturgis a little something extra to think about.

The stakes were high, and Ed Sundberg, the new sports columnist in town, was all sorts of fired up: "Shakespeare wrote something about 'All the world's a stage' and Friday football fans in the Northern Black Hills will be watching the gridiron stage in Deadwood and all of its associated sideshows when the Bears meet the Scoopers in something more than a ball game."

On the Scoopers side was a team clocking fourteen consecutive wins, with a powerful line and a precision offense featuring a talented backfield headlined by Ross Bottum and Jerry Merritt. The opposing Bears would likely counter with a return to a wide-open game featuring its own skilled backfield trio of Palmer, Smiley, and Gene Whitelock alongside all-everything tailback Jones. Sprinkle in a

Deadwood team that had never gone undefeated or won a conference title, and a match-up that would likely determine this year's Black Hills conference championship—coupled with the festive Bear Day celebration—and yeah, it felt like something more than a ballgame.

Even Ferguson, uncharacteristically, said the Bears would play every second of the game with the idea of defeating Sturgis and making the Bear Day celebration perfect. With the *Deadwood Pioneer-Times* predicting a Bears victory and the *Rapid City Journal* calling for a Scoopers win, it was undeniably a toss-up game in an as-predicted toss-up season.

In a strange start under an intermittent drizzle, the Deadwood community packed themselves around the rodeo grounds and watched both teams fumble on the second play of their opening possessions. The game soon settled down and Sturgis manufactured a solid drive beginning at Deadwood's forty-one-yard line, leading to a first down one foot from the Bears' end zone. The Bears' line held firm until the Scoopers' Jerry Merritt finally plowed over on the fourth down for the opening score. Sturgis tried to pass for the extra point, but the Bears gobbled up quarterback Jerry Bachleitner before he could make an attempt.

After the Scoopers' kickoff fell out of bounds, the Bears took over on their own forty. Deadwood struggled to move the ball and on fourth and nine, Billy Jones dropped back into punt formation, but he didn't kick. Behind a group of blockers, Jones took off around right end and scampered to the Sturgis thirty-five for a new set of downs. On the next play, Jones let one fly and talented junior halfback Richy Sears hauled it in at the five for another first down. Two Jones rushes up the gut put Deadwood on the board. Ed Morris kicked wide on the extra point attempt, keeping the game tied, 6–6.

Sturgis struck right back. On its next possession, speedy Ross Bottum broke free off tackle, bursting into Deadwood territory. The Scoopers then sprang a bit of their own razzle-dazzle, hitting the Bears with a reverse that went all the way to the three-yard line. Jerry Merritt finished things off with his second rushing score of the night, and this time Bachleitner booted through the extra point.

Down a touchdown in the second quarter, the Bears immediately answered. They mixed it up with a few runs and quick-strike passes, and a Jones to Palmer connection netted a first down at the Scoopers twenty-six. Jones hit Palmer again in stride over the goal line for Deadwood's second score. Fellow backfield mate John Smiley passed to Jones for the successful conversion, and the game was even again, 13–13. The first half ended as it started, with both teams trading turnovers.

The Bears received the kickoff to start the third quarter, and a strong Billy Jones return gave his team terrific field position at their own forty-five. Then disaster struck Jones and his Bears. An off-tackle run play to Jones never got going as the ball slipped out of his grasp and bounced toward midfield, directly into the waiting hands of Jerry Merritt, who outran the Bears to the end zone for his third touchdown of the game. Another successful Bachleitner kick left the Bears behind 20–13.

The swift turn of events seemed to give the Scoopers added life. They bottled up the Bears on the ensuing possession, forcing a Billy Jones punt—not a spot to risk a fake—and grabbed great field position near midfield. The Scoopers line took control and led the way for the backs to drive down the field. Eventually, Ross Bottom went over from a foot away to extend Sturgis's lead. Bachleitner, however, missed his first extra point kick of the game.

Still, it was nearly the fourth quarter and Deadwood was down thirteen points to the defending Black Hills champions who had won fourteen consecutive games and had emphatically snatched the reins as the conference's new top dog with Rapid City's recent departure. Not to mention a head coach who would not have minded turning the tables on his nemesis across the sidelines.

On the following kickoff, halfback Gene Whitelock woke up the Bears with a strong return to their forty-nine-yard line. Ferguson kept his crew in a spread formation and the offense started to click. After a short run on first down, quarterback Reece Palmer—seeing no open receivers—found some free space and sprinted for a first down. Two Billy Jones strikes to Palmer and Sears moved the Bears to the Scoopers' eleven. From there, Jones found Sears open in the end zone for their second scoring hookup of the game. A Jones to Sears extra point attempt failed, however, leaving the Bears down 26–19 early in the fourth quarter.

The Bears' line bent once more on the Scoopers' next drive, but after two first downs, the Scoopers stalled and a failed fourth down pass turned the ball over to the Bears on their own forty. Ferguson had that feeling again; time to change things up. He switched his offense out of the spread and moved tackle Jerry Sternad from the line to fullback. Catching the Scoopers off guard, Sternad powered his way up the middle for a twenty-yard gain. Jones then zipped around right end, bringing another first down at the Scooper twenty. And then something told Ferguson it was sleeper time.

Whitelock "quietly trotted away from the huddle unnoticed by the Scoopers," while the Bears raced to the line. Jones lofted one to a wide-open Whitelock down the sideline, who snared it in stride and darted into the end zone. The "most perfect sleeper in memory" brought the Bears within one, and Billy Jones hammered up the middle for the extra point, tying the game for the third time with the clock running down. Both the Bears and the Scoopers had one more shot but couldn't sustain drives. The instant classic finished deadlocked, 26–26.

So, Deadwood and Sturgis remained unbeaten and tied at the top of the conference with two games left to play. The Bears' next opponent was an underdog Custer team. Though the Wildcats were a surprising 3–1 on the year (2–1 in the conference), they were undersized and missing running back Jim Kelley, their most explosive player, out with a knee injury. After falling easily to Sturgis, Custer was coming off a dominant victory against the still-winless Belle Fourche Broncs. The Wildcats had lost five straight to Ferguson's Deadwood teams, and this one played out as anticipated.

The Bears scored on three consecutive possessions in the first half and forced two early turnovers, while the Wildcats struggled to move the ball. Never one to run up the score, Ferguson removed his starters in the third quarter in a game the Bears won comfortably,

42–6. The fourth quarter fun was highlighted by little Deadwood freshman Jerry Harmon holding up his pants with one hand, in a Wandering Weevils-esque attempt to tackle Custer's Jim Gibson with the other, as Gibson whizzed by to get his team on the scoreboard.

There was one game left; fifty years after the Lead Golddiggers and Deadwood Bears officially met for the first time on the football field, the teams were ready to get after it again. Heading into the season, Lead had lost a whopping sixteen lettermen to graduation, but Coach Wendell Handley remained upbeat during the team's weeklong late August training camp about twenty miles away at Camp Columbus. He said the boys were "working hard, training hard, and having a good time doing it." So far, they were 2–2 in conference play and had just lost 13–6 at home to Spearfish after leading 6–0 at the half.

By Thursday, it was evident both teams were banged up and some starters would miss the game. Lead was down two halfbacks, including the loss of top back Bud Kornmann, who was injured in Tuesday's practice and ruled out for the remainder of the season. For Deadwood, senior guard Al Johnson hurt his wrist against Custer, thinning the front line.

In Friday's *Pioneer-Times*, both coaches were asked about their chances. As a wise and wary Coach Ferguson observed, "On paper, it looks like we should win it, but you know how these conceded games many times pan out, and we can't count on anything in this rivalry." With two upsets in the last four meetings, this statement rang true. On the other side, Coach Handley was undaunted. "We had a good workout last night, and if the Bears think they're going to take it, we're going to make them earn it. If the boys put out full effort—and they really want this game—it'll be a good battle."

As the kickoff approached at a quarter to eight, the Deadwood versus Lead weather gods, for a change, delivered calm skies and unseasonably mild temperatures. A sea of about five thousand fans from the twin communities enveloped themselves around Deadwood's football field. What they witnessed was the coronation of a special team.

The Deadwood Bears lit up (or more accurately, chalked up) the scoreboard, putting an exclamation point on the first undefeated football season in school history. Though much closer than the 45–6 final would indicate, it was by far the biggest margin of victory for the Bears during the fifty-year rivalry. It was a team win all the way, and a particularly sweet climax for the exceptional group of seniors. Big Ed Morris sparkled at center, booming punts and banging through two more extra points. Quarterback Reece Palmer and fullback John Smiley flourished on offense and defense. And, of course, Billy Jones completed his Deadwood football career in style. After his first game as a freshman, *Pioneer-Times* columnist Jack Cannon had said the kid "showed promise of making good in the Deadwood backfield." Jones then announced his arrival to Lead with two electric touchdown bursts. Now that kid who had worked so hard to become a better person and a leader on and off the field, blossoming into the best player in the conference, was back on his favorite stage one final time.

Jones ran for four scores and threw for another. For an encore, he rose to pick off a Golddigger pass at his own forty-six-yard line and followed a bunch of Bears into the end zone for Deadwood's final touchdown. Heading into the battle against Lead, Ferguson, brimming with pride, wanted to talk a bit about Billy: "Having Bill out there on the gridiron is just like being out there myself. He knows football and he knows the way I want it played."

For the tight-knit community, Deadwood's first ever undefeated season—finishing 6–0–1 and 5–0–1 in the conference—and a share of the Black Hills Conference crown with Sturgis (who had just beaten Spearfish and had not lost a game since September 1951) was plenty. But those local football gods were still shining brightly on these Deadwood Bears. The Scoopers sat at 4–0–1 in the conference with one more game left, a Friday trip down to the southern Black Hills to play the Hot Springs Bison, who had nearly stunned the Bears in the final seconds earlier in the season and were coming off a win against Custer. In a game they never trailed, Hot Springs upset Sturgis 20–18. Ferguson's 1953 Deadwood Bears were Black Hills Conference champions for the first time in school history.

Ed Sundberg, for his *Pioneer-Times'* "Dope Sheet" column, reached out to the coach to offer congratulations and found a delighted

Ferguson. He started by saying that every member of the team should be proud of their accomplishment and added, "The team was characterized mostly by the intense determination, the will to win, and the ability to master quickly difficult assignments." The force of Ferguson's close was unmistakable: "This team will be remembered for as long as football is played in Deadwood."

CHAPTER 39

SIDELINED

The glow of Deadwood's first ever football title lasted through the rest of October. To wrap up the season, the chamber of commerce hosted a festive team banquet, and every member of the Bears shared in the celebration. Ferguson introduced the backfield and commended the boys' "fine teamwork." Glenn Burgess announced the line and said it was a "pleasure" to work with the crew, and Billy Jones—who a few months later would be an honorable mention on the National High School All-American Football squad—followed by thanking the chamber for its support, before turning his attention to the team: "The backs get the glory, but the line does the work." Representing that line, "Big" Ed Morris added a few words.

The evening culminated with sportswriter Joe Langston from the *Deadwood Pioneer-Times* and *Lead Daily Call* announcing the papers' 1953 all-conference selections. Billy Jones, Ed Morris, and Richie Sears earned first team honors; an astounding ten members of Deadwood's starting eleven were honored in all.

As the sports calendar circled on, thoughts shortly turned to the upcoming basketball season. With Deadwood returning all five starters from last year's emerging squad, the team's outlook looked promising. Coach Stewart Ferguson, however, would not be returning. For the first time since his 1944 arrival in Deadwood, Ferguson handed over the keys of the Bears basketball A team to another coach. While Ferguson felt relieved by the lower workload, the actual switch still felt a bit strange. As for the players, the transition from Coach Ferguson to Coach Burgess meant a significant change in styles.

Hank Frawley, now a six-foot-three junior (a smidge shorter than Big Ed), offered an insightful perspective on the two coaches years later. Reflecting on the "laid back" Ferguson, Frawley observed, "Some coaches would get excited, and chew you out one side down the other. That never happened with Coach Ferguson. . . . I just remember him being very calm, cool, and collected even under exciting or tense situations." Though Ferguson was "very quiet and gentle, he was a good coach and always very clear and precise about his instruction." Coach Burgess, as Frawley recalled, took a starkly different approach. "Well, Burgess was a lot more intense. If you made a mistake, you'd hear about it. He was a good coach, but he was a real taskmaster. If you didn't measure up to his expectations, you heard about it." When asked about what Coach Burgess thought was important on the court, Frawley smiled and instantly responded: "Winning."

And that was what immediately transpired. Coach Burgess's Bears amassed six straight conference wins before finally falling at home, 68–50, in a late January showdown with likewise unbeaten Rapid City, which remained part of the Black Hills conference for basketball. Four more league victories kept the Bears within range of the Cobblers, but a late-season loss to middle-of-the-pack Belle Fourche handed the Cobblers the inside track for the conference title. The Bears' regular season wound down with a much tighter loss to Rapid on the Cobblers' home court and a convincing victory over Custer. Burgess's crew finished a robust 11–3 in the conference, second to the 14–0 Cobblers, and headed into sectional play as the clear favorite to advance and earn a berth in the Class A state tournament for the second time in three years.

Section eight went as predicted. The Bears followed an easy win over Spearfish with a bounce back 57–50 triumph over Belle Fourche. But in a stunner, the undefeated Rapid City squad was beaten by Custer 73–55 in the finals of section seven, ending Rapid's season. More shock waves came out of the east as the Eastern South Dakota Conference (ESDC) champion Brookings Bobcats, who had knocked out Ferguson's Bears in the 1952 Class A tourney en route to becoming state champs, fell in their section two opener. In a blink, the two top ranked teams in the state were out of contention and the Class A state title was up for grabs.

The Bears earned another trip across South Dakota, to Huron's Civic Arena, where they matched up against the Sioux Falls Warriors, a close runner-up to ESDC champ Brookings. Down three points at halftime, the Bears took the lead at the end of the third quarter, pushed it to seven with three and half minutes left in the game and held on for a 47–44 win.

Next up was the hometown Huron Tigers, who had gone only 6–8 in conference play but had just blasted Aberdeen, last year's Class A state champs, to open the tournament. Once again, the Bears were down three at the half before rebounding for a three-point lead entering the fourth quarter. This time the game stayed close, and the Tigers had the ball, down 50–48 with under a minute to go and stalling for a final shot to tie the game (a common tactic in the days before a shot clock). Then, Billy Jones (who else?) picked off a pass and fed it to "Big" Ed Morris for a dunk and the final basket. The Bears needed one more win. Their opponent was the Parkston Trojans, located about eighty miles to the south of Huron and the tourney's second smallest school, next to Deadwood.

Parkston had stunned two ESDC teams, Mitchell and Yankton, to win sectionals and stayed hot, easily beating fellow small school Madison, another surprise entrant, in its first game. Parkston followed up with an impressive win over Custer, eliminating the chance for a Saturday night all-Black Hills final. In front of a capacity crowd of 6,800 fans, the Bears trailed at the half for the third straight time, 27–25, and a sluggish third quarter by both teams kept Deadwood behind 33–29. But the fourth quarter was all Bears. They exploded for nineteen points and held the Trojans without a basket, pulling away in a 52–38 final. Five months after the Bears won their first ever football conference championship, they were back on top—1954's Class A state basketball champions. The town was once again ready to celebrate.

But before Deadwood's welcome home, the Sturgis community returned the favor from two years earlier when Deadwood showered Sturgis in celebration of the Scoopers' 1952 hoops title. Upon reaching Sturgis, the Bears' five-car team caravan was greeted with welcome flags dotted along Main Street and a high school band salute from the steps of City Hall. From there, Deadwood Chamber of Commerce president Charles Waters proudly told the paper, "several hundred cars" led the team's victory ride home through the Black Hills and into town. For the final approach, Deadwood's police car and fire truck flipped on their sirens and escorted the robust caravan uptown to the Franklin Hotel. Among a packed crowd, a short ceremony ensued—comprising both Deadwood's city and high school bands, along with a flag escort from the American Legion—plus a promise of a more formal ceremony to come.

Through all the basketball hoopla of the last few months, climaxing with the school's first ever Class A state championship, Coach Stewart Ferguson quietly taught his history and civics classes and worked to develop and coach the B team, many of whom would move up to the A squad the following season. While Coach Burgess molded the varsity boys with his own methods, Ferguson easily morphed into a fan and followed each of the tournament radio broadcasts on local station KDSJ, set up by A. H Shoemaker, Homestake's new general manager. R. E. Whitmyre, the sports editor of the *Deadwood Pioneer-Times* and *Lead Daily Call*, acknowledged Ferguson in his column after the Bears win, dusting off the "Rome wasn't built in a day" line to discuss Ferguson's dedicated effort in building the team. Ferguson, however, knew this wasn't his moment and stayed in the shadows.

The Deadwood Chamber of Commerce sponsored a formal celebration for the basketball team the following Monday at the Bodega Café, a popular postgame hangout with a separate gambling hall. Coach Burgess, after being introduced to the 140 guests, graciously reflected on the last several months. "It's been a banner year for Deadwood High School athletics. First Stewart Ferguson and the football record and then this honor. In order to play basketball, boys must have ability, and these boys had it and had a good background." The evening closed with the presentation of autographed team photos taken at the tournament and a bouquet of flowers presented by

South Dakota's official coyote Tootsie, trained to be a household pet as a pup by a local business owner.

One more big night remained to cap Deadwood High School's unprecedented sports year. In April, the Deadwood Jaycees put on a second consecutive all-sports banquet, providing a final forum for Ferguson and Burgess to speak on their championship teams and to call up the lettermen from their respective squads. Before the school year closed, there was one last piece of sports hardware to hand out. Ferguson presented Billy Jones, the football star and four-year letterman in basketball and track, with the Norman Oestreich Memorial Trophy as the outstanding athlete of the senior class.

The summer of 1954 was a chance for Ferguson to reset. It began with a trip to Mitchell to attend his thirty-year college reunion at Dakota Wesleyan. The ghosts of Mitchell past had faded, as the former prodigal son returned for the second time in three years. The summer wound down with another leisurely August family trip to the California coast.

Upon his return, Ferguson received a happy anniversary in the paper. Sort of. Leading off the August 20 daily "Memory Lane" column was a reminder that a decade earlier Stewart A. Ferguson had "accepted a position as athletic director and coach for the Deadwood high school." Ten years later, Deadwood meant one thing for Ferguson, Edna, Freddie, and their youngest, feline family member, Bomber: home.

The annual call for football was just a few days away, and a friendly face showed up for the Bears' return to the field. Cecil Stoner was recently returned from a four-year stint in the U.S. Navy and Marine Corps as a medical specialist, including an extended stay with the fleet deployed in Korea. The former Deadwood quarterback, whom Ferguson had an instant feeling about as an eighth grader messing around at recess, was eager to catch up with his coach. Years later, he distinctly remembered the surreal encounter.

Cecil mentioned he was "gonna go to Black Hills [Teachers College] this year," and then switched to an excited Ferguson voice. "He says, 'Are you gonna play football?' Of course I am," Cecil answered.

'Well, I'll talk to the coaches over there and let them know you're coming.'"

Cecil shot back, "Why you gonna do that?" The response was quintessential Ferguson: "Because they need to know you're coming."

Stoner hung around for some more early practice work. For the first time, the Deadwood Bears were defending champs. But the graduation of Billy Jones, Reece Palmer, and John Smiley left a gaping hole in the starting backfield; additionally, the loss of "Big" Ed Morris at center put Ferguson in a challenging spot. Eight returning lettermen would need to form the glue of these 1954 Bears. While plenty of spots were up for grabs, the role of number one team fan was already filled by a recently turned seven-year-old who also happened to be the coach's son.

Over the last couple of years, Freddie Ferguson had become a Bears superfan, and Hank Frawley, who had played some football earlier in high school before turning his attention to basketball, clearly recalled Freddie's growing bond with the team. "I remember him at the games. He must've been four or five years old. Freddie would get dressed up in a football uniform. He'd have a helmet and he had some pads and orange and black shirt and jersey and stuff. He was kind of our mascot. . . . He'd ride the bus when we were going out of town. He was pretty special you know."

Fellow Bears alumnus Willie Steinlicht, who was logging his second season as manager of the football team, had a more succinct, colorful recollection on Freddie's assistant role with the team. "He used to help [us] carry s—t."

With Freddie strolling the sidelines, Ferguson's 1954 Bears debuted at home on Friday night, September 3, and survived the annual opening tussle against Gillette, 6–0, thanks to another late goal line stand. A tweaked conference schedule had them off for the next two weeks before hosting Hot Springs. Though a ten-game undefeated streak was on the line, Ferguson was more concerned about his team lacking energy due to the layoff, along with illness and injuries of key players. But the biggest issue before the game was the coach's own physical condition. Ferguson was hit with pneumonia Thursday evening and was ordered on Friday to check into Deadwood's St. Joseph's Hospital. But Friday was game night, so only *after* watching his Bears topple the Bison 25–6 did Ferguson check himself in for treatment.

Ferguson was confined to the hospital heading into the week's Bear Day festivities and Friday night's battle with Belle Fourche. Freddie filled the void. As part of the local merchant theme to include a different Bears player in each of the plentiful *Deadwood Pioneer-Times* Bear Day ads, the team's superfan posed in his uniform for Robley's Grill's "BEAT THE BRONCS" call. He also stood proud and puffed out next to his dad in a team photo recently taken by the paper. The Broncs entered the game 1–1 in the conference, having just been beaten by a reloaded and undefeated Sturgis squad, and the Bears were looking to keep pace atop the conference standings.

On a chilly but clear evening, the Broncs, behind their perennial power running attack, scored on the opening drive and didn't look back. Although the Bears tightened up their defense and ended up outgaining the Broncs, the team looked out of sync. A staggering four fumbles and two interceptions, one returned seventy yards for a touchdown, was too much to overcome and the Bears fell 19–6.

Deadwood's first loss in almost exactly two years was not the biggest news of the night. Ferguson couldn't completely stay away from his Bears. As broadcast over Deadwood's KDSJ's airwaves by sports announcer Vincent Coyle, an ambulance carrying Ferguson cruised into the Rodeo Grounds during halftime and found a spot for the coach to take in the second half action. While not a night for a storybook comeback, the players and huddled Deadwood fans were pleased to see their coach back on the field.

Ferguson was finally discharged on Wednesday, just two days before Deadwood's next game at Spearfish. With the coach leading only one practice before his return to the sidelines, it wasn't too surprising to see an animated Spearfish group—in front of their homecoming crowd and coming off their first win of the season—bolt to a 12–0 lead at halftime. The Bears fought back to take a 13–12 lead halfway through the fourth quarter. In the final minutes, Spearfish drove down the field to the one-foot line. The Bears defensive front held strong for three plays before the Spartans nudged the ball across on fourth down for the winning score. The loss was a heartbreaker for the Bears, and things wouldn't get any easier the following week, as a hungry, dominant Sturgis squad awaited.

Since Sturgis's astonishing loss to end the 1953 season, they had steamrolled through this year's schedule—6–0 overall and 4–0 in the conference, with a frightening 228–32 point differential. In addition, five of Ferguson's starting eleven were expected to be out; the Bears' prospects to reasonably compete couldn't have looked much bleaker. Traditional defenses, with five to seven linemen, were hardly stopping Sturgis, so Ferguson dug into his bag of tricks and unveiled an unorthodox defensive formation to open the game—debated afterward as a 4–5–2, a 4–1–4–2, or even a 4½–4½–2 setup—featuring a large hole in the middle of the line. The Bears guards and center were pulled back, the next level covered the gaps in the line, and the defensive backs inched up.

Surprised Sturgis quarterback Jerry Bachleitner immediately called a timeout to discuss things with his coach. Ferguson's new defensive scheme, along with some Sturgis miscues, helped stymie the high-powered offense throughout the first half, and the undermanned Bears—a heavy underdog—played the Scoopers to a scoreless tie. The second half was a different story, though, as the Bears wore down and lost handily, 34–0.

Lifted by the return of starting quarterback Woody Williamson from a hip injury, the Bears bounced back in their final home game of the season, beating Custer 21–0. Next up: Lead week. Though the actual Lead–Deadwood games were generally becoming more civil, the rivalry was as fiery as ever. Years later, when a conversation with Hank Frawley turned to his reflections on Lead, he grinned and leaned in:

> Well, I'll tell you a story about the Delicate family. They had all these good looking daughters in Lead." Hank's friend and former classmate, Janet (Chyba) Thoresen, fighting off the giggles,

couldn't help herself and added, "That was a problem, yes." As Janet lost it on the side, Hank steadied and continued. "And I finally got a date with one of the Delicate girls. [The plan was] I'd pick her up in the afternoon, go to a movie. So I drove up in front of the house and this car pulls in across the street full of Lead football players. And they put the window down. They said, 'Frawley, get your butt back to Deadwood! You're not dating any of our girls.' I figured there were more of them than me, so I got back in the car and headed back to Deadwood and got to a phone and called this Dianne or whatever [her name] was and of course she was just furious and I guess she figured out . . . her brother—she had a brother in the family—he must've found out about the date from the football players." Hank trailed off for a moment before finishing. "So that's the kind of rivalry that we had. I mean they were dead serious. They just told me to get back into the car and go back to Deadwood.

The Golddiggers sat in second place, 4–1 in the conference, and were an experienced squad led by senior Bert Roesler, a triple-threat halfback. Heading into the season, Coach Ferguson spoke glowingly of Roesler to the *Pioneer-Times*, saying, "Lead should be tough, as they have the best back in South Dakota." The Bears were expecting a boost from bulldozing fullback senior Jerry Sternad, who had returned to action against Custer, and was the team's top offensive threat.

On Thursday, the opposing coaches weighed in, painting a complete role reversal from the prior year. Lead coach Wendell Handley said his Golddiggers were in strong physical shape heading into the game, but he was certainly wary of the underdog Bears: "This game should really be a tough one and I expect it to be tight all the way through." Coach Ferguson, noting the strength of this Lead outfit but possibly feeling a bit better about the health of his team, remarked, "We have a tough night ahead of us . . . but the game should be close."

No longer the little brother that got pushed around by its up-gulch rivals, Ferguson's crew had taken two straight against Lead and five of the last nine, all tight contests outside of last year's 45–6 Bears triumph. Finally, it was game day. Or rather game night, as this was Deadwood's first game at Lead's Mountain Top Field since the floodlights were added the prior season. Dropping temperatures, whipping winds, and an ice-crusted playing surface played right into Ferguson's hands; the difficult field conditions and a healthy Sternad convinced Ferguson this was not the night for his beloved fancy football.

The teams battled on the ground and a Lead drive to open the third quarter concluded with a one-yard touchdown by Roesler, knotting the game 6–6 as each team fell short on a rush for an extra point attempt. The game then swung wildly to the Bears, with Jerry Sternad and Richy Sears teaming up for a little thunder and lightning to lead the way. Sternad finished off the next Deadwood drive with a thirteen-yard scoring bulge and after the Bears recovered a botched Golddiggers pitch attempt two plays later, he worked forward with three straight rushes, completing the quick twenty-yard possession with a three-yard score. A bit later, Sears broke through for a forty-five-yard burst, down to Lead's twenty-five. From there, the two in-rhythm backs pushed the Bears closer, and Sternad's third touchdown of the evening gave Deadwood a 24–6 cushion. Lead rallied for another score and even recovered an onside kickoff to retain possession, but for the third year in a row it was Deadwood's night.

Battling his health, Ferguson found a way to get through the season. But this time around, he would not be making the usual wrap-up awards festivities. A week after the victory over Lead, Ferguson was admitted again at Deadwood's St. Joseph's Hospital. He needed emergency surgery to remove a cancerous left lung, and was immediately transported to the Rochester, Minnesota Mayo Clinic, fighting for his life.

CHAPTER 40

BACK IN ACTION

Edna Ferguson flew to the hospital on Friday, November 12. Stewart Ferguson's procedure was scheduled for Monday morning. Later that day, Edna reported to the *Pioneer-Times* that his condition "was as well as can be expected." The school soon announced that Merlyn Veren, a recent graduate of the University of South Dakota's school of education and a former Sturgis High School track and football star, would coach Deadwood's B basketball team and teach Ferguson's classes during his anticipated extended recovery.

The coach rested at home, his first Bears sports season not on the sidelines. While the Deadwood community awaited Ferguson's return, Camille Yuill reported on several encouraging developments in her "Backlog" column. Heading the list was the opening of a re-built theater, appropriately named the Flame. The town had been without a movie house since January 1952, when the second of two devastating fires about a month apart had destroyed the existing the-ater, city hall, and nine other businesses.

More welcome news included the continued construction of a J. C. Penny's, along with the anticipated return (from the two fires) of other popular local businesses such as Don's Slipper Shop. Also in motion, through a near-unanimously approved $175,000 bond is-suance, was an overdue two-part school building program for Dead-wood. A new grade school annex—to contain three classrooms, a multi-purpose room (designed to enable the school's first cafete-ria), an office, and lavatories—was underway, and contracts were imminent for a new armory-auditorium to house a larger gymnasium and serve as a meeting center for the South Dakota National Guard.

To help pass the time while Ferguson was recuperating at home came one other exciting announcement for the Deadwood community. A giddy Yuill got right to it in her January 7, 1955, *Pioneer-Times* column: "Deadwood has its first television!"

Eight years after the introduction of full-scale commercial television broadcasting—and twenty months after television arrived in South Dakota—approximately two thousand folks stuffed themselves into the Deadwood City Auditorium to watch the first television programs ever broadcast into the city. Extensive local research from representatives of Seattle-based Western Television System had come to the decision to run a closed-circuit system in which television cable wire, emanating from a downtown studio, was strung along existing power and telephone lines throughout the city. Due to the challenging mountainous terrain and climate, location testing for an antenna-based system had resulted in too many issues with picture quality and two-way radio interference.

More local history occurred a week later as the Deadwood gymnasium was set up with coaxial cable for the A and B basketball games, the first ever televised basketball games in the Black Hills. In the weeks ahead, the conveniently named WTVS held at least five hours of varied afternoon and evening programming and ran ads encouraging residents to see their favorite twin cities TV dealer about getting connected to the new station. As an added sales boost, the station ran a limited time promotion for a lower connection cost and tapped an eager promoter—Coach Stewart Ferguson.

As a long-standing consumer of media, it was hardly surprising that Ferguson was one of the community's first purchasers of a television set and was happy to provide a testimonial. "We enjoy the programs very much and feel TV is worth many times the cost. Television is very educational, especially in my subjects of history and social sciences. We like to boost any new enterprise that puts Deadwood and Lead in leadership in Western South Dakota." While Ferguson would not have minded the full seven-channel selection bundle in Los Angeles or even the four available channels in Greeley, Colorado, WTVS shows like *Nerves of the Nation* and *So This Is Washington* certainly held his attention. Overall, television provided a terrific lift for Ferguson, and as winter wore on, he started to feel more like himself.

Ferguson took on teaching a Saturday morning BHTC extension class in beginning philosophy and was regaining his strength just in time for an upcoming special event sponsored by the Deadwood Chamber of Commerce that he of all people couldn't miss. Instead of the usual spring basketball banquet, chamber president Allan ("Birdie") Arnold arranged a Saturday night trip for both the A and B basketball squads and the coaches to the new Belle Fourche gymnasium for an evening with the world-famous Harlem Globetrotters.

Although this was the Trotters' western team—not their main eastern unit, featuring such stars as Reece ("Goose") Tatum—the Bears contingent was quite familiar with all the players, having just seen them on the big screen at the Flame in *Go, Man, Go!*, the "all new, all true" Globetrotters movie playing across the country. The opponent was the Boston Whirlwinds, an all-white professional team of former college stars who played it pretty straight and enabled the Globetrotters to do their thing, dazzling the crowd with their dribbling prowess and vast array of scripted and unscripted antics—a perfect night for the fun-first coach taking it all in.

Ferguson continued to feel stronger into the spring and attended another Jaycee-sponsored sports banquet. KDSJ sports announcer Vince Coyle, the master of ceremonies, introduced the coaches. Ferguson finally got the chance to present each member of the 1954 football team, while Coach Burgess introduced the A basketball team (who slipped to a 6–8 conference record and lost to Lead in the first round of sectionals). A month later brought the promising news that Ferguson was feeling healthy enough to fully return to the classroom. He was scheduled to teach two classes, education and social sciences, during BHTC's first summer session beginning June 1.

By Thursday, August 25, it hardly felt like football weather. Deadwood temperatures had hit ninety degrees for four straight days, but

Coach Ferguson wasn't complaining about the heat. He was home, back on the practice field and sizing up his new group for the 1955 season. A week later, the coach and his Bears owned the local sports page, beginning with a familiar sounding headline spread across the top: "Ferguson Formula to Be Wide Open Style." A light, youngish squad led by five seniors after losing ten to graduation had Ferguson preaching "a variety of formations" and "more wide open football than ever before."

The 1955 Deadwood Bears preview was the first of three local high school football features by Bert Cameron, the latest, greatest *Deadwood Pioneer-Times* and *Lead Daily Call* sports editor, and a Lead local who had just graduated from BHTC. He also included a biography of the coach to kick off his daily column, "Cameron's Comments." It was the first time in a while that the paper covered Ferguson's Arkansas A & M years, and though the young pup editor got most of the facts right—including the crazy contract, stipulating that the coach did not have to win a game for three years as long as the players were having fun—the recap ended with a real doozy: that Ferguson, "of course, built the squad into a championship team." Humorous revisionist history aside, a little extra Ferguson time felt right.

The following week included a return trip for the coach as a luncheon guest of the Deadwood Rotary Club, and a peppy Ferguson spoke enthusiastically about his team one day before the season start at Gillette. But for the first time in seven matchups, Ferguson's Bears were thoroughly outplayed by the Gillette Camels and lost 19–6. The Bears had a week off before their September 23 game at Hot Springs, which pleased the coach, who told the *Pioneer Times* "It will give us a chance to sharpen up." The Bison had opened with two wins and, impressively, had just defeated Sturgis, last year's unchallenged conference champion. The time off did seem to help as the Bears ran effectively and clicked on several short passes—significantly outgaining the Bison—but were undone by eight turnovers in a 14–0 defeat.

Despite a tough start, Ferguson remained positive and supportive of his Bears. Heading into a third straight road game, against Belle Fourche, Ferguson was encouraged by the state of the team. He reported to the paper that "the boys feel good over last week's show-ing, even though we lost . . . and we're going to do our best to show the Broncs that they've been in a ballgame Friday night." The Broncs, behind fifteen returning lettermen, were the talk of the conference heading into the season but stood a disappointing 0–2 after a close nonconference loss and a defeat against Spearfish.

This one stayed tight, and a 20–13 Bears lead shrunk to just one in the final minute after a fifteen-yard Broncs score. With time wind-ing down and the Broncs needing a point to tie, halfback Sandy Huff-man took a pitch to the right, but was immediately stuffed by two charging Bears linemen, junior Jerry Pontius and sophomore Dale Hansen, preserving the Bears' first win of the season. Bear Day was on deck and senior Walter ("Woody") Williamson—chosen by his coach as a co-captain for the game—was, appropriately, at the center of the festivities.

Class president and vice president the prior two years, Woody was selected as president of the student council for his senior year. The highlight of his Bear Day responsibilities was to crown Dead-wood's all-school queen on behalf of the student body and the foot-ball team. Over the last four years, Woody had also developed into a leader on the football field. A four-year letterman, he easily bounced as needed between line and backfield positions on both offense and defense and was now the team's top overall player. So far, he had been alternating between halfback and quarterback and had just romped for an eighty-yard score in the win against Belle Fourche.

This year's homecoming celebration was also especially meaning-ful for the Bears coach. Stuck in the hospital for the previous year's Bear Day festivities, Ferguson seemed remarkably passionate when it was his turn in the ceremony to say a few words: "We will be out-weighed, out-sized, and out-numbered, but we will not be out-fought." It was an embellishment, for sure—though homecoming opponent Spearfish was a bigger bunch—but there was no doubt how Ferguson felt about his team's heart.

Spearfish was looking to regroup after its first loss of the season, 6–0, to still undefeated Hot Springs. After a sloppy, fumble-laden start, the team settled down and played to an entertaining 13–13 draw, with the Bears driving to the Spartans' twenty-yard line before time ran out. The Bears split the next two games, getting overpowered on the ground against Sturgis and then holding on for their second one-point win of the season, 13–12, over a still winless but much improved Custer team.

The end of the Custer game signaled the beginning of Lead week, and the launch of an inspired addition to the twin cities sibling rivalry. But news coming out of Hot Springs demanded immediate attention. The Friday night combination of Lead's 19–6 home win over Spearfish and Belle Fourche's 13–9 upset victory at Hot Springs meant that the Golddiggers, 4–0–1 in the conference, had just clinched the title; all the other teams had at least two losses.

Over the weekend, however, Hot Springs football coach Keith Roberts had filed a protest to the South Dakota High School Athletic Association requesting the game against Belle Fourche be replayed due to a claim of poor officiating. Since the protest did not involve a state championship, the issue was forwarded to the current president of the Black Hills Conference, Maurice Fitzgerald, Lead head coach for basketball and line coach for football. Fitzgerald knew an overall officiating complaint was not cause to grant a protest, but he also wanted to eliminate any hint of prejudice since Lead was currently entrenched as conference champ. Fitzgerald decided to call an impromptu meeting with the other head coaches in the conference, who voted to dismiss the protest.

With the issue closed, focus quickly returned to the exciting rivalry news: the introduction of a travelling trophy. Similar to the storied little brown jug trophy—which was neither little nor brown—that went to the annual winner of the matchup between the University of Michigan and the University of Minnesota, or even the actual goat that a couple of Ferguson's Arkansas A & M teams fought for against Magnolia A & M, the Deadwood Jaycees wanted to create a new award that would go to the Deadwood–Lead winner each year.

Plans had been developing in the weeks leading up to this year's game, and the Jaycees invited both coaches to a Wednesday buffet dinner to provide an update and get their thoughts on the football game with forty-eight hours to go. Coach Handley and Coach Ferguson were strong proponents of the new award, and amid the night's light banter, found some time to talk seriously about the upcoming match-up. Lead's Handley was up first and said that "past records do not mean anything. The eleven boys who want to play will win." Ferguson followed and simply said he was "very optimistic about his team's chances."

With a day to go, the *Deadwood Pioneer-Times* headline read: "Annual Lead-Deadwood Classic May Be Photo Finish Contest." This was a fairly surprising take since Lead, after two early season non-conference losses, was on a roll with four straight wins, including a 13–12 home thriller over previously unbeaten Hot Springs earlier in October that had vaulted the Golddiggers into the conference top spot, while Ferguson's Bears stood 2–2–1, with the two wins coming by a measly point each. On the other hand, the forecast made complete sense: every year, this game was simply different than any other.

One piece of the rivalry you could almost set your watch to, however, was some wild, wintry weather. Naturally, Tuesday's clear skies with temperatures in the seventies were a distant memory by Thursday. The temperatures plunged to the twenties and the clouds thickened; a crew pushed hard on Friday to clear about four inches of overnight snow from Deadwood's Amusement Park field and get it as dry as possible for kickoff at a quarter to eight.

By game time, near-blizzard conditions engulfed the field, and the weather remained the story throughout the first half. Ten fumbles, including five in the first twelve plays, kept any real scoring threats to a minimum. Beyond a slippery football, sudden updrafts of swirling snow popped many of the large, hot floodlight bulbs late in the second quarter, almost ending the game due to darkness. As soon as the scoreless affair reached halftime, the floodlights were shut off and allowed to cool. By the start of the third quarter, the snowstorm had subsided, and the sufficiently rested lights held for the remainder of the evening.

The story returned to the players on the field as the action picked up. Still scoreless late in the third quarter, the Bears started a new possession on their own thirty-yard line and not even Ferguson could have cooked up what happened next. Halfback Larry Mitchell spotted fellow back Donnie James open in the flat and zipped one his way. The ball deflected off James's fingertips and headed to the ground. Just before ball met grass, Woody Williamson cut behind James, snatched the ball, and motored sixty-four yards to the end zone. The pass for the extra point was good, putting the Bears up 7–0 with one quarter to go.

Lead instantly responded. Starting from their own thirty, the Golddiggers' ground game began to hum, churning to the Bears' two-yard line before Deadwood's defense stiffened and forced a fourth down. Needing a yard for a first down, fullback John Ward, Lead's go-to power back all season, drove straight ahead and wound up on the bottom of a massive pile-up. Once the heap was cleared, the officials ruled Ward made his yard, giving Lead new life. On the next play, Ward charged up the middle and into the end zone, setting up a critical point after play call. The call remained the same—Ward bolted straight ahead and across the goal line to even the score, 7–7.

As the final quarter wore on, no real scoring threats materialized, and the game ended knotted at seven. For the first time in sixteen years, and the third time in its official fifty-two-year history, Deadwood versus Lead finished in a tie. And this time, the proceedings were not quite complete. The Jaycees decided that the first annual Deadwood-Lead travelling trophy would be split; the safekeeper for the first six months would be resolved on the field by a flip of the coin. Deadwood co-captain Tommy Gorder called "heads," but the coin landed "tails" and Gorder, along with fellow co-captain Don James, handed the game ball—symbolizing the trophy, which was not quite ready—to Lead's captain, Gene Raetz.

In the center of the ceremony, captured by the *Pioneer-Times*, stood the two coaches, shaking hands. The snapshot of a beaming Ferguson—who had become famous for his determination to play football for fun—lit up the field; he was one proud papa and precisely where he was meant to be.

CHAPTER 41

CELEBRATING FERGIE

The next few weeks continued a pleasant period for Ferguson and his family. The coach celebrated his team at the annual football banquet, while Edna helped organize and lead the school's yearly declamatory contest. The best night of all came at an Elks Club candlelight ceremony, as Ferguson and Edna watched Freddie join the latest group of Deadwood boys to be inducted as Cub Scouts.

Without any warning, on Thursday morning, December 29, Ferguson woke up around half past seven and told his wife he couldn't breathe. By the time medical assistance arrived, he was already gone. Coach Stewart A. Ferguson died of a sudden heart attack, two weeks before his fifty-sixth birthday. Services were set for Monday afternoon and a stunned, saddened Twin City community packed into Deadwood's Methodist Church to say goodbye.

Six former Bears players, spanning Ferguson's first Deadwood team to his last, served as pallbearers. Among the six were Billy Jones, Norman Lee, and Fred North, who paid respects to his namesake, Ferguson's son, Freddie. Years later, Bob Sjomeling, a senior who had just completed a strong season playing end for Ferguson, remembered the day well. "It was nice out and the Methodist Church was so full, a lot of us—even players and kids—had to stand outside." The coach's friends and family were considered honorary pallbearers. Inside the church, Edna made sure one detail was not forgotten. Ever since a railroad factory accident years prior, Ferguson remained conscious of losing part of his little finger on his left hand, hiding it whenever possible. So, Edna covered his left hand in the casket.

The day after the funeral, Camille Yuill, who had welcomed Stewart Ferguson to Deadwood in September 1944 and watched him leave an indelible imprint on the community, dedicated her "Backlog" column to Ferguson. Yuill championed his work as an educator, and how he shared with his students the "great adventure of learning." In athletics, she commended Fergie's focus on how the game was played over results on the scoreboard, and when the wins did start to pile up, how the praise always centered on the players. Camille went on to paint a picture of a man who had left far too soon:

> Quietly, modestly, he went about his work, faithful to his creed, quick to praise, equally quick to resent injustice and come to the defense of any he believed were being treated unfairly; compassionate and understanding. No one ever can know the effect or extent of his influence.
>
> Our spirits are lifted, our ideals strengthened, and our faith and hope in man's promise and power renewed, even as with heavy hearts, we say farewell to him— "Fergie," husband, father, citizen, coach, teacher—and friend.

The Deadwood community's heavy hearts quickly moved from words into action, and the Jaycees knew exactly where to strike first. The group crafted a resolution to change the name of the Deadwood Amusement Park grounds to Ferguson Field. The Jaycees also announced that the traveling trophy had arrived—to be presented in an official ceremony in Lead's gym before the following week's Lead–Deadwood basketball game—and that the placeholder game ball would be signed by the Deadwood football team and presented to Edna Ferguson. Upon accepting the snazzy new trophy, Ross Oates, president of the Lead Student Council, asked the crowd to rise for a moment of silent prayer "in memory of Deadwood's great football coach, Stewart A. Ferguson."

In early April, Deadwood's city council officially approved the football field in the Deadwood Amusement Park to be dedicated as the Stewart A. Ferguson Memorial Field. The council also endorsed the request of the Jaycees and representatives of Deadwood High

School's faculty and student body for Mayor Ray L. Ewing to issue a proclamation naming and dedicating the field. A week later, the Jaycees' annual Deadwood High School sports banquet provided another opportunity to honor Ferguson. His absence still stung, but his presence loomed large.

Several Black Hills coaches, including Ferguson's good friend Don Young, BHTC's athletic director, were among a two-hundred-person overflow crowd who drank in Ferguson reflections across the series of speakers. The banquet opened with the mayor's proclamation designating Ferguson Field and followed with KDSJ's Vince Coyle, once again serving as the master of ceremonies, reading a letter from Edna thanking the people of Deadwood, the mayor, and the Jaycees for honoring her husband in renaming the field: "This is one of the rarest things in life so valuable that it has no purchasing power—money would not buy this great honor, and few of us could earn it."

Before the end of the school year, one more vital tribute accompanied a resplendent photo of Ferguson on page two of the 1956 Deadwood High School yearbook:

We of the 1956 Bear Log staff wish to dedicate this annual to the memory of Coach Stewart Ferguson who died suddenly on December 29, 1955. For eleven years, "Fergie" gave his best to us not only as a coach but also as a history teacher. His industriousness, kindheartedness, sympathy and understanding won for him a place in the hearts of all who knew him.

Hustle and bustle emanated from the Deadwood Amusement Park grounds two days before the Bears' first home football game of the 1956 season. Supported by a Jaycees funding campaign, furious work continued to get a few sections of the brand-new bleachers ready for Friday night's official dedication of Ferguson Field. The bleachers were built above the retaining wall on the north side of the field and splashed across the fifty-yard line, giving Bears fans a new home side and a now unobstructed view of all the action below.

At the end of June, Edna had announced her resignation after twelve years at Deadwood High School to become the new high school librarian in Sheridan, Wyoming, about two hundred miles away in the backdrop of the Bighorn Mountains. While ready for a change, Edna planned to keep her house up the hill and return for vacations during the year. She also decided to stay home in Deadwood through the summer, enabling Freddie to keep busy with his friends during a difficult time.

Freddie's Cub Scout events and award ceremonies flowed into the Deadwood Junior Softball season, played under the lights at the ball field within the Amusement Park grounds. Thanks to a famous cowboy organization, almost nine-year-old Freddie also attained formal mascot status. Selecting Deadwood for their annual South Dakota Stock Growers Association Convention, forty-three members of the 1902 Cowboys chose Freddie as a mascot and included him in their distinguished *Deadwood Pioneer-Times* page one photo.

Now, on a cool September night, after a short time getting acclimated at her new school, Edna was back in Deadwood for Ferguson's ultimate tribute. In addition to the new name and new bleachers, a large memorial flanked midfield with an inscribed bronze plaque due to arrive soon. The Bears were hosting another group of Cowboys, from Lemmon, and at a special halftime ceremony, the formal dedication of Ferguson Field got underway.

Mayor Ewing opened with a look back on Ferguson's football life and stressed his emphasis on sportsmanship in teaching the game. Paul Thompson, president of the Jaycees, then introduced Edna Ferguson to her hometown crowd. She thanked the Jaycees and the Deadwood community for the memorial to her husband, and accentuated one lasting point: Coach Ferguson, across his entire colorful life, loved the sport of football.

AUTHOR'S NOTE

Edna and Freddie Ferguson did not leave Deadwood for long. After the 1956–1957 school year, Edna returned to run Deadwood's public library; she stayed for two years, left to teach junior high English at Rapid City's Ellsworth Air Force Base, remarried to Harry Robinson (a former player of Fergie's at Dakota Wesleyan) in 1960, and came back in the fall of 1961 for a second stint as English teacher and librarian at Deadwood High School. Edna felt strongly that Freddy (as he now spelled his name) should attend DHS. For his part, the apple didn't fall far from the trees; Freddy joined the debate team and the drama club, became an all-state drummer, and progressed from Bears football superfan into a talented halfback and captain of his 1964 senior year squad.

Five decades later, I counted down the days to take in a game at Deadwood's stunning Ferguson Field, though it wouldn't be *Bears* spread across the school's jerseys. The Lead Golddiggers and Deadwood Bears are now the Lead–Deadwood Golddiggers and have been for some time. The integrated Lead–Deadwood Independent School District took effect in the 1971 school year, the result of a 1970 state commission for elementary and secondary education intended to offer a more robust educational program for both communities. On a chilly September evening, I watched Rapid City's Saint Thomas More High School dominate the up-down gulch boys for a 42–0 lead at halftime. But the image that stays with me occurred a bit later. As a Lead–Deadwood defender turned a fumble recovery into a 33-yard touchdown romp, on the sideline the former ancient rivals erupted in unison and ran alongside.

The same day that Lead and Deadwood high schools officially integrated (July 1, 1971), Arkansas A & M College merged with the University of Arkansas to become the University of Arkansas at Monticello. Over the years, Boll Weevils football has enjoyed many winning seasons, and in another uncanny coincidence, celebrated its first conference title in 1953, the same year as Fergie's Deadwood Bears. In 2010, the school also celebrated Buddy Carson, who seamlessly transitioned from Wandering Weevil to "Mr. Weevil." He received the Continuing the Connection Award, presented to the person who best maintains the connection between A & M and UAM.

I wonder how Fergie would connect to today's game, starting with the seismic shifts across the landscape of college football. Concerned foremost with the overall well-being of his players, he'd likely support the evolving (and overdue) changes to more equitable compensation for college players, and the relaxed restrictions on players transferring to new schools. He would certainly applaud the ongoing efforts, at all levels, to make football safer. I wholeheartedly agree. Though we can't eliminate the sport's extreme risks, put me in the camp of flag over tackle at younger ages, along with limited contact in high school practices—and yes, also at the college level. Contrarian endeavors like that of Dartmouth's head coach, Buddy Teevens, to practice smarter and improve technique—eliminating live tackling and instead using various dummies, including a robotic moving version—are worthy of further conversation and consideration.

ACKNOWLEDGMENTS

To begin, I need to talk about Bill Bell. Dubbed by his family as "the thing in the basement," Bill had the unique ability to do a crossword, play guitar, read, watch college football, belt out Johnny Cash, and nap, all at the same time. Yeah, and as a lifelong newspaperman, he could also bang out stories with the best of 'em.

Raised in Arkansas, Bill's first gig, in 1953, was sports editor of the *Pine Bluff Commercial*. He went on to literally span the world for United Press International—from South America to Europe and Africa—before settling down in Connecticut and starting up at the New York *Daily News*. Spending years as the religion editor and City Beat columnist, he was a witty, gritty, wise, and beloved newsroom figure. In a touching tribute, legendary *Daily News* cartoonist and columnist Bill Gallo captured the essence of Bill: "Bill interviewed everybody, be it the baker, shoemaker, ice cream parlor owner or the high and mighty. His way of getting something out of someone was with an easy voice, the questions all in the best of taste."

Bill also kept the newsroom loose with his rapid-fire, endless supply of "Bell-isms," including a family favorite: "I never knew what true happiness was until I got married—and then it was too late." While his *Daily News* buddies knew how excited Bill was about his second act as an author, I only became acutely aware after stumbling upon a document during some additional Connecticut basement book research. Circa 2004, Bill Bell typed up the not-so-little, therapeutic ditty *It Didn't Take _____ This Long to...* Enjoy one of the 53 beauties, a nod to Fergie's religion-centric musings in the book: "*It*

Didn't Take Adam This Long to convince Eve they should be more than friends." Wait no longer, Billy Bell, and thank you for lighting the path for all of us you touched along the way.

As I alluded to in the Preface, this book simply couldn't have happened without the ardent support of Deadwood High School alumni Dick Dunwiddie (1954) and Bill Beshara (1955). I found Dick through his wonderful Deadwood High School Classmates blog, and I can't thank him enough for responding to my letter, chatting with me soon after, and putting me in contact with Bill Beshara. Bill, based in Rapid City and a member of Deadwood's champion 1953 football squad, connected me with many former Deadwood players and an absolute gem of a human being, Jill Tiffany.

Previously, Jill was married to Freddy Ferguson, who developed diabetes-driven health complications shortly after their wedding in 1993 and succumbed to his failing health just a few years later, in June 1996. Jill remarried, but she and Edna remained close. Over the years, Edna became "like a grandma" to Jill's two kids. Further, Edna left all rights of Stewart Ferguson's story to Jill. Sitting, listening, and laughing with Jill—immersed in Edna's family photos and keepsakes—I could see the entire book take shape. Jill's endorsement that Bill and I were the right team to tell Fergie's full story meant everything and kept pushing me to see it through. I couldn't wait to share with Jill the great news on the book contract and was extremely saddened to learn of her recent passing.

I want to sincerely thank the former Deadwood Bears who made the time to speak with me: Hank Frawley and Janet Thoresen, Sheldon Jacobs, Maurice Etem, Cecil Stoner, Willie Steinlicht, Bob Sjomeling, and Don Gross. Special thanks to Hank and Maurice for welcoming me into their homes and to Willie, Bob, and Don, who met me up the hill in Deadwood during some historically brutal Black Hills winter weather.

I'd also like to recognize a few people who provided invaluable support during my time in the Black Hills. At the Deadwood Public Library, Carol Hauck lugged up stacks of the *Deadwood Pioneer-Times* until she finally found her savior, the hidden cart! And I'm so appreciative of Carol's spearheading the painstaking effort to digitize the paper, which was an immense help in finishing the book.

Deadwood's City Archivist, Michael Runge, was incredibly patient, laying out all the relevant files, along with prepping and sending me copies of the Deadwood Oral History project (including an enlightening interview with Edna Ferguson Robinson).

Lynn Larsen, the Lead–Deadwood School District's long-time all-star administrator, organized my Deadwood and Lead school visits, scanned numerous pages from Deadwood's *Bear Log* yearbook, and enthusiastically met my assorted follow-up requests.

An additional thank you to the supportive staff of the Rapid City Public Library.

For the Mitchell area, I owe a big thank you to Dakota Wesleyan University's ace archivist, Laurie Langland. Laurie was overwhelmingly friendly and accommodating, no matter how much material I requested before and during my Dakota Wesleyan visit; I was happy to recently reconnect over the book's publication. Courtesy of Laurie, I also must sneak in an exchange from Dakota Wesleyan's 1925 *Tumbleweed* (Professor Owens: *What right do you have to swear before me?* Fergie's response: *How did I know you wanted to swear first?*).

One other thank you to Pam Range, who pointed me to valuable content at the Mitchell Area Historical Society.

Bill and I want to thank several crucial individuals who further informed Stewart Ferguson's extended stay at Arkansas A & M, including his remarkable run with the Wandering Weevils. Thank you to A & M's former players and family members who shared their stories (and a couple of scrapbooks) with Bill: Annie Robinson, J. P. Leveritt, Buddy Carson, Teddy McKinney, Oscar Dove, Verl Gill, and Sara Stegall. Thank you to Jim Brewer, University of Arkansas at Monticello's long-time media services director, who sent Bill initial material and article clips. Jim published a wonderful book of his own, *They Played for Laughs: The True Story of Stewart Ferguson and the Arkansas A & M Wandering Weevils, College Football's Marx Brothers*, in 2021. Thank you to UAM's Special Collections Librarian, Mary Heady, who warmly provided Bill and me with school newspapers, yearbooks, and the trove of Stewart Ferguson school files. Additional thanks to the Arkansas library staffs in Monticello, Pine Bluff, and UA Little Rock; the Ashville-Buncombe, North Carolina library system staff; and the West Virginia University library staff.

I'd also like to acknowledge some folks from my travels to Louisiana. Pati Threatt, McNeese Archivist and Special Collections Librarian, graciously instructed me to don gloves and sharpen pencils for Lake Charles High School's delicate old newspapers and yearbooks. And thanks to Pati's predecessor, Kathie Bordelon, who sent Bill some Stewart Ferguson mentions from the student paper and the (Lake Charles) *American Press*. Faith Johnson and Candice Hamilton from Alexandria's Rapides Parish Main Library were terrific, supporting my various needs. My visit to the Dry Creek Baptist Camp— former site of Dry Creek High School—was a real treat; thanks very much to Meghan and Debra for hosting me. Unfortunately, the former schoolhouse was subsequently lost to a devastating 2021 fire, but the camp has survived and continues its mission. And thanks to the team at LSU's Hill Memorial Library for pulling old editions of the Summer Bulletin.

A huge thank you to the fantastic team at the South Dakota Historical Society Press: to Cody Ewert for shepherding me through the book's acquisition and production process; to lead editor Slater Sabo; and to editor-in-chief Dedra McDonald Birzer, who also oversaw the book's marketing.

I'd like to thank Curt Chaplin for his unwavering encouragement and belief in the book and Bryan Dunn for finding time to read and discuss a preliminary draft.

And thanks to my longtime biggest fans—my parents and my wife Amanda. Finally, a heartfelt thank you to Di, who put up with my amateur basement detective work, traded laughs across the table over Bill's helpless handwriting, and always answered the Bell on my questions throughout the writing process.

NOTES

A NOTE ON SOURCES

To provide a more complete portrait, Bill and I include excerpts (with sometimes controversial opinions and language) from Stewart Ferguson's unpublished memoirs (ca. 1947) throughout the first two parts of the book. Bill obtained a copy of these memoirs from Edna Ferguson Robinson; we have revised a few word usages, for clarity, and added words to some sentences with cut-off text. For simplicity, I use the abbreviation *SFM* for Stewart Ferguson memoirs citations not referenced in the book.

We have relied on archival newspaper coverage to provide a foundation for the narrative. The *Mount Vernon News* and Mitchell's *Evening Republican* were especially helpful in the telling of Coach Stewart Ferguson's adolescent years, while the *Deadwood Pioneer-Times* and *Rapid City Journal* were instrumental in detailing his return to Deadwood. For Ferguson's prolonged period in Arkansas, including the 1939–1941 Wandering Weevils era, we leaned on the *Arkansas Democrat*, the *Advance-Monticellonian*, and local papers whenever possible. Dakota Wesleyan University's *Phreno Cosmian* and Arkansas A & M's *Weevil Outlet* provided vital college newspaper coverage. Other essential sources included the *Drew County Historical Journal* and several school yearbooks (Dakota Wesleyan University, Arkansas A & M, Deadwood High School, and Lead High School).

Driven by the book's narrative focus, Bill and I include historical context as deemed appropriate. Raymond Schmidt's *Shaping College*

Football: The Transformation of an American Sport, 1919–1930 was particularly useful. For those interested in a comprehensive telling of college football through the 1980s, I highly recommend John Watterson's *College Football: History, Spectacle, Controversy*.

For Bill's interviews included in the book, comprising former Arkansas A & M players (Annie Robinson, J. P. Leveritt, Buddy Carson, Teddy McKinney, and Oscar Dove) and a wonderful conversation with Edna Ferguson Robinson, I reference dates wherever possible. My interviews with Deadwood High School alumni (Hank Frawley, Janet Thoresen, Sheldon Jacobs, Maurice Etem, Cecil Stoner, Willie Steinlicht, Bob Sjomeling, and Don Gross) were conducted during 2014, mostly in person.

In addition, I use the following abbreviations in these detailed Notes: DWU (Dakota Wesleyan University), WO (*Weevil Outlet*), AD (*Arkansas Democrat*), DPT (*Deadwood-Pioneer Times*), RCJ (*Rapid City Journal*), DHS (Deadwood High School).

CHAPTER ONE

SFM: Reflections around Stewart's rebellious sixteen-year-old ways; attending his first football game; and convincing family that football was the way to the Methodist pulpit.

Reverend William T. Ferguson filling in when needed as editor of the local newspaper, Paul's scary bout with Polio, and other details on the Mount Vernon High School come from 1916 accounts (June 16, Aug. 18, Aug. 25, Sept. 1, Sept. 22, Oct. 6, Oct. 13) in *Mount Vernon News*. Mary Ferguson's mysterious crib death is sourced from the Dakotas Conference Archives and History Library. Overview of the 1916 polio epidemic draws from https://www.historyofvaccines.org/content/new-york-city-polio-epidemic.

The size of the Reverend's congregation and his annual salary figure are referenced from the *1914 Annual Conference Journal*. The details around the 1917 accidental school fire are found in the *Dakota Dateline: 1881–1981, The Story of Mount Vernon, South Dakota* (10).

CHAPTER TWO

SFM: Stewart's characterizations of growing up in Gregory; his daily chores and continued rebellious ways; and his musings about the colorful Professor Wilds.

The *Dakota Dateline: 1881–1981, The Story of Mount Vernon, South Dakota* (47) provides a parody version of the hymn 'Beulah Land,' describing the "wind-swept prairie town of Mount Vernon." The hymn's original version begins: "I've reached the land of corn and wine, And all its riches freely mine." It can be found at https://hymnary.org/hymn/HHOF1980/517. Details of Reverend Ferguson's accomplishments and varied professional responsibilities in Mount Vernon stem from 1916 accounts in *Mount Vernon News* (Apr. 2, May 5, July 14). Additional content from *The Dakota Dateline* details the setting and commercial activity in the town of Mount Vernon upon the Ferguson family's arrival in 1913. Information on Reverend Ferguson's weekly sermons in Gregory, South Dakota comes from *Gregory Times-Advocate*, Oct. 16, 1913, and the town's population is pulled from the 1909 Gregory Business Directory. James E. Fraser's biographical sketch is taken from https://www.usacoinbook.com/encyclopedia/coin-designers/james-earle-fraser/. The information on Mitchell's origin is from James D. McLaird's engrossing *DWU Memory Book, 1885–2010*.

Although I could not confirm the reference, Bill likely spotted Reverend Ferguson's and Stewart's visit to the Canton, South Dakota asylum in his thorough newspaper research. Information on the Canton asylum comes from Steve Young, "S.D. revisits past at Native American insane asylum," *Argus Leader*, May 5, 2013, and Elizabeth Stawicki's piece, "A Haunting Legacy: Canton Insane Asylum for American Indians," https://sites.rootsweb.com/~sdlincol/hiawatha.htm, Dec. 9, 1997.

Depiction of the growing popularity of college football comes from Raymond Schmidt, *Shaping College Football: The Transformation of an American Sport, 1919–1930* (Syracuse, N.Y.: Syracuse University Press, 2007), pp. 40–41; and https://pac-12.com/content/

about-pac-12-conference. The principle sources behind the birth of the flying wedge and later efforts to lessen the ritual violence in college football are: Scott A. McQuilkin and Ronald A. Smith, "The Rise and Fall of the Flying Wedge: Football's Most Controversial Play," *Journal of Sport History* 20, No. 1 (Spring 1993): 57–64; *Washington Post*, Oct. 15, 1905; New-York *Daily Tribune* (Nov. 26, Dec. 29, 1905); *Chicago Tribune*, Jan. 26, 1907; and *New York Times*, Nov. 12, 1908. An article from the *Ithaca Journal*, Oct. 7, 1916, highlights concern around the rapidly rising financial costs to compete at the highest levels of college football.

The *DWU Memory Book* (15, 37) is also sourced to explain the "oddly named" school newspaper (*Phreno Cosmian*) and the school's 1904 name change. The origin of DWU football stems from two sources: https://www.dwu.edu/about-dwu/why-dwu/history; and https://dwuathletics.com. Stewart's spirited football play draws from *Phreno Cosmian*, Dec. 14, 1916.

Details concerning Reverend Ferguson's failing health, the extensive coverage of his funeral, and associated tributes are taken from the following sources: *Mount Vernon News* (Apr. 27, May 11, 1917); *Daily Republican*, Apr. 23, 1917; DakotaWest At Bankwest, "Pastors Of The Church"; 33rd Session of the Dakota Annual Conference (189); and https://oddfellowsguide.com.

CHAPTER THREE

SFM: Stewart's reputation for rough play; and his sense that Ray McLean thought he was too inexperienced to make any impact on the field.

After Reverend Ferguson's death, the pensions provided to Edith Ferguson are sourced from the Methodist Church Annual Conference Journal. The number of male students at DWU in fall 1917 is taken from Sept. 2017 articles in the (Mitchell) *Evening Republican*.

Stewart's notification of entering the Student Army Training Corps comes from *Evening Republican*, Aug. 27, 1918. Local coverage of World War I, along with anti-German propaganda and new laws in 1918 is pulled predominantly from *Evening Republican*: "Mitchell boys cover selves with glory, says Col. Shade," and "German language forfeited by law on phone or streets," July 1; "Yaw'sa, Dem Dere Darkey Boys Sure Can Battle Some," July 8; "Mitchell Soldier Gassed in Battle," July 25; Aug. 21; and Oct. 18, 1918. Stories on the influenza pandemic are also covered extensively in *Evening Republican* (Sept. 19, Oct. 18, Nov. 6, 1918). A group of articles are referenced from the Nov. 11, 1918, *Evening Republican*, covering the armistice, the reopening of local schools and churches, and the 31 influenza deaths in Mitchell. The overall 1918 South Dakota death toll is taken from "A Brief History of Epidemics in South Dakota," Mar. 23, 2020, https://www.sdpb.org/blogs/images-of-the-past/a-brief-history-of-epidemics-in-south-dakota/. The number of estimated fatalities attributed to the 1918 Pandemic—globally and in the U.S.—is sourced from https://www.cdc.gov/flu/pandemic-resources/1918-pandemic-h1n1.html.

The description of Stewart's broken ankle in the 1918 season is sourced from *SFM* and the 1919 *Tumbleweed*, DWU's yearbook.

CHAPTER FOUR

SFM: Stewart's attempt to break Mark Payne's drop kick record; job and family updates; reflections on his college career and thoughts on big vocational choice ("teaching or preaching"); and decision to accept job offer in DeRidder, Louisiana.

Biographical sketch of Richard ("Bud") Dougherty draws from two sources: "New Coach Secured for Dakota Wesleyan," *RCJ*, Feb. 2, 1919, and the 1921 DWU *Tumbleweed*. News of Ray McLean's death in Germany comes from "State News Notes," *DPT*, Mar. 29, 1919.

Complimentary appraisal of Stewart's football skills is referenced from DWU's 1919 *Tumbleweed* and the quote that "he is showing up well" on the field comes from DWU's *Phreno Cosmian*, Oct. 9, 1919. Other sources contributing to the drop kick section are: *Argus*

Leader, Nov. 16, 2015; "100 year anniversary of Mark Payne's world's record drop kick," https://www.dwu.edu/news/100-year-anniversary -of-mark-paynes-worlds-record-drop-kick, Oct. 8, 2015; NCAA Record Book; http://www.luckyshow.org/football/field%20goals%20 of%2060%20yards%20or%20more.htm; and The Pro Football Hall of Fame.

The exploits of Stewart's band, The Dakota Kings, are pulled from one of the band's handbills, which Bill unearthed in his research (but which I was unable to locate). During this period, Stewart began dating Ione Raben; her biographical sketch is sourced from the 1923 *Tumbleweed*. More positive mentions of Stewart's football play, along with his earning a 'W' are taken from two *Phreno Cosmian* entries (Jan. 15, Mar. 11, 1920).

Stewart's departure from and eventual return to DWU in fall 1922 is confirmed through his DWU transcript and the Mitchell Directory. Stewart's accident at work, surprising return to the field, and "sly grin" in the team photo are referenced from three additional *Phreno Cosmian* entries (Oct. 20, Dec. 4, Dec. 15, 1922). Details surrounding DWU's new nickname, the Tigers, come from the 1925 *Tumbleweed* and the *RCJ*, Nov. 4, 1923. Content on the 1923 DWU Tigers football season is pulled from the *Argus Leader*. Stewart's selection as a conference first team all-star is taken from the *RCJ*, Dec. 4, 1923. His Rhodes Scholarship nomination comes from *Phreno Cosmian*, Nov. 27, 1923, and *Argus Leader*, Dec. 6, 1923. The 1923 DWU football program's $601.42 shortfall is from *Phreno Cosmian*, Dec. 11, 1923.

CHAPTER FIVE

SFM: Ferguson's discussion with Superintendent Lunsford; reflections on his years at Dry Creek High School, Lake Charles High School, and Bolton High School; his wonder at DWU's offer to return as athletic director, particularly given his college days indiscretions; and reflections on the story of the Prodigal Son.

Depiction of the town of DeRidder, ca. 1924, and area's historical Catholic missionaries' influence draw from: http://www.Beaurrgard-Dailynews.com, July 19, 2013; Mrs. Lether Edward Frazar's "Early Annals of Beauregard Parish," 1933; and http://theusgenweb.org/la/calcasieu/block/deridder.html. Ferguson's description of Dry Creek, Louisiana is from his letter to DWU Professor Owen: "Ferguson Tells of South," *Phreno Cosmian*, Mar. 23, 1925.

The biographical sketches of Bill Banker, Don Zimmerman, and Walter ("Dobie") Reeves are sourced from: the Lake Charles High School newspaper (*The Wild Cat*), the (Lake Charles) *American Press*, http://tulanegreenwave.ocsn.com; and https://lsusports.net.

Additional content on Ione Raben is referenced from the 1923 *Tumbleweed*. Stewart and Ione's elopement is confirmed from ancestry .com.

Columbia University's recruitment of Percy Barber is taken from the (Alexandria) *Town Talk*, Sept. 5, 1929. Details on Ferguson's year teaching and coaching at Bolton High School come from the school's 1929 *Bruin* yearbook. Ferguson's return to DWU as athletic director is sourced from the following articles: "Ferguson, Class of '23, Named Director of Athletics," *Evening Republican*, Feb. 28, 1929; "Ferguson Is D.W.U. Coach," The (Huron) *Daily Plainsman*, Mar. 1, 1929; "Wesleyan Names Athletic Head," *RCJ*, Mar. 1, 1929; "Ferguson named DW Coach," DWU *Phreno Cosmian*, Mar. 5, 1929; and "Ferguson, Bolton Hi Coach, Gets Job At Alma Mater," *Town Talk*, May 24, 1929. Further details on Elliott Hatfield's two-year stint as DWU's athletic director are from dwuathletics.com.

CHAPTER SIX

SFM: Ferguson's thoughts on new role as DWU athletic director; his recruitment of Glenn ("Hub") Hubbard and motivational plan for 1929 DWU football team; Yankton game external pep talks and Ferguson's Kiwanis Club invitation; his comments on packed Corn Palace DWU basketball games and reflections on fast-passing playing style at Dry Creek; memories of DWU's Sept. 1930 train ride to Louisiana State University; obtaining President Roadman's approval for DWU's first ever Athletic Guide and sending applications to larger universities; Ferguson's fall 1931 DWU contract negotiations; and details on the "goods and services" that comprised part of his DWU salary, due to the Great Depression.

The biographical sketch on President Roadman comes from: "Waterloo Man Named Dakota Wesleyan Prexy," *RCJ*, Aug. 25, 1927; "Kiwanis Club Honors Dr. Roadman," *The Morningsider* (Morningside College Alumni Newsletter), Jan. 1949; "Roadman to Be Baccalaureate Speaker At 'Aggie' Graduation," *Argus Leader*, Mar. 3, 1929; and "School of Mines Graduation Events to Commence Sunday," *Argus Leader*, May 24, 1929.

The account of Ferguson's DWU formal lakeside welcome is from "New Wesleyan Coach Honored At Dinner," *Evening Huronite*, Sept. 7, 1929. Additional details on Coach Hubbard joining DWU as an assistant coach draw from the *Evening Huronite*, Nov. 12, 1929. Ferguson's optimistic feeling about the team is referenced from *Phreno Cosmian*, Sept. 18, 1929. The overview of DWU's 1929 football season prior to the big Yankton game stems from Oct.–Nov. coverage in *Argus Leader* and *Evening Huronite*. Recap of the scoreless tie with Yankton is taken from *Argus Leader*, Nov. 29, 1929. DWU basketball results for the 1927–1928 and 1928–1929 seasons are sourced from dwuatheltics.com; and the comment on overall popularity of college basketball comes from timetoast.com/timelines/the-history-of-college-basketball.

The history of the World's Only Corn Palace is sourced from the following: lewisclark.net/biography; Mitchell Chamber of Commerce's Welcome to the World's Only Corn Palace pamphlet; *Evening Huronite*, Sept. 10, 1929; and *Argus Leader*, Sept. 19, 1929. William Clark's reference to the "Deserts of America" comes from his May 26, 1805, journal entry, found in Gary E. Moulton and Thomas W. Dunlay, eds., *The Journals of the Lewis and Clark Expedition: Volume 4, April 7–July 27, 1805* (Lincoln: University of Nebraska Press, 1987), p. 205.

DWU's first ever intersectional college football game, along with game preview and recap, comes from: "Wesleyan Grid Team Will Play At Baton Rouge," *Argus Leader*, Jan. 13, 1930; *Evening Huronite*, Sept. 15, 1930; and *RCJ*, Sept. 17, 1930. Additional coverage of DWU's 1930 football season draws from: *Argus Leader* (Sept. 28, Nov. 28) and *Evening Republican* (Nov. 9). Further information on intersectional college football, along with commentary on Coach Glenn ("Pop") Warner, is sourced from Raymond Schmidt, *Shaping College Football*, pp. 35, 86.

Details of the 1930 DWU football team banquet are referenced from *Phreno Cosmian*, Dec. 3, 1930, and *Argus Leader*, Dec. 22, 1930. Highlights of 1930–1931 DWU basketball season, including (exclusive) invitation to the annual National Amateur Athletic Association's tournament, are taken from Mar. 1931 articles in *Evening Huronite*, *Argus Leader*, and (Kansas City) *Journal-Post*. Results of Ferguson's track team at the Minnesota Relays come from *Evening Republican*, Apr. 2, 1931. Ferguson's puffed-up quotes on DWU's recent athletic prowess are from the "DWU Athletic Review: Two Remarkable Years."

The DWU P.K. (Preachers' Kids) event is sourced from *Evening Huronite*, Jan. 22, 1931. News of Ferguson submitting his master's thesis is referenced from *Phreno Cosmian* and his Louisiana State University transcript. The details surrounding Stewart and Ione's 1931 divorce are taken from Davison County, South Dakota Fourth Judicial Circuit Court report, July 23, 1931. Mention of rising unemployment in fall 1931 comes from https://the-balance.com. Ferguson's DWU salary is from *Evening Huronite*, Mar. 25, 1932, and *Argus Leader*, Nov. 7, 1932.

Coverage for DWU's 1931 football season and Ferguson's unprecedented travel plans for the team—including the White House visit—draw from the following: "New Plays Add Color In Dixie," *Monroe News-Star*, Nov. 6, 1927; *Evening Huronite*, Aug. 27, 1931; *Argus Leader* (Aug. 31, Sept. 29, Oct. 4, Nov. 27, 1931); *Phreno Cosmian* (Sept. 8, Sept. 29, Oct. 6, Oct. 13, 1931); https://dwuathletics .com; Christopher J. Walsh, *Who's #1?: 100-Plus Years of Controversial*

National Champions in College Football (Maryland: Taylor Trade Publishing, 2007), p. 10; and Schmidt, *Shaping College Football*, pp. 88–89.

Highlights of a third straight DWU championship basketball season, including undefeated 1931–1932 regular season and Corn Palace match-up with the unique House of David touring basketball team, are sourced from: *Phreno Cosmian* (Feb. 23, Mar. 15, 1932); *Evening Huronite* (Mar. 8, Mar. 20, 1932); and "House of David hoops team held court," https://www.newsleader.com/story/news/history/2017/07/17/house-david-hoops-team-held-court. Ferguson's interview at Drake University draws from: "Wesleyan Coach Among Applicants for Drake Job," AP, Mar. 24, 1932; *Evening Huronite*, Mar. 25, 1932; and "Williams Named Drake Coach," *Des Moines Register*, Apr. 5, 1932.

CHAPTER SEVEN

SFM: Ferguson's summer 1932 stance de-emphasizing DWU football player recruitment; growing unease heading into 1933 DWU football season; news that President Roadman's son wanted to play quarterback; Ferguson's 'drifting' feelings about playing to win; his souring relationship with DWU administration and Mitchell townspeople; his opinion that DWU's athletic committee had unfairly punished most of his track team, resulting in impetuous decision to share his thoughts with local newspaper; and Roadman convincing Ferguson to attend welcome breakfast for Lester Belding.

DWU's 1932 football content is sourced from: *Evening Huronite*, Oct. 4, 1932; *RCJ*, Nov. 12, 1932; and https://dwuathletics.com. DWU's stellar 1932–1933 basketball season overview is from: *Argus Leader* (Feb. 27, Mar. 12, 1933); *RCJ*, Mar. 8, 1933; and https://dwuathletics.com. Details of DWU's fall 1933 football season, along with fallout from the annual Methodist Episcopal church state conference, draw from: *Argus Leader* (Sept. 5, Oct. 1, Oct. 9–10, Oct. 12, Oct. 15, Nov. 12, 1933); *Evening Republican* (Sept. 27, Nov. 1, 1933); and *DPT*, Oct. 8, 1933. Details of DWU's 1933–1934 basketball season come from: "Ferguson Uneasy As Wesleyan's Real Championship

Test Nears," *Evening Huronite*, Jan. 25, 1934; "Augustana And Wesleyan Fight For Lead Tonight," *Argus Leader*, Feb. 5, 1934; "Vikings Pass Champs In Title Race with 34–33 Win," *Argus Leader*, Feb. 6, 1934; and https://dwuathletics.com.

News that the majority of track team was declared ineligible for Apr. 28, 1934, meet, and the end of Ferguson's tenure as DWU's athletic director are sourced from: "Wesleyan's Track Squad Is Crippled for Scalper Meet," *Evening Huronite*, Apr. 27, 1934; "Ferguson Quits As Dakota Wesleyan Coach!," *Evening Republican*, May 1, 1934; *Argus Leader*, May 29, 1934; and *Phreno Cosmian*, May 29, 1934.

CHAPTER EIGHT

SFM: Ferguson's travails betting on horses; news of a job opening at Monticello Agriculture and Mechanical College (hereafter called Arkansas A & M or A & M); description of trip to Monticello, his initial impression of the town and his assessment of the campus; chat with A & M student; and A & M President Horsfall bullying Ferguson into signing contract.

Ferguson's Missouri Pacific train route is also sourced from 1934 Missouri Pacific Railway Map. The depiction of Monticello, Arkansas is referenced from the June 1931 Monticello Sanborn Map; https://monticelloarkansas.us/monticellos-history/; and https://encyclopediaofarkansas.net/entries/drew-county-courthouse-7765/.

Arkansas A & M's setting, history, and controversial tenure of President Horsfall come from a number of sources: the 1935–1936 Arkansas A & M handbook; Horace G. Porter, "A Brief History of A. & M. College; History of Arkansas A. & M. College (uncredited article); "Hail to the Chief: Frank Horsfall and His Campus of Controversy," *Drew County Historical Journal* 11 (1996): 4–8, 11, 17–18; "The Final Conflict: Frank Horsfall and His Campus of Controversy," *Drew County Historical Journal* 11 (1996): 5, 7–10, 13; and Dallas Tabor Herndon, *Centennial History of Arkansas* (Chicago: S. J. Clarke Publishing Company, 1922), pp. 454–55.

The details of Coach Hammons' Arkansas A & M football

record and his 1934 resignation are from: https://www.uamsports
.com/documents/2020/4/28//All_Time_Records_2020.pdf?id=1090
and "Hammons Quits As Coach At A. & M.," AP, July 3, 1934.

CHAPTER NINE

SFM: Ferguson's anxiousness and frustration upon taking over Arkansas A & M's football team; his antagonistic meeting with the Athletic Committee and his pep talk with President Horsfall; reflections on "Swinging Gate"; decision to send resumes to many colleges after 1934 football season and his references to Monticello's downtown "wolves"; initial portrayal of Hugh Critz, his detailed dialog of their first meeting, and highly charged 1935 public meeting with Monticello's townspeople; Ferguson's emergency appendectomy; and his reflections around loss of love for the game of football.

The announcement of Arkansas A & M's 1934 football schedule and the news that spring football practice had been cancelled due to a shortage of players come from the school's student newspaper, the *Weevil Outlet*, spring 1934 (hereafter abbreviated as WO). Description of Ferguson's first practice with 1934 A & M football team is referenced from Donald Holley, "The Final Conflict: Frank Horsfall and His Campus of Controversy," *Drew County Historical Journal* 11 (1996): 8, 30. Ferguson's attempt to downplay expectations for the season, along with his deeper explanation of the "Swinging Gate," comes from *AD*, Oct. 1, 1934.

The origin of the Boll Weevils name is sourced from https://onlyinark.com/%20sports/the-history-of-arkansas-mascots/ and "Stewart Ferguson, the Wandering Weevils, and Why They Played Football for Fun," *Drew County Historical Journal* (1998): 15. Lowlights of A & M's 1934 football results come from articles in the Oct.–Nov. *AD*.

Coverage of President Horsfall's fight to hang on to his position, news of his January 1935 resignation, and the interim appointments to run the school draw from the following: Donald Holley, "The Final Conflict: Frank Horsfall and His Campus of Controversy," *Drew*

County Historical Journal 11 (1996): 25, 29, 31–32; "Horsfall Resigns From Monticello," AP, Jan. 11, 1935; *Pine Bluff Commercial*, Jan. 11, 1935; and Arkansas A & M Board Meeting, Jan. 9, 1935. Announcement of new A & M president Hugh Critz, along with the commentary on Critz's son, Hughie, comes from: *AD*, Mar. 26, 1935; Arkansas A & M Board Meeting, Mar. 25, 1935; *New York Post*, Sept. 15, 1934; and baseball-reference.com.

CHAPTER TEN

SFM: 1935 A & M football slush fund and roadshow caravan; secret raid of Duke Wells; reflections on the new football recruits, their transition to A & M, and his resigned acceptance to passing all of them in his freshman history class; assessments of the recruits' rough play; and school sendoff for A & M's first 1935 football game, in Monroe, Louisiana.

The biographical sketch of Eugene ("Bo") Sherman, the details driving his Dec. 1934 suspension as an Arkansas college coach, and the news of his hiring at Arkansas A & M draw from the following: Nov. 1934–Feb. 1935 coverage in *AD*; *Arkansas Gazette* (Mar. 8, May 22, 1935); and *WO* (May 22, Nov. 4, 1935).

Specifics around Monticello Tomato Festival are based on: (Gentry) *Journal Advocate*, June 27, 1935; *Hope Star* (Feb. 27, June 27, 1936); *Madison County Record*, July 1, 1936; *Advance-Monticellonian*, June 6, 1940; *Delta Democrat-Times*, June 15, 1941; and *Arkansas Gazette* (likely June 29, 1951).

Ferguson's and Coach Sherman's salary figures come from the Aug. 21, 1934, Arkansas A & M Board Meeting. A & M's 1935 football season schedule additions are referenced from the *AD*, Sept. 16, 1935. The psychological testing given to incoming A & M students aged 21 or older is sourced from the 1939–1940 A & M Catalog.

CHAPTER ELEVEN

SFM: Shocking news that 1935 A & M football team lost first game; increasing ire of Monticello's businessmen as A & M continued to lose; Ferguson's appreciation for President Critz's honesty on doing whatever it took to have a winning football team, and his initial thoughts of A & M's incoming president, Marvin Bankston; Ferguson's depiction of the developing slush fund scandal, portrayal of the new 1936 A & M football recruits, and unsuccessful job offer idea for the school's football players; Bankston's actions to eliminate the slush fund; description of football players' dorm and Bankston's decision requiring the entire team to leave A & M; "small and raw" 1937 A & M football team; and Ferguson's private gloating over potential end of A & M's football program.

A & M's fall 1935 enrollment information is sourced from Donald Holley, "The Final Conflict: Frank Horsfall and His Campus of Controversy," *Drew County Historical Journal* 11 (1996): 31. The brief sketch of Hendrix College comes from two sources on the school's website: "History in Brief," https://www.hendrix.edu/collegehistory/ and "The history of Hendrix football," https://www.hendrix.edu/news/news.aspx?id=10456, reprinted from James E. Lester Jr., *Hendrix College: A centennial history* (Arkansas: Hendrix College Centennial Committee, 1984).

President Critz's resignation, along with discussion of his abbreviated A & M tenure is based on: *Hope Star*, Dec. 30, 1935; *Pine Bluff Commercial*, Jan. 11, 1935; Donald Holley, "The Final Conflict: Frank Horsfall and His Campus of Controversy," *Drew County Historical Journal* 11 (1996): 15; and 1936 Arkansas A & M annual yearbook. February 1936 announcement of new Arkansas A & M president Marvin Bankston and description of huge school celebration come from *WO*, Feb. 28, 1936.

The brief overview of A & M's lackluster 1936 football results is sourced from Oct.–Nov. 1936 AP game recaps and the University of Arkansas at Monticello's (UAM) extremely informative website: https://www.uamsports.com/documents/2020/4/28//All_Time_Records

_2020.pdf?id=1090. Coach Sherman's clairvoyant quote on likelihood of A & M losing 100–0 in team's 1937 opening game and mention of team's eventual 1–6 record are from: *Monroe News-Star*, Sept. 24, 1934; *Monroe Morning World*, Sept. 26, 1937; and UAM's website.

CHAPTER TWELVE

SFM: President Bankston's plan to save A & M football by re-hiring Ferguson; Ferguson's contentment as a history teacher and disinterest in coaching again; Ferguson's car and his anticipation for a summer 1938 romance (at LSU) with a "Frenchy" schoolteacher; Ferguson's and Bankston's dueling letters; fateful meeting on LSU campus with C. C. Smith; and Ferguson's "conflicted" feelings on returning as A & M's football coach.

The mention of Sherman's marriage to a Monticello woman is referenced from the Arkansas A & M Bulletin, Mar. 1934. The overview of Bankston's *Barnyard Battery* special dairy program and his quote asking A & M students to show more love to cows comes from WO, Jan. 28, 1938. Ferguson's mild reputation among A & M students and details on his roles and responsibilities are sourced from the following: 1937 A & M yearbook; WO (Feb. 11, Feb. 25, Mar. 11, Apr. 9, May 6, 1938); Arkansas A & M Board Meeting, June 23, 1938; and the Arkansas A & M Bulletin (1937, 1938).

The mention of Ferguson's third straight summer at LSU comes from the Louisiana State University Summer Bulletin (1936–1938 editions). Update on Bolton High School principal S. M. Brame and news of Brame's job offer to Ferguson (as a top assistant coach) is from *Town Talk*, Aug. 17, 1938.

CHAPTER THIRTEEN

SFM: Ferguson's reflections on not preparing for second tour as A & M's football coach; his memory of the first practice of 1938 football season, and rebuke of Monticello businessmen who attended;

perspective across campus that Ferguson was rehired to dismantle football program; Ferguson's belief that returning players missed Coach Sherman; ruminations on prioritizing character over winning; his strategy to build offense around Tom Curry, and last minute telegram that Curry was ineligible to play opening game; and initial overview of Ferguson's "going crazy" 1939 A & M football schedule.

Official news of Ferguson's second tour as A & M's football coach comes from "Athletic Director To Be Monticello's Coach," AP, July 27, 1938. Ferguson's comments concerning upcoming 1938 A & M football season are sourced from "Weevils Hope For Comeback: New Coach Faces Rebuilding Task at Arkansas A. & M.," AD, Aug. 28, 1938. First day of A & M's fall semester, along with overview of the thirty players at opening football practice is from AD, Sept. 8, 1938, and WO, Sept. 16, 1938. Reverend James R. Sewell's biographical sketch is referenced from: 1937–1940 A & M yearbooks; WO entries on Oct. 6, 1939, and Mar. 28, 1940; and from Sewell's obit, *Arkansas United Methodist*, Jan. 5, 1996. The biographical sketch of J. P. Leveritt stems from: A & M yearbooks (1937–1939, 1941); WO, Sept. 30, 1938; and Clara B. Kennan's "Trainer to President," AD, June 6, 1948.

News that Sherman's A & M contract was not renewed, along with his new job as a high school coach is from "Sherman Relieved As College Coach," AP, July 26, 1938 and "Sherman Is Named Coach At Nashville," AP, Aug. 4, 1938. Preview and recap of opening 1938 football game against Mississippi State Teachers College in Hattiesburg is sourced from AP, Sept. 24, 1938, and WO, Sept. 30, 1938. Coverage of game at Millsaps College comes from: "Millsaps Faces 'Swinging Gate' Formation Here Tonite," *Clarion Ledger*, Sept. 29, 1938; Stewart Ferguson's "Inside the 10-Yard Line," *Athletic Journal*, Oct. 1936 issue; UP, Oct. 24, 1937; and *Clarion Ledger*, Sept. 29, 1938.

Overview of Arkansas' 'Little Big Three' mini-conference and news that Magnolia A & M had suddenly dropped out in 1937 draw from AP (Sept. 22, Nov. 29, 1937); and WO, Sept. 16, 1938. The spoof on A & M's game against fictional Pine Ridge University, along with student body's lack of team spirit is sourced from WO, Oct. 21,

1938. Highlights of the game at Louisiana College are from *AD*, Oct. 22, 1938, and *WO*, Oct. 28, 1938.

Details of A & M's winless 1938 football season are referenced from Oct.–Nov. game recaps in *AD*, *Arkansas Gazette*, https://home pages.cae.wisc.edu/~dwilson/rsfc/RuleChanges.txt, and https://www .uamsports.com/documents/2020/4/28//All_Time_Records_2020. pdf?id=1090. The events encapsulating Ferguson's end-of-season trip with the team to New Orleans and Baton Rouge are pulled from *WO*, Dec. 9, 1938.

CHAPTER FOURTEEN

SFM: Ferguson's concerns about readiness for A & M's 1939 "insane football schedule"; reflections on first practice and further thoughts (plus dialog) of candidates Terry Field and Annie Robinson; frenzied attempt to teach football basics and how to avoid serious injuries; scramble to find uniforms for opener against Louisiana Tech; Ferguson finding bathroom privacy to vent at A & M's Athletic Committee declaring most of his team ineligible for first game and gathering himself to immediately fix matters with President Bankston; reflections on conversation with Ruston, Louisiana hotel manager; and ill-advised Louisiana Tech pregame pep talk.

Discussion of Ferguson overhauling A & M's health and physical education program and the associated additional attention draws from a number of sources: "Physical Exam Is Thorough: New Program To Promote Health Begun At A. & M.," *Advance-Monticellonian*, Oct. 7, 1937; Arkansas A & M Bulletin, 1937; *WO*, Feb. 25, 1938; *WO*, Feb. 10, 1939; 1939 A & M yearbook; "A. & M. Phys. Ed. Attracts Attention," *Advance-Monticellonian*, Feb. 2, 1939; Sam G. Harris's, "Monticello A. & M. Grid Experiment Paying Dividends," AP, Feb. 2, 1939; "Weevil Coach Will Serve on Revision Board," *AD*, Feb. 7, 1939; *Journal of Health and Physical Education*, Vol. 10, Issue 6 (1939); "Athletics in New Concept: Personal Benefits, Rather than Victory, Ideal at A. & M.," *AD*, Mar. 12, 1939; Allen Tilden, "Game is Given 'Back to the Boys' Under New System of Athletic Director Ferguson,"

AD, Sept. 24, 1939; and "A. & M. College Among Leaders In Physical Education: Southern Physical Education Convention Recognizes Work Of College," *Advance-Monticellonian*, Apr. 13, 1939.

The additional sketch on J. P. Leveritt is referenced from the 1937–1939 A & M yearbooks. The inspiring story of Eddie McLane, Louisiana Tech's 1939 athletic director and mention of team's current coach, Ray Davis, are from: *Monroe News-Star*, Feb. 15, 1938, and two articles from *Shreveport Times*, Sept. 1, 1938, and Jan. 27, 1939. The background on Annie Robinson comes from: Ben Epstein, "Picturing Personalities," *Arkansas Gazette*, Nov. 24, 1939; *Harrisburg Telegraph*, Oct. 2, 1940; and Bill's phone interview with Annie (unknown date).

Details of A & M's 1938 opening game, including having to borrow Louisiana Tech's spare uniforms, is referenced from *WO*, Sept. 17, 1939, and *AD*, Sept. 17, 1939. Additional details on the gaudy new A & M uniforms (displayed later in the season) are sourced from *Philadelphia Record*, Oct. 1, 1939. Commentary on A & M's daunting 1939 road schedule, along with the associated $1,500 in expected game guarantees comes from "Boll Weevils To See The Country," *WO*, Feb. 10, 1939.

CHAPTER FIFTEEN

SFM: Ferguson's reflections on moment he officially decided to play 'football for fun'; his labeling Memphis "the Sodom and Gomorrah of the delta," and thoughts on decision to not worry about travel schedule and strict arrival times; the team's dinner in Jackson, Tennessee, and Ferguson's value-driven restaurant selection; characterizations of A & M players; frustration with YMCA night attendant in Nashville, Tennessee; Green Dawg's ongoing problems and related testiness among team; Ferguson's rationale for unregulated chaperone approach; the boys' religious backgrounds; Ferguson's humorous responses to the two Tennessee Polytechnic coaches' bewilderment that A & M was actually a college football team; Ferguson's catch-up with Russ Cohen; team's misadventures in Charlottesville, Virginia; team's trip to Washington, D.C., ending on uplifting visit with Postmaster General Jim Farley; Ferguson's solution to Hotel Normandie's dining room policy and A & M player's quote upon sticker shock of dinner cost; responses to questions from a *Philadelphia Enquirer* sportswriter; Ferguson's explanation why St. Joseph's athletic director couldn't pay the agreed on game guarantee; wiring C. C. Smith for salary advance; and retelling of A & M's invitation to join the Philadelphia Eagles on their team bus and sidelines for professional football game.

Ferguson's formal "football for fun" declaration comes from Allen Tilden, "Game is Given 'Back to the Boys' Under New System of Athletic Director Ferguson," *AD*, Sept. 24, 1939. Additional details on A & M's Coy Brown, Tunis Bishop, and J. P. Leveritt are sourced from the 1937–1942 A & M yearbooks and *WO* (Mar. 25, 1938; Sept. 30, 1938; and Sept. 22, 1939).

Coach Russ Cohen's biographical sketch is referenced from http://www.thetruecitizen.com/news/2015-10-28/Front_Page/Russ_Cohen_the_pointaminute_team.html. The biographical sketch on Davey O'Brien comes from https://www.pro-football-reference.com/players/O/OBriDa21.htm and https://www.sports-reference.com/cfb/players/davey-obrien-1.html. The Davey O'Brien Award, for the best college quarterback each year, is named in his honor.

Complete coverage of A & M's wild Sept. 30, 1939 'football for fun' debut at St. Joseph's College draws from: *Philadelphia Enquirer*, Sept. 30, 1939; Frank O'Gara, "Easy Win Gained By St. Joseph's," *Philadelphia Enquirer*, Oct. 1, 1939; UP, Oct. 1, 1939; and Don Lambert, "Those Wandering Weevils," *Drew County Historical Journal* 27 (2012): 30. Dutch Meyer's "you may fire when ready" quote is from an article Meyer co-wrote with Amos Melton, "Pass! Pass! Pass!," *Collier's*, Oct. 7, 1939. The characterization of the running game as still dominant in college football is taken from Francis Wallace's annual "Pigskin Preview" in the *Saturday Evening Post*, 1937–1939.

CHAPTER SIXTEEN

SFM: Ferguson's Oct. 9, 1939 catch-up chat with President Bankston, including testy exchange with a fellow A & M professor; decision to release two unhappy boys from football team; mention of some Odessa service clubs providing Ferguson financial guarantees for game versus Daniel Baker College; reflections on travel across Texas; his thoughts on Carlton Spears (mistakenly) lateralling football to referee; game versus Louisiana College; team's hotel stay in Hollister, Missouri, resulting in his searching bus for stolen items; Ferguson's accolades for Springfield, Missouri; his unenthusiastic perspective on Rolla, Missouri, and the fans' shenanigans during game against the Missouri School of Mines; the team's St. Louis stopover, including one of his players finding true love; reference to snow fences en route to Chicago, along with team's exploits upon arrival; Ferguson's negative opinion of the University of Chicago's Dec. 1939 decision to drop football program; Nov. 1939 visit to Notre Dame, including effusive praise for Elmer Layden and the team's entrancement watching Notre Dame's practice; unappealing take upon arrival in Toledo and decision to move on after the local university ignored his request for a workout on team's field; team's visit to University of Michigan, especially his admiration for its athletic director, Fielding Yost; Terry Field's solution to rid Green Dawg of pungent garlic smell; Ferguson's thoughts on team's second half comeback against John Carroll College and team's decision to head directly back to A & M after the game.

Details of team's stay in Odessa, coverage of its well-received game versus Daniel Baker College, and Carlton Spears' biographical sketch are sourced from the following: "Hillbillies Meet Bollweevils Here Saturday: Unorthodox Style Of Play Used By Men From Monticello May Upset Hillbillies From Baker," *Odessa News-Times*, Oct. 13, 1939; "Hillbillies Swamp Bollweevils 33–13," *Odessa News-Times*, Oct. 14, 1939; AP, Oct. 14, 1939; and 1940 A & M yearbook.

Preview and recap of A & M's Oct. 20, 1939, home game against Louisiana College, including overview of head coach Jack Walker, is referenced from: *Town Talk* (Feb. 5, 1938; Oct. 18, 1939); and *AD*, Oct. 21, 1939. Additional details of A & M's manic Nov. 4, 1939 game versus the Missouri School of Mines, including biographical sketch of Gale Bullman and nickname of Coy ("Feller") Brown, come from: the *Rolla Herald* (Aug. 3, 1939; Nov. 9, 1939); *Sports Illustrated*, Sept. 18, 1961; *St. Louis Post-Dispatch*, June 26, 1977; *AD*, Nov. 5, 1939; and 1937 A & M annual yearbook.

Further information on University of Chicago's December 1939 announcement cancelling football program, and its illustrious former president, Robert Hutchins, is sourced from: "Hutchins Views Education As A Pathway To Life," *Chicago Tribune*, Oct. 1, 1939; "Chicago U. to Drop Football: 'Students Get No Special Benefit,' Trustees Say," AP, Dec. 22, 1939; "College Football Is An Infernal Nuisance," *Sports Illustrated*, Oct. 18, 1954; and "Robert M. Hutchins, Long a Leader In Educational Change, Dies at 78," *New York Times*, May 6, 1977.

The biographical sketches of Elmer Leyden and Joe Boland are from: http://www.und.com/sports/mfootbl/mtt/elmer_layden_95318.html; Elmer Leyden's obit, *New York Times*, July 1, 1973; and https://archive.org/details/FightingIrishFBJHMC. The brief overview of the legendary Fielding Yost, and the fake kick play Yost demonstrated during the team's practice come from: "Fielding Yost, godfather of UM sports," *Detroit News*, Oct. 28, 2017; *Detroit Free Press*, Nov. 26, 1939; and https://michigansportshof.org/inductee/fielding-harris-yost/. Additional color on A & M's Terry Field is referenced from the 1940 A & M yearbook.

Account of the media coverage surrounding A & M's Nov. 1939 game against John Carroll College, along with the momentous game recaps sparking the nickname "the Marx Brothers of Football" draws from several sources: Gordon Cobbledick, "Arkansas A. & M. Gives Football Back to Boys: Haven't Won in 2 Years—and Don't Care," *Cleveland Plain Dealer*, Nov. 7, 1939; *Cleveland Press*, Nov. 10, 1939; "Arkansas Aggies Throw All the Passes But Opponents, Alas, Win All the Games," *Cleveland News*, Nov. 10, 1939; AP, Nov. 10, 1939; Gordon Cobbledick, "These Arkansas Travelers Play Football for Fun," *Cleveland Plain Dealer*, Nov. 11, 1939; *Cleveland News*, Nov. 11, 1939;

Gordon Cobbledick, "Carroll Romps, 49–7" and "Blue Streaks Rip Arkansas A. & M. for Two Periods: Subs play in Last Half and Boll Weevils Passes Start to Click," *Cleveland Plain Dealer*, Nov. 12, 1939; *AD*, Nov. 12, 1939; AP, Nov. 12, 1939; and Harry Grayson, "High Pressure Football Is Out for Arkansas Aggies: Do They Have Fun?" *NEA Service*, Nov. 17, 1939.

CHAPTER SEVENTEEN

SFM: Ferguson's plastering A & M's campus with Boll Weevils newspaper clippings and his summary of the varied reactions from faculty and students; team's corny practices and Monticello business community's bitterness concerning the team; Ferguson's giddy double-cross that drove the downtown gamblers to lose their bet in A & M's homecoming game against Northwest Mississippi, A & M's second half antics, and reflections on the contrasting football philosophies between the two schools; letting players decide how to handle breaking a key team rule on eve of departure for game against Missouri State Teachers College and the comical recap of rain-soaked affair; thoughts on maintaining A & M's football program, culminating in a university vote and the 10-point football manifesto.

The supportive A & M football newspaper quotes come from *Pampa Daily News*, Nov. 14, 1939, and *Orlando Sentinel*, Nov. 19, 1939. Additional detail on Northwest Mississippi College and further highlights from A & M's win are referenced from https://resources.finalsite.net/images/v1595962973/northwestmsedu/nuzij7w6qsdauiyof8f6/Bulletin2020-2021-v19.pdf and "Weevils Win on Homecoming," *AD*, Nov. 18, 1939. More moments of A & M's final two games in 1939 season, featuring Annie Robinson's monumental passing and the team's likely taking a page from vaudeville star Joe Penner draw from: "Robinson's Smoke Ball Baffling to Warriors At Times," *Arkansas Gazette*, Nov. 24, 1939; "Weevils Give Fans a Show, but Warriors Win the Game, 32–14," *AD*, Nov. 25, 1939; "Rain Grounds Monticello Aerials, Bears Win," *Springfield Daily News*, Dec. 1, 1939; *AD*, Dec. 1, 1939; *WO*, Dec. 8, 1939; and https://walkoffame.com/joe-penner/.

Additional details on Ferguson's quest to keep football alive at A & M come from various sources: *WO*, Oct. 6, 1939; Stewart Ferguson, "Busology—New Subject In Education—Gains Popularity," *WO*, Oct. 20, 1939; *WO*, Jan. 12, 1940; *Minneapolis Tribune*, Jan. 14, 1940; Jack Keady, "'Football for Fun' Becoming Profitable Business at Monticello," *AD*, Sept. 16, 1940; and 1940 A & M yearbook.

CHAPTER EIGHTEEN

SFM: Ferguson's miscalculation that external, talented athletes would appear at A & M's first 1940 season practice; commentary around Annie Robinson's departure and surprising return to A & M; disenchantment with disciplinarian football coaches, such as Eastern Kentucky's Rome Rankin, and A & M's wild, multi-lateral play against Rankin's squad; team's trip to Hershey, Pennsylvania for a game against Lebanon Valley, capped off by a *Collier's* photographer spending time with team; visiting Gettysburg battlefield site; exhausting night in Roanoke, Virginia, mistaking a "whorehouse" for a hotel; and depleted funds as team headed back to A & M campus, along with the warm welcoming committee upon arrival.

The overview of A & M's eye-popping 1940 football schedule and Ferguson's associated blitz of press materials, plus competing buzz from campus scavenger hunt are sourced from: "13 Games for Boll Weevils," *WO*, Feb. 2, 1940; *WO*, Mar. 28, 1940; "Monticello Gridders to Travel Even Farther Next Season," *AD*, Feb. 20, 1940; and aforementioned *AD*, Sept. 16, 1940. Snapshot of team's opening 1940 football practice, including biographical sketch of Stanley Cheshier, is from: *WO*, Jan. 12, 1940; "40 Candidates for Weevil Eleven," *Arkansas Gazette*, Sept. 8, 1940; and *AD*, Sept. 16, 1940.

Additional coverage of A & M's first two 1940 games, including overview of Eastern Kentucky's undefeated 1940 football season, is sourced from: "Widely Traveled, Colorful Aggies Are Coming," *Town Talk*, Sept. 14, 1940; "Big Crowd Pleased With Wildcats In Opener," *Town Talk*, Sept. 17, 1940; *AD*, Sept. 17, 1940; and (Louisville) *Courier Journal* (Sept. 27-28, Nov. 18, 1940).

Depiction of team's momentous trip to Hershey comes from several sources: *AD*, Sept. 16, 1940; *Harrisburg Telegraph*, Oct. 1, 1940; Jack Conlin, "In Reverse," *Harrisburg Telegraph*, Oct. 2, 1940; "Lebanon Valley Plays At Hershey Tonight," (Harrisburg) *Evening News*, Oct. 4, 1940; *AD*, Oct. 5, 1940; Kyle Crichton, "Football is for Fun," *Collier's*, Nov. 23, 1940; 1989 Wandering Weevils Reunion (part of UAM's Homecoming Celebration); Ralph Stegall's and Verl Gill's Wandering Weevils Scrapbooks; and Bill's Community Inn pricing research.

CHAPTER NINETEEN

SFM: Annie Robinson's final departure from A & M; reflections on frantic 48 hours to complete to do's before Wandering Weevils' big western trip; bubbling ire of A & M's main bus driver, senior Joe Coker, and fonder recollections of team's creative solution to resolve embarrassment with group bathroom breaks; reflections on team's stay in Denton, Texas, including its entertaining game against North Texas; reflections on sites and stops as the Green Dawg pushed westward, including the Grand Canyon and Las Vegas; amusing retelling of hitting up cheap orange juice stops just outside of Los Angeles and team's action-packed two-day stay.

Much of the specific content capturing the team's exploits on fall 1940 trip west to Los Angeles (Oct. 10–17) comes from Verl Gill's daily diary, namely: A & M's Phi Sigma Chi fraternity providing Ferguson with a carton of cigarettes and team with a sack lunch amid rowdy cheerleader squad send-off; Mount Pleasant, Texas supper at the Hillbilly Café; stay at Denton, Texas's Southern Hotel and movie excursion to see *City of Conquest*; Flag Ranch breakfast in Tucumcari, New Mexico; Grand Canyon visit, including returning stolen souvenirs; midnight visit to Boulder (Hoover) Dam; and Los Angeles adventures to Grauman's Chinese Theater and Hollywood's Hawaiian Hut. Paul Stegall's quotes on team's visit to Grand Canyon and Boulder Dam come from "Local Weevil Players Like To Play For Fun," *Advance Monticellonian*, Nov. 7, 1940.

Brief details of North Texas football program and additional commentary of A & M's game against North Texas are sourced from the 1940 *Denton Record-Chronicle* (Oct. 11–12).

Biographical sketch of Bob Burns is referenced from http://www.encyclopediaofarkansas.net/encyclopedia/entry-detail.aspx?entryID=2185 and http://www.oldstatehouse.com/collections-blog/the-radio-man-arkansan-bob-burns. Brief overview of actress Dorothy Lamour comes from www.imdb.com/name/nm0483787/bio and http://www.cmgww.com/stars/lamour/bio2.html. Press account of A & M's visit to Los Angeles stems from Paul Zimmerman, "Sports Post-Scripts," *Los Angeles Times*, Oct. 17, 1940.

CHAPTER TWENTY

SFM: Difficult mountainous ride to Reno; contentious pregame and postgame interactions with the University of Nevada football team and administration; and Ferguson's approving stance on city of Reno and nighttime stroll.

Full coverage of A & M's Oct. 19, 1940, game in Reno versus the University of Nevada draws from: four Oct. 1940 *Reno Evening Gazette* articles; "Overconfidence Is Main Nevada Danger: Aiken Unable To Scout Screwball Arkansas Offense," *Nevada State Journal*, Oct. 18, 1940; "Nevada Plays Barnstorming Bollweevils Here Today: Clowning Visitors Are Underdogs In Homecoming Event," *Nevada State Journal*, Oct. 19, 1940; and "Nevada Scores 78–0 Victory to Climax Homecoming Day," UP, Oct. 20, 1940.

CHAPTER TWENTY-ONE

SFM: Dangerous mountain trek to Arcata, California and fun Oct. 23, 1940, game versus Humboldt State, taking a cue from two days of driving rain; reflections on Weevils' exhausting 1,700 mile drive to Rapid City, South Dakota; and team's joyous stay in Rapid City, peaking with J. P. Leveritt's show-stopping touchdown against South Dakota School of Mines.

Further details of team's travel to Arcata and following push to Rapid City are sourced from Verl Gill's diary and his Wandering Weevils scrapbook. Pete Cheshier's quote on the giant California Redwoods comes from *Advance Monticellonian*, Nov. 7, 1940. More information on Edith's Home Café is referenced from *RCJ*, June 8, 1940.

Additional commentary on Rapid City's Alex Johnson Hotel and Gutzon Borglum's work on Mount Rushmore National Monument, along with full coverage of A & M's Oct. 28, 1940, game against the South Dakota School of Mines come from: *Argus Leader*, May 19, 1939; *RCJ*, Nov. 20, 1941; "Little Fergy (Remember Him?) Preaches Fun Football," *Daily Argus Leader*, Oct. 15, 1940; "Miners Prepare for Arkansas 'Fun Team' Monday," Oct. 22, 1940; "Miners Await Arkansas Grid Shenanigans Monday: Stage Is Set For Grid 'Vaudeville' Of Boll Weevils," *RCJ*, Oct. 26, 1940; "Arkansas Gridders Trim Hardrockers, 26–7: Weevils Pass Their Way to First 1940 Win," Oct. 29, 1940; and blackhillsbadlands.com.

CHAPTER TWENTY-TWO

SFM: Bus trip across South Dakota and thoughts on brief return to Mitchell; planned lunch stopover in Sioux City, Iowa to purchase twenty copies of recent *Sioux City Tribune*; team's return to A & M campus and Ferguson's reflections on game against Hendrix College; and overview of Ferguson's plans for team's upcoming east coast trip.

The enhancements made to the Corn Palace come from the aforementioned Mitchell Chamber of Commerce pamphlet. The summary of Ferguson's interview with a Sioux Falls, South Dakota sportswriter is referenced from J. D. Ashley, *Daily Argus Leader*, Oct. 30, 1940. Details on the newspaper feature that prompted Ferguson to purchase 20 copies are from "Former Dakotan, Most Envied Coach in United States, Brings Screwiest Grid Eleven Back for Homecoming This Week," *Sioux City Tribune*, Oct. 27, 1940.

Added color on the team making their own music aboard the Green Dawg comes from Bill's interview with former Wandering Weevil Teddy McKinney (unknown date and location). Details on the team's midnight arrival at A & M's campus and next day's home game versus Hendrix College are referenced from *WO*, Nov. 1, 1940, and *AD*, Nov. 2, 1940.

CHAPTER TWENTY-THREE

SFM: Various visits as team headed up the east coast via Mississippi, Alabama, Georgia, and the Carolinas; Green Dawg's nearly disastrous accident near Plymouth, North Carolina, and aftermath in local police station; efforts to secure various housing for the night; and Greyhound bus trip to New York, highlighted by crafty work in Washington, D.C. to outwit new bus driver, plus early morning arrival in New York City.

The festive campus send-off for A & M's Wandering Weevils comes from the 1941 A & M yearbook. The brief biographical sketches of Paul ("Bear") Bryant and Don Hutson are sourced from https://www.thefamouspeople.com/profiles/paul-william-bryant-804.php and http://www.encyclopediaofarkansas.net/encyclopedia/entry-detail.aspx?entryID=2978.

CHAPTER TWENTY-FOUR

SFM: Team's bungling subway and LIRR trip to Hempstead, overview of arrival at the Garden City Hotel, and Nov. 16, 1940, football game against Hofstra College; additional NYC experiences; travels to St. Louis and Springfield, including game against Southwest Missouri State Teachers College; and return to A & M's campus for a homecoming 'win' against Northwest Mississippi.

Coverage on Wandering Weevils' arrival in New York, in conjunction with the *Collier's* feature draws from: Arthur J. Daley, "On College Gridirons," *New York Times*, Oct. 22, 1940; *Newsday*, Nov.

13, 1940; *Nassau Daily Review-Star*, Nov. 13, 1940; "Hofstra Team Maps Crazy Plays: It's Only Way To Match Arkansas Aggies," *New York Post*, Nov. 14, 1940; and Kyle Crichton, "Football is for Fun," *Collier's*, Nov. 23, 1940.

The team's exploits in NYC and additional commentary on Hofstra game come from: Verl Gil's scrapbook and Bill's interview with Teddy McKinney; Dick Gordon, "Watch for the Passes...," Hofstra College Football Program, Nov. 16, 1940; "Hofstra Routs Aggies, 32–14, On Air Attack," *Long Island Daily Press*, Nov. 18, 1940; http://keepingupwiththejones-markjones.blogspot.com/2011/02/today-in-black-history-smalls-paradise.html; and https://www.pro-football-reference.com.

Additional details on A & M's final two 1940 football games are sourced from "Bears Scrap Madcap Weevils Here Tomorrow," *Springfield Leader and Press*, Nov. 20, 1940; *Springfield Leader and Press*, Nov. 22, 1940; *Arkansas Gazette*, Nov. 28, 1940; and WO, Nov. 29, 1940.

CHAPTER TWENTY-FIVE

SFM: Ferguson's initial student invitation to join A & M's travelling band of Boll Weevils for 1941 season and follow up recruitment effort; his sizing up new crew and unexpected glee with Lawrence Lavender's wild tackling display in opening game.

The overview of Ferguson's plans for A & M's 1941 season, alongside the news of several players' induction into the U.S. Army is referenced from WO, Jan. 10, 1941, and "Boll Weevils Plan To Really Wow Grid Fans in 1941," *Arkansas Gazette*, Jan. 1941 (unknown specific date). Depiction of the St. Mary's football team and its coach, J. C. ("Mose") Simms, draws from: Kyle Crichton, "Backs in Motion: St. Mary's (San Antonio) Footballers, on the Loose," *Collier's*, Dec. 2, 1939; UP, Oct. 10, 1940; Henry McLemore, "It's Honest Mose Simms Now, After Colorful St. Mary's Mentor Puts On His Act For New York Sport Scribes," UP, Oct. 22, 1940; George Kirksey, "Mose Simms Gives Team Back To College, Wants to Work for Salary, Nor

Pay 'Em," UP, Mar. 11, 1941; and "Simms Resigns Athletic Post At St. Mary's Job," AP, Apr. 15, 1941.

The section introducing Edna McAdams comes from the following: Bill's Mar. 10, 2002, interview with Edna; "South Dakota Aggie Is Well Pleased With The South," *WO*, Sept. 30, 1938; *WO*, Mar. 28, 1940; 1939–1942 A & M yearbooks; 1989 Wandering Weevils Reunion; and Edna's obit, *RCJ*, Aug. 13, 2009.

Further details on the start to A & M's 1941 football season are sourced from: *WO* (Sept. 12, Sept. 19, 1941); *Town Talk*, Sept. 18, 1941; *AD*, Sept. 19, 1941; "Louisiana College Cats Blank Aggies, 60–0," *Town Talk*, Sept. 22, 1941; and 1942 A & M yearbook.

CHAPTER TWENTY-SIX

SFM: Ferguson's fuming over newspaper recap of game versus Mars Hill; reception in Boone, North Carolina, ahead of game versus Appalachian State, along with postgame dressing room visit from Dr. B. B. Dougherty; team's meandering trip to next game versus Bradley Technological Institute in Peoria, Illinois, including impromptu detour into Canada, memorable visits (with new squad) to Michigan and Notre Dame, and sightseeing in Chicago; rescheduling rained-out game in Peoria; fortuitous Memphis run-in with Eldon Roark; team's stay in Mobile, Alabama, and antics-galore game against Spring Hill College; and team stops in New Orleans and Baton Rouge, en route to Denton, Texas, for nutty affair against North Texas State Teachers College before finally returning to A & M.

Coverage of Sept. 25, 1941, game against Mars Hill Junior College draws from Paul Jones, "Speculatin' in Sports," *Asheville Citizen-Times*, Sept. 21, 1941; "Arkansas Aggies 'Clown' Against Lions Here Tonight," *Asheville Citizen-Times*, Sept. 25, 1941; and "Arkansas Aggies Handed 19–0 Trimming By Mars Hill Lions: Turnout of 1,000 Is Disappointed In Night Contest, Aggies Not Regarded As Funny By Customers," *Asheville Citizen-Times*, Sept. 26, 1941. Additional commentary of A & M's visit to Appalachian State Teachers

College comes from Benny Gaston's journal, published in *WO*; Verl Gil's scrapbook; and AP, Sept. 28, 1941. Brief biographical sketches of Benny Gaston and Dr. B. B. Dougherty are referenced from 1942 A & M yearbook and https://chancellor.appstate.edu/installation/history/.

Further highlights of the Boll Weevils' wanderings upon leaving North Carolina and coverage of next game in Mobile, Alabama, are sourced from: Benny Gaston's journal; Harold Boian, "'Arkansas Travelers' In Person Here," *Dayton Daily News*, Sept. 30, 1941; http://research.sabr.org/journals/history-of-chicago-city-series; Mill Marsh, "Boll Weevils Of Ark A. & M. Hold Workout At Ferry Field," *Ann Arbor News*, Oct. 1, 1941; John Hix's syndicated cartoon, *Strange As It Seems*, Oct. 6, 1941; Eldon Roark, "Strolling with Eldon Roark," *Memphis Press-Scimitar*, Oct. 7, 1941; Vincent Johnson, "Good Morning," *Mobile Register*, Oct. 7, 1941; and "Spring Hill Crushes Clown Team Of Arkansas A. & M.," *Mobile Register*, Oct. 9, 1941. Additional details from A & M's game versus North Texas draws from: *Denton Record-Chronicle*, Oct. 10, 1941; Frank Tolbert, "Worst Of All the Boll Weevils Holds North Texas to 60–0," *Fort Worth Star-Telegram*, Oct. 12, 1941; and Frank X. Tolbert, "Tolbert's Texas," *Dallas Times Herald*, Jan. 1967 (unknown exact date).

CHAPTER TWENTY-SEVEN

SFM: A & M's return trip to Peoria to play Bradley Tech; travelling to and playing game in Bethlehem, Pennsylvania, versus Moravian College; game in torrential rain versus Upsala College, followed by team's jubilant arrival in New York.

The detailed coverage of A & M's Oct. 27, 1941, game versus Bradley Tech is from "Arkansas Team Starts 8,000 Mile Grid Trip," AP, Oct. 24, 1941; Ralph Deatherage and Clint Eckstrom, "Tech Talk," *Peoria Journal-Transcript*, Oct. 27, 1941; and Russell Perry, "Tech Whips Clowning Arkansas: Weevils Run Through Repertoire Of Antics," *Peoria Journal-Transcript*, Oct. 28, 1941.

The section starring A & M's celebrated cow, Oscar, comes from "Blue-Ribbon-Oscar Demands Fanfare," *WO*, Oct. 10, 1941; *The Camden News*, Jan. 21, 1939; and 1942 A & M yearbook. Further discussion of A & M's games against Moravian College and Upsala College is sourced from Bill's fall 2004 interview with former Wandering Weevil Buddy Carson; (Allentown) *Morning Call*, Oct. 30, 1941; (Bethlehem) *Globe-Times*, Oct. 31, 1941; AP, Nov. 1-2, 1941; "Upsala Gets First Win Over 'Daffiness' Boys," (Newark) *Star-Ledger*, Nov. 1, 1941.

CHAPTER TWENTY-EIGHT

SFM: Team's stay in NYC and impromptu visit to Yale; travels to game against St. Francis College and unexpected rough play from opponent; sightseeing in Philadelphia and Washington, D.C.; reflections on final leg of trip, including games against Davis & Elkins College and Evansville College.

The latest Wandering Weevils features, additional details on the boys' NYC adventure, and further information on Yale's 1941 football team draw from Herbert Allan, "College Grapevine," *New York Post*, Oct. 30, 1941; "The Wandering Weevils," *Newsweek*, Dec. 1, 1941; Bill's phone interview with J. P. Leveritt (unknown date); 1941 A & M yearbook; "Bodybuilder Bert Goodrich - The First Mr. America," https://www.fitflex.com/bert-goodrich.html; https://blogs.shu.edu/nyc-history/minskys/; nypl.org; and https://www.sports-reference.com/cfb/schools/yale/1941-schedule.html.

Additional coverage of game against St. Francis College comes from: (Pottsville) *Republican and Herald*, Nov. 6, 1941; "Wandering Boll Weevils Wander Into Pottsville," *Evening Republican*, Nov. 7, 1941; "Football's Craziest Team To Tangle With St. Francis," *Johnstown Tribune*, Nov. 7, 1941; *Pittsburgh Post-Gazette*, Nov. 10, 1941; Bill's interview with Buddy Carson; *WO*, Jan. 31, 1941; and James R. Leonard Sr. obit, AP, Dec. 2, 1993.

Further details on the team's visit to Philadelphia and its games against Davis & Elkins and Evansville are referenced from Bill's 2005 interview with Oscar Dove (unknown exact date); 1941 *Elkins Inter-Mountain* (Nov. 12, Nov. 17); *Portsmouth Daily Times*, Nov. 17, 1941; and "Purple Aces Swamp Screw-Boll Weevils From Arkansas, 26–6," AP, Nov. 23, 1941.

CHAPTER TWENTY-NINE

SFM: Ferguson's reflections on Wandering Weevils' final game on Nov. 26, 1941, against Magnolia A & M.

Full coverage of A & M's 1941 homecoming game versus Magnolia A & M is sourced from the following: "Hendrix Praised For Grid Policy," *AD*, Jan. 8, 1941; "Monticello Zany' Weevils And Magnolia Muleriders To Battle for Goat Wednesday," *AD*, Nov. 23, 1941; Burne Bennett, "Aggies And Muleriders Clash Today," *AD*, Nov. 26, 1941; Burne Bennett, "Weevils Provide Show, But Magnolia the Touchdowns, And Muleriders Win, 25–0," *AD*, Nov. 27, 1941; *WO*, Nov. 27, 1941; and Bill's interview with Buddy Carson.

CHAPTER THIRTY

The news on the widespread 1942 cancellation of college football in Arkansas comes from "Top Colleges of State to Drop Football," AP, Sept. 14, 1942.

The section covering Ferguson's new job with the Civilian Pilot Training Program draws from: Theresa L. Kraus, "The CAA Helps America Prepare for World War II," https://www.faa.gov/; Patricia Strickland, *The Putt-Putt Air Force: The Story of The Civilian Pilot Training Program and The War Training Service (1939–1944)*, (Washington, D.C.: Federal Aviation Administration, 1971), pp. 99–112; Jane G. Birch, *They Flew Proud*, (Jane G. Birch, 2007, Part 1); "C.P.T. Moved to Lafayette," *Current Sauce*, Oct. 2, 1942; "C.P.T. Program on Campus Has New Instructor- Stewart A. Ferguson Becomes Head of Flying School Here This Week," *Current Sauce*, Dec. 17, 1942; and

Suzanne Julin's interview with Edna Ferguson Robinson, City of Deadwood Oral History Project, May 16, 2007.

The news around A & M's new 1943 football program and Ferguson's 'set the record straight' response is referenced from "Monticello Flabbergasted With Gridders," AP, Oct. 14, 1943; and Joe R. Carter, "Raspberries and Cream," *Shreveport Times*," (Nov. 14, 1943; Nov. 18, 1943). Word about the impending closing of all of the Navy Flight Schools across U.S. campuses comes from "Naval Flight School At College To Be Discontinued About July 1- New Navy Program May Be Set Up Here," *Current Sauce*, Apr. 15, 1944.

Mention of the Fergusons' Deadwood apartment and later updates on their Deadwood housing are predominantly from interviews (Suzanne Julin; Bill) with Edna Ferguson Robinson.

CHAPTER THIRTY-ONE

The initial overview of Deadwood and the events culminating in the news of Stewart and Edna Ferguson's new positions at Deadwood High School (DHS) are sourced from the following: *SFM*; interviews (Suzanne Julin; Bill) with Edna Ferguson Robinson; 2010 Deadwood Wall of Fame Inductee: Harry Stone Berger, http://www.dhsclassmates.com/; *DPT*, Aug. 15, 1944; "Former Wesleyan Coach Accepts Deadwood Post," *DPT*, Aug. 20, 1944; and *DPT*, Aug. 27, 1944.

Coverage of the 1944 DHS football season is referenced from: *DPT*, Sept. 5, 1944; "Football Practice Starts For First Game With Custer," *DPT*, Sept. 9, 1944; "Bears Lose Opener To Custer 39–0," *DPT*, Sept. 23, 1944; additional Sept.–Oct., 1944 articles in the *DPT*; the 1944 *RCJ* (Oct. 12, Oct. 26); and http://www.bellefourche.org.

The extended discussion of historical rivalry between Deadwood and Lead draws from: 1897–1900 *Deadwood Evening Independent* and *DPT* (Daily and Weekly); *Daily DPT* (Nov. 20, Nov. 22, 1900); "The Metropolis of the Black Hills," *Lead Daily Call*, Mar. 7, 1903; "Challenge To Lead," *Daily DPT*, Nov. 1, 1908; 1909–1922 *Daily DPT*; *DPT*, July 12, 1917; *DPT*, June 6, 1923; *DPT* (Oct. 4, Nov. 11, Nov. 13, Nov.

27, 1924); *RCJ*, Oct. 30, 1943; 1945 *Bear Log* (DHS yearbook); 1945 *Goldenlode* (Lead High School yearbook); https://www.cityofdead-wood.com; https://www.leadmethere.org/history/; and Census data.

CHAPTER THIRTY-TWO

The content covering the rest of Ferguson's first school year in Dead-wood is referenced from *Black Hills Weekly* (Mar. 2, Mar. 16, June 1, 1945); 1945 *Bear Log*; and the 1945 *Goldenlode*.

News concerning the critical reopening of the Homestake Mine comes from *Black Hills Weekly*, May 25, 1945; *Lead Daily Call* (May 12, June 18, 1945); "Homestake To Resume Operations On July 2nd," *Black Hills Weekly*, June 22, 1945; and *Argus Leader*, July 26, 1945. Description of Deadwood's joyous reaction to official end of World War II is referenced from the *DPT*, Aug. 15, 1945.

Coverage of DHS's 1945 football season, including return of Bear Day homecoming celebration, is sourced from several Sept.–Nov. 1945 articles in *DPT*; three others in the Oct. 1945 *RCJ*; *RCJ*, May 23, 1946; and the 1942–1945 *Bear Logs*. Details on the Fergusons' 1945 Thanksgiving and Christmas plans, and Deadwood's celebration of peace-time holiday season come from *DPT* (Nov. 25, Dec. 21, Dec. 23, 1945).

CHAPTER THIRTY-THREE

The depiction of Stewart and Edna's life together in Deadwood draws from: Bill's interview with Edna Ferguson Robinson; my Feb. 27, 2014, interview with DHS alumni Hank Frawley and Janet Thoresen; *Black Hills Weekly*, Jan. 11, 1946; *DPT* (May 7, July 4, 1947); 1945–1947 *Bear Logs*; Clara B. Kennan, "Trainer to President," *AD Magazine*, June 6, 1948; *DPT*, Feb. 14, 1969; https://www.cityofdeadwood.com/; and https://www.deadwood.com/history/.

News of Stewart Ferguson's summer positions at the Black Hills Teachers College, and additional details on the school and the greater

Black Hills region is sourced from *DPT*, May 21, 1946; (Spearfish) *Queen City Mail*, July 11, 1946; *RCJ*, July 25, 1946; Paul Haivala, Professor of History, https://www.bhsu.edu/aboutbhsu/bhsuhistory/tabid/85/default.aspx; https://www.sdpb.org/blogs/images-of-the-past/ the-early-history-of-black-hills-state-university/; https://www.archives .gov/milestone-documents/servicemens-readjustment-act; https:// www.legendsofamerica.com/sd-blackhills/; and blackhillsknowledge network.org.

The discussion of the merger between the *Deadwood-Pioneer Times* and the *Lead Daily Call* is referenced from *DPT* (July 27, July 31, Aug. 1, 1946).

The biographical sketch of Melvin M. Minton is referenced from: 1930–1942 articles in the DPT; "Minton Continues Physical Training Work, Army Hospital," DPT, Oct. 5, 1944; DPT, Oct. 14, 1945; and DPT, Oct. 17, 1945.

Coverage of DHS's 1946 football season comes from Aug.–Oct. 1946 articles in *DPT*; two from *Black Hills Weekly* (Apr. 12, Nov. 22); and the 1947 *Bear Log*. Deadwood's 1946–1947 basketball season, highlighted by longest high school tournament game in South Dakota's history comes from Feb.–Mar. 1947 articles in *DPT*; and (Huron) *Daily Plainsman*, Mar. 12, 1953.

Commentary on spring and summer 1947 good news for Stewart and Edna, as well as the whole Deadwood community, along with overview of *National Geographic* feature story on the Black Hills is sourced from Mar.–July 1947 articles in *DPT* and *Black Hills Weekly*, June 6, 1947.

CHAPTER THIRTY-FOUR

Brief description of Deadwood's annual Days of '76 celebration comes from *DPT*, July 6, 1947. News of the passing of Edith Ferguson is from "Mrs. Edith B. Ferguson Dies Near Carthage," *Joplin Globe*, Aug. 17, 1947; *DPT*, Aug. 18, 1947; and the Dakota Conference, 64th Annual Session, (98).

Coverage of DHS's 1947 football season is sourced from Aug.–
Nov. 1947 articles in *DPT*. The detailed preview and recap of game
against Lead draws from: "Injuries Mark Deadwood's Bid For Win
Over Diggers' 'Hard-Scrimmaged' Eleven," *DPT*, Oct. 24, 1947;
"Bears Take Diggers In Annual Classic By 18–7 Score," *DPT*, Oct. 26,
1947; and the 1948 *Goldenlode*. The overview and expected publication of Ferguson's book, *Football Madness*, is referenced from Norman Thomas, "Story-Book Football Coach, Stewart Ferguson, One
Of The Most Colorful In State," *DPT*, Jan. 14, 1948.

The content on Ferguson's increasing connection to his players
and his lasting impact on Sheldon Jacobs comes from: my June 19,
2014, interview with Sheldon Jacobs; *DPT* (Apr. 18, May 9, May 13,
1948); and the 1948 *Bear Log*.

Coverage of DHS's 1948 football season through the team's
homecoming game against Belle Fourche is sourced from the following: my Feb. 28, 2014, interview with Maurice Etem; Apr. 6, 1947, *Argus Leader*; several *DPT* articles from Aug. 26, 1948, through Oct. 17,
1948; and the 1949 *Bear Log*. The detailed depiction of Deadwood's
game against Lead is referenced from: *Lead Daily Call*, Aug. 24, 1947;
DPT, Aug. 20, 1948; "Golddiggers And Bears Clash In Annual Tilt,"
DPT, Oct. 21, 1948; "Golddiggers Hammer Out Victory Over Bears,
6–0," *DPT*, Oct. 24, 1948; and the 1949 *Goldenlode*.

The illustrious high school sports career of Norman Oestreich
comes from *DPT*, May 18, 1949.

CHAPTER THIRTY-FIVE

News of Norman Oestreich's fatal accident and how his brother and
coach helped each other cope with their loss draw from: "Norman
Oestreich, 18, Deadwood Athlete Killed in Hill City Accident," *DPT*,
Aug. 30, 1949; *DPT*, Sept. 2, 1949; *DPT*, Dec. 12, 1951; and Al Oestreich's Letter to Ferguson, Nov. 22, 1951.

Details of DHS's 1949 football season through the team's game
at Belle Fourche, along with the special bond between Ferguson and

Cecil Stoner, is sourced from Sept.–Oct. articles in *DPT* and my Mar. 1, 2014, interview with Cecil Stoner. Coverage of the game against Lead and highlights of other important team events come from: "Deadwood, Lead Teams Are Ready," *DPT*, Oct. 21, 1949, "Diggers Top Bears, 12–7, In Traditional Contest," *DPT*, Oct. 23, 1949; Jack Cannon, "Black Hills Sports Scene," *DPT*, Oct. 23, 1949; *DPT*, Oct. 28, 1949; *DPT*, Nov. 29, 1949; *DPT*, Dec. 4, 1949; *DPT*, Mar. 7, 1950; and the 1950 *Goldenlode*.

The detailed comparisons between Ferguson and Minton are referenced from: DPT, Mar. 22, 1951; DPT, Aug. 15, 1952; and my interviews with Maurice Etem and Cecil Stoner.

Coverage of DHS's 1950 football season through the team's game at Belle Fourche comes from: *DPT*, Mar. 7, 1950; Aug.–Nov. 1950 articles in *DPT*; and the 1951 *Bear Log*. Recaps of the game against Lead, last game versus Lusk, and the annual team banquet draw from: *RCJ*, Oct. 21, 1950; "Long Runs Pave Way For Deadwood Bear Win Over Lead Golddiggers 13–7," *DPT*, Oct. 22, 1950; Jack Cannon, "Black Hills Sports Scene," *DPT*, Oct. 22, 1950; *DPT*, Oct. 27, 1950; *DPT*, Oct. 29, 1950; and *DPT*, Nov. 7, 1950.

CHAPTER THIRTY-SIX

The overview of DHS's 1950–1951 basketball season is sourced from: https://amhistory.si.edu/polio/; *DPT*, Jan. 21, 1951; *DPT*, Apr. 4, 1951; and the 1951 *Bear Log*.

Coverage of DHS's 1951 football season through the team's home game versus Belle Fourche comes from: "Deadwood Jaycees Receive Charter At Elaborate Banquet," *DPT*, May 20, 1949; *DPT*, Aug. 15, 1951; "Bear Grid Prospects Are Bright," *DPT*, Aug. 26, 1951; and additional Sept.–Oct. 1951 articles in *DPT*.

News of Ferguson's roof accident is referenced from Bill's interview with Edna Ferguson Robinson; Al Oestreich Letter to Ferguson; and *DPT*, Oct. 8, 1951. Coverage of the game against Lead, including brief sketch of Wendell Handley and Rapid City's departure from

Black Hills football conference, draws from: *DPT*, Oct. 24, 1950; *DPT*, Aug. 15, 1951; "Bears, Diggers Are Ready For Crucial Game at Deadwood Homecoming, Friday," *DPT*, Oct. 18, 1951; and "Lead Trips Deadwood 8–0 in Crucial Black Hills Conference Grid Contest," *DPT*, Oct. 21, 1951. News that Deadwood's last game was cancelled is referenced from *DPT*, Nov. 2, 1951.

The story of DHS's memorable 1951–1952 basketball season comes from several sources: *DPT*, Apr. 4, 1951; Nov. 1951–early Mar. 1952 articles in *DPT*; Camille Yuill, "The Backlog," *DPT*, Mar. 11, 1952; Marv Kebschull, "Black Hills Sports Scene," *DPT*, Mar. 12, 1952; "Cage Fans Follow Snow Plow To State Meet at Mitchell," UP, Mar. 13, 1952; *DPT*, Mar. 13, 1952; Jerry Tippens, "Deadwood's Stewart Ferguson Has Had Illustrious Career: Believes In 'Playing For Fun,'" (Mitchell) *Daily Republic*, Mar. 14, 1952; Dick Dozier, "'For The Fun Of It' Philosophy Is Stu Ferguson's Way of Play," *Argus Leader*, Mar. 15, 1952; and daily *DPT* stories from Mar. 13–20, 1952.

The mention of Ferguson hosting Easter and news of Minton's resignation are sourced from *DPT*, Apr. 13, 1952; "Minton Resigns From Deadwood Faculty," *DPT*, Aug. 14, 1952; and Jack Cannon, "Black Hills Sports Scene," *DPT*, Aug. 14, 1952.

CHAPTER THIRTY-SEVEN

Ferguson's quote praising Coach Minton and details on Minton's replacement, Glenn Burgess, are referenced from Bill Hockstedler, *RCJ*, Sept. 9, 1952, and *DPT*, Aug. 25, 1952.

Overview of DHS's 1952 football season through the team's homecoming game versus Custer, along with information on Billy Jones, comes from Aug.–Oct. 1952 articles in *DPT*. Coverage of the thrilling game against Lead is sourced from: Jack Cannon, "Cannon Reports," *DPT*, Oct. 14, 1952; "Deadwood Bears Fight From Behind to Claw Lead Golddiggers 19–14," *DPT*, Oct. 17, 1952; and the 1953 *Goldenlode*.

Ferguson's Christmas holiday schedule, including final trip to Carthage, Missouri, stems from *DPT*, Dec. 30, 1952, and *DPT*, Jan. 3,

1953. Highlights of DHS's 1952–1953 basketball regular season are referenced from Dec. 1952–Feb. 1953 articles in *DPT*.

News of change in DHS coaching roles for 1953–1954 school year, depiction of Ferguson's full teaching and coaching slate, reflections from former DHS players and students, and coverage of DHS's 1953 basketball post season draw from: *DPT*, Nov. 13, 1951; *DPT*, Oct. 12, 1952; Jack Cannon, "Cannon Reports," *DPT*, Mar. 11, 1953; *DPT*, Mar. 13, 1953; *DPT*, Mar. 15, 1953; my interview with Hank Frawley and Janet Thoresen; and the 1953 *Bear Log*. Notes on DHS track and annual sports award event are from *DPT* (Apr. 22, May 12, 1953).

CHAPTER THIRTY-EIGHT

Mention of Ferguson family trip to California and coverage of DHS's 1953 football season through the home game versus Spearfish are referenced from: "Toss A Coin For Black Hills High School Champ This Fall," *RCJ*, Sept. 10, 1953 and Aug.–Sept. articles in *DPT*. Coverage of DHS's epic Bear Day game against Sturgis is sourced from: 1951–1953 football recaps in *DPT*; "Deadwood Faces Big Sturgis Hurdle In Bid For First Black Hills Championship," *DPT*, Oct. 1, 1953; Ed Sundberg, "The Dope Sheet," *DPT*, Oct. 1, 1953; *RCJ* (Oct. 2–3, 1953); and Joe Langston, "Bears Roar Back in Last Quarter To Tie Sturgis: Battle for Conference Crown Ends In Bitter 26–26 Stalemate," *DPT*, Oct. 4, 1953. Highlights of DHS's game versus Custer, come from *DPT* (prior football recaps, Oct. 8, Oct. 11, 1953); and the 1954 *Bear Log*.

Coverage of Deadwood's game against Lead is from: *DPT*, Aug. 26, 1953; "Deadwood Can Clinch Top Spot With Win Over Lead," *DPT*, Oct. 15–16, 1953; *RCJ*, Oct. 16, 1953; and Joe Langston, "Bears Finish Undefeated Season by Drubbing Lead: 45 to 6 Win Over Diggers Completes First Perfect Year," *DPT*, Oct. 18, 1953. The news of Sturgis's season-ending loss and Ferguson's reaction to Deadwood's first ever conference title comes from: earlier 1953 football recaps in *DPT*; *RCJ*, Oct. 24, 1953; "Bison Trip Sturgis And Deadwood Takes

Crown," *DPT*, Oct. 25, 1953; and Ed Sundberg, "The Dope Sheet," *DPT*, Oct. 25, 1953.

CHAPTER THIRTY-NINE

Deadwood's community celebration of DHS's football championship is from "Deadwood Bears, Coaches Honored At Chamber Banquet Tuesday Night," *DPT*, Oct. 25, 1953 and "Three Deadwood Players On All-Conference Team," *DPT*, Oct. 25, 1953.

Highlights of DHS's 1953–1954 basketball season through sectionals, including perspective on transition to Coach Burgess, plus news of huge sectional upsets across the state are referenced from my interview with Hank Frawley and Janet Thoresen; and Nov. 1953–Mar. 1954 articles in *DPT*. Coverage of 1954 Class A state basketball tournament, celebration of DHS's first ever State A title, and commentary on Ferguson's significant impact in shaping team draw from: *DPT*, Mar. 17, 1954; *DPT*, Mar. 19, 1954; *Argus Leader*, Mar. 20, 1954; "Bears Win State Basketball Crown," *DPT*, Mar. 21, 1954; *DPT*, Mar. 22, 1954; R. E. Whitmyre, "Whitticisms," *DPT*, Mar. 23, 1954; and "Deadwood Salutes State Champions At Banquet," *DPT*, Mar. 30, 1954. Overview of the second straight DHS sports banquet is from *DPT* (Apr. 20, May 11, 1954).

Coverage of the early part of DHS's 1954 football season, including the content on Ferguson's "superfan" son, Freddie, comes from: my interviews with Cecil Stoner, Hank Frawley, and Janet Thoresen; my Feb. 27, 2014, interview with Willie Steinlicht, Bob Sjomeling, and Don Gross; Aug.–Sept. articles in *DPT*; and Cecil Stoner's obit, *RCJ*, Oct. 5, 2020. Overview of the next part of the season, through DHS's home game versus Custer, is referenced from Oct. 1954 articles in *DPT* and *RCJ*, Oct. 17, 1954. Coverage of Deadwood's game against Lead and the news of Ferguson's emergency surgery are sourced from: my interview with Hank Frawley and Janet Thoresen; *DPT*, Oct. 27, 1954; "Golddiggers Host Bears Friday in Traditional Battle," *DPT*, Oct. 28, 1954; *DPT*, Oct. 29-30, 1954; Nov. 8, 1954,

DPT; "Coach Ferguson Undergoes Surgery At Rochester," *DPT*, Nov. 16, 1954; and the 1955 *Bear Log*.

CHAPTER FORTY

The update on Ferguson's surgery and the brief bio of Merlen Veren come from *DPT*, Nov. 16, 1954, and *RCJ*, Nov. 21, 1954.

Deadwood news (rebuilt theater, new construction, and the debut of television) draws from: several Dec. 1951–Jan. 1955 articles in *DPT*; https://www.lib.niu.edu/1993; http://www.nyu.edu/; and http://northern.edu/. Additional WTVS details and Ferguson's enthusiastic support of the area's new television system are sourced from: the *Los Angeles Times*, Jan. 10, 1955; *Lead Daily Call*, Mar. 26, 1955; and the *Greely Tribune*, Apr. 23, 1955. News of Ferguson's gradual spring 1955 return to teaching, the special DHS basketball trip to see the (western) Harlem Globe Trotters, and DHS's Apr. 1955 sports banquet are referenced from: Feb. 1955 articles in *DPT*; *DPT*, Apr. 13, 1955; and *Queen City Mail*, May 26, 1955.

Depiction of DHS's 1955 football season through the game against Custer, including biographical sketch on "Woody" Williamson, comes from: *DPT*, Aug. 22–25, 1955; "Ferguson Formula To Be Wide Open Style," *DPT*, Sept. 1, 1955; Bert Cameron, "Cameron's Comments," *DPT*, Sept. 1, 1955; Sept.–Oct., 1955 articles in *DPT*; 1952–1954 *DPT* football recaps; and the 1956 *Bear Log*.

Coverage of Deadwood's game against Lead, including resolution of a conference protest handled by Maurice Fitzgerald and details on the rivalry's inaugural travelling trophy are sourced from: Oct. 1955 *DPT* articles; "Annual Lead-Deadwood Classic May Be Photo Finish Contest," *DPT*, Oct. 27, 1955; "Bears And Golddiggers Battle To 7–7 Tie: Deadwood and Lead Deadlock for Third Time in 52-Year History," *DPT*, Oct. 29, 1955; and *RCJ*, Oct. 29, 1955.

CHAPTER FORTY-ONE

The overview of the Fergusons' activities after the football season is from: *DPT*, Oct. 29, 1955; *DPT*, Nov. 23, 1955; and "Cub Scouts Use America The Beautiful Theme," *DPT*, Nov. 30, 1955.

News of Fergie's passing and depiction of the days that followed draw from: "Death Claims Prominent Deadwood Man," *DPT*, Dec. 29, 1955; "Funeral Services for Ferguson Held," *DPT*, Jan. 3, 1956; Camille Yuill, "The Backlog," *DPT*, Jan. 3, 1956; Bill's interview with Edna Ferguson Robinson; and my interview with Willie Steinlicht, Bob Sjomeling, and Don Gross.

Tributes to Ferguson and honors through the remainder of the 1956 DHS school year are sourced from: *DPT*, Jan. 7, 1956; "Jaycees Want Football Field Be Named to Honor Ferguson," *DPT*, Jan. 12, 1956; *DPT*, Jan. 18, 1956; "Deadwood Field To Be Named In Honor Of Coach Ferguson," *DPT*, Apr. 3, 1956; "Deadwood Honors Athletes, Pays Tributes To Ferguson," *DPT*, Apr. 13, 1956; and the 1956 *Bear Log*.

The spring and summer 1956 commentary on Edna and Freddie, including the news of Edna's resignation from DHS, are referenced from: Feb.–July 1956 articles in *DPT*.

The update on addition of new bleachers for DHS's football field and overview of the formal Sept. 1956 re-naming ceremony of Ferguson Field, including Edna's return to Deadwood, come from *DPT*, Sept. 10, 1956; *DPT*, Sept. 19, 1956; and "Game Includes Dedication of Field To Former Coach," *DPT*, Sept. 22, 1956.

AUTHOR'S NOTE

The 1956–1964 Edna and Freddie content stems from: *DPT*, June 21, 1957, and Apr. 20, 1959; the 1962–1965 *Bear Logs*; and Edna's obit. News of newly integrated Lead-Deadwood school district and recap of 2014 football game at Ferguson Field are from: Sept. 1970–Aug. 1971 articles in the *Black Hills Weekly* and the Sept. 15, 2014, *Black Hills Pioneer*. The additional information on Arkansas A & M College and Buddy Carson draw from: two articles in the 2011 *UAM Magazine*:

(Vol. 18, No. 1; Vol. 18, No.3); and https://www.uamsports.com/doc-uments/2020/4/28//All_Time_Records_2020.pdf?id=1090. My commentary on the college football landscape and efforts to make the overall game safer are especially derived from: 2021–2022 *Sports Illustrated* college football coverage; Tabatha Wethal, "Study: Limiting Contact in Practices Reduces Youth Football Head Injuries," https://www.athleticbusiness.com/, Oct. 13, 2022; and Leana Wen, "Here's one way to make football safer," *Washington Post*, Nov. 28, 2022.

FOR FURTHER READING

Bacon, John U. *Fourth and Long: The Fight for the Soul of College Football*. New York: Simon and Schuster, 2013.

Benedict, Jeff, and Armen Keteyian. *The System: The Glory and Scandal of Big-Time College Football*. Palatine, Ill.: Anchor Book Press, Ltd, 2014.

Birch, Jane G. *They Flew Proud, Part 1*. Jane G. Birch: 2007.

Bissinger, H. G. *Friday Night Lights: A Town, a Team, and a Dream*. 25th Anniversary Edition. Cambridge, Mass.: Da Capo Press, 2015.

Brewer, Jim. *They Played for Laughs: The True Story of Stewart Ferguson and the Arkansas A&M Wandering Weevils, College Football's "Marx Brothers"*. Outskirts Press, 2021.

Bronson, William. *Homestake: The Centennial History of America's Greatest Gold Mine*. Homestake Mining Company, 1977.

Cavanaugh, Jack. *The Gipper: George Gipp, Knute Rockne, and the Dramatic Rise of Notre Dame Football*. New York: Skyhorse Publishing, 2010.

Gaul, Gilbert M. *Billion-Dollar Ball: A Journey Through the Big-Money Culture of College Football*. New York: Penguin Books, 2016.

Gola, Hank. *City of Champions: An American story of leather helmets, iron wills and the high school kids from Jersey who won it all*. Croton-on-Hudson, NY, 2018.

Herndon, Dallas Tabor. *Centennial History of Arkansas*. Chicago: S. J. Clarke Publishing Company, 1922.

McLaird, James D. *Dakota Wesleyan University Memory Book, 1885-2010*. Mitchell: Dakota Wesleyan University, 2010.

Nocera, Joe, and Ben Strauss. *Indentured: The Battle to End the Exploitation of College Athletes*. New York: Portfolio, 2018.

Robinson, Ray. *Rockne of Notre Dame: The Making of a Football Legend*. Oxford: Oxford University Press, 1999.

Schmidt, Raymond. *Shaping College Football: The Transformation of an American Sport, 1919-1930*. Syracuse: Syracuse University Press, 2007.

Soderstrom, Robert M. *The Big House: Fielding H. Yost and the Building of Michigan Stadium*. Ann Arbor: Huron River Press, 2005.

Strickland, Patricia. *The Putt-Putt Air Force: The Story of The Civilian Pilot Training Program and The War Training Service (1939-1944)*. Federal Aviation Administration, 1971.

Walsh, Christopher J. *Who's #1?: 100-Plus Years of Controversial National Champions in College Football*. Maryland: Taylor Trade Publishing, 2007.

Watterson, John. *College Football: History, Spectacle, Controversy*. Baltimore: The Johns Hopkins University Press, 2000.